SECOND EDITION

SUPERVISION AS A PROACTIVE PROCESS

SECOND EDITION

SUPERVISION AS A PROACTIVE PROCESS

CONCEPTS AND CASES

JOHN C. DARESH   MARSHA A. PLAYKO

WAVELAND
PRESS, INC.

Prospect Heights, Illinois

For information about this book, write or call:

Waveland Press, Inc.
P.O. Box 400
Prospect Heights, Illinois 60070
(708) 634-0081

Contents

PART III
The Realities of Supervision

Preface

In the first edition of this book, the argument was advanced that, in order to be effective as an educational leader, school supervisors and administrators need to be proactive. Effective supervisors do not simply react to situations but plan ahead and anticipate proper ways of behaving in advance. In short, we defined effective educational supervision practices in terms of a leader's ability to maintain *perspective* while appreciating the *people* in the organization to understand supervision as an ongoing *process*. Supervision, therefore, must be based on values and thoughtfulness, not simply adherence to slogans, popular perspectives, and packaged programs.

As a large number of people have reviewed the first edition and put some of our suggestions into actual practice, we have gotten a great deal of very important and helpful feedback which has served to guide our development of this volume. In the past six years, discussions of organizational behavior and leadership have expanded to include new descriptions and frameworks. The work of W. Edwards Deming, while certainly not "new" in many ways, has been linked with such terms as "Total Quality Management" (TQM)—a concept that has become an important issue in literature about management. Deming's principles have guided many conversations among leaders in recent years, both in education and in the private corporate sector. In addition, concepts such as Bolman and Deal's organizational frameworks and Block's notion of stewardship as a legitimate goal of effective leaders have become popular contributions to current philosophies of supervision. As a result, we have included information about these topics, none of which were as highly visible at the time of the first edition. We do not claim that our treatment of any single topic is necessarily comprehensive or exhaustive. Again, our goal here is to provide you with an overview of a very broad and complex topic, namely how to improve organizations through more effective supervision. We are not, therefore, committed to a detailed analysis or promotion of terms such as "Quality Schooling" or "Supervisors as Stewards."

Those who have made use of our work in the past have indicated they are pleased that our focus has been on the role of leaders and their interactions with people, taking into account the structural components of organizations to achieve desired outcomes. Others who write about supervisory practice in schools often take a different perspective by looking at supervision primarily as part of the curriculum and instructional practices of schools. As a result, many describe supervision as an activity carried out by educators with no formal leadership role or responsibility. We believe that supervision involves much more than curriculum development, and it has been our continuing view that supervision is a process that is the responsibility of a wide variety of educators—both those with and those without formal power and authority. Nevertheless, earlier users of this book have pointed out something with which we wholeheartedly concur: A big part of supervisory work in schools necessarily deals with the core technology of schools. Normally that technology is defined as teaching, learning, and curriculum. Therefore, in this second edition, we have included a new chapter (14) which deals with the issue of how an educational supervisor or administrator might provide leadership in the domain of curriculum development.

Finally, we were pleased to note that users of the first edition reported it included material that was both practical and readable. Many have told us that we achieved our objective of presenting a clear conceptual base with equally clear applications to issues faced in the "real world" of schools. In this regard, we have retained the "Suggested Activities" sections which are found at the end of chapters 1–18. However, we felt the linkage between theory and practice could be made even more powerful if we were to include specific examples which readers could use to apply some of the theoretical material to realistic settings. Thus, in addition to the "Suggested Activities," you will note that we have tapped into the collective memories of many colleagues and also called upon our own professional experiences to provide two "Cases to Consider" at the conclusion of each of these chapters as well. The cases are not designed to present complex, detailed narratives. Rather, we have attempted to provide enough material to provoke students to look at some events that have happened in real schools, apply some of the concepts covered in the text, and then project potential resolutions which are in line with the fundamental assumptions in proactive supervision.

Throughout our efforts to modify and improve our presentation of material in this second edition, we have tried to ensure that basic beliefs held in our first effort have not been altered. We continue to hold firmly our view that more effective educational programs will result from more effective leadership practice; we also continue to believe that effective leadership and proactive supervision are synonymous terms; and we cling to the belief that the work of leaders can always be enhanced in many different ways. We hope that the additional topics we have included in this updated text combine with the substance of the first edition to represent viable ways to become a proactive supervisor.

Acknowledgments

Our work on this second edition is largely a reflection of the insights and assistance that have come from many friends and colleagues. We begin our recognition by noting the many students who have enrolled in courses where the first edition of this book has been used. We specifically speak of classes at the University of Northern Colorado for the past five years, and also at The Ohio State University, the institution where much of what is included was first used. As this manuscript for the second edition is in its final stage of preparation, yet another institution must be identified, namely Illinois State University, where one of the co-authors will soon work. We acknowledge other places where the first edition has been used and where colleagues have given us much appreciated feedback and suggestions. One example has been The Pennsylvania State University, where our friend and colleague Paula Short has been a true supporter.

Those who have worked with us in Ohio and Colorado have also been quite instrumental and helpful to our efforts to launch this second edition. In Colorado, Bruce Barnett, Rosemary Caffarella, Gary Galluzzo, Gene Hall, and Carol McGrevin offered support and encouragement as well as valuable insights into the revision process. In Ohio, Newark superintendent Les Johnson and assistant superintendent Susan Hatcher joined with the parents and pupils of Hazelwood Elementary School in providing support and understanding.

We have also gained encouragement and important ideas that are included from other friends across the nation who have devoted their time and talents to the improvement of educational leadership in so many ways. We pass along our thanks to Donn Gresso of East

Tennessee State University, Ron Areglado of the National Association of Elementary School Principals, James LaPlant at the University of Cincinnati, and Scott Thompson of the National Policy Board for Educational Administration. All of these individuals not only offered ideas that could be included in our work but, more importantly, provided constant examples of the kinds of educational leadership that we hope will be followed by readers of this book.

In the actual production of this book, we thank Neil Rowe of Waveland for having faith in our work, and Jeni Ogilvie, our editor who spent to many hours working with us in revising individual chapters, and then putting the whole effort together. Finally, we send along our continuing appreciation to Naomi Silverman, now at St. Martins Press, for her belief in this work so many years ago when she was still at Longman.

While the numerous professional friends and colleagues that we have listed here have been truly important to us as we worked on this revision, we must note in closing that the most critical actors who deserve our thanks have been our families who put up with so much as we worked on this second edition. Thanks, Bridget and Stephanie. And that you to Kelly, Nick, Mark, and Rich.

Introduction

Imagine two different supervisors or school administrators facing the same question: What is required to encourage veteran teachers to explore the new research on effective teaching strategies? The first supervisor announces a plan for all teachers to study the topic in inservice workshops, and the experienced teachers immediately and clearly voice their resistance—the program will mean more work, and besides, they are competent and effective teachers already. The supervisor reacts to this resistance by hastily putting an inservice program together, hiring an outside consultant to run it, and requiring the entire faculty to attend the sessions.

The second supervisor approaches the problem differently. In fact, the task may not become problematic in the first place, for this supervisor has taken time throughout the year to talk with all the teachers on a one-to-one basis. As a result, the supervisor is neither surprised nor frustrated when some teachers express little interest in the plan to acquaint them with new research on teaching. This second supervisor already knows where probable sources of dissatisfaction exist among the teachers and constructs the inservice agenda to accommodate this fact. Expert teachers are consulted and given leadership roles; workshops are geared to actual needs; potential resistance is defused.

This brief example illustrates two very different approaches to the exercise of supervisory responsibilities. The first supervisor approaches the job *reactively*. As long as the school seemed to be moving along reasonably well, the supervisor left things alone; but conflict erupted suddenly and unexpectedly when experienced teachers were presented with an inservice agenda for which they were unprepared and which they felt was being forced them. This

1

supervisor, who believed in the need for teachers to keep up with research, was no doubt angry and frustrated because plans for good, professional inservice training had been "sabotaged."

The second supervisor practices *proactive* supervision. Through constant involvement with staff throughout the year, even when everything was running smoothly, this supervisor could anticipate and plan for negative reactions to a particular decision. In fact, the second supervisor would probably have avoided making a unilateral decision about a topic for inservice training in the first place and instead would have spent considerable time during the year getting to know the *people* in the organization and the *nature* of the organization. As a result, the supervisor could *proactively* anticipate problems in advance and minimize their negative consequences for the organization.

In this book, which emphasizes the development of skills, knowledge, and attitudes consistent with proactive supervision, we make a number of fundamental assumptions about the nature of supervisory responsibilities in general. First, we assume that our understanding of educational supervision must be based on a knowledge of historical definitions and perspectives. Second, we assume that supervision today represents a blend of many earlier as well as current perspectives. As a result, we begin in chapter 1 by reviewing the development of educational supervision in the United States and some of the most important trends that have guided that development. Finally, and most importantly, we assume that the most productive and effective way to define educational supervision today is as a *proactive process*. This central assumption underlies virtually all of the arguments advanced in this text.

What do we mean by proactive supervision? We believe that there are six major components to this view of leadership practice in schools. To be an effective proactive supervisor, you need to:

1. Know your own beliefs.
2. Understand the nature and characteristics of organizations.
3. Understand that supervision is not an event or a series of events; it is an ongoing *process*.
4. Examine and understand alternative perspectives, even those that you do not fully accept.
5. Be consistent in your own behavior; "walk your talk."
6. Be capable of analyzing the people in your organization and their patterns of behavior.

The chapters in this text are not designed to teach you each of these characteristics independently. Rather, these six concepts are woven into a total pattern of supervisory behavior throughout the 19 chapters of this book. We believe, and stress throughout this volume, that effective supervisors look at their responsibilities *holistically* and not as a series of tasks and responses to the various emergencies that arise in the life of a school or a district. The effective proactive supervisor must develop a total understanding of what is being done, to whom, and with what likely consequences.

Supervision, as you will discover by reading this book, is not a neutral or reactive process where things simply "happen." Rather, *good* supervision changes people and their organizations for the better. Supervision is a critical responsibility in schools, and effective supervision can be extremely rewarding to the educator who chooses to follow this career route. We hope this book will assist you in deciding if in fact you *want* to follow the supervisory path and, if you do select educational supervision as your career, we hope that this text will help you be as good an educational supervisor as you can be.

Part I

Educational Supervision
Tradition and Context

The single most important attribute for any educator, and particularly for those educators who engage in supervisory practices, is an understanding of his or her own basic attitudes, values, and assumptions concerning both supervision and education. This understanding can derive only from a knowledge of history and context—how supervision has developed in American education—and of theories of educational supervision.

1 In Search of a Definition

Educational supervision is a field in search of a definition. Although supervision has been a normal school-based activity for as long as there have been public schools in America, no real consensus has ever been reached concerning what supervision should be or what educational supervisors should do. Attitudes about schools, teachers, and learners have changed periodically since the seventeenth century. As a result, views of what constitutes proper and effective supervisory practice have also shifted.

In this chapter, we review the different approaches to supervisory practice that have paralleled changing perceptions of public education and educational management and that serve as examples of the transitory nature of definitions. To clarify the particular approaches that dominated specific historical periods of supervisory practice, we note some of the basic assumptions, definitions, and characteristics typical of each period and provide examples of how supervisory practice has been affected by these predominant definitions and assumptions. Before beginning this review, however, we make an important point: Although this chapter appears to describe an orderly, sequential, and basically rational development of the field of supervision, in fact, the history of supervision has never really been as clear-cut as it might seem. Overlaps exist from one period to another, and features of most of the early views of supervision are still alive and very much with us today.

One important assumption underlies this review of alternative definitions and serves also as a crucial foundation for the concept of proactive supervision that is espoused throughout this text. The field of educational supervision is greatly influenced by the ways in which individuals and groups define that field on a day-to-day basis. A brief review of perspectives from the past enables us to see how supervision has developed over time and how some of our present practices and beliefs originated. This understanding of history will help you make consistent choices about proper supervisory behavior—an important component of the authenticity that must underlie proactive supervisory practice.

Throughout this book we will suggest that effective supervisors are *proactive* in their approach to supervisory responsibilities. What we mean by this is that they plan ahead and anticipate proper ways of behaving in advance; they are not simply reacting after a situation forces a response. It is an easy concept to define, but as the chapters ahead will show, a difficult one to effect.

Supervision as Inspection

The issue of providing supervision for teachers in American schools is as old as the history of formal education in this country. In fact, the year 1642, when the first Massachusetts School Law was enacted, also marks the beginning of educational supervision in American schools. The first stage of supervisory development lasted until approximately the conclusion of the Civil War in 1865.

During these years, supervisors were primary engaged in inspection (or, as some call it, snoopervision)—an approach based on the assumption that an educational supervisor's job was to find out all the wrong things that teachers were doing in their classrooms. While this description seems rather harsh, we need to recall some historical facts before judging seventeenth and eighteenth century supervisors as insensitive ogres who lacked compassion or basic respect for teachers. During the earliest days of American education, teachers often were not well educated and frequently stayed only a step or two ahead of their students in basic skills. Teachers in those years often needed monitoring to make certain that minimally acceptable levels of performance were being maintained in classrooms and schools. Individual supervisors did not always agree with their assigned responsibilities. In fact, the judgmental nature of supervision during this time rested in job descriptions, not in personal interpretations.

The first stage of supervisory practice (roughly 1642–1865) can be further subdivided into two distinct eras: the first religious control and the second of a more secular involvement. The first years of American public education were characterized, particularly in the New England colonies, by the assumption that local religious beliefs and values should be both preserved and transmitted from one generation to another. Supervision, then, was defined largely in terms determined and accepted by religious leaders. The Massachusetts Bay Company of 1642 provides the earliest known description of educational supervision:

> This Court, taking into consideration the great neglect of many parents and masters in training of their children in learning and labor, and other implyments which may be proffitable to the common wealth, do hereupon order and decree, that in every town ye chosen men appointed for managing the prudentiall affaires of the same shall henceforth stand charged with the redress of this evill . . . and for this end, they, or the greatest number of them, shall have the power to take into account from time to time of all parents and masters, and of their children, especially of their ability to read and understand the principles of religion and the capital laws of this country.

These chosen men were typically either ordained ministers or elders in local congregations—an understandable phenomenon in light of the fact that the teaching and learning they reviewed was tied directly to matters of religion. If students were not learning how to read the Bible, their paths to eternal salvation were blocked because they would never be able to gain insights into the Scriptures and to learn about their God.

After the American revolution, the duty of monitoring classroom procedures was increasingly entrusted to committees of laymen who were not associated with any specific religious group. This switch no doubt occurred as part of the general secularization of American society taking place at this time. As the years went on, school officials placed less emphasis on the supervisor's responsibility to verify the quality of religious instruction and more emphasis on the supervisor's responsibility to oversee the quality of secular instruction. What remained constant, however, was the assumption that teachers lacked basic competency. Two popular definitions of supervision illustrate this shift in focus. Theodore Dwight and James Wickerman noted:

> Visitation and careful examination are necessary to discover the teacher's merits in teaching and governing the attention, deserts, and improvements of the children. To render a teacher, in the first place, to convince him that he can, are the principal objects to be offered by a friend of education. (Dwight, 1835, p. 21)

> Such visitations (by supervisors) are necessary to secure the
> caretaking of the grounds, buildings, furniture, and apparatus;
> necessary to secure the most rapid progress on the part of the
> pupils; necessary to encourage competent teachers and to detect
> incompetent ones; in short, necessary to ensure the well-working
> of the whole school machinery. (Wickerman, 1864, p. 9)

As these definitions show, the religious orientation in educational
supervisory practice had given way to a more worldly and secular
view by the mid-nineteenth century. On the other hand, these
definitions continue to demonstrate some striking similarities in
supervisory practice derived from a common set of assumptions
held by educators throughout the first stage of supervisory development in American education.

Assumptions and Related Practices

Teachers were not to be trusted. Perhaps the most basic
premise of the earliest descriptions of supervision was simply that
teachers were, for the most part, incompetents who could not be
trusted to do their assigned jobs. At first, this assumption suggested
a lack of trust in teachers' abilities to provide instruction in religion.
The supervisor's responsibility, then, was to be present in classes
as often as possible to guard against the spread of any religious
heresy, either intentional or unintentional. Instruction was moni-
tored closely, not so much to guarantee proper methods of teaching,
but rather to make certain that proper interpretation of the Bible
was maintained. Even when this religious focus became blurred and
finally disappeared, however, teachers were still viewed as essentially incompetent employees who needed to be carefully watched.

***Supervisors had the right to intervene directly in the class-
room.*** During both stages of these early years, supervisors often
engaged in activities that were descriptive in their own right; they
deliberately tried to catch teachers in the act of making mistakes.
Supervisors made frequent, usually unannounced, classroom visits,
often intimidating even the most confident or competent of
instructors. Supervisors of the time frequently entered a classroom
while a lesson was in progress and then openly and defiantly
debated with a teacher about the accuracy of the information he
or she was imparting.

Supervisors were meant to be inspectors. Supervisors were
expected not only to monitor instructional processes and correct

incompetent teachers in the midst of leading their classes, they were also expected to review the characteristics of the total school, not as consultants or facilitators, but solely as inspectors. They performed functions, such as overseeing the upkeep of school buildings, instructional materials, and equipment. They were supposed to make sure, for example, that the schoolhouse roof did not leak, that the fire in the stove was well stoked, and that there were sufficient slates and benches for all the pupils.

Supervision as Science

From approximately the end of the Civil War until soon after World War I (around 1920), teaching procedures and educational practices in general were greatly influenced by experts whose interest was primarily the improvement of organizational efficiency. William Payne set the stage for employing management principles with his 1875 definition which reflected the notion of precision and certainty of performance in schools:

> The theory of school supervision . . . requires the superintendent to work upon the school through teachers. He is to prepare plans of instruction and discipline, which the teachers must carry into effect; but the successful working out of such a scheme requires constant oversight and constant readjustments. Hence arises the necessity for conference, instruction in methods, and correction of errors. The teachers of a graded school should be under continual normal instruction. (p. 4)

In 1914, E. C. Eliot offered this view: "Supervisory control is concerned with what should be taught, when it should be taught, to whom, how, and to what purpose" (p. 23).

Both of these views of supervision strongly imply that there is a single right way of doing things in education and that once this path is identified, it is the supervisor's responsibility to ensure that teachers know and follow it. The supervisor is also charged with the responsibility of planning—that is, of finding the most efficient and economical ways to attain organizational goals.

The views of various writers on corporation management, particularly Frederick W. Taylor (1916), whose scientific management principles were advocated as the way to ensure good practice in industrial organizations, also affected the beliefs of educators. A review of Taylor's major tenets provides a context for our discussion of this second period of supervisory thought and practice.

Raymond Villers (1960, p. 78) outlined the essential points of Taylor's views below.

Time-study principle.   All productive effort should be measured by accurate time study and a standard time established for all work done in the shop.

Piece-rate principle.   Wages should be proportional to output and their rates based on the standards determined by time study. As a corollary, a worker should be given the highest grade of work of which he is capable.

Separation-of-planning-from-performance   principle.   Management should take over from workers the responsibility for planning the work and making the performance physically possible. Planning should be based on time studies and other data related to production, which are scientifically determined and systematically classified; it should be facilitated by standardization of tools, implements, and methods.

Scientific-methods-of-work principle.   Management should take over from workers the responsibility for their methods of work, determine scientifically the best methods, and train the workers accordingly.

Management-control principle.   Managers should be trained and taught to apply scientific principles of management and control (such as management by exception and comparison with validated production standards).

Functional principle.   The strict application of military principles should be reconsidered, and their industrial organization should be so designed that it serves the purpose of improving the coordination of activities among the specialists.

These principles of scientific management imply that certain features of organizational life are so predictable that specific laws can be formulated to guide behavior in virtually every circumstance. Thus, in both educational and corporate views of supervision during this period, the belief reigned that behavioral formulae, when faithfully followed, would necessarily and automatically lead to predictable outcomes and products.

Scientific management principles clearly influenced the development of educational supervision during this period, but other facts also played a role. For example, many schools grew rapidly in both size and complexity, to the extent that larger organizational arrangements—districts and systems—were established across the nation, particularly in urban centers in the north and east. This increased organizational complexity was a major factor in the creation of a more segmented view of educational supervision. Larger school systems began hiring two individuals—a business manager as well as a supervisor of instruction—who would function as equal partners in the hierarchical structure of the school district. Both were responsible to a third person in another newly created role, the superintendent of schools. This concept of dual administration (business and instruction) greatly influenced the development of modern administrative and supervisory practice. One product of this era in educational history, then, is what might be called the institutionalization and professionalization of the educational supervisor's role. In later chapters, we will look at the problems that separation of functions has created.

Assumptions and Related Practices

Great faith was placed in educational laws. Organizations throughout society were awakening to the possibility that rules and principles derived from research, could be established to guide practice. School administrators in particular were open to this line of thinking, because at this time a variety of problems were emerging from over two centuries of rather confused development. The notion that the educational practices of the past could be understood and even improved upon if some key facts and laws were learned was indeed tempting.

The outcome of this view, in terms of supervision, was that increasingly, the educational supervisor became a reviewer who checked to see if employees conformed to procedures which were determined and handed down by experts. The supervisor's job was to make sure that the scientific rules of schooling were being followed. Thus, the emphasis in supervision was on the maintenance of acceptable teaching behaviors, and particularly on ensuring that these were carried efficiently.

The supervisory staff of a school system would determine the proper methods of instruction. This scientific approach to supervision emphasized a "top-down" orientation to defining and communicating information concerning instructional practices, and the supervisory personnel of a school or district became the legitimate experts in the field of instruction. Scientific management principles urging separation of management from employee control made unthinkable the possibility that teachers might work together to influence or define proper instructional techniques. Quite simply, teachers were viewed as the implementors of administrators' policies, and supervisors were around to make certain that the policies were being implemented faithfully.

To summarize, the overriding aim of educational supervision as it was practiced during this era was to develop teachers to be professionally efficient—that is, capable of self-analysis, self-criticism, and self-improvement in order to conform to stated standards of performance. Those standards were determined at higher levels of the school district organization and then transmitted to the teachers. A primary activity of educational supervisors, then, was to provide either condemnations or commendations to teachers after classroom visits. Compromises between these two extremes were not possible.

Emphasis on Human Relations

One consequence of the scientific era of supervisory practice was the tendency to value organizational goals more than the interests and needs of the people who worked in the organization. Scientific management often emphasized the notion that all organizational components—employees included—were best understood as replacement parts. "One teacher is as good as another" could have been a motto of the time. Predictably, a vigorous reactive movement eventually emerged. In the human relations era (approximately 1920 to 1960) a supervisory philosophy that focused on needs of individuals who worked in schools and emphasized satisfying their personal interests took root. Widespread support developed for cooperative group efforts as both an end and a means for change in schools.

Supervisors were encouraged to use every means possible to stimulate and encourage classroom teachers, with the assumed outcome being more effective instruction. Terms found in the literature describing supervision during this era included such words as coordinating, integrating, creativity, stimulating, and democratic relationships. Again, a glance at some definitions of supervision from the time provides insights to guide our understanding of the era. For example, the National Education Association (NEA) in 1930 stated:

> [The following is a] fundamental philosophy of supervision:
> Supervision is a creative enterprise. It has for its objective the

development of a group of professional workers who attack their problems scientifically, free from control of tradition and actuated by a spirit of inquiry. Supervision seeks to improve an environment in which men and women of high professional ideals may live a vigorous, intelligent, creative life.' (p. 47)

What is truly remarkable about this definition, when compared to those in the earlier era of scientific supervision, is the sudden shift in emphasis from segmentation toward allowing employees to work together to define organizational goals and to create appropriate activities to meet those goals. The top-down emphasis on supervisory control had given way to a more democratic process. Two additional definitions support this view.

The supervisory function is described not much toward teachers and their methods as it is toward practices of advisement, student activities, pupil control of defensible subject matter, and personality adjustments of pupils and teachers. (Cox, 1934, p. 33)

In general, to supervise means to coordinate, stimulate, and direct growth of teachers in the power to stimulate and direct the growth of every pupil through the exercise of his talents toward the richest and most intelligent participation in the society and world in which he lives. (Biggs and Justman, p. 21)

A review would be incomplete if it did not include a description of the work of Kimball Wiles, often characterized as the chief advocate for the human relations approach to educational supervision. In 1967, he provided the following definition of what supervisors should do:

They [the supervisors] are expediters. They help establish communication. They help hear each other. They serve as liaisons to get people into contact with others who have similar problems or with resource people who can help. They stimulate staff members to look at the extent to which ideas and resources are being shared, and the degree to which persons are encouraged and supported as they try new things. They make it easier to carry out the agreements that emerge from evaluation sessions. They listen to individuals discuss their problems and recommend other resources that may help in the search for solutions. They bring to individual teachers, whose confidence they possess, appropriate suggestions and materials. They serve, as far as they are able, the feelings that teachers have about the system and its policies, and they recommend that the administration examine irritations among staff members. (p. 11)

Clearly there is a great difference between the perspectives of this human development era of supervision and those of the inspection and scientific eras. In the first two centuries of American education, very little concern was expressed about the individual needs of teachers and others in school systems. In Wiles's words, on the other hand, we find little or no concern for the priorities and needs of the organization. The focus had shifted dramatically from things to people.

Assumptions and Related Practices

If people are happy, they will be productive. This is the fundamental premise of this era, and it is the key ingredient of any approach to supervisory or managerial practice that endorses the fulfillment of human needs. If happy employees are better, more effective employees, then supervisors must focus on the needs and interests of the workers. Thus, educational supervisors must spend a good deal of time seeking input from teachers and staff members concerning working conditions and other issues related to the quality of life in the organization. Supervisors must also emphasize discussion groups, shared decision making activities, and group-process skill development.

The improvement of the psychosocial climate of the school is a legitimate concern of supervisors. The human relations movement, which emerged quite forcefully during the 1920s and 1930s, was heavily influenced by the research and theory bases that were increasingly popular in the social sciences. During this time period, the overall tenor of supervision was altered; it became acceptable for educational leaders to expend energy toward effecting positive feelings within an organization. Previously, only the measurable outcomes of organizations were considered to be the legitimate concerns of supervisors and administrators.

The supervisor is an in-between person in school systems. Whether it was a conscious modification or not is unclear and probably unimportant, but during this period the formal role of the supervisor changed drastically from that of an authority figure to that of a process helper and consultant. In contrast with earlier periods when supervisors were either inspectors or efficiency experts, supervisors became supporters, facilitators, and consultants to teachers. Two reasons might explain this shift. First, educational organizations and curricula were becoming more complex, and increasing specialization took place in many professional roles. The job of the supervisor probably reflected this change more than any other. Increasing demands for more varied curricula in school districts created the need for subject area specialists— one frequent conceptualization of the role of supervisors—to work with teachers and provide expert assistance to help solve classroom instructional problems.

Second, a prevailing philosophical orientation of human relations management was that teachers and other workers needed supportive people to help them with their jobs. The supervisor's role was ideally suited to that function.

The nature of the supervisor's role continues to be debated. In chapter 3, we will see how supervisors are often categorized as being neither-fish-nor-fowl, characteristic of their many ambiguous roles.

Current Perspectives

Supervisory thought and practice today in some ways result from all three of these earlier perspectives, but in many ways bear no resemblance to any of them. Some educators now lean toward supervisory practices that stem from the earlier inspection and scientific philosophies of supervision; others have expanded the concept of human relations to develop an approach often referred to as human resource development. In recent years, there has been a great interest in concepts associated with client-driven managerial behavior (giving a high priority to keeping the client happy) and a commitment to quality. In the remainder of this chapter we will briefly discuss the current application of these stances to provide you with alternative definitions of educational supervision which you need to understand if you are to practice proactive supervision.

Return to Inspection

You would not expect to hear any modern supervisors openly suggest that most teachers in their districts are incompetent and that supervisors are supposed to catch people teaching incorrectly or providing incorrect information to pupils. Yet this approach to supervision persists, frequently veiled in jargon such as "getting tough with those teachers who aren't performing." When school districts are faced with the unhappy need to reduce the number of teachers or administrators because of budget shortfalls, declining enrollments, or other environmental pressures, there is often talk about the need to lay off incompetent teachers and administrators—

not just those unlucky enough to be the most recently hired. This kind of rhetoric can lead to a climate where virtually all teachers feel threatened, and supervisors and administrators feel compelled to look for the worst rather than the best characteristics of their staffs.

The increasing acceptance of competency tests for teachers, which are required in a number of states and local school districts, is a very real manifestation of this approach. The unstated belief behind the calls for such testing is clearly that some teachers—an undetermined number—are doing a poor job and that these ineffective individuals must be weeded out from the ranks of public school teachers. The best way to do this, say proponents of competency testing, is to subject all teachers to an assumption of inadequate professional performance by requiring them to take tests or else lose their teaching certificates.

In some school systems, the percentage of widespread teacher incompetence has led supervisors and administrators to define their jobs once again as those of inspectors. Such educators are likely to engage in behaviors indicating a general lack of trust in their teaching staff. For example, they may call for unannounced classroom visits to gather information about classroom activities. Discussions of procedures that require a collaborative relationship between teachers and supervisors become pointless. Clinical supervision, a model that requires open communication (see chapter 16) would be impossible.

Return to Scientific Supervision

A blind faith in the certainty that scientific laws can guide educational practice is by no means dead and buried. While the pontifications of the disciples of scientific management, such as Frederick Taylor, may seem to be foolish overstatements today, many educators continue to believe that educational practice can be understood according to predictable relationships among predictable variables. If we know how to mix chemicals to produce compounds in life-saving medicines, why can't we know exactly which ingredients should be mixed to form children who can read, write, and cipher?

The press for a return to scientific management in education comes from many sources. School boards, whose members often have strong ties to the world of private business still heavily influenced by the heritage of scientific management, wonder why educators do things so inefficiently while those in the private sector effectively change raw materials into finished products. There is a great desire to find predictability in educational practice. The number of products becomes an indicator of organizational effectiveness, and the assumption is often made that more is better.

Educational supervisors who agree with the assumptions of this approach would probably attempt to produce more visible signs of productiveness in their schools, possibly in the form of higher scores on standardized achievement tests. A conception of teaching influenced by Eisner's and Rubin's "artistic" views (see chapter 17) would be unacceptable.

Human Resource Development

Rather than an outright return to human relations supervision equivalent to the revivals of inspection and scientific supervision, proponents of this approach have incorporated the basic assumption of human relations (namely that people in an organization hold the key to more effective supervision or management) into a variation known as *human resource development*. This approach has dominated the literature of the past twenty years.

As its name implies, human resource development suggests that the most important activity of a supervisor is to help people within an organization—human resources—become as skillful and effective as possible. The organization will be improved because its most important features—employees—will be more effective.

There is a good deal of overlap between human relations and human resource development. Both approaches place tremendous emphasis on the needs of the people who work in an organization, and both views hold that organizational effectiveness is a desirable outcome of intervention by a supervisor. In addition, both views suggest that the key to organizational effectiveness is the extent to which workers can feel satisfied in their jobs.

Some important differences, however, keep human resource development from being a mere rehash of the earlier concept. Human relations advocates believed that emphasizing the happiness of an organization's employees would almost automatically guarantee that those employees would work harder, thereby increasing the overall effectiveness and productivity of the organization: "Happy people are productive people." The principal duty of the supervisor, manager, or administrator, then, would be to guarantee that workers are content and satisfied with the workplace and would therefore want to work harder. In school settings, the supervisor would ensure that teachers had what they want in terms of supplies and equipment and that they are reasonably satisfied with how they are being treated. By contrast, the human resource development approach advocates that employees will be happier, more satisfied, and ultimately more productive only if they are first satisfied through working in a productive organization: "Happy employees are productive employees if they work in a productive place." Thus, the supervisor becomes primarily interested in bringing about greater organizational effectiveness, thereby creating a setting where employees can feel satisfied through their association with productivity. In many ways, then, human resource development supervision is an outcome of the human relations movement. The key distinction is in the emphasis selected by the supervisor.

Proponents of human resource development criticize the earlier human relations perspective as highly manipulative because it assumed that a supervisor could be nice to employees and thereby make them buy into organizational goals without hesitation. Human relations believers, on the other hand, suggest that, because of its emphasis on organizational productivity, human resource development is but a thinly disguised return to scientific management. The real distinction seems to be more subtle, however. In human relations supervision, organizational effectiveness is a by-product of satisfying people's needs immediately. People tend to be comfortable in a human relations environment. The human resource development advocates, however, claim that people will eventually be happy if the organization is productive, even though the immediate impression may be that the supervisor is ignoring individual needs and that the results will be longer lasting. In fact, meeting the concerns of employees is a long-term goal for human resource development supervisors, who believe that immediate energy needs to be directed toward organizational effectiveness.

Client-Based Supervision and

Total Quality Management

If there is any single movement that epitomizes management philosophy development in the past ten years, it is clearly the concept of Total Quality Management (TQM), sometimes described in the literature as emphasizing the development of organizational plans and priorities directed toward increasing the sense of satisfaction felt by those who are the clients or customers of organizations. In other words, when the external environment perceives that it is satisfied with what happens within an organization, then the organization is, in fact, effective.

Actually, focusing on the need to engage in absolute dedication to customer satisfaction is only one part of the philosophy of TQM. Dan Ciampa (1992, p. 7) noted that TQM is directed toward producing results which fall into the following four categories:

- *Customers* are intensely loyal. They are more than satisfied because their needs are being met and their expectations are being exceeded.
- *The time to respond* to problems, needs, and opportunities is minimized. Costs are also minimized by eliminating or minimizing tasks that do not add value. Moreover, they are minimized in such a way that the quality of the goods or services given to the customer and the way the customer is treated is enhanced.
- A *climate* is put in place that supports and encourages teamwork and leads to more satisfying, motivating, and meaningful work for employees.
- *There is a general ethic of continuous improvement*. In addition, there is a methodology that employees understand for attaining a state of continuous improvement.

These basic assumptions of structuring organizations to reflect a commitment to the needs of clients and total quality are drawn in large measure from the earlier work of W. Edwards Deming. Deming, prepared academically to be a physicist, has achieved most of his fame as the individual largely responsible for the rebirth of Japanese industry after World War II. He was recruited by the Supreme Command for Allied Powers in 1947 to join a team of individuals working with Japanese officials in planning for programs that would bring about national stability after the massive destruction brought on by the war. Deming noted that a complete redefinition of the ways in which people viewed organizational roles and relations would be needed to rebuild the national economy. In short, Deming realized that his role was to foster a new way of thinking about management, perhaps even more importantly than finding new ways to manage.

The result of this initial effort to promote restructuring the Japanese managerial culture has been the identification of Fourteen Points (Walton, 1986) for effective practice which seem to define Deming's conceptualization of a more effective way in which organizations might operate:

Point 1.   *Create constancy of purpose for improvement of product and service.* Effective organizations do not simply try to earn a lot of short-term success through immediate increases in profits, rather they promote long-term success by focusing on organizational maintenance through promoting (and funding) innovation, research, constant improvement, and maintenance.

Point 2.   *Adopt the new philosophy.* This new philosophy must be one of intolerance toward poor service and complacency. The goal must be one in which mistakes and negativism are unacceptable.

Point 3.   *Cease dependence on mass inspection.* The identification of problems in manufactured products implies that the system of production is designed so that flaws are acceptable. As a result, designing a system dedicated in total to the elimination of errors is more effective than one that is designed to inspect and seek errors as production occurs.

Point 4.   *End the practice of awarding business on price tag alone.* Selecting products solely on the basis of lowest cost is shortsighted. This often leads to selecting products of low quality; "you get what you pay for."

Point 5.   *Improve constantly and forever the system of production and service.* Management is obligated to continually look for ways to reduce waste and improve quality.

Point 6.   *Institute training.* It is irrational to expect that people would be able to do their jobs if they are not properly prepared.

Point 7.   *Institute leadership.* Leadership consists of helping people do a better job and of learning by objective methods to determine who needs to receive individualized help.

Point 8.   *Drive out fear.* It is not wrong to make mistakes. It is a mistake to develop a culture where people believe that it is impossible to try without always achieving immediate success.

Point 9.   *Break down barriers between staff areas.* Collaboration, not competition, among work groups is the key to success.

Point 10.   *Eliminate slogans, exhortations, and targets for the workforce.* The "rah-rah" spirit shown in old movies about great coaches never really helped teams win. Only the skills of individuals did any good. Effective leaders recognize this fact and downplay the reliance on slogans or other "grandstand" efforts to promote "spirit" and "a winning attitude."

Point 11.   *Eliminate numerical quotas.* Quotas promote the achievement of numerical goals, which are simply symbols of reality. They do not enhance quality. The effective organization seeks quality, not symbols.

Point 12. *Remove barriers to pride of workmanship.* The fundamental belief is that people really want to do a good job.

Point 13. *Institute a vigorous program of education and retraining.* The only way in which an organization will grow and prosper is if the people who make up the organization continue to grow and learn.

Point 14. *Take action to accomplish the transformation.* People in the organization must function as a team at all times.

In addition to these Fourteen Points associated with effective organizations, Deming also noted what he referred to as the "Seven Deadly Diseases of Organizations" which must be addressed:

1. Lack of constancy of purpose
2. Emphasis on short-term profits
3. Evaluation by performance, merit rating, or annual review of performance
4. Mobility of management (i.e., leaders are moved frequently without reason).
5. Running a company on visible figures alone
6. Excessive medical costs
7. Excessive costs of warranty, fueled by lawyers who work on contingency fees

As one reflects on the vision of proper supervision and administration suggested by this emphasis on TQM and the needs of customers, it becomes clear that certain practices are exhibited by those who adhere to this approach. For example, top-down management is no longer valid, nor is any effort to use immediate and visible indicators of effectiveness. As a result, in school settings, it becomes increasingly difficult to imagine successful practice being identified solely in terms of increases in student achievement scores.

There is little doubt that school supervisors and administrators in recent years have been inundated with proposals to improve schools by adopting principles of TQM. The pages of professional journals are filled with stories about how to apply TQM to schools, and dozens of special training sessions are sponsored at professional association meetings each year to describe how to make schools more responsive to clients. There is a bewildering array of terms and programs that appear to offer effective strategies to make use of the fundamental principles of Deming's work in schools. Consequently, programs such as site-based management (or collaborative decision making or school-based management or school-based decision making or any one of a number of similar popular terms) and the ever-elusive concept of "Outcomes-Based Education" litter the scene as proposed strategies to make school management more consistent with effective practice that is suggested by reformers.

We doubt that there will be an immediate end in sight to school supervisors and administrators (and managers in many other organizations) attempting to apply TQM techniques and principles. We are also equally unsure about whether or not this trend will continue well into the future and form another major approach to management philosophy in the same way scientific management or human relations have. As we review the various descriptions of TQM and customer-driven management, we find at least four areas in which we believe there are inconsistencies between this popular perspective and the reality of schools.

- TQM, above all, is not a specific strategy for managing, but rather, an overall philosophical orientation to the ways in which organizations and people interact. TQM holds that people are to be heard, valued, respected, and viewed with a degree of importance. This perspective may be novel in many industrial and manufacturing organizations where the historical goal has been to turn out more product at any cost. By contrast, schools (and school personnel) have typically held a much different set of values concerning their societal roles and responsibilities. Simply stated, school people already view the satisfaction of human needs as central to their vision. As a result, the central belief of TQM is one that has been familiar to most educators for many years.
- The identification of customers and clients is central to TQM. If one cannot specify who the customers of an organization are, how can one develop a set of organizational activities and procedures to meet their needs? In the case of schools, the identification of customers is not a simple task. Are primary clients the pupils? Parents? Teachers? Taxpayers? State legislators? All of the above, or none of the above?
- There are many cases where TQM simply does not fit the reality of public schools (or perhaps most other not-for-profit organizations). For example, Deming's Points 4 ("Eliminate the practice of awarding business on price tag alone.") and 11 ("Eliminate numerical quotas.") are consistent with the wishes of many

educators. Yet are they realistic in today's climate which seems to be constantly seeking ways to force public agencies to become more cost-effective and efficient? Would it be likely that many school systems would be able to ignore lowest bidder provisions when purchasing materials?

- There are many undefined (or at least ill-defined) concepts and practices associated with TQM. As a result, a philosophical orientation that has power for some might become so open to interpretation by others that its individual concepts become virtually meaningless. Deming is often credited with stating that effective organizations are those which downplay supervision and replace it with leadership, implying that supervision cannot be viewed as an act of leadership. We vigorously disagree with this assertion, provided that we understand what is meant by leadership in the first place.

Total Quality Management and attention to customer needs have many benefits to assisting educational leaders improve practice. On the other hand, we are not totally convinced that this perspective is sufficiently articulated at present to make it an enduring or a very useful concept.

What Is Supervision?

In this chapter we have provided a general overview of the development of educational supervision over the years. We noted that the field has been influenced by the tendency to find the worst in people and later by the assumption that people are the most important component in any organization. Currently, several perspectives on the roles and responsibilities of those charged with supervisory duties compete for our attention. Numerous definitions have been offered, but none was endorsed without reservation.

You may find a bias in this book toward the basic belief that human resource development, or even the recent emergence of Total Quality Management, is a reasonable perspective in most cases. An even more fundamental view, however, is that anyone with supervisory responsibilities should understand as many alternative views as possible and then choose a perspective that is the most consistent with one's own basic set of values. The most important thing to do after making an initial selection of acceptable options, then, is to behave in a fashion that is faithful to that orientation. As we noted in the introduction to this section, a key ingredient in the process of proactive supervision is the maintenance of *authentic* and *consistent* behavior. While there are clear strengths and weaknesses inherent in all orientations to supervision, there is probably nothing more damaging to supervisory effectiveness than to pretend to have a particular perspective and then act in a way that suggests an entirely different view. Time and again teachers report great frustration with what they perceive to be behavior that is not authentic or consistent on the part of supervisors and administrators. While it is probably true that few teachers would be overjoyed with the prospect of working for someone who espoused the beliefs of the inspection era, such a condition would be more acceptable than one where a new supervisor claimed to be a human relations proponent or a believer in Total Quality Management while really being a closet inspector. People value predictable, consistent, and authentic behaviors.

We make one additional comment. There are probably times and situations in the life of any organization that make different supervisory practices more (or less) acceptable and effective. The prospect of supervisors as inspectors—and the inherent assumption that teachers are not competent—is not typically attractive; on the other hand, there are times when incompetent teachers require greater scrutiny. Human relations supervision may be criticized as manipulative, but there might be a time, for example, after a particularly autocratic administrator has just departed, when an overemphasis on human relations would be effective and important.

Is there, then, a single, acceptable definition of supervision? The ones that we have introduced thus far have faults, although they may be useful from time to time. The answer to this question, particularly in this volume's context of proactive supervision, is not easy. If proactive supervision calls for you to select a perspective and stick with it, then our espousal of a single definition of supervision that is tied too closely to one set of assumptions will contradict a fundamental value of this text. The basic definition presented here represents an attempt to go beyond educational settings and focus on essential features of supervision in any situation. The following simple definition will be used here: *Supervision is the process of overseeing the ability of people to meet the goals of the organization in which they work.*

A key feature of this definition is its suggestion that supervision needs to be understood as a *process* and not as a specific professional role. It is also related to the concept of *proactive supervision*, the foundation of this book, which holds that the best supervision is based on a set of fundamental values and assumptions possessed by the individual serving in a supervisory capacity. The major problem of current school supervisory behavior is its undue emphasis on *reactive* performance—doing things as a result of a crisis orientation rather than through careful, logical planning and preparation. The remaining chapters of this text are devoted to suggesting that effective supervision is based on the development of a more predictable strategy to guide action, and that strategy must emerge no matter which definition, philosophy, or overall orientation an individual adopts.

Summary

In this chapter we reviewed several alternative perspectives of supervisory practice to enable you to question your own personal assumptions regarding the proper definition of supervision. The hope is that you will be able to begin formulating a personalized but authentic perspective of effective supervisory behavior. Further, we pointed out that the development of a personalized understanding of supervision is the first step forward in proactive, rather than reactive, supervision.

Suggested Activities

1. Interview at least four supervisors or school administrators to determine their predominant views of supervision. You might start by asking for their definition of supervision. Propose a supervisory situation, such as "reasons for evaluating staff." Interpret their responses according to the historical views presented in this chapter. Were there any responses that leaned toward inspection? Toward scientific supervision? Toward the human relations philosophy?

2. Look at the job descriptions of supervisors in two or more different school districts. Can you determine if there are any prevailing views of how supervisors are supposed to behave, according to the historical definitions reviewed in this chapter?

Cases to Consider

The following brief cases are based on actual situations which have taken place in schools. Please read each case and consider the following:

a. What are the critical issues raised in each case, as they relate to the topics covered in this chapter of the text?
b. How do these cases relate to the development of the concept of proactive supervision as it is explained in this chapter?
c. In what ways might you suggest a resolution to the issues raised?

Case 1.1:

The Tiger Is Always Changing Stripes

Pat MacMillan has been the principal of Hazel Hills Elementary School for sixteen years. As a result, she has become a kind of institution in that part of the city, where recently a lot of things have changed. What used to be a semi-rural part of town that was surrounded by empty plains and only a few housing developments has become a very busy community since the opening of the Hazel Hollow Mall seven years ago. The total school district has changed, too, but not in the same physical sense. The last sixteen years have seen four superintendents come and go. In fact, the school board is currently carrying out yet another national search for a new district administrator.

As each new superintendent has come on board, a new organizational plan and operating philosophy have been put in place, and building administrators have been expected to get in line with the district's vision. The first person brought with her a strong emphasis on increasing student achievement scores and a no-nonsense philosophy of discipline. Three years later, the board hired a man who stated that the welfare of the people in the district should come above all other concerns. Next, there was a superintendent who pushed for (but did not get) a system where teachers were expected to evaluate peers, and principals were supposed to spend at least 51 percent of their time in classrooms to make sure that effective teaching was taking place. It was at that time that many of Pat's colleague principals opted for early retirement or found jobs in other school systems. The superintendent was delighted to be able to hire several new administrators who could get tough with teachers and weed out all incompetence.

The most recent superintendent was an enigma. He had been in his role for about two years before leaving for a bigger district near the state capital, but while in office, few saw him because he was so heavily involved with serving as a national speaker and consultant. It seemed like he used each new buzz word, and the key to school restructuring became a focus of his speeches around the country.

Pat had seen a lot of different managerial philosophies and building principals come and go, but Pat MacMillan was certain that she liked the community of Hazel Hills, and she did not intend to leave on someone else's terms. It was her home, and she would do whatever it took to stay until retirement in three years. Her bookcase in her office contained books and materials that reflected the administrative style of each past superintendent. Last week, she made certain that there was an empty shelf so that she could stock up on readings that were consistent with the next district administrator.

Everything, then, was great at Hazel Hills Elementary School and in the professional life of Pat MacMillan. So why has her school had the highest rate of teacher turnover in the district? Why did she always feel so isolated from her teachers?

Case 1.2:

I Thought This Was Heaven

When the job of district math coordinator became available in the Rocky Bluff School District last year, Cliff Gilcrest could hardly wait to apply. He had been a middle school principal in a neighboring district for five years, and he really enjoyed the job. The faculty, parents, staff, and students had an emotional farewell party for him when he left. The plaque they gave him, which hangs on his office wall now, shows that people viewed him as "the leader with a heart." However, he was anxious to advance his career and get a job where he could impact on the quality of instruction across the total district, particularly a very good and highly respected school district. There is no question that Rocky Bluff is a district that emphasizes student achievement and performance. When Cliff worked in the other district, he was always looking for a chance to work in a place like Rocky Bluff where they "really know about high standards." When Cliff came to Rocky Bluff, he looked forward to having his ideas for instructional improvement heard and appreciated. What he has started to recognize, however, is that no matter how hard he pushes for higher math scores and other indicators of student achievement, he always feels the pressure from the superintendent and school board to increase scores even more.

Now that Cliff has been in his new job for about six months, he is starting to look at his wall plaque more and more, wondering if he made a terrible mistake.

References

Briggs, Thomas H., & Justman, Joseph (1952). *Improving instruction through supervision.* New York: Macmillan.

Ciampa, Dan (1992). *Total quality: A user's guide for implementation.* Reading, MA: Addison Wesley.

Cox, Philip W. L. (1934). *High school administration and supervision.* New York: American Book Company.

Cubberly, Elwood P. (1916). *Public school administration.* Boston: Houghton Mifflin.

Dwight, Theodore (1835). *The school-master's friend of the committee-man's guide.* New York: Roe Lockwood.

Eisner, Eliot W. (1979). *The educational imagination.* New York: Macmillan.

Eliot, E. C. (1914). *City school supervision.* New York: World Book Company.

Massachusetts Bay Company in New England: Records of the Governor and the Company. (1642). (Vol. II).

National Education Association, Department of Superintendence (1930). *The superintendent surveys supervision.* (Yearbook 8). Washington, DC: The Association.

Payne, William H. (1875). *Chapters on school administration.* New York: Wilson Hinkle and Company.

Rubin, Louis J. (1985). *Artistry in teaching.* New York: Random House.

Taylor, Frederick W. (1916). The principles of scientific management. *Bulletin of the Taylor Society.*

Villers, Raymond (1960). *Dynamic management in industry.* Englewood Cliffs, NJ: Prentice-Hall.

Walton, Mary (1986). *The Deming management method.* New York: Perigree Press.

Wickerman, James P. (1864). *School economy: A treatise on the preparation, organization, employments, government, and authorities of schools.* New York: Lippincott.

Wiles, Kimball, & Lovell, John T. (1967). *Supervision for better schools.* Englewood Cliffs, NJ: Prentice Hall.

Additional Readings

Deming, W. Edward (1986). *Out of the crisis.* Cambridge: MIT Press.

Dobyns, Lloyd, & Crawford-Mason, Clare (1991). *Quality or else: The revolution in world business.* Boston: Houghton-Mifflin.

Glickman, Carl D. (1990). *Supervision of instruction: A developmental approach* (2nd ed.). Needham Heights, MA: Allyn and Bacon.

Sergiovanni, Thomas J. (Ed.) (1982). *Supervision of teaching.* Yearbook of the Association for Supervision and Curriculum Development. Alexandria, VA: Association for Supervision and Curriculum Development.

2 Personal Assumptions Guiding Supervisory Practice

Several important concepts underlie the process of proactive supervision. In chapter 1, for example, we introduced the notion that the effective supervisor reviews and considers many different perspectives concerning supervision but ultimately selects one point of view and remains true to it. Such adherence to a particular perspective is encouraged, even if your stance reflects an approach to supervision based on scientific management or some other relatively unpopular view. Of course, you will change or modify a position from time to time, depending on a wide array of reasons. However, your authenticity and your clarity in espousing a particular supervisory philosophy are the first important ingredients in effective proactive supervision.

Even more critical in developing a framework for successful supervisory practice is an ability to analyze your own personal beliefs, attitudes, and values, as components of a clear philosophy of education. The practitioner of educational supervision who is unable to articulate basic thoughts concerning professional issues will find successful leadership difficult. Equally important, without the capacity to reflect on the beliefs that form the basis of a personal educational philosophy, you will be unable to provide your staff and teachers with modeling and leadership to help them grow and develop in their own roles.

In this chapter we examine how supervisors build effective practice on personal assumptions. First, we review fundamental concepts such as beliefs, attitudes, and values. Second, we develop the concept that an educational philosophy clarifies action planning. Third, we briefly examine the concept of reflective practice as it relates to individual philosophy formulation. Finally, we consider the practical implications of individual philosophy and action planning.

Beliefs, Attitudes, and Values

An important first step in defining your personal philosophy is to become more familiar with the meaning of such frequently used words as *beliefs*, *attitudes*, and *values* and to understand how these affect how you behave.

Beliefs

The primary component in a general system of values is a belief or a set of beliefs, or what Milton Rokeach (1971) defined as "any simple proposition, conscious or unconscious, inferred from what a person says or does, capable of being preceded by the phrase 'I believe that'" (p. 61). We all have hundreds, perhaps thousands of beliefs about an equally large number of things, places, people, or ideas. These notions are often short-lived because we find out that they are not correct, or because we simply do not find them important enough to grasp for very long. A person may wake up in the morning, for example, believing that the weather is hot, cold, or any one of dozens of other adjectives. That belief may be shed after hearing the radio report the day's temperature, when the person actually goes outside, or when the individual gets sufficiently absorbed in some other belief that the temperature outside becomes unimportant. In schools, much of what teachers and others do is based on beliefs. Teachers are quick to explain their approaches to classroom management issues in terms related to the ways in which they believe students will act under most circumstances.

Attitudes

Attitudes are, in a sense, the next step in a hierarchy. Again, note Rokeach's (1971) definition: "An attitude is a relatively enduring organization of beliefs around an object or situation predisposing one to respond in some preferential manner" (p. 180). Attitudes are clusters of individual beliefs that survive the immediate moment.

The belief that it is hot or cold outside may be fleeting, but our belief about temperature generally may create a particular attitude about the weather. Some people are happy to believe that it is cold outside because their attitude toward cold weather, built on personal theory, is positive.

We can certainly have incorrect attitudes based on false beliefs; this does not make the potency of the attitude any less real, however. Consider, for example, a belief acquired as a child based on an image in a movie or television, that politicians are corrupt. As the child grows, the belief may unite with other incorrect beliefs to form an attitude of prejudice toward politicians in general. The attitude may be wrong, but it is real and may continue to influence the person for a long time unless a deliberate effort is made to change it.

Values

Rokeach (1971) defined values as "types of beliefs, centrally located within one's belief system, that address how one ought or ought not to behave, or about some end state of existence worth or not worth attaining" (p. 202). In many ways, values represent our permanent view of reality, formed and fashioned out of our more temporary beliefs and attitudes as well as the beliefs and attitudes of others in our family, neighborhood, or larger societal environment.

Awareness of some unique characteristics of individual values can increase our understanding of this concept. Values represent a person's beliefs about ideal modes of conduct. They are generally more permanent than attitudes or beliefs, and a hierarchical order exists among our personal values. This order is based on the relative potency, durability, and stability of the values we hold. The values that are more likely to shift over time are lower in the hierarchical order. Values are not typically articulated directly by their bearers; more often than not, our behavior is the strongest demonstration of our values.

We are convinced that a recognition of the importance of values is an important skill for those who would engage in proactive supervisory practice. First, if you are aware of values and how they affect human behavior, you will become more appreciative of your own values about a given issue. Even the activity of talking about values tends to make us more sensitive to them and to the role they play in shaping our behavior. Thinking about the fact that people have attitudes, beliefs, and values that differ from our own is the first step toward accepting those differences.

Second, supervisors must examine the issue of values because, as educational leaders, they will be called upon to analyze the values of people who work in, around, and with schools. Developing personal competency in how to interpret the values, attitudes, and beliefs of the people associated with any organization is a critical skill; a supervisor who is unable to sense those things that people hold dearest to them will almost certainly be an ineffective leader. All people have absolute points beyond which they will not compromise or change. Attempting to push people beyond those limits is a serious blunder. Appreciating the value orientations of others is necessary for perceiving and dealing with those non-negotiable issues.

Third (and perhaps most directly related to the overall concept of proactive behavior), supervisors need insights into many value orientations because organizational leaders are often the most visible people in the organizations. Supervisors represent to many people, not only their own personal value systems but also the orientation of the entire school or district. Frequently, we think not of "the elementary school down the block," but of "Mrs. X's school," where Mrs. X is the principal. The leader, a values witness, provides the members of the organization with an implicit identity and a sense of "what's right," or "what we do around here."

McGregor's Assumptions

In chapter 1 we considered a number of definitions and perspectives on educational supervision. At different times, supervision has been viewed as a means to correct incompetent teachers, to promote better human relations in schools, or to increase the measurable productivity of schools. In this book we do not espouse any of these three views, but we recognize that, because each is based on a total value system supported by some people in supervisory roles, each is a legitimate way of thinking. We also suggest that a critical responsibility of those of us in supervisory positions is to examine our personal values and determine how they align with other perspectives. We must do this openly, so that people who work in the school are aware of where we are "coming from." Most of us like to work with others who hold similar values; most of us can work with others with whom we openly disagree; but no one can work effectively with those who attempt to hide their true value orientations.

A useful framework for analyzing individual values regarding supervisory responsibility is Douglas McGregor's (1960) Theory X/ Theory Y Assumptions which are often used to illustrate how people in organizations can be motivated. A review of McGregor's basic assumptions is a good starting place for the supervisor intent on forming a personal and honest view of what supervision implies.

Theory X Assumptions

1. People are naturally lazy; when faced with a choice, they normally prefer to do nothing.
2. People work mostly for money and status rewards.
3. The main force keeping people productive in their work is fear of being demoted or fired.
4. People remain children grown larger; they are naturally dependent as learners.
5. People expect and depend on direction from above; they do not want to think for themselves.
6. People need to be told, shown, and trained in proper methods of work.
7. People need supervisors who will watch them closely enough to be able to praise good work and reprimand errors.
8. People have little concern beyond their immediate motivational interests.
9. People need specific instruction on what to do and how to do it; larger policy issues are none of their business.
10. People appreciate being treated with courtesy.
11. People are naturally compartmentalized; work demands are entirely different from leisure activities.
12. People naturally resist change; they prefer to stay in the same old ruts.
13. Jobs are primary and must be done; people are selected, trained, and fitted to predefined jobs,
14. People are formed by heredity, childhood, and youth; as adults they remain static.
15. People need to be "inspired" through pep talks; they must be pushed or driven.

Theory Y Assumptions

1. People are naturally active; they set goals and enjoy striving to attain them.
2. People seek many satisfactions in work; pride in achievement; enjoyment of process; sense of contribution; pleasure in association; stimulation of new challenges, and so forth.
3. The main force keeping people productive in their work is the desire to achieve their personal and social goals.
4. People are normally mature beyond childhood; they aspire to independence, self-fulfillment, and responsibility.
5. People close to the situation see and feel what is needed and are capable of self-direction.
6. People who understand and care about what they are doing can devise and improve their own methods for doing work.
7. People need a sense that they are respected as capable of assuming responsibility and self-direction.
8. People seek to give meaning to their lives by identifying with nations, communities, companies, or causes.
9. People need ever-increasing understanding; they need to grasp the meaning of the activities in which they are engaged; they have cognitive hunger as extensive as the universe.
10. People crave genuine respect from others.
11. People are naturally integrated; when work and play are too sharply separated both deteriorate.
12. People naturally tire of monotonous routine and enjoy new experiences; in some degree everyone is creative.
13. People constantly grow; it is never too late to learn; they enjoy learning and increasing their understanding and capability.
14. People need to be encouraged and assisted.

We can make two general observations about the pairs of items shown in the above lists. First, most people will not agree with every item under either Theory X or Theory Y; one list will be preferable, but a few statements from the other list will probably seem more accurate. Second, our true professional feelings about a particular item may not be reflected in the statements of either list; we might prefer a middle ground. Very few of us could be classified as absolute Theory X- or Theory Y-type supervisors. However, we can gain considerable insight into our own values by determining which of these items seem more accurate and acceptable. Such insight is the first step toward developing a personal educational philosophy.

Individual Action Planning

Each of us has an established set of beliefs and attitudes that shape our values. The next step is to put these concepts together into a meaningful statement to guide our behavior in a supervisory role. In this section, we suggest some ways to assemble your most important value statements into a working *personal philosophy*, one that can be translated into an individual action plan.

Construct Theory

The assumptions that underlie individual action planning come from a body of theory that has recently begun to influence the field of preservice teacher education, called Construct Theory. Developed by George A. Kelly (1965) as a way to explain actions in terms of mental constructs, it attempts to explain how people derive signs used in making decisions about how they conduct their lives.

Antoinette Oberg (1986) said of Construct Theory:

> It is the major premise of Construct Theory that people's actions are based on the ways in which they anticipate future events . . . Future events are differentiated on the basis of constructs which are attributes or qualities the events are expected to exhibit. (p. 57)

Construct Theory can help us understand why effective supervision is not always "knowing all the answers," but rather developing a way of thinking through problems and asking the right questions. Donald Schön (1983) in *The Reflective Practitioner*, observes that the critical responsibility of a professional is often to recognize the nature of problems and not always to determine perfect solutions to all dilemmas. Construct Theory and the concepts of reflection-in-action by Schön are important bases for the development of personalized guides to supervisory action.

Educational Platform Development

The supervisor's educational platform, developed by Thomas Sergiovanni and Robert Starratt (1993) is a model designed to help professional educators assess their views about a series of educational issues by stating their views in a straightforward manner, akin to the platform statements made by political candidates in an election campaign. The major difference between a politician's and an educator's platform is that the latter is structured to communicate the educator's deepest and truest beliefs, attitudes, and values, even if these are contrary to the sentiments of the public. (An individual educational platform is very similar to a personal, informal theory, a concept explained in greater detail in chapter 4.)

There is no single, perfect format for an educational platform. For example, Bruce Barnett (1991) has suggested that a platform may consist of a written statement which articulates educators' viewpoints on issues ranging from desired student outcomes to preferred school climate to expectations for community involvement in schools. Sergiovanni and Starratt's model (1993) for formulating a supervisor's educational platform includes twelve major elements. Ten of these deal with general educational themes, and as a result, they can serve as the basis for any professional educator's platform. The last two are linked directly to the role of a supervisor.

1. The aims of education
2. The major achievements of students this year
3. The social significance of the student's learning
4. The supervisor's image of the learner
5. The value of the curriculum
6. The supervisor's image of the teacher
7. The preferred kind of pedagogy
8. The primary language of discourse in learning situations
9. The preferred kind of teacher-student relationships
10. The preferred kind of school climate
11. The purpose or goal of supervision
12. The preferred process of supervision

The following excerpts from two particularly well-developed statements—the first by an experienced classroom teacher contemplating a supervisory career and the second by a beginning elementary school principal—illustrate how writing a platform helps define personal views.

Aims of Education

(Teacher) The aims of education are threefold. First, the schools must help each student to acquire a sense of self-fulfillment and self-worth in which all children can discover and realize their own unique talents, gifts, and abilities . . . Secondly, the schools must help students create and maintain meaningful relationships with others. They must help students learn how to communicate

. . . their needs, attitudes, concerns, and appreciations . . .
Finally, educators should enable students to become productive,
responsible citizens in our society. Schools need to impart the
basic knowledge, develop creative expression, and provide a
variety of experiences that will enable each student to assume a
role within one's community, one's country, and one's world . . .

(Principal) I believe it is the responsibility of education and
educators to develop students' self esteem and self-worth,
combating the situations and/or environment when necessary . . .
we must use extra effort to improve students' self-esteem when
the home situation or personal environment is abusive,
unnurturing, or uncaring; develop students' ability to get along
in society . . . ; give all students the opportunity to build a
foundation of basic knowledge and develop strategies to enable
them to achieve future goals; help students understand the
advantages of developing a life-long learner attitude.

Major Achievements of Students This Year

(Teacher) The major achievements I would hope to have my
children display by the end of the year include both academic
achievements and personal achievements. As a first-grade
teacher, I hope that my children will acquire the basic skills,
concepts, and information that they will need in order to
continue in their educational pursuits . . . Along with an ability
to receive and absorb specific facts, concepts, and skills, I hope
that my children will achieve the necessary work habits that they
will need in order to accomplish their present and future goals . . .
In order to meet the personal objectives that I deem important for
my children I hope to create a safe and comfortable environment
in which they can explore and discover themselves.

(Principal) I believe that a major achievement of a student at any
age is to be satisfied with his or her learning accomplishments
and yet to strive to do his or her best. As students mature,
education must put more emphasis on the process of setting
learning goals or life goals and to develop certain attitudes and
beliefs toward the learning process. Educators, along with
parents and communities, must help students realize the
importance of their educational accomplishments and the
importance of feeling good about them.

Social Significance of the Students' Learning

(Teacher) Our children are our future. Therefore, student learning
profoundly affects us in that students' views of the world begin to
take shape during the school years. Out of the student population
will come the future leaders and decision makers of our country.

Thus, the future quality of life in our society is directly related to the quality of education we provide for our students today.

(Principal) I believe that part of what students are expected to learn in the educational setting involves societal behaviors, and there are certain requirements that society dictates. Education is partly responsible for developing productive individuals . . . I believe we all need to do a better job helping students understand the importance of developing interpersonal relationships with a variety of different personalities. Our . . . existence . . . involves interpersonal relations with various individuals or systems: families, teams, groups, organizations, and governments. These systems are . . . comprised of individuals having diverse beliefs and values . . .

The Image of the Learner

(Teacher) Children are unique. Therefore, their ability to acquire and retain new knowledge and skills is unique. One method of instruction, although it may be appropriate for a percentage of the children within a classroom, cannot adequately meet the individual needs and learning styles of the remainder of the children. Thus, in order to motivate children to greater degrees of personal success, it is necessary to provide a variety of learning strategies within a classroom . . .

(Principal) Educators perceive the learner in a variety of situations and in a variety of performance modes. Through experience and observation, educators make assumptions of students' visual, auditory, tactile, and kinesthetic learning styles and should help students understand their most preferred learning style. Educators see students as individuals who want to gain knowledge or understanding through study, instruction, and experience. Adjectives that describe the learner are responsible, enthusiastic, inquisitive, attentive, hard working . . . and the opposite of each adjective as well . . .

Value of the Curriculum

(Teacher) In essence, the curriculum is a composite of all experiences, planned and unplanned, that constitute the learning of the individual. These learnings occur both within and outside of the classroom. Those experiences which children encounter through the interaction with their families and peers, through the mass media, such as television, radio, magazines, and newspapers, and through social and religious organizations strongly impact the curriculum that is presented in schools. Therefore, in designing and developing curricula for schools, this "hidden" curriculum needs to be recognized, acknowledged, and planned for specifically. In so doing, the teacher can be proactive rather than reactive in providing the optimal learning experiences for each child . . .

(Principal) By articulating the curriculum (the vision, mission statements, proficiencies, outcomes, objectives, etc.), the focus and direction of the school become evident. The curriculum is a means through which educators can reflect on the value or importance of the information taught, make recommendations for adjustments, and be more accountable for the results. The curriculum is also a means to communicate to parents and communities the nature of desired educational goals . . .

The Image of the Teacher

(Teacher) A teacher is an individual with a specific purpose or mission. A teacher with a mission has a deep underlying belief that students can grow and attain self-actualization. Teachers believe that they have something of significance to contribute to other people, especially students, and believe with every fiber of their being that they can "make a difference." Teachers believe that children can and want to learn and are driven from within to find the technique or strategy that will assist each child to learn . . . Teachers also receive high personal satisfaction and inner joy from the growth of their students. They seek out the resources necessary to stimulate and activate learning with the student and are excited when students think, respond, and learn . . . A teacher is also a contributing member of the larger school setting and should value working closely with the principal and other staff personnel.

(Principal) Since teachers work with . . . our children, I expect teachers to:

- Possess a certain set of high standards and moral values
- Be caring and concerned about the education and welfare of the students
- Be service-oriented and have a high sense of achievement
- Have a positive attitude about people, especially children
- Be a dispenser of knowledge and a translator of culture
- Be knowledgeable, enthusiastic, and hard working
- Be challenging and understanding
- Be a friend, advisor, and counselor
- Be an observer, facilitator, and role model
- Work miracles

Preferred Kind of Pedagogy

(Teacher) As a first grade teacher, I enjoy a multitude of ideas, materials, and experiences when helping my children to learn.

Because of the age, experiences, and socialization of first-graders, at the beginning of the year I find it necessary to assume a more directive role within my particular classroom. I feel that this is appropriate and necessary in order to help six- and seven-year olds feel safe and secure in their new environment and to help them make a transition from a more home-centered world into a more school-centered world . . . As I work within my classroom, encouraging children to strive for higher degrees of personal and academic achievement, I also utilize the larger resources of the school. These include other students, the principal, the media specialist, the special area teachers . . . the guidance counselor, the psychologist, and our teacher aides. I believe that it takes many caring and concerned individuals to help a child learn and grow into a healthy, productive adult . . .

(Principal) I am discovering that personality styles and temperaments affect all that we do. I can't state that one teaching style is preferable over another. Different kinds of pedagogy can be effective depending on . . . situations, subject areas, skills to be taught, educator style, and temperament of student groups. The important issue is how educators use their own temperament to establish and maintain a facilitative relationship with the differing temperaments of the student groups . . .

Primary Language of Discourse in Learning Situations

(Teacher) Children learn best when they are involved and when the material presented is relevant to their interests and needs. Therefore, the language within the classroom should foster communication. This communication can take many forms: discussion, lecture, questions and answers, dialogue, and role-playing. But whatever form that it takes, it should have at its base the interests and needs of the child . . .

(Principal) Communication is the essence of education, possibly in all industries. Communication can be orderly and thought provoking, imaginative and open, feeling and nurturing, or conflicting and confusing. Communication involves sending and receiving messages. An educator must give praise; give instructions; ask and answer questions; deal with conflict and emotions; and be friendly, positive, stern, caring, and aware of students' needs. With the interests of the child in mind we need to improve our skills in active listening, observing, interpreting messages, using acceptance messages, using appropriate acknowledgments, using door openers, paraphrasing, giving feedback, and maybe sometimes just being silent. Communication is both verbal and nonverbal. The educator must realize the importance of nonverbal communication and be consistent in the conveyed messages. Effective communication is a vital and complex process and not easily accomplished.

Preferred Kind of Teacher-Student Relationship

(Teacher) The relationship established between the teacher and the student has a profound effect upon the child's ability to function and learn to his or her optimal level. A teacher's priority is to foster a safe environment in which each child feels a sense of belonging, importance, and acceptance. If this is established, the child is able to channel his or her energy into positive learning rather than withdrawing from the learning situation in a negative way . . . It is important for the teacher to understand that each child is unique and that a teacher's expectations for one student might not be the same for another student . . .

(Principal) The interpersonal relationships that occur and the bonds that are formed between teacher and student are very special. We must admit that our children spend a great deal of their time at school. In addition to the time involved in daily academic instruction, we have to consider all the extracurricular activities, practices, and athletic events which contribute to the overall growth and development of the whole child. By nature people become involved in such activities to satisfy the need for group belonging and interpersonal relationships. Students often look up to educators with admiration. Educators who give praise and encouragement might be the only positive influence in some students' lives. It is not surprising that strong bonds and relationships are formed.

Preferred Kind of School Climate

(Teacher) An atmosphere of trust and safety must be created within a classroom. Within this environment, each child's unique needs and interests can be met. Because all students are different, they have different requirements for openness and structure, for movement and control, for an opportunity to work in groups, or for the need to work alone. It is important to meet these differences and to help children create an awareness and understanding of the similarities and differences that they share . . . A teacher needs to realize that no one best environment will meet the needs of every student . . . A positive climate is essential throughout the total school building and should be realized districtwide.

Allowing for and appreciating the special needs, interests, and styles of our colleagues—feeling valued and important as professionals and as people—ultimately transfers itself into an atmosphere that profoundly affects children and stimulates their capacity to learn.

(Principal) The school climate is affected by educator attitudes, how staff relates to administration, the amount of collegiality that exists, teacher-student relationships, and school-community relationships. I believe that attitudes might be the key to a positive climate. The students are able to feel the general attitudes of the staff, which will be filtered to the parents and into the communities. The teachers will produce a more comfortable and safe climate for the students if these attitudes consist of openness, trust, and honesty. Likewise, when community groups are not positive about school issues or staff members, this will have an effect on the students and staff and their climate as a whole. Educators need to be continually aware of the relationship between school and community and present an open-door policy at all times. Schools need the support of parents and communities and should do what they can to nurture and develop this relationship.

Purpose of Supervision

(Teacher) The purpose of supervision is to maximize children's learning. This is accomplished by directly improving the quality of a teacher's instruction within the classroom. A supervisor, therefore, is an individual whose responsibility and desire are to help teachers recognize and capitalize on their strengths. A supervisor must also understand and assume responsibility for the goals and priorities of the organization as a whole. This requires that the supervisor often bridge the gap between the interests and needs of the teachers and those of the administration. Thus, the supervisor's role often entails effective communication and advocacy—advocacy of the teacher and advocacy of the administrator. The supervisor must clearly visualize how each separate part of the organization fits together for the benefit of the whole and be able to take the steps necessary to accomplish this end. Thus, the supervisor must be genuinely concerned and comfortable with each group and be able to effectively merge their varied concerns and transcend the difficulties to a level of greater excellence for the total organization. In order to accomplish this, supervisors must clearly understand their personal platforms. This has the potential of creating a climate of trust and credibility between supervisors and all parties involved. When this is achieved, the needs of the child are enhanced, and that is our primary focus as educators.

(Principal) I have some administrative colleagues who really believe that supervision should be a way to find out what's wrong in a school. They use it as a kind of quality control process that can help them weed out teachers and staff who are not doing the job. I disagree with that perspective. Instead, I think that the real purpose of supervision should somehow be to

identify the strengths that people have and build on those. If
people make mistakes and need help, that should also be
something that occurs in the supervisory process. Dealing with
mistakes can be done in a way that promotes growth and
professional development, not simply finding fault with others'
performance.

Preferred Process of Supervision

(Teacher) As I grow in my understanding of supervision and the
various modes of supervisory practice, I believe that there is no
one best way to supervise. I realize that each institution is
different and that each individual is unique. It would be my
responsibility as a supervisor to evaluate and to respond to each
condition by gathering and accessing the data surrounding that
particular situation.

I would respond to the inherent worth and value of each
individual, and this belief would be a strong guide within me as I
interact with my colleagues. I believe that growth is attained
most completely when the strengths of an individual are
determined and those strengths are developed and encouraged.
By identifying and developing strengths, I believe that the
personal dignity of the individual is preserved and that this is the
foundation upon which change and growth can occur. I feel that
as I would direct and encourage teachers to utilize their strengths
to their greatest potential, they would, in turn, direct their
abilities to more productive instruction of the children.

I realize that, at times, it would be necessary to supervise a
staff member who is minimally effective with children. I hope
identifying the person's strengths with him or her would increase
the person's self-worth and possibly minimize any confusion or
anxiety that might hinder the individual's effectiveness in the
classroom. If it became apparent that this person's strengths
could be utilized more appropriately in a different direction,
working together with him or her to explore possible alternatives
would be appropriate. I am aware that a high degree of trust
needs to be established before this is even possible.

I see myself applying the human resources philosophy. When
members of an organization understand the goals of that
organization, and become the agents by which those goals are
achieved, then growth within those members is attainable to a
higher degree. Personal self-attainment is energizing, both to the
individual and to the organization, and creates an atmosphere of
good will, trust, and greater cooperation. This has a cyclic effect.
Within the organization, participation should be encouraged at
the level at which an individual is capable; understanding that
each person has his or her own "timing" and will develop
accordingly. It would be necessary to stimulate learning for each

staff member by offering many opportunities for personal and professional growth, such as inservices, workshops, conference attendance, and involvement in specific interest and support groups. Staff who had interest and skills in a particular area would be encouraged to share them, formally or informally, with their peers. In this fashion, a network of in-house expertise is developed for the recognition and the evolution of the presenter, the growth of the staff, and the benefit of the children. In this manner, supervisors can, by acknowledging the control of the growth of the teachers with their colleagues, internalize and expand the ownership of the goals of the district.

(Principal) The main challenge that I face as an educational leader is to promote learning in my school. That learning, of course, is most directly related to children. However, it also includes the promotion of effective learning among all who work in our school— teachers, classified staff, and me. As a result, the kind of supervisory process that I believe that I follow is one that does not emphasize making judgments about others' competence. Instead, what I hope that I emphasize is always a supervisory style that encourages individual growth and development. In other words, I encourage people to do what it takes to become all that they can be . . . even if that means making mistakes from time to time.

Preparing and periodically revising an educational platform is useful for a number of reasons. Writing a formal educational platform requires you to articulate many of the ideals that you may take for granted as you go about your business in a particular role. Highly experienced educators praise the platform-writing process because it is a disciplined way to express sets of beliefs, attitudes, and values they may have forgotten over the years; it results in a formal agenda that allows you to see and then confront ideas that are rarely stated; and it allows you to make your values more visible to others. Although we don't recommend circulating copies of a personal platform as a standard practice, a well-prepared platform can be a useful tool for sharing important personal feelings with others who need to know your beliefs. In addition, a formal statement can help you gain greater insights into your fundamental non-negotiable values.

Finally, the articulation of a personal educational platform can be a most valuable experience for anyone who may be contemplating making a career shift into the field of school administration or supervision. This is consistent with the recommendation of the National Policy Board for Educational Administration (1989) which noted that it is important for aspiring educational leaders to explore their personal values and attitudes as they consider new career options.

> . . . students [of educational leadership] must be pushed to examine their own belief systems, their reasons for wanting to be administrators, their images of the mission of schooling as a social process. The curriculum should be designed to provide frameworks and tools to assist students in assessing the moral and ethical implications of administrative decisions in schools. They must come to understand the concept of public trust and to realize how values affect behaviors and outcomes. (p. 9)

Everyone who works in any organization wonders from time to time whether or not to stay in a particular position. Sometimes an organization changes to the extent that it no longer seems to represent values that were once appealing. A formal platform statement is a visible and constant reminder of what an educator holds in greatest esteem. Its real value may be to help you answer the question, "What is so important to me that I would quit rather than compromise?"

Reflective Practice and the Action Plan

Articulating an individual educational platform is an extremely powerful activity for reviewing professional and personal values, but it is little more than an exercise unless it is combined with an action plan. An action plan need not be a formal statement with a predetermined number of elements as in a platform, but it should list actions that will enable you to look at your present role to determine how personal behavior actually matches both the platform and the characteristics of the job.

Let us see how action plans are developed as the result of individual reflection of platform statements. Consider how the elementary teacher quoted earlier moved from her initial platform statement to a statement of analysis, and then to a personal action plan.

Platform Analysis

The writing of my platform has been a challenging and valuable undertaking. I feel these beliefs and assumptions, but have never articulated them until now. This has been an affirming exercise, but at the same time, I realize that I am also in process. I am not the same person today that I was yesterday. Nor will I be the same person tomorrow as I am today . . . I know that should I ever step out of the process, I will stop growing as an individual and will lose any effectiveness that I might have as a teacher and a supervisor . . . I found as I placed my thoughts on paper that there was an element of interrelatedness among the different themes. In order to achieve one aspect of my platform. I need to build upon the others. As a result, I sense a unified direction for myself. It is as though I have developed a focus, and that the confusion that accompanies indecision is removed. As a teacher, I know what I'm about and feel that what I do is valuable. Yet, as I began to express my thoughts regarding supervision, I found myself searching for clarity. My experience in personnel, in facilitating both student and adult groups . . . has given me a background of understanding. There are still gaps in this understanding. This is what is directing me to gain a better understanding of the field of supervision.

Personal Action Plan

I plan:

1. To exercise my belief that learning is a lifelong adventure. This would include my present goals . . .
2. To become a more effective classroom teacher, and to continually seek the resources that will permit children to reach their greatest potential
3. To encourage and assist in the development of staff within my particular school and within the district. To plan and implement with my principal a specific plan for staff support and supervision
4. To evaluate my growth and needed areas of growth with my supervisors and the participants involved in my experience
5. To continually clarify my educational platform by asking the question, "What is best for children?"

The principal concludes with the following statement of actions that she wishes to carry out for her professional development in the future:

1. Work on becoming more of a visionary leader who can pull the group together for a common goal . . .
2. Improve my evaluation techniques, time management skills, and legal knowledge
3. Improve my communication skills and interpersonal skills
4. Be a good model for the students and the staff
5. Develop trusting and open relationships with students and the staff
6. Spend more time expressing appreciation and acceptance of the staff and students
7. Become a proactive leader

These two action plans allow the teacher and the principal to examine the major non-negotiable issues described in their original platform statements and to select a series of important personal professional development objectives. Action planning allows the platform writer to come full cycle from an original statement of philosophy to a statement of action.

One last issue that we mention regarding the development of an educational platform is an important item to remember. It is relatively easy to fill a platform statement with many commendable, nice-sounding, or even politically correct items. One example might be the stated belief that "all children can learn." While we certainly do not wish to disagree with that belief, we raise the question here as to whether all such blanket statements are always supported by behaviors that a teacher or supervisor can witness on a day-to-day basis. We firmly believe that it is important to espouse one's educational philosophy in a way that can be shared with others. We believe more firmly in the notion that such statements must be honest and consistent with actual practice. Nothing could be worse than saying one thing and not "walking the talk."

Summary

This chapter introduces the most critical and basic aspect of supervision as a proactive process: *To be most effective, supervisors must be aware of their personal assumptions, beliefs, attitudes, and values.*

Beliefs and attitudes change frequently during our lives; values are more permanent. However, values can also be modified over time. Personal values can be put together in a coherent statement to guide supervisory practice, using procedures involving two separate but related tools: an individual educational platform and an action plan. Writing these as a formal activity helps individual educators to understand and to demonstrate their most important values. Becoming aware of our personal values benefits both us individually and the organizations in which we work. Excerpts from the educational platforms and action plans of an elementary teacher and a principal illustrated how the formulation of a personal statement can guide future practice.

Suggested Activities

1. Formulate your own educational platform, using either the formats that are presented in this chapter or a design of your own creation. As preservice students, many of you will not be able to address every element suggested here, but try to define your feelings about as many important educational issues as possible. What do you consider to be the primary aims of education? What is your image of the learner? What pedagogical methods do you prefer? Why should people be supervised?

2. Review the educational platform that you have developed. In what ways can your values and beliefs about education be put into action in supervisory practice? Make a brief, informal list of actual behaviors or objectives that would enable you to put your beliefs into action.

3. As you review your platform, write down one or more observable behaviors you demonstrate, allowing others to recognize that you consistently put your beliefs into action. By contrast, identify any of your value statements in the platform that are often contradicted by your normal practice and behavior.

4. Share your platform statement with someone who knows you quite well and ask him or her to provide a critique. Is what you say you believe reflected in what you do on a regular basis?

Cases to Consider

The following brief cases are based on actual situations which have taken place in schools. Please read each case and consider the following:

a. What are the critical issues raised in each case, as they relate to the topics covered in this chapter of the text?

b. How does each case relate to the development of the concept of proactive supervision as it is defined in chapter 1?

c. In what ways might you suggest a resolution to the issues raised?

Case 2.1:

Always a Friend of the Schools?

Steve Albright has been the principal of Green Mountain High School for the past twelve years. Prior to that, he was the head football coach who frequently led his team to league championships. In addition, he was a social studies teacher who worked exceptionally well with many students who had trouble adjusting to school life. He spent many hours out of school helping "lost kids" find their way. With all of these accomplishments, it is not hard to see why, three years ago, the local Rotary Club provided Steve with a special plaque celebrating his devotion to the needs of students in the community.

Since the plaque was awarded, a few things have happened in Steve's life. He applied for the position of superintendent two years ago when Carl Spencer left the district. He was shocked and angry when the school board passed him over in favor of another district administrator who was working on his Ph.D. at a local university. It was rumored that there was a feeling that this person would present a better image of the school system than "ex-coach" Albright would. Steve was hurt but continued to work at the high school. He continued to express his public view that "Kids always come first in my life."

Recently, the new superintendent started to experience some problems with the community, and it was increasingly apparent that the next school tax referendum might not pass, thus sending the school district into a rather serious financial bind. If the levy did not pass, many programs for students would be curtailed, bus service would end, and there would be no extracurricular programs. As the date of the referendum approached, community interest grew, and Steve Albright began to receive a lot of phone calls from parents and sports boosters he had known for many years. Most calls were for advice regarding how people should vote. More than a few suggested that, if Steve agreed, there would be a strong move by many of his supporters to vote against the tax levy, increasing the likelihood that "the wonder boy" superintendent would be discredited in front of the school board, and thus assuring that Steve would get the job he really deserved all along. It was a very tempting scenario to Steve.

Case 2.2:

The First Job

Gretchen Callahan was really excited about the phone call she just received. The superintendent of the Climbing Vine Schools called her to say that he and the assistant superintendent decided to offer her the job as an elementary principal in their school system. Gretchen, a primary grades teacher in her present school district for sixteen years, had worked really hard to complete the administrator certification at the local university. Now she was eager to get out of the classroom and put her ideas to work as a real-life principal.

Her first inclination was to accept the position at Climbing Vine. The pay sounded good, it wasn't too far from home, and the building in which she would serve was very attractive. Something inside of her told her to delay a decision.

When the superintendent called, he made no mention of any of the input he had gotten from the team of teachers and parents who had interviewed Gretchen last Monday afternoon. In fact, there was no mention of any of the ideas that she shared with the team or any of the other central office administrators with whom she talked. And what about the feedback that the superintendent must have received from the other district principals who had visited with her? Although it was a fairly good experience, she knew that at least two of the other principals obviously disagreed with her position on inclusion for children with special needs. The district administrator acted as if he had received no feedback from the other people.

As Gretchen reflected on the interview process that she had gone through, she recalled how careful she had been to point out that she would always seek input concerning any important decisions she would make as the principal. Building a strong sense of teamwork in her school through promoting consensus would be at the heart of her approach to problem solving in her building.

References

Barnett, Bruce (1991). *The educational platform: A developmental activity for preparing moral school leaders*. Paper presented at the Annual Meeting of the American Educational Research Association, Chicago, IL.

Barnett, Bruce (1992). Using alternative assessment measures in educational leadership programs: Educational platforms and portfolios. *Journal of Personnel Evaluation in Education*, 6:141–151.

Kelly, George A. (1965). *A theory of personality: The psychology of personal constructs*. New York: Norton.

McGregor, Douglas (1960). *The human side of enterprise*. New York: McGraw-Hill.

National Policy Board for Educational Administration (1989). *Improving the preparation of school administrators: An agenda for reform*. Charlottesville, VA: NPBEA.

Oberg, Antoinette (1986). Using construct theory as a basis for research into teacher professional development. *Journal of Curriculum Studies*, 19(1): 55–65.

Rokeach, Milton (1971). *Beliefs, attitudes, and values: A theory of organization and change*. San Francisco: Jossey Bass.

Schön, Donald A. (1983). *The reflective practitioner: How professionals think in action*. New York: Basic Books.

Sergiovanni, Thomas J., & Starratt, Robert J. (1993). *Supervision* (5th ed.). New York: McGraw-Hill.

Additional Readings

Argyris, Chris (1982). *Reasoning, learning, and action: Individual and organizational*. San Francisco: Jossey Bass.

Kottkamp, Robert (1982). The administrative platform in administrative preparation. *Planning and Changing*, 13:82–92.

Raven, J. (1981). The most important problem in education is to come to term with values. *Oxford Review of Education*, 7(2): 50–67.

Sanders, Donald P., & McCutcheon, Gail (1986). The development of practical theories of teaching. *Journal of Curriculum and Supervision*, 2(1): 253–272.

Schön, Donald A. (1987). Educating reflective practitioner. San Francisco: Jossey Bass.

Sergiovanni, Thomas J. (1987). *The principalship: A reflective practice perspective*. Boston: Allyn and Bacon.

3 Continuing Controversies

In this chapter, we review some major, continuing controversies that typically surround discussions about the nature of supervision in schools. Understanding these controversies will help you clarify your own view of educational supervision.

Is There Such a Thing as a Supervisor?

There is an old saying that goes, "If you say something often enough and with enough conviction, whatever you say will eventually become true—or at least, believed to be true by a lot of people." A little of this logic has crept into discussions concerning educational supervision. The literature has generally treated supervision as if it were a field with clear boundaries and well-accepted definitions and assumptions. In truth, supervision is a highly ambiguous field of which no clear view is generally held. Supervision is not easy to define.

We can see the vague and fluid nature of educational supervision by comparing and contrasting two different educational roles— those of the school principal and supervisor. Most people recognize and understand what a "school principal" is. We may even have an image of what a principal looks like, how his or her office is arranged, what he or she usually does, how students and teachers interact with a principal, and so forth. Furthermore, tremendous similarities exist in the principal's role from school to school, district to district, state to state, or even nation to nation. Rural, suburban, and urban school principals lead very different lives in many ways, but their basic job descriptions appear very similar. In addition, the public perceptions of what or who a principal is remain fairly stable: We have generally had enough encounters with individuals who are called "principals" to lead us to believe we know what they do.

By contrast, there is no similar automatic or universal recognition of what supervisors "usually" do for several reasons, First, what supervisors do in Chicago may not at all be what supervisors do in Boston; second, those who carry out supervisory duties in one school district may have substantially different job titles than those in similar positions in other settings; and third, many school districts have no formal supervisory positions at all. A number of people who have spent a lot of time around schools have simply never met anyone who holds the title of "supervisor." We could not, in all likelihood, find anyone who had never encountered a principal.

Where supervisors exist, they are responsible for a wide variety of tasks. The following list indicates the responsibilities assigned to individuals specifically designated as supervisors in five different school districts. Clearly, no single person could be expected to undertake all of the prescribed activities, and we might even ask if all of these duties should really be considered "supervisory" in nature. The fact is, however, that these tasks are listed in the formal job descriptions of people who needed state certification as "supervisors" in order to get their jobs.

The supervisor of instruction:

- assists in assessing needs at the local school and citywide levels
- provides consultant help to individuals and staffs
- keeps current on developments in education and in the fields of specialization; attends professional conferences
- conducts the piloting and implementation of new instructional materials and strategies
- serves as advisor-representative to various professional organizations
- interviews prospective teachers
- prepares demonstrations, programs, and reports on the work of the school for professional, parent, and community groups
- works directly with students in educational projects
- assists in the evaluation of teaching performance, instructional programs, and materials
- designs, develops, and conducts inservice activities

- designs and develops goals and objectives for new curricula
- works with principals, teachers, pupils, and parents in an effort to accomplish the improvement of instruction
- plans opportunities for continuing education for all certificated personnel
- works to improve communication within the system and between schools and the public
- works toward a curricular and educational philosophy that strongly emphasizes the children's needs
- keeps the records and makes the reports required by law, by state regulation, and by the state superintendent and school board
- provides consultative services in subject areas
- reviews and evaluates requests for changes in course offerings
- keeps abreast of research trends, innovations, and other aspects of the various subject areas
- disseminates information pertaining to research trends and innovations as well as reminders of sound teaching practices
- maintains a program of visitation at regular intervals at all schools
- attends meetings of administrative and supervisory personnel
- serves as a total resource person in the educational process
- screens requests from outside special interest groups for student participation in community activities
- performs such other duties as assigned by the superintendent

Supervisors are expected to do different things in different places, and to compound the confusion, many of these same things are often done by people who hold job titles other than supervisor. In recent years, many school systems have deliberately used different job titles to designate individuals who undertake tasks historically assigned to the area of supervision. We now find numerous settings where people are called "coordinators," "resource personnel," "specialists," or "directors." These titles have been modified over the years for many reasons, including the desire to find terms more descriptive of what individuals actually do, or to avoid the negative connotations conjured up by the "inspectors" and "managers" of previous supervisory eras. No matter how good the motivation, however, changing names can cause problems. A supervisor is not always a supervisor. In some school districts, formally designated supervisors undertake work duties that are not clearly supervisory in nature, while other individuals in the same district are given supervisory duties, but not the equivalent titles. Further, more so today than ever, administrators are focusing on providing instructional leadership; school principals, superintendents, and other educational administrators are more involved in the core technology of schools—the curricular and instructional practices and teaching-learning processes.

This last statement underlines the difficulty many educators have in understanding and defining the field of educational supervision: The job simply does not exist in many settings. A great many people have not had any direct contact with a supervisor because many school systems are just too small to employ supervisory personnel; other systems have deliberately eliminated supervisors as "frills" whose traditional responsibilities can best be carried out by principals or other administrators. In these districts, the typical organizational arrangement might include a superintendent, an assistant superintendent or two, a business manager or treasurer, building principals, and teachers. If we view supervision as a process rather than as an isolated role, we can say that anyone who works with teachers and provides them with feedback concerning their classroom performance is engaging in supervisory behavior.

Possible Responses

Based on these observations, the immediate answer to the question "Is there such a thing as a supervisor?" is no. Yet there are supervisors in education. We clarify this issue in two ways. First, we can understand supervision not as an identifiable and stable role, but as an ongoing *process*. Second, we can analyze the generic tasks, duties, or responsibilities commonly associated with supervisory activities.

Describing supervision as a process rather than as a particular organizational role is a useful way to bring some clarity to a discussion of supervisory practice. If we consider individuals, regardless of their specific job titles, who engage in a process of supervision, we can free ourselves from worrying whether a supervisor in District A is the same as a supervisor in District B, or whether a curriculum coordinator is the same as a supervisor of curriculum. In addition, a process orientation to supervision reduces needless distinctions between such things as "generalist supervisors" and "specialist supervisors," or "school-based supervisors" and "central office supervisors." While distinctions such as these exist in various school systems, and some understanding of their similarities and differences is probably useful under some circumstances, a general understanding of the foundations of educational supervision is hardly enhanced by emphasizing subtle differences in supervisory practice. Rather, our knowledge base is substantially increased when we can find and focus on similarities among the activities of all who either formally or informally "supervise."

We can break down the distinctions that cloud our understanding of what supervision entails by looking toward the unique features of different supervisory roles and searching for the overlapping or similar duties undertaken by those who practice supervisory processes. The following list, frequently cited as a framework for describing generalized supervisory duties, was prepared by Ben Harris (1985) of the University of Texas at Austin. Performance in the nine distinct areas can be used to assess supervisory effectiveness. More importantly, the nine areas indicate the essential ingredients of effective supervisory practice, regardless of the supervisory context or the job title of any specific individual who engages in supervisory duties.

Supervisory Competency Areas

1. Developing curriculum
2. Providing materials
3. Providing staff for instruction
4. Organizing for instruction
5. Relating special public services
6. Arranging for inservice education
7. Developing public relations
8. Providing facilities for instruction
9. Evaluating instruction

Is There a Difference between Administration and Supervision?

One theme that recurs in virtually every discussion of educational supervision is the differences that exist, or do not exist, between those who are called school "administrators" and those who are called school "supervisors." A quick answer to the question "Is there a difference between supervisors and administrators?" is yes; a distinction is made between the two fields. We made the point in the previous section that immediate recognition normally follows when we talk about an administrative role such as that of the school principal. We also noted, in contrast, that confusion often reigns when we talk about supervision. A review of the precise nature of the differences between supervision and administration may prove helpful.

One important and traditional distinction is that administrators are typically referred to as "line officers" while supervisors are "staff members." Figure 3.1 is a line-staff organizational chart describing the governance structure and relationships in a typical school district.

The key distinction between those who serve in line positions and those in staff positions is that the former usually enjoy the formal, or statutory, authority to make decisions on behalf of the organization in which they are members. Staff members, by contrast, are responsible for acting on directions provided by line officers and for implementing decisions made by those in line positions. While this seems like a relatively simple distinction, it is not entirely accurate. Consider, for example, the fact that school principals are classified as administrators, or "line officers," which suggests that principals make decisions and are not required to respond to the direction of others. In fact, few modern school principals would view their jobs in these terms. A common view of the modern school

Figure 3.1. Typical line-staff organizational chart. (Solid lines indicate line positions.)

principal is that he or she serves as a "middle manager," that the position lies somewhere between the imperatives expressed by the central administration and school board and by the wishes of teachers who understand that they must carry out those imperatives in their classrooms. In addition, teachers today rarely accept unreservedly the notion that they must respond "upward" to the dictates of formal authority figures in the organization. The classic distinctions between line versus staff, and supervisor versus administration, then, are considerably blurred.

Despite this blurring of distinctions, administrators do have organizational and often statutory responsibilities that supervisors do not. At least on paper, administrators have greater formal authority and control over the people who work in their organizations than do other individuals in the same organizations. Those "other individuals" include the supervisory staff. In the real world of schools, the distinction gets played out in a variety of ways. Teachers may be observed formally, for instance, by people designated both as administrators (usually the building principal) and supervisors (a subject area specialist from the central office). More often than not, however, if an unfavorable personnel decision must be made based on data gathered through classroom observations, the person legally responsible for making the decision and then communicating it to the teacher is an administrator. The supervisory staff may be asked to provide additional supporting documentation to assist the administrator in making his or her decision, but the authority resides at the administrative level.

The majority of encounters between supervisors and teachers, or administrators and teachers, are not as dramatic as a negative personnel review. There are numerous situations, however, where the differences between supervisors and administrators are reflected in their respective roles in working with teachers. In many school systems, supervisors are perceived as somewhat "closer" to teachers; in fact, they are still teachers in the minds of many people. Administrators, on the other hand, have moved to a world outside teaching, and some imaginary barriers seem to separate them from classroom teachers. Clearly, these unfortunate views tend to reinforce the stereotypical divisions between administration and teachers and hinder the search for conditions that will contribute to schools becoming more productive and effective places.

Good school administrators must first have served as good teachers; effective principals must have been effective teachers (although effective teachers do not automatically become effective administrators). In any case, while the distance between administrators and teachers is certainly lamentable, suggesting that such separations do not exist would be a serious mistake. The persistence of this characteristic of school life needs to be recognized as a genuine part of the differences that exist between administration and supervision because it often drastically changes the nature of supervisory practice in school settings. In many ways, the educational supervisor is truly neither fish nor fowl. A supervisor is associated with teachers but no longer serves in the classroom. A supervisor is also given duties consistent with a formal leadership position but does not enjoy formal authority in the governance structure of the typical school system, unless the building administrator is described as a supervisor in a specified setting.

The final distinction made between supervision and administration is a bureaucratic and legislative one related to the licensure and certification requirements imposed by various state education agencies. Many states treat supervisory certification as a first step toward becoming licensed as a school administrator. Requirements for supervisory certification are often less demanding than those for an administrative certificate and require fewer courses and university credits. In some states this is beginning to change, and the role of the supervisor is being defined more or less apart from any other educational role.

Possible Responses

Differences exist between educational administration and educational supervision that are truly felt in the real world of schools. These distinctions need not serve as dysfunctional barriers, however, to the ability of schools to operate effectively and serve the needs of learners. One observation in this regard seems particularly relevant. Schools today are demanding people who are capable and talented, regardless of job titles. These people will need to assume a variety of duties along the way. Thus, it is fair to say that school administrators will continue to need additional skills and sensitivities related to effective supervisory behaviors and processes, and supervisors will need to be aware of their managerial and administrative responsibilities.

Can Supervisors Ever Really Get Anything Done?

To what extent do supervisors have the formal authority and power to see to it that anything is accomplished by the people who work in the schools or district? More will be said·about this in chapter 10, but a few comments concerning the nature of supervisory power and authority are offered here.

We argue that supervisors can, in fact, "get things done." Certain limitations, however, have traditionally been placed on people who serve in supervisory roles in schools. As we noted earlier in this chapter, supervisors are typically described as staff, and regardless of the fact that distinctions between "line" and "staff" are not often entirely clear, the prevailing expectation is that staff personnel are not able to give orders to others, or to make decisions to which others in the organization can be expected to respond. On a formal organizational chart, therefore, supervisors are limited because they cannot require people to behave in a particular way. We should consider, however, whether it is realistic to suggest that any position found in a modern school system chart, either a line officer or staff member, truly possesses total control over the other members of the organization. Teachers' associations and unions have increasingly sought input into school system decision-making processes, and it seems increasingly unlikely that anyone—from superintendent to principal to instructional supervisor—can command total control over the members of that school system. Nevertheless, it remains true that statutory and other formal control mechanisms exist in all school districts, and these to a large extent dictate that certain individuals will be legally designated as "in charge." Typically and traditionally, those individuals are not supervisors but administrators.

Nevertheless, there are more subtle ways in which educational supervisors are able to see that things get done. These methods rest in informal control and influence rather than in the control and power that derive from relationships depicted in a line-staff chart. The primary ways in which educational supervisors exert influence results largely from a consistent demonstration of what others in the organization perceive to be expertise concerning a given curricular area. A reading supervisor's influence rarely derives from the fact that he or she holds a certain position in the school district's organizational chart or has an office at central headquarters. Instead, reading supervisors are respected or consulted because teachers believe that the supervisor *knows something about reading that is relevant to the concerns of teachers.*

In addition to influence derived from their subject area expertise, of course, supervisors also get things accomplished through the exercise of interpersonal influence. People tend to follow other people's direction if they find those people appealing. However, too much reliance on interpersonal and charismatic avenues of influencing others can be fraught with dangers. Building support entirely on personality styles and compatibility can lead to supervisory practices devoid of any substantive content. In schools, teachers look to colleagues who can provide answers and help in a real way to assist them in solving their real problems. At such times, likeable people are simply in the way unless they can help solve someone's immediate problems.

Possible Responses

The question "Can a supervisor really ever get anything done?" has been answered to the extent that we believe a person in this role can be effective. However, such effectiveness requires skills that go far beyond traditional channels of formal control, power, or authority. Perhaps the ultimate answer to our question is found not in the analysis of influence patterns—based on expertise or personality—that are utilized, but instead on a concern essential to the basic assumption of proactive supervision. That assumption holds that a person will function at a much more effective level with a clear personalized understanding of what should be accomplished. If the goals of a supervisor are simply to enforce policy that has been formulated by others, and if there is no personal attachment or commitment to that policy, there is little likelihood that the supervisor will be able to convince those people with whom he or she works that the policy is worth following. On the other hand, tremendous power clearly rests in the sharing of other individuals' values and visions.

Summary

In this chapter we advanced our basic understanding of what supervision is all about through a review of some of the fundamental issues, or continuing controversies, related to the field. These controversies include the need to understand who educational supervisors are, distinctions that exist between supervision and administration, and finally, the extent to which the nature of supervision actually allows you to achieve your goals and objectives.

In response to these issues, we proposed that supervision should be understood not as a job responsibility designated by a specific role and title, but rather as a process carried out by many different actors in an effective organization. In addition, we endorsed the need to seek areas of similarity between administration and supervision rather than dwell on differences that separate these two fields. Finally, consistent with the overall view expressed throughout the chapters of this text, we indicated that your effectiveness as a supervisor will be greatly enhanced if you have a strong internalized understanding of what your agenda for action will be. If you merely define your role as speaking for the organization, little will happen to benefit that organization. If, however, you take a proactive supervisory posture in deciding what goals and objectives of the organization are of greatest personal value and if you communicate that value orientation openly, honestly, and often to the school staff, more effective organizational performance is likely to result.

Suggested Activities

1. Conduct a local analysis of supervisory jobs in your area. Interview one or more local school district personnel administrators to determine whether there are specific "supervisor" jobs. If jobs are not referred to as "supervisory," how are they classified in different districts?

2. Interview both a person who has a clearly defined supervisory position and a school principal about the ways in which they might carry out a similar task, such as leading a curriculum evaluation project. Listen for differences in the ways in which these two individuals approach the same task. Are there any apparent differences between the strategies used by an administrator and a supervisor?

3. Ask a supervisor for examples of the ways in which she or he must engage in administrative behavior. Talk to an administrator about supervisory duties.

4. Collect the organizational charts of three or more local school systems to determine the expressed differences between "line" and "staff" personnel.

Cases to Consider

The following brief cases are based on actual situations which have taken place in schools. Please read each case and consider the following:

a. What are the critical issues raised in each case, as they relate to the topics covered in chapter 1?

b. How do these cases relate to the development of the concept of proactive supervision as it is explained in this chapter?

c. In what ways might you suggest a resolution to the issues raised?

Case 3.1:

You Can Trust Me, Can't You?

Hank Flagler, a teacher with more than fifteen years of experience in the Apple Valley Schools, had recently received word that, for the next year, the district wanted to designate him as a Teacher on Special Assignment. He would be responsible for visiting different elementary schools in the district each week to share his considerable expertise about working with children with special needs. This was considered a high priority for Apple Valley because it had just adopted one of the strongest stances supporting inclusion for special needs students in the state. Hank was known as a teacher respected by co-workers across the system, and the school board assumed that he would be most welcome as a consultant and resource person to help his colleagues in all the schools.

Soon after the school year began, however, it became clear that convincing the teaching staffs to accept inclusion would not be easy. Regular classroom teachers were not interested in becoming special education teachers, and special education teachers expressed a concern that they would soon lose their ability to serve as experts if they did not continue to focus on special education. To put it mildly, Hank did not feel welcome when he walked to the front doors of the schools in the district.

The overriding concern that Hank expressed to his closest friends was that somehow teachers around the district seemed to forget suddenly their long involvement with Hank as one of their colleagues. People who had started their careers with him, worked in the same schools, served on many different committees together, and even attended parties in Hank's home now seemed to look at him as if he had crossed some sort of invisible line. He was now "one of them," and not "one of us."

It was only mid-October, but Hank had pretty much decided

that next Monday he would stop in to see the superintendent and get a release from his special assignment. He simply wanted to get back to his classroom where he knew everything would be safe and sound, and where he could be trusted again. Or could he?

Case 3.2:

I Want to Be Important

Mary Fletcher recently earned her administrative certificate after taking classes for several summers at State Teachers College. She was quite pleased to hear that, almost immediately after she received her certificate in the mail from the state department, the district curriculum coordinator wanted to talk to her about an opening in her division. She told Mary that if all worked out, she would soon be in a "key leadership position."

The selection process for the new position of elementary curriculum coordinator, a new supervisory position designed to enable someone from the central office to spend time in the field observing teachers in their classrooms working with new curriculum, didn't take very long, and it didn't take long for Mary to accept it. Mary was really pleased. After eleven years as an elementary school teacher, she now looked forward to stepping into a position of prominence and importance.

Mary soon discovered, as she began making visits to schools around the system, that her presence was rarely recognized by those who worked in the individual schools. Principals and teachers were pleasant, and they allowed her to roam freely in their buildings. Nevertheless, no one really paid much attention to her unless she happened to be accompanied by the director of curriculum. On a few occasions, the superintendent also came with her. On those days, she was also noticed by school staff.

The pay was good, the working conditions were nice, and it was really impressive to go to state meetings wearing a badge that designated her as a member of the district leadership team. Somehow, however, this was not the kind of life that Mary had expected to find after landing her first "important" job.

References

Harris, Ben M. (1985). *Supervisory behavior in education* (3rd ed.). Englewood Cliffs, NJ: Prentice Hall.

Theory into Practice

Throughout Part I we argued that the most practical way to understand educational supervision is as a set of process skills, rather than as a specific job or role. In Part II, we present and analyze a series of analytic "tools"— theories advanced by various perspectives in the social sciences—to help those of you engaged in supervisory activities. Only through this use of theory to guide action can supervisors function in a dynamic, proactive way.

4 The Role of Theory in Improving Supervisory Practice

An important assumption throughout this text is that an understanding of theory in the social sciences represents a critical step toward enhancing our appreciation and understanding of effective supervisory practice; it is a way to gain important new insights into how things work in organizations. One very practical consideration serves to support this assumption. When our perspectives are rooted in theory, we also have access to a way of guiding our behaviors in everyday problems and situations. As a consequence, our actions will be based on something other than the same tired answers to the same tired questions. Developing a basic understanding of what theory is and how it can be applied to local school settings will greatly contribute to your mastery of proactive supervision.

Definition of Theory

What is theory? To many, a standard and rather negative view of what theory is prevails in the field of education. Our discussions with numerous school practitioners suggest that educational theory is often viewed as a synonym for speculation or supposition or as an attempt to represent some ideal with little relevance to the real world. For many people actually working in schools, theory is anything that does not possess an immediate, practical value.

There are many things that theory is not. It is not, for example, part of axiology (the branch of philosophy which deals with values)—although you may develop a personal theory based on your own values to guide your supervisory practice, as we discussed in chapter 2. In the strictest sense, mixing "theory" with "values" and "philosophy" represents an incorrect application of all these terms. Nor is theory simply the individualized application of one person's common sense. The problem we face whenever we talk about common sense is that what we label with this term is often neither "common" nor "sensible" to everyone at the same time; common sense is, in fact, often a fiercely individualistic and personal view of reality. We need only think of the bit of sense commonly held in the Middle Ages that the earth was flat. Ultimately, such common sense views have little practical use to any decision maker.

What is theory, then? *Theory is an attempt to describe phenomena and interrelationships found in the real world in terms that reflect the true nature of the world.* In its most fundamental form, theory is an attempt to collect elements of knowledge and truth from multiple sources—authority, tradition, intuition, common sense, observation, structured empirical research—to guide practice by informing decision makers of likely (if not always absolutely certain) consequences of their actions under certain conditions. The view of theory in the field of educational supervision, consistent with the view in the wider field of social sciences, holds that theory is a type of generalization based on observable and verifiable reality. The assumptions of theory in the social sciences, then, have been borrowed extensively from the physical sciences.

For educational supervision in particular, the contemporary literature provides several useful definitions. Thomas Sergiovanni and Robert Starratt (1983), for example, define theory as "a mode of thinking that leads to the generation of propositions amenable to testing either in the laboratory or in practice. It is a systematic, conceptual framework to be used in understanding present phenomena and in gaining insights into how to behave in the future, when faced with the same phenomena" (p. 121). Wayne Hoy and Cecil Miskel (1988) offer a similar, related definition by noting that theory is "a set of interrelated concepts, assumptions, and generalizations that systematically describes and explains regularities in educational organizations" (p. 155). This second definition is particularly interesting because it suggests three important characteristics of social science theory: First, that theory is logically composed of concepts, assumptions, and generalizations; second, that the major function of theory is to describe, explain, and predict the nature of regularities in human behavior; and finally, that theory is heuristic—it stimulates and guides the further development of knowledge. Both definitions suggest that theory is based on present reality, but usable in building future understandings. These notions are consistent with and applicable to our view of proactive supervision.

It would be misleading to suggest that theories always appeal to us because of their clarity and precision as descriptions of present reality. They are, in fact, frequently full of terms and concepts difficult for us to grasp. Theories are, by their very nature, general and somewhat abstract, and more importantly, they are never absolutely true or false. A theory is always open to some individual interpretation.

Functions of Theory

Based on the definitions of theory we have cited, we can begin to identify specific outcomes to be accomplished through the application of theoretical perspectives to a field such as educational supervision.

Ultimately, the function of a theory in the social sciences is to provide generalizations and, eventually explanations of the ways in which phenomena appear in the "real world." As a result, theory often serves as the basis for further empirical research, in which "theory-testing/theory verification" is a stated goal. One function of theory has traditionally been to set up future research questions and to provide suggestions about which research results may be relative to a defined, specific issue. Consider, for example, the researcher who conducts a study based on an established theory of motivation, such as Abraham H. Maslow's (1970) view of need-satisfaction, which holds that people will be motivated only as their lowest levels of need are met. If the researcher finds that people seem to be motivated in this way, Maslow's view is supported. If people do not respond in the way predicted by the theory, further studies with different assumptions will be carried out.

A second widely accepted function of theory is to provide an integrating, common feature in the further development of the knowledge base in a given field. Theory often leads to the generation of research; the findings of research lead to action; action leads to further theory refinement, and so on. Research emerges from a theory base, and this often stimulates the researcher to build upon the assumptions and generalizations of an earlier theory and research base. The use of theory in this type of clarification and building process often leads to new issues. Researchers might investigate, for example, how a certain theory is reflected in the ways teachers think about instruction. As research is conducted, the researcher will see an increasingly clear picture of how thinking takes place. As a result, the theory may be revised to reflect this research finding, and new and separate issues discovered in the process may be reserved for further study.

Finally, and perhaps most relevant to our presentation of supervision as a proactive process, theory in the social sciences often guides action. Theory can help us make wise, reality-based decisions. Theory allows us to make sense out of the complex and often contradictory behavioral patterns that we so often see in the real world. While the first two functions of theory related primarily to the needs of most educational practitioners engaged in systematic research in schools, this last function is a cornerstone for effective supervisory practice, which reflects proactive rather than reactive or crisis-oriented behavior. The third function of theory captures the most straightforward of its uses—it describes the nature of present conditions and events in a most accurate and economical fashion and predicts the likelihood of the same events and conditions occurring in a similar, predictable way in the future. A teacher who is aware of a child development theory that suggests children learn best when they are personally ready to learn, for instance, may design a classroom environment where children with varying personal interests can find a variety of things to do.

Steps in Theory Development

Another way to clarify how theories are used to link present realities with future practice is to consider how they develop over time. Most theories appear to develop as the result of a movement through at least three identifiable, sequential steps: first, the discursive treatment of a topic; second, the development of a simple listing of characteristics; and third, the creation of a juxtaposed taxonomy of observed events. These first three steps are often followed by the building and sharing of theoretical models, also known as graphic depictions of theoretical statements. We will return to each of these steps in the next few pages to examine how they fit together and how they may be used by the practitioner of supervision interested in the improvement of practice in schools.

Discursive Treatment of a Problem or Topic

This step, usually considered a starting point in the theory development cycle, basically consists of brainstorming" or even "idle chit-chat" about some specific topic, issue, trend, or event. No attempt is made to offer any connection between and among random, disjointed observations.

As an example, consider the type of talk that can be heard in teachers' lounges in schools across the nation. Dozens, even hundreds, of random observations are made each day about how a particular group of students behaves, about the latest memo from the administration, or about the policies recently formulated by the school board at a public meeting. This kind of real-world, random discussion might well serve as the beginning for the theory-development cycle.

Let us imagine that a group of teachers makes some random observations about how the students in their classes tend to behave. Most teachers may comment that "the kids are pretty good here," while a few might note that some students "cause a lot of problems" in the school. Names of individual students will probably emerge. Comments from other staff members range along a continuum stretching from "the kids here are angels" to the "kids are terrors." These comments come fast, without advance thinking; they are not offered in any specific order, but randomly represent what at least a subset of the teaching staff in a particular school believes about the nature of students in their care. They are "true" statements insofar as they represent the honest beliefs of people; they derive from each teacher's perceptions of the reality that he or she experiences each day. Theory in the social sciences often begins this way, even when the participants have no realization, and certainly no conscious desire in that direction, that they are laying the groundwork for the development of a theory in any formal sense.

Development of a Simplified Listing

Eventually, observations made in random fashion begin to be repeated with enough frequency that a list becomes apparent. Although this activity is the second step in a linear theory-building process, it is actually quite similar to and often simultaneous with the "discursive treatment" stage. Listings of phenomena begin to take shape almost immediately from random observations.

As we suggested above, random observations about student behavior are virtually nonstop in most teachers' lounges throughout the year and across the nation. The same general observations occur with sufficient frequency to suggest that simplified listings of observed characteristics could easily be compiled. Unfortunately, the random observations of professional educators are not generally recorded in any systematic manner; therefore a relatively small amount of formal theory is actually built upon the observations of classroom teachers, but a very personal informal level of theory building is in fact going on continuously in schools. What rarely takes place is the type of codification and formalized listing described as the characteristic of this step in the formal theory-building cycle.

Formulating a Juxtaposed Taxonomy

At a certain point in the theory-building cycle, the random, limited observations of existing phenomena are placed in relationship to other features of the observed environment. In other words, discursive treatment is placed in context, and a juxtaposed taxonomy is created.

Returning to our teachers and their observations of student behavior, simple statements such as "The kids are terrors" are usually quickly followed by qualifying statements such as "right before spring break." Teachers frequently make use of context-based statements to guide their own professional behavior. Within a relatively short time, beginning teachers note that students tend to behave one way on Monday mornings, somewhat differently late in the afternoon on Wednesdays, and in a completely different fashion on Friday afternoons. One year "in the trenches" is usually time enough to show a teacher that students will react to directions differently before a long vacation break from how they act after that same break. This series of random observations of student behavior, then, when placed in the context of the school-year calendar, provides considerable guidance for the teacher who is planning instructional activities. Most instructors learn quickly that a major examination on the last afternoon before spring break will result in low grades and high frustration for students. For years, teachers have tended to search for hands-on activities that call for high physical involvement when they know students are preoccupied with thoughts of an upcoming week away from school.

A good theory must be able to describe the present with a high degree of accuracy; more importantly, it must be useful in terms of suggesting and predicting future events. The fact that students tend to be disengaged from classroom activities on days before vacations is in itself an interesting piece of descriptive information. However, this information is much more important in terms of what it offers to the classroom teacher for lesson planning at vacation times. The observation placed in context allows teachers to change their behavior to accommodate what they have learned. The real value in understanding theory is not simply that a theoretical perspective offers a novel way to describe real situations. Rather, the long-term value is that theory enables us to engage in proactive practice.

Model Building

Although the steps just covered constitute the basic theory-building cycle, one additional activity is often included in this process, namely the building of a theoretical model. This may sound like a mysterious activity, but all we mean is that the interrelationships of variables or factors in a theoretical statement are depicted graphically. Although not an absolutely essential part of theory development, models are nonetheless an integral part of most conceptualizations that influence practice in the social sciences. We will include a number of these graphic depictions or theoretical models as we review theories in later chapters.

Characteristics of "Good" Theory

A good, usable theory in the social sciences—that is, one which fulfills the assigned functions of describing present reality while also predicting the likelihood of events occurring in the future—should have at least some of the following identifiable characteristics:

- A "good" theory must be based on observed (and observable) events that are grounded in reality. Theories cannot be so conceptually abstract or divorced from common reality that no one besides the individuals who formulate the theories can understand what is meant. Theories must communicate bits of reality to a relatively wide audience. Thus "good" theories cannot be mere suppositions of a chosen few; they must be born of and tested in a reality that is shared by many at a time.

- A "good" theory should explain things found in reality in a complete, yet succinct fashion. A statement that must use many qualifiers to explain exceptions to the rule is probably not a particularly "good" theory. A theory should say much in a few words, or in the case of a theoretical model, in as simple a graphic design as possible.

- A "good" theory must be amenable to some type of systematic verification, validation, or testing process. It is not enough, for example, for a small group of teachers to note the behavior patterns of the students in a single elementary school. Someone else needs to be able to witness the same behaviors; in a sense, a person must be able to walk in off the street and verify whether or not students do behave as the teachers claim. More important, a good theory must "hold up" when it is transported to other settings. Is it true that students do not act seriously the day before a vacation? If this question can be answered similarly in a wide variety of different sites, then this theoretical assumption is likely to be a "good" one.

- A "good" theory must have a future-time orientation, because it ultimately needs to be an accurate predictor of the way things will probably be. As we mention throughout this text, understanding and applying the theories of the social sciences to educational supervision will be of little value unless this understanding somehow improves practice in the schools at some point in the future.

One way of thinking about what social science theory is, is to conclude that a good theory is like a pair of glasses worn to aid our vision. Theory should help us see the relationships between the goals of the organizations and the abilities of the people who work in those organizations more clearly. We wear "glasses" to get a better look at things—the situations and events that might occur from time to time in the world of practice related to educational supervision. The corrective lenses of a good theory help us develop generalizations and reactions, and, more importantly, to aid future planning and anticipation of events. The application of good theories does indeed permit more proactive, less reactive, behavior. The ultimate importance of theory, and perhaps its stiffest test of goodness, is that it provides consistent ways of looking at similar, but not wholly alike, events that are part of the world at work. Theory in this sense can be viewed as an important part of an educational leader's "bag of tricks."

Restrictions on the Use of Theory

There are some important cautions that need to be voiced about reliance and usage of theory in the field of educational supervision. These cautions are in no way meant to detract from the value of theory as an ongoing guide to practice in supervision; rather, we list them only to suggest potential problem areas to those who might develop too great a reliance on theoretical formulations as guides to all behavior.

- Although many elements of current supervisory practice date back to the origins of American public education in general, the field of educational supervision as currently practiced is still an emergent discipline. As a result, the events from which the initial observations and assumptions come are highly limited. There is no long-established history from which we can draw sufficient inferences for use in formal theory-building processes.
- We need to recognize that biases are a constant threat to objectivity in the collection of sound observations. Idiosyncratic interpretation of reality is bound to enter the field of theory development at one point or another, and listings will remain the products of personal observation, wherein we can never be sure that the observers are totally free of prejudice.
- Educational supervision is a complex and widely interpreted field. As a result, the totality of educational supervision can never be represented by one finite set of theoretical assumptions and models. In the chapters that follow, we will underscore this point by selecting for intensive review a handful of theoretical perspectives that might prove useful to you in guiding supervisory practice. There are many other perspectives, models, and theories that might be useful to those who serve as educational leaders; no one theory can answer all our questions.

We have focused our discussion of theory up to this point almost exclusively on formal theoretical formulations in the social sciences. Before we move on, we should glance quickly at the applications of less formal, more personal theories to the enhancement of supervisory behavior.

Distinctions between Formal Theory and Personal Philosophy

Much of what we have just said about the functions and characteristics of formal theory, along with the steps followed in the theory-building cycle, has relevance to the development of a personal philosophy as a way to guide and improve supervisory practice. While we have tended to suggest that theories are developed in a more or less conscious fashion by those who wish to contribute to a general, widespread clarification of practice in the social sciences, theory also emerges in a considerably less visible and grandiose fashion. Most people periodically observe events in their personal reality, form simple lists, and then place their observations in a context that enables them to behave in a more or less predictable way over time. We can cite again our examples of the individual classroom teacher who, after some experience, knows that students tend to behave one way at certain times and differently at other times. The ability to accumulate such theories to guide personal practice is often pointed to as a characteristic that differentiates between "average" and "good" teachers. We can use the knowledge accumulated in one year to help us improve the next year—or we can simply repeat the same year, over and over. Cumulative learning is another way to describe what we refer to as the development of personal philosophies, theories, platforms, or guides to action.

Structurally, then, great similarities exist between the steps followed in formal theory building and individual or personal philosophy construction. Perhaps the greatest single difference is the extent to which we can generalize from the initial random observations. In the case of the formal theory building, the "discursive treatment" step might include random observations made by many different individuals in numerous settings over a long period of time; our own observations, on the other hand, are simply that—our own.

A potential danger exists in developing too rigid a stance toward a personalized theory. There is a fine line between taking a stance on a particular issue, based on highly personalized observations that are not necessarily shared by many in the general population, and closed-mindedness. Personal observations can produce prejudices and biases. A teacher whose classes have included only a few Hispanic children might generalize based on observed behavior that Spanish-speaking students are (1) very ambitious, (2) very lazy, (3) very talkative, (4) very shy, (5) very bright, or (6) any one of thousands of other characteristics that might be assigned to all students based on the witnessed behavior of a very few in a highly limited setting. (Of course, merely increasing the number of observations does not guarantee that a theoretical formulation will be free of bias. For example, during the earliest days of our nation, "theories" of witchcraft were "proven" by a multitude of "observations" reported by reliable citizens about their neighbors.)

Formal theory, then, does not differ from personalized, informal theory solely because observations are made by many people rather than one. Other distinctions need to be recognized. Formal theory, for instance, is open to ongoing testing and verification in an objective fashion. If those subscribing to the theories of witchcraft had been open to a dispassionate review of their assumptions, their theories might have had a much smaller audience. The theories used as the basis for much of our thinking in the social sciences are formal; they have been tested through empirical research and, as a consequence, have undergone periodic modifications. In addition, what are most often classified as important theories in educational supervision have been generalized across many different settings. A review of the Axiomatic Theory of Organizations by Hage in the next chapter, for example, demonstrates that it is as usable in schools as it might be in hospitals or private industry. To be sure, there is considerable value in developing individualized, personal, and informal theory, and it is a process that occurs with or without specific recognition. However, there are limitations in allowing our behavior as leaders and supervisors to be guided too much by informal patterns. We also need knowledge of formal statements of theory.

Summary

In this chapter we have explored the role of theory in the social sciences as a way to improve supervisory practice. As an introduction to this concept, we offered a number of definitions for theory and noted that theory is not, as often described, solely abstraction or philosophy. Rather, *theory attempts to reflect the nature of reality based on observable phenomena.* Steps in the theory-building cycle were described and related to the major functions and characteristics of "good" theory in the social sciences: the description and explanation of present events and the prediction of the likely occurrence of future events and behavior. The chapter concluded with a review of some typical restrictions and limitations associated with the use of formal theory and with a summary of the differences between formal and informal theory. We noted that both personal, informal theory development and formal theory building in the social sciences are important tools for use in educational supervision. However, formal theory makes use of widespread generalizations of observable phenomena and is normally subjected to some degree of objective testing and verification. As a result, some special features of formal theory make it particularly valuable to those who need to understand "the way things work" in organizations.

Understanding and relying on theories is certainly not the only way for practitioners of educational supervision to function. There are many unfortunate examples of supervisors living solely in the world of theory who are very ineffective when faced with making decisions concerning "real-world" issues. On the other hand, we firmly believe that some appreciation of theory is an important characteristic of successful followers of proactive supervision processes.

Suggested Activities

1. Analyze the way in which you or a colleague deals with parents, students who have discipline problems, or some other situation faced by school teachers to determine how your approach is guided by the development of a personalized theory as described in this chapter.
2. Interview a supervisor or school administrator concerning the way in which he or she handled some sort of recent "critical incident." In your analysis, try to determine the steps that were followed by the person. Was there a similarity between his or her expressed behavior and the steps in the theory-building cycle described in this chapter?
3. Ask a number of people how they would define "theory." Determine from their responses the extent to which these individuals have a positive or negative view of theory.

Cases to Consider

The following brief cases are based on actual situations. Please read each case and consider the following:

a. What are the critical issues raised in each case, as they relate to the topics covered in this chapter?

b. How does each case relate to the development of the concept of proactive supervision?

c. In what ways might you suggest a resolution to the issues raised?

Case 4.1:

So, Here's the Answer

For the past three years, Washington Terrace Elementary School had been gaining a reputation as a school with a lot of problems. There were no great discipline problems with the students; rather, the problems at Washington Terrace revolved around a growing sense of conflict between the teachers and the parents. Recently, an ultra-wealthy subdivision opened near the school, and the new local residents were extremely rich and, for the most part, well educated. This represented quite a change in the past few years. Teachers at Washington Terrace had a long history of working with a very different type of community.

Ann Smith, a young principal with two years of very successful experience in another school district, was considering a career change. She applied for and became a finalist for the position of principal at Washington Terrace where the principal of eight years had just left to take position in the northern part of the state. Ann was extremely interested in the job because of the outstanding reputation of Washington Terrace and the suburban school district in which it was located. The only apprehension she had concerned the things she now started to hear about the turmoil taking place between parents and teachers.

Ann was just a few days away from the final set of interviews that would decide who would get the Washington Terrace principalship. As she reflected on the likely questions which would be posed concerning her ability to handle conflict between teachers and parents, she felt increasingly comfortable with the notion that she could respond to any concern. After all, she had sixteen years of teaching experience, and during that time she had many confrontations with unhappy parents in her middle-class school district. As a principal for the past two years, she was called upon to deal with a lot of situations where the working-class parents objected to some of the practices of her teaching staff. Her experience as an educator would truly help her with the kinds of issues that were likely to surface at Washington Terrace. After all, parents are parents and teachers are teachers.

Case 4.2:

I Thought I Knew . . .

The faculty of Mountain State University, a major research institution with a strong national reputation for the quality of its academic program in educational administration and supervision, was universally happy with one of its recent graduates, Dr. Peter Greene. Pete was one of those really rare students who came along only once every ten years. He was someone who truly stood out as an outstanding scholar, even at a place as prestigious as MSU. It was not surprising that he was able to land a principalship at Olive Tree Elementary School, one of five highly regarded elementary schools in the Peaceful Branch District, a well-respected system near the campus of Mountain State. It took a little bit of work on the part of the MSU faculty to convince Bob Davidson, the Peaceful Branch superintendent and another graduate of their doctoral program, to hire Pete, even with his strong academic record. Pete had only three years of prior professional experience as a primary teacher in a small private academy in another state. For the past six years, he had been enrolled as a full-time graduate student at MSU where he completed his masters degree and doctorate. The faculty convinced Bob that Pete was a bright young star who could truly bring a fresh perspective to the system. Besides that, it was hard to dispute the fact that over the years, MSU had produced so many examples of first-rate administrators like Bob.

Pete had been on the job for less than a month, but the signals were already becoming clear that something was not right. Bob Davidson was starting to hear a number of complaints by parents, and he noted on his calendar that he was meeting next Monday with Shirley Kincaid, the Peaceful Branch Teachers' Association building rep at Olive Tree. His secretary's notes stated that Shirley was coming to express some faculty concerns about the way in which this school year had started. Beyond that, Bob had been hearing some concerns regarding the fact that Pete did not seem to be able to make decisions very quickly. Even relatively simple things appeared to be taking longer than they should to be resolved. The other principals were beginning to make comments to Bob about the "rookie" at Olive Tree.

Pete was aware that there was some tension in his building, but he was not really concerned. After all, he felt confident that the findings of his doctoral dissertation which dealt with the micropolitics of education would help him in his work. He would be able to tell exactly what the issues were in the community. Further, he had learned quite a bit from Dr. Jackson's excellent class in conflict resolution back at MSU. Finally, he had been reading a number of other studies on the issue of community unrest and its impact on staff morale conducted by researchers all over the country. Pete felt confident that, as he studied and analyzed the problems that were emerging in his building, he would be able to provide a reasonable explanation for what was happening, and the rest of his principalship would be very successful.

References

Hoy, Wayne K., & Miskel, Cecil G. (1988). *Educational administration: Theory, research, and practice* (2nd ed.). New York: Random House.

Maslow, A. H. (1970). *Motivation and personality* (2nd ed.). New York: Harper and Row.

Sergiovanni, Thomas J., & Starratt, Robert J. (1983). *Supervision: Human perspectives* (3rd ed.). New York: MGraw-Hill.

Additional Readings

Halpin, Andrew (Ed.) (1958). *Administrative theory in education*. Chicago: Midwest Administrative Center, University of Chicago.

Owens, Robert G. (1987). *Organizational behavior in education* (3rd ed.). Englewood Cliffs, NJ: Prentice-Hall.

5 Organizational Analysis

In this chapter we review the theory-based analysis of complex organizations presented through two analytical approaches. The first we call *formal* analysis, and the second *informal* analysis. Formal organizational analysis refers to the structure of organizations, including their stated and institutionally defined purposes and objectives. Informal organizational analysis deals with the characteristics of people who work in the institutions, along with the less visible and tangible features of the organization such as the psychosocial climate or "feel." The practitioner of effective and proactive supervisory processes needs to be aware of both the formal and informal levels of analysis.

In the first part of the chapter, we present some theoretical perspectives that describe and predict behavior associated with formal organizations. Included are Gerald Hage's Axiomatic Theory of Organizations, Jacob Getzels's Social Systems, Gareth Morgan's Organizational Metaphors, and Lee Bolman and Terrence Deal's Organizational Frameworks. In the second part of the chapter, two perspectives in informal aspects of organizations, Matthew Miles's view of Organizational Health, and Organizational Climate as conceptualized by Andrew Halpin and Donald Croft, will be described. Throughout the discussion, we indicate how these theoretical perspectives offer opportunities for the educational supervisor to improve his or her practice, and more importantly, the quality of life in schools.

Hage's Axiomatic Theory of Organizations

An enduring theoretical analysis of the formal characteristics of organizations was proposed by sociologist Gerald Hage (1965).

While the term "axiomatic" (i.e., so obvious as to be self-evident) may be open to some debate, we include this framework for two reasons. First, the development and application of this theory directly follow the rational, linear theory-building cycle which we set forth in chapter 4. Second, the theory offers some important insights into the operation of organizations to the extent that supervisory behavior can be greatly enhanced through an understanding of the assumptions and properties found in this theory.

Historical Development

Hage's focus throughout his work as a sociologist has been to determine how societal institutions function. He began by simply looking at a wide array of organizations—hospitals and nursing homes, private companies, and educational institutions, among others. By reviewing the characteristic components in diverse locations, Hage and his colleagues were able to note conceptually similar features that existed in all types of organizations. Thus, the process of the discursive treatment of a topic (random observations) and the development of a simplified listing of phenomena were completed as nearly simultaneous activities. In this earliest phase of the historical development of Hage's theory, then, the first descriptive function of a theory was completed.

Structural and Outcome Variables

Hage's examination of complex organizations yielded a primary, simple finding: All organizations, regardless of their type and purpose, may be conceived of as having two basic characteristics: *structure* (or the way in which they are put together) and *outcomes* (the purposes for the organization). Further analysis indicated that all organizations have at least four common structural components: centralization, complexity, formalization, and stratification. These may be defined as follows:

Centralization.   A measure of the proportion of jobs in an organization that participate in decision-making processes. An organization where only a few people tend to make all or most decisions is highly centralized, whereas an organization where there is widespread and broad-based involvement in decisions is low in centralization, or decentralized.

Complexity.   The number of occupational roles and specialities, and the level of training required by people in an organization to fulfill the roles and specialities needed. Organizations with many complicated jobs requiring advanced training are high in complexity.

Formalization.   The proportion of jobs that are codified, along with the range of individual variation and interpretation that is allowed in the performance of jobs. An organization where people are expected to comply with the features of a very specific job description is high in formalization. If there are opportunities for many employees to do many different tasks without regard to official responsibilities, an organization is low in formalization.

Stratification.   The differences that exist in income levels and prestige found within an organization. When there are gaps between employees in terms of salary levels and other forms of organizational rewards, there is high stratification.

A few additional comments need to be made concerning these structural variables. First, some organizations are typically relatively high or low in terms of each factor. For example, a large modern hospital is normally very high in complexity, given the tremendous amount of specialization now found in the field of medicine. Moreover, hospitals are also institutions with high stratification: Cardiac surgeons make more money and have greater prestige and visibility than do general surgeons, emergency room physicians, or radiologists; physicians stand far apart from nurses, orderlies, or any of the other scores of jobs found in most hospitals. By contrast, consider the characteristics of another type of organization, the mom-and-pop grocery store. Here, decision making is highly decentralized, there is little complexity, and stratification does not exist. In many instances, when something needs to be done, everyone (owner or employee) pitches in to get the job done. We should be aware, however, that there can be gradations in each of these structural components in the same types of organizations. For example, not all hospitals are the same; some are more stratified than others.

As do hospitals, schools have different gradations of structural components. While schools might, in general, fall somewhere around the middle of a continuum of all organizations, some schools are obviously different from others in terms of centralization, complexity, formalization, and stratification. Some schools feature opportunities for greater participation by teachers in schoolwide decision making. Other schools have greater job specialization and, perhaps as a result, more levels to increase discrepancies in terms of prestige. In fact, the nature of the size and grade levels served by a school also has a good deal to do with the relative degrees of any of Hage's structural elements that might be present. High schools, particularly ones with a strong departmental structure and many specialists on the staff (nurses, guidance counselors, librarians, and so forth) are much higher in their degree of complexity than are the majority of elementary schools. On the other hand, some elementary schools serving many students across a range of several grades will be more complex than elementary schools enrolling pupils in only two or three grades. In addition, the degree of formalization and stratification will vary in schools where there are many specialized roles, as contrasted with a setting where there is but one administrator and, perhaps, no more than ten classroom teachers.

Organizations may also be understood through their outcome characteristics. Hage described four: production, efficiency, job satisfaction, and adaptiveness.

Production.   In most organizations, production is defined simply as the number of things that are produced during a given period of time. High production means that many things are created or built in a relatively short period of time, and low production occurs when a small number of items are produced during a certain time frame.

Efficiency.   This outcome variable is a measure of the cost associated with the production of the items produced. High efficiency results when the ratio of cost-per-item or unit is low. Low efficiency is the reverse: An individual item costs a great deal to produce. Incidentally, cost is defined here as the amount of any resource—money, time, labor, and so forth—that is expended.

Job Satisfaction.   This was originally indicated by the rate of turnover of employees. However, nowadays people tend to stay on their jobs whether they like them or not. Thus, in many institutions job satisfaction currently might be viewed as a condition where there is a continuous, deliberate focus on the needs and interests of employees.

Adaptiveness.   Also referred to as "innovativeness," adaptiveness describes the number of new products developed within an organization during a given period of time. A manufacturing company would be considered high in adaptiveness if it introduced many new products in a calendar year. By contrast, a company that tended to "stand pat" and stay with the same merchandise year in and year out would be low in adaptiveness.

As was true of structural variables, organizations may also be generally high or low in these four outcome variables. Employees in a manufacturing company might not enjoy the daily routine on the assembly line but experience job satisfaction because the company's policies reflect a caring attitude. For example, the company might provide pay increase incentives, insurance benefits, profit-sharing plans as well as display a caring attitude—all factors which can affect job satisfaction. On the other hand, an employee working for a small firm, performing challenging tasks that vary every day, might feel isolated and unappreciated by co-workers and management. The firm might not provide extra benefits or other incentives. Job satisfaction, in this case, might be low. A research and development institute might place great emphasis on adaptiveness because the company was created primarily to develop an abundance of new ideas and products. A very "old line" and stable producer of one identifiable product line, such as high quality watches or writing instruments, might never be inclined to bring out something "new and different." Variations may occur, however, even among organizations with similar titles and interests.

Similarly, individual schools differ significantly in terms of the outcome variables. One school may have a reputation for very high standardized test scores (an indicator of productivity), while a neighboring school system has a history of much lower scores. One system may produce X number of National Merit Scholars at a per-pupil expenditure of $4,800, while another district, spending only $4,500 per student, boasts of even more scholars—a difference in efficiency.

Mechanistic versus Dynamic Organizations

After Hage analyzed organizations in terms of structures and outcome, he essentially finished the stage of the theory development cycle that we referred to earlier as the simplified listing. In the next stage of theory formulation, Hage related two prototypic organizational patterns that could be described in terms of the structural and outcome variables. These two organizational types are defined as *Dynamic* (open to constant change) and *Mechanistic* (tending to maintain existing practice). Table 5.1 indicates the relative degree of structural and outcome variables possessed by each type.

Neither the Mechanistic nor the Dynamic organization should necessarily be viewed as better or worse than the other; these two designations serve only to describe two polar opposite organizations. Table 5.2 compares two opposite organizational structures by Richard Wynn and Charles Guditis (1984). If we ask, "Should a school tend to be a Dynamic or Mechanistic organization?" two answers are possible. First, individual schools are already best understood as Dynamic because they emphasize widespread involvement in decision making (low centralization), little reliance on formal job descriptions (low formalization), few distinctions among staff members in terms of prestige or income differences (low stratification), but many special technical skills demonstrated by teachers and other staff (high complexity). Other schools typify the Mechanistic model because they have the opposite structural characteristics.

Second, perfection for schools, as for any organization, depends largely on the goals of that particular school. Different structural characteristics yield different outcomes. If a school's goals include stability (low adaptiveness), high test scores (high productivity), without spending too much money (high efficiency), but without concerns for the needs of staff (low job satisfaction), the appropriate model would be the Mechanistic organization. Other goals might suggest that the Dynamic model is more appropriate. As the nature of organizations tends to change in the 1990s and on into the twenty-first century some of the assumptions of Hage's theory might change. For example, we note that in many cases smaller businesses now tend to be less formalized, demonstrate less centralization, and show virtually no stratification. Nevertheless, they show great productiveness while remaining efficient. It could very well be that the economies traditionally associated with large-sized organizations drove Hage's analysis of organizations in the 1960s and 1970s, while we now operate from a different paradigm. Those who make policy regarding schools, however, tend to remain driven by traditional views which suggest that "large is better."

Illustrations of Actual Applications

The ultimate educational value of any theory is that it can help us make decisions that improve the quality of what takes place in schools. Hage's Axiomatic Propositions listed below represent little more than an academic exercise unless they serve to direct our supervisory behavior so that we can more effectively guide school district personnel to achieve their goals. Let us look now at a few propositions of the Axiomatic Theory of Organizations and an

TABLE 5.1. "DYNAMIC" VERSUS "MECHANISTIC" ORGANIZATIONS, AS DESCRIBED ACCORDING TO THE RELATIVE AMOUNT OF FOUR STRUCTURAL VARIABLES AND FOUR OUTCOME VARIABLES.

Dynamic Organizations	Mechanistic Organizations
Structural Variables	Structural Variables
High Complexity	Low Complexity
Low Centralization	High Centralization
Low Formalization	High Formalization
Low Stratification	High Stratification
Outcome Variables	Outcome Variables
High Adaptiveness	Low Adaptiveness
Low Productivity	High Productivity
Low Efficiency	High Efficiency
High Job Satisfaction	Low Job Satisfaction

SOURCE: Reprinted from *An axiomatic theory of organization*, *By Gerald Hage, published in* Administrative Science Quarterly, *10, 3 (December 1965) by permission of* Administrative Science Quarterly.

TABLE 5.2. COMPARISON OF TWO MODELS OF ORGANIZATIONS ("DYNAMIC" VERSUS "MECHANISTIC") IN TERMS OF 10 SELECTED CRITERIA.

	Mechanistic (Bureaucratic)	Dynamic (Professional)
Decision Making	Centralized	Widely participative
Work	Individual jobs are self-contained and isolated	People function in face-to-face groups collaboratively
Control	Through hierarchical structure	Through interaction of involved persons
Tasks	Specialized and differentiated with precise specifications of jurisdictions	Continuously enlarged through consensus in context of total organization
Authority	Determined by hierarchical status	Shared and determined by consensus
Relationships	Unilateral management action based on passive conformance	Emphasis on mutual dependence and cooperation based on trust and confidence
Mood	Competition and rivalry	Cooperation
Nature of Organization	Rigid	Flexible
Commitment	To superiors	To the task and "ethos of progress"
Climate	Closed	Open

SOURCE: *Reprinted with the permission of Macmillan College Publishing Company from* Team management: Leadership by consensus *by Richard Wynn and Charles W. Guditus. Copyright © 1984 by Macmillan College Publishing Company, Inc.*

explanation of how an understanding of this theory might lead to a more proactive approach to supervisory practice.

- The higher the centralization, the higher the production
- The higher the formalization, the higher the efficiency
- The higher the centralization, the higher the formalization
- The higher the stratification, the lower the job satisfaction
- The higher the stratification, the higher the production
- The higher the stratification, the lower the adaptiveness
- The higher the complexity, the lower the stratification
- The higher the complexity, the higher the job satisfaction

Suppose that an educational supervisor is assigned the task of working with a school where there has been a long history of low staff morale, and where little attention has been paid to the human dimension of the organization. In Hage's terms, the school would be described as low in the outcome variable of job satisfaction. If the supervisor's goals include increasing this variable so that teachers and staff feel their personal needs are being addressed, the Axiomatic Theory might suggest a number of avenues for change, all in the structural characteristics of the school. Job satisfaction can be increased by raising the level of complexity in the organization, or by lowering centralization, formalization, and stratification. While any of these changes is likely to have a positive effect on the job satisfaction variable, the most readily modified structural characteristic of a school is probably the extent to which people believe that they are involved in organizational decision making. Thus, the proactive supervisor interested in increasing satisfaction among school employees might increase opportunities for teachers and staff to participate in making important relevant decisions. Many successful educational leaders make the kind of structural shift to achieve different outcomes almost intuitively. Effective supervisors need not make use of Hage's technical, theoretical language to act in this way. The essential understanding of the principle that job satisfaction tends to be higher when people are involved in making relevant decisions is all we really need.

If Hage's theory is valid, however, modification of one structural component might cause undesirable effects in terms of other outcomes. Remember, for example, that the productivity and efficiency levels of organizations are generally lower in organizations where centralization is lower. The net effect of involving people in a school's decision-making processes might indeed be a happier staff, but one that does not "produce" as much or as efficiently as a staff in a school where one person makes most of the decisions. The reason for this is simply that, when many are involved in a consensus-seeking approach to decision making, it takes longer to reach a decision. It is not an efficient approach. When one makes all decisions alone, it takes little time. However, note that this is only a statement about the *ease* of decision making, not an assessment of the quality of decisions that might be made.

The real practical value of a theoretical framework such as Hage's, then, is not that it tells us what we are supposed to do in all cases. No theory is meant to serve as a cookbook. To the contrary, understanding a given theory should provide us with an awareness of the possible outcomes of a set of actions that we might follow. In the case we just examined, no one can say whether it is better to have a "satisfied staff" or a "productive and efficient staff." Such a choice must be made by the leader in a way that is consistent with goals, objectives, vision, values, and individual philosophy.

Getzels's Social Systems

Jacob Getzels developed another theoretical model that supervisors may find useful in understanding what takes place in formal organizations.

Historical Development

Getzels's initial work was carried out largely in the years immediately after World War II and involved the analysis of such diverse settings as the military, hospitals, universities, private businesses, and public schools. Getzels isolated essential properties of all these different organizations and was able to conclude that, regardless of the organizations' stated purposes, all such units possess two common dimensions, one that describes the structure of the organization and the other that provides a review of the people who work in it. Observing and analyzing the interaction of these two dimensions helps us understand much of the human behavior in organizations.

The Structural Dimension and

Component Elements

The dimension of social systems that deals with the structure of organizations is referred to in Getzels's theory as the *nomothetic*, *normative*, or *sociological* dimension. The component elements of this dimension are the institution, roles and expectations (Getzels and Guba, 1957).

Society has created many different *institutions*, each of which is theoretically designed to carry out some identified and required function. Because society requires that there be ways of helping sick people, hospitals (and other health-care organizations) have been created. Schools exist largely because society has indicated that there shall be organizations that educate people. Police agencies have been created to deal with the need to protect people and their property.

When institutions are thus formed, the *roles* within them are also created and institutionally defined. "Roles represent dynamic aspects of positions, offices, or statuses within the institution" (Lipham and Hoeh, 1974, p. 66). Schools have a number of standard roles: students, teachers, administrative personnel, supervisory staff. In fact, institutions and roles form an intense interrelationship: Institutions would not exist without the presence of certain roles (e.g., schools would not exist without students), and roles are meaningless without institutions (e.g., a teacher would be lost, to some extent, without a school).

The third component element of the nomothetic dimension of Getzels's social systems model is the *expectation* that exists for the performance of any particular institutionally defined role. Teachers, students, and others serve in roles within the school, which is a social institution, and each of these roles evokes certain types of behavior. Teachers act in certain ways (with some limited variation allowed); students do other things to play out their institutional responsibilities, and so forth.

The "People" Dimension and
Component Elements

The second dimension of the social systems model is concerned with the nature of people who serve within organizations. This aspect is called the *idiographic, personal*, or *psychological* dimension and is also composed of thee elements: the *individuals* (corresponding to the institution in the nomothetic dimension) who belong to the organizations, each of whom has a unique *personality* that, in turn, is defined largely in terms of particular *needs*. The two dimensions of the social systems model are represented by the model in Figure 5.1.

The pictorial representation of Getzels's model illustrates a number of concepts that are useful to the educational supervisor.

NOMOTHETIC (normative) DIMENSION

Institution ⟶ Role ⟶ Expectation

Individual ⟶ Personality ⟶ Need-disposition

IDIOGRAPHIC (personal) DIMENSION

Figure 5.1. Representation of the Social Systems model of Getzels showing the two component dimensions and their elements. (Reprinted from J. W. Getzels and E. G. Guba, 1957. Social Behavior and the Administrative Process. *School Review, 65,* 429 by permission of the University of Chicago. Copyright © 1957 by the University of Chicago.)

The congruence demonstrated between the component elements of the two dimensions in the model suggests a neat, parallel alignment of individual personalities and institutionally defined roles. As the model suggests, this type of clear overlap is a strong indication of organizational effectiveness because people who work in the organization are doing what they want, and their jobs are fulfilling their needs. Unfortunately, in many organizations and at many times, the definition of a role is far from consistent with the personality and needs of the individual who fills it. At such times, conflict occurs, and the extent to which this conflict is serious is a critical indicator of whether or not a particular organization will achieve the kind of balance between institutional demands and human needs that leads to effectiveness.

Illustrations of Actual Applications

Understanding Getzels's central ideas allows the educational supervisor to be more effective, particularly in the context of our definition of supervision: *Supervision is the process of overseeing ability of people to meet the goals of the organization in which they work.* Throughout this book, we suggest that the supervisor has a legitimate stake in maximizing the match between people and organization. As suggested by Getzels's model, we assume that people who are involved with and interested in their jobs will do these jobs better, and that the organization will benefit through increased productivity and effectiveness.

Examples are plentiful in most school settings of the mismatches between institutional roles and individual personalities. Teachers are frequently assigned such duties as "cafeteria patrol," which are at best tolerated and at worst seen at totally opposed to their view of professional responsibility. Many teachers define their role as working constantly with highly motivated students, whereas in fact the role of the teacher in most schools today requires working with some kids who do not want to come to school, let alone learn. Frequently a lack of congruence exists between assigned roles and individual responsibilities. The value of a theoretical model such as the social systems paradigm is not that it tells the supervisor that conflicts will occasionally occur, but that it allows us to predict such conflicts in certain cases, conflicts that can make the operation of the school or district a likely failure. Once again, the model of organizations as social systems has the potential of increasing more proactive behavior on the part of the supervisor.

Morgan's Organizational Metaphors

Yet another perspective of formal organizations is that of Gareth Morgan (1986) who attempted to provide managers, supervisors, and other leaders with ways to learn how to "read" what is going on in the organizations in which they work. He suggested that *metaphors* provide a useful way of understanding the subtle differences among the purposes, practices, policies, and underlying philosophies of organizations.

> It is easy to see how this kind of thinking has relevance for understanding organization and management. For organizations are complex and paradoxical phenomena that can be understood in many ways. Many of our taken-for-granted organizations are metaphorical . . . For example, we frequently talk about organizations *as if* they were machines designed to achieve predetermined goals and objectives, and which should operate smoothly and efficiently. And as a result of this kind of thinking we often attempt to organize and manage them in a mechanistic way, forcing their human qualities into a background role. (p. 13)

Listing of Major Metaphors

Morgan suggested eight predominant metaphors that describe organizations.

1. *Organization as machines* derives from the era of scientific management and suggests that organizations resemble machines because of the prevailing expectations for reliable, durable, and predictable behavior. People who work in such organizations are seen as expendable and wholly interchangeable components. The usefulness of this metaphor is that it suggests we can design organizations to maximize predictability, especially in designing problem-solving strategies, but its major shortcoming is that creative approaches to problem solving are destroyed, and the people who work in such settings participate in a dehumanized environment that provides little support for individual creativity.

2. *Organizations as organisms* suggests that organizations have needs, interests, and life cycles, just as living organisms do, and that we can better understand the workings of organizations by considering them in terms of features like cellular structure. The usefulness of this metaphor is that we become increasingly aware of such things as the "social ecology" in which organizations exist; this metaphor emphasizes our need to appreciate the dynamic nature of the relationships between organizations and their environments. This organization as a living, breathing organism dissolves, however, as we realize the level of abstraction necessary to create it.

3. *Organizations as brains* emphasizes the organization's capacity to be guided by conscious rationality while still safeguarding such characteristics as flexibility and creative action. Its usefulness lies in its suggestion that organizations are capable of learning and self-organization—of creating, for instance, a series of appropriate responses to problems and "storing" that creation for future use. The major shortcoming of this metaphor is that, in its emphasis on rationality, it may prevent us from recognizing the important reality that much of what occurs, especially in the struggle for power and control of organizations, is in fact irrational.

4. *Organizations as cultures* suggests that we can best understand organizations by examining them in the context of culture. Understanding value components is thus a critical factor in organizational analysis; we cannot understand how Toyota operates, for example, without understanding how Japan operates. This perspective places a premium on subtle behaviors, but it is limited in that understanding a culture is impossible. Cultures are fluid, their values, beliefs, and

traditions constantly changing; we are prevented, then, from ever entirely understanding the working of an organization.

5. *Organizations as political systems* suggests that we can best understand organizations by recognizing that they represent ongoing attempts to gain control over finite resources. The analyst must discover the nature of special interests, conflict, power, and authority because it is these processes, and not more rational or logical ones, that finally lead to organizational action. This is a particularly realistic view of what takes place in organizations, but its danger is that too much emphasis placed on political agendas may increase the amount of political activity within an organization. Hidden agendas can become operating practice, and honesty and openness abandoned.

6. *Organizations as psychic prisons* suggests that organizations frequently construct views of reality that cause their members to be trapped, because they lose contact with larger, more accurate visions of reality. Organizations often create their own assumptions about what is and what is not possible for members to attain, and these assumptions limit the extent to which members feel free to explore new avenues of behavior. Examples of this kind of "group think" occur regularly in politics, as for instance in the Watergate or Iran-Contra scandals, where those "on the inside" were convinced by the assumptions of the group that their behaviors were appropriate, even though those same behaviors seemed entirely inappropriate to virtually all outside observers. The metaphor's strength is that it encourages critical analysis of what the organization considers "real"; its weakness is that it suggests that members of organizations are often "trapped" when in fact they have consciously selected the view of reality that underlies their actions. We must ask, then, who controls "reality?"

7. *Organizations as emblems of flux and transformation* suggests that organizations constantly change and must be understood as symbols of a larger, unending evolutionary process. Traditionally, change has been viewed as a process that organizations must endure; this metaphor suggests that organizations are proactive and create their own constant change. The weakness of this view is that organizations, like people, in fact frequently change in reaction rather than pro-action; people do not always create their own vision of change.

8. *Organizations as instruments of domination* suggests that organizations can best be understood in terms of elites that use organizations to promote selfish interests through the manipulation of others. It serves as the basis for a radical critique of organizations. The constant danger in this metaphor, however, is that it can move us toward cynicism by suggesting that conspiracies of elite, controlling classes abound, and that the control of lower social classes is the sole focus of organizations. In short, a belief inheres in this metaphor that organizations (and the people who control them) are entirely rational in both purpose and action.

Practical Applications

Morgan's organizational metaphors represent another tool that supervisors may use to increase their personal insights into how organizations function. As Morgan notes in his work, the metaphors provide a "road map" that leaders may use to "read and understand" strengths and weaknesses in various organizations. For those in supervisory roles that require working with many different organizations (i.e., different school buildings, districts, or multiple educational agencies such as state departments of education, universities, and so forth), the ability to sense the nature of differences among these organizations can be critical to successful relations. You will no doubt find some metaphors more appealing than others. Those in control of organizations make the same choices; they often view their organizations as one (or a mixture) of Morgan's models. The reality of a description comes largely from a leader's perceptions of its characteristics. Whether the supervisor likes it or not, therefore, some organizations must be understood as "political systems" or even "systems of domination." You may find this awareness useful in understanding why things happen as they do in different settings.

You may also find Morgan's framework useful in assessing your own personal assumptions regarding the nature of organizations and building an individual philosophy and action plan. When we pause to consider our basic views concerning the "goodness" or "badness" of organizations, "rationality" versus "irrationality," "openness" or "closedness," or any of the other issues that are raised through the metaphors, we become involved in an important reflective process that may lead to increasing the clarification of our beliefs and the identification of nonnegotiable values.

Finally, as Morgan noted, examining competing metaphorical

descriptions of organizations encourages us to confront the paradoxes that exist in the world around us and to think in new and more expansive ways about them. We can "imaginize" or attempt to see the world in completely untested ways, and our creativity may lead to the formulation of new metaphors. Only through this type of thinking can more creative solutions to existing problems be found, a process entirely consistent with our view of proactive supervision.

Bolman and Deal's Organizational Frames

Our review of the ways in which the formal properties of organizations have been applied has taken us through the ideas of Hage, Getzels, and Morgan. It is clear that, over the years, there has been a decided movement away from a technical-rational approach to the analysis of organizational structure to an increasingly artistic perspective. Whereas Hage developed an analytic perspective wherein aspects of the organization could be measured and counted, Morgan moved to the use of literary techniques such as metaphors as a way to describe reality.

Even more recently, Bolman and Deal (1991) advanced the artistic approach to organizational analysis through their conceptualization of four alternative interpretations of organizational structures and processes which they refer to as *frames*. As was true of the theorists listed earlier, Bolman and Deal developed their schema after studying numerous public and private organizations. We believe that an awareness of the four frames has considerable potential value to the educational supervisor.

Alternative Frames

The four alternative frames developed by Bolman and Deal (1991, pp. 15–16) are explained in the following terms:

1. *Structural frame.* This perspective emphasizes the understanding of organizations through an appreciation of formal roles and relationships. In terms of other approaches we have reviewed, this perspective would be quite consistent with those who believe that scientific management, or perhaps Morgan's metaphor of organizations as machines, might be the most useful way to understand and explain what is happening in a particular institution.

2. *Human Resource frame*. Here, the emphasis is on the people who inhabit an institution. An underlying belief in this perspective is that it is critical to understand the needs and feelings of people, rather than what an organization looks like on a formal line and staff chart. This view is similar to the human relations and human resources perspectives to management that we reviewed in chapter 1.

3. *Political frame*. In this approach to the analysis of organizations, the emphasis is on developing an understanding of the ways in which competing groups tend to strive for control over power and scarce resources. The assumption is made that conflict is a normal and expected reality in all organizations. In terms of Morgan's work, this perspective is similar to viewing organizations as political systems.

4. *Symbolic frame*. This frame is the most unique perspective offered by Bolman and Deal, and it differs greatly from any other view that we have reviewed. The symbolic frame "treats organizations as tribes, theater, or carnivals . . . [Organizations] are cultures that are propelled more by rituals, ceremonies, stories, heroes, and myths than by rules, policies, and managerial authority."

Practical Applications

We believe that there are at least two reasons for learning more about this approach to organizational analysis. First, each frame makes extensive use of a variety of established social science disciplines as a way to describe what is taking place in an organization. For example, the structural frame borrows greatly from sociology, the symbolic frame is related to anthropology, the human resource frame is based on ideas from social psychologists, and political science defines the political frame. Thus, the supervisor who would use the alternative frames is able to rely on several well developed paradigms that have long histories of use in studying a variety of social issues.

We also believe that the Bolman and Deal perspective warrants our attention, if for no other reason than it introduces the concept of the symbolic frame as a usable part of the supervisor's analytic "tool kit." The symbolic frame, in our mind, legitimizes the use of many subtle signs of organizational life which we recognize exist, but which often become ignored because they do not "fit" established social science descriptions. Yet we know that cultures, traditions, and even myths often drive much of what takes place in schools and school districts. Bolman and Deal provide us with words and a framework to appreciate these real features of the world of education.

Miles's Organizational Health

The theoretical perspectives of Hage, Getzels, Morgan, and Bolman and Deal differ considerably from one another. However, they are similar in the sense that they all represent descriptions of the formal characteristics of organizations with an emphasis on structure and predictable interrelationships rather than sensations or feelings. In the following sections, we look at the contributions of Matthew Miles, Andrew Halpin, and Donald Croft, all of whom examined informal features of organizations.

Matthew Miles is not the only theorist to suggest that organizations can be seen as *healthy* or *unhealthy*. Chris Argyris (1965) used this construct and suggested that, in order to be effective and healthy, an organization must accomplish the following core activities:

> Achieve its goals
>
> Maintain itself internally
>
> Adapt to its environment

Miles (1965) built on these characteristics and defined a healthy organization as one that "not only survives in its environment, but continues to cope adequately over the long haul, and continuously develops and extends its surviving and coping activities. Short-term operations on any particular day may be effective or ineffective, but continued survival, adequate coping, and growth are taking place" (p. 162). The analogy exists, then, with healthy people who are able to respond positively to whatever barriers occur in their pursuit of long and prosperous lives. Healthy people are not always without illness; rather, they are able to avoid prolonged stages of being incapacitated. The immune system remains intact because of overall good health.

By contrast, the unhealthy person has numerous, recurring encounters with illnesses, some of which are relatively minor, some life-threatening. The long-term prognosis for such individuals is poor; they will probably enjoy shorter life spans than other, healthier people. Robert Owens (1987) described "unhealthy" organizations in much the same way.

> The unhealthy organization . . . is steadily ineffective. It may
> cope with its environment effectively on a short-term basis with
> a "crash program," a concentrated drive to meet a particularly
> threatening situation, or "administration-by-crimes" tech-
> niques, but in the long run the unhealthy organization becomes
> less and less able to cope with its environment. Rather than
> gaining in its ability to cope with its situation, it declines in this
> capacity over time and it tends to become dysfunctional. (p. 218)

The unhealthy organization is one with a continually ineffective
"immune system." The unhealthy organization uses crisis orientation just as the ineffective supervisor uses reactive leadership.

Miles identified ten dimensions that indicate the relative health
of an organization.

1. *Goal focus* is the extent to which people in an organization
   understand and accept the goals of the organization. In a
   healthy organization, these goals are further defined as being
   appropriate, achievable, and well accepted by organizational
   members.

2. *Communication adequacy* is the ease and facility of
   communication that takes place within the organization as well
   as between the organization and its external environment. In
   healthy organizations, the flow of information is not
   constrained from one level to another, and shared information
   is accurate.

3. *Optimal power equalization* is the balance among organizational members that ensures that no one party can coerce and
   corrupt other members. Healthy organizations demonstrate a
   relatively low degree of informal influence-seeking behavior by
   their members.

4. *Human resource utilization* is the effective use of organizational personnel, to the end that they feel as if they are growing,
   developing, and being satisfied in their jobs. In healthy
   organizations, there is evidence that members are working as
   hard as they believe they can and, more importantly, are
   experiencing personal and professional pride in this effort.

5. *Cohesiveness* is the extent to which members like their
   organizations and want to remain a part of them. Healthy
   organizations are those in which all members make a firm
   commitment to invest personal energy toward the goal of
   increasing the strength of the total organization.

6. *Morale* pertains to feelings of well-being and satisfaction
   expressed and demonstrated by organizational members.

People express happiness at being part of healthy organizations.

7. *Innovativeness* is the tendency of an organization to grow, develop, and become "better" over time, as demonstrated by a general willingness to try new programs and procedures. Healthy organizations are those that indicate openness to new ideas that may be tried as a way to stimulate continued growth toward meeting external environmental changes.

8. *Autonomy* is the tendency of an organization to determine its own standards and behaviors in harmony with external demands but without acquiescing to those demands. Healthy organizations show a consistent independence from other organizations, but without rebellion or other potentially destructive behaviors.

9. *Adaption* is the ability of an organization to anticipate changes in environmental demands and engage in self-corrective behaviors that indicate an ability to adapt to these demands. Healthy organizations provide evidence of ongoing sensitivity to changes in environmental pressures, and they make change accordingly with great regularity.

10. *Problem-solving adequacy* involves the maintenance of strategies for sensing problems, along with techniques for regularly dealing with organizational crises in a rational fashion. When a healthy organization has problems (as all organizations do, from time to time) it has established ways of dealing with these issues.

Practical Applications

The concept of organizational health has some useful applications in educational supervision. We can conclude from the above review, for example, that there is probably no organization that is high in all areas at all times. In other words, there probably has never been and never will be a completely healthy organization. Schools will never be perfect, just as no human being will ever be without periodic bouts with illness. The value of a conceptual frame of reference such as the one proposed by Miles is that it permits the proactive supervisor to serve as a diagnostician by reviewing the nature of some critical features of schooling. Are people communicating openly? Is there obvious involvement and commitment being demonstrated by teachers to the stated goals of the school? Is there a spirit present suggesting that people want to try new approaches to instruction? If the answer to these questions is yes, the supervisor has a fundamentally healthy organization. If most questions yield a no response, there is a lot of work to do.

Organizational Climate

A frequently discussed characteristic of organizations in recent years is *climate* or the *psychosocial feel* of an organization, and one of the earliest and most familiar attempts to gain a handle on this characteristic was the work of Halpin and Croft (1963).

Halpin and Croft based their work on the simple notion that schools and other organizations have unique personalities just as do human beings. The researchers developed an instrument, the Organizational Climate Description Questionnaire (OCDQ) (Halpin, 1967), to measure the relative absence or presence of eight factors determined to have an impact on the informal feel, or climate, of a school. These factors, or dimensions, were grouped into two categories, one descriptive of teachers' behavior, and the second of principals' behavior. The individual dimensions related to teachers are *disengagement* (tendency to be uninvolved in school activities); *hindrance* (sense of being burdened by too much inconsequential work); *esprit* (morale); and *intimacy* (friendly social relations). The behaviors of principals include *aloofness* (formal and impersonal actions); *production emphasis* (preference for tight monitoring of staff performance); *thrust* (effort to "move the organization"); and *consideration* (tendency to treat staff in a warm and humane fashion). The climate of these dimensions is measured (through the interpretation of the OCDQ administered to teachers and principals) as "high," "medium," or "low."

Halpin and Croft suggested six different profiles of organizational climate, which reflect the degree to which an organization is high or low in the eight dimensions reviewed above.

1. *Open climate.* An energetic organization that is moving toward its goals while its staff members are satisfied in their personal social needs.
2. *Autonomous climate.* An organization in which leadership emerges primarily from the groups, and the formal leader exerts little control over the staff.
3. *Controlled climate.* An environment that is impersonal and highly task-oriented.

4. *Familiar climate.* A highly personal, but undercontrolled environment in which personal needs are satisfied, but with little attention paid to task accomplishment.

5. *Paternal climate.* An organization in which the formal leader tries consistently to constrain leadership emerging from the group; the leader tries to do it all alone.

6. *Closed climate.* An organization that demonstrates considerable apathy by all members.

Practical Applications

Halpin and Croft's organizational climate concept is not meant to be used as a tool for judging the quality or lack of quality of a particular school, even if some climate profiles may seem more appealing to us than others. For example, a "closed climate" is not necessarily less desirable than an "autonomous climate" or an "open climate." Rather, the true value of the organizational climate conceptualization rests in the useful perspective it provides for analyzing the organization and understanding how to introduce new concepts to school groups and how to compel school employees to engage in more goal-related behavior. For example, if you determine that a particular school reflects the "paternal climate" (where the principal tries to do everything), you will probably need either to seek ways to help the principal delegate some activities or to be satisfied with a limited set of goals and objectives. By contrast, in an "autonomous climate" you would be well advised to work directly with individual staff members interested in engaging in particular types of work.

Summary

In this chapter we provided several theoretical models for supervisors who want to become more proactive through the use of organizational analysis. Organizational analysis, as we noted earlier, is but one of a number of theory-based perspectives that supervisors may find useful.

The first part of the chapter reviewed four theories that describe the *formal* nature of organizations. The first, Hage's Axiomatic Theory of Organizations, suggests that complex organizations are best understood as dynamic or mechanistic, depending on the relative amounts of eight different variables, four related to

TABLE 5.3. PROFILES OF SIX DIFFERENT ORGANIZATIONAL CLIMATES, DESCRIBED IN TERMS OF THE RELATIVE ABSENCE OR PRESENCE OF EIGHT TYPES OF ORGANIZATIONAL BEHAVIORS.

Climate:	Disengagement	Hindrance	Esprit	Intimacy	Aloofness	Production Emphasis	Thrust	Consideration
Open	low	low	high	medium	low	low	high	high
Autonomous	low	low	high	high	high	low	medium	medium
Controlled	low	high	medium	low	high	high	medium	low
Familiar	high	low	medium	high	low	low	medium	high
Paternal	high	medium	low	low	low	high	medium	high
Closed	high	high	low	medium	high	high	low	low

SOURCE: Andrew W. Halpin and Donald B. Croft (1963, March). The Organizational Climate of Schools, Administrator's Notebook, 11, 1–2. Reprinted by permission of the publisher.

structure and four to outcomes. The major relevance of this theory for supervisors is the indication that, while changes in structure and outcome may be a part of daily organizational life, such modifications have a great likelihood of altering much of what goes on in an organization.

The second theory, Getzels's concept of social systems, suggests that organizations must be understood in terms of a constant, dynamic interaction that takes place between two dimensions: nomothetic (institutional) and idiographic (personal). A congruence between institution and individual, role and personality, and expectations and needs is a strong indication of overall organizational effectiveness. Getzels's concept encourages supervisors to look at practices in their schools or districts to determine if a sufficient "fit" exists between the system and the people who work in it. An absolutely perfect match can never be achieved, but an awareness of serious discrepancies can help supervisors head off major, dysfunctional conflict.

Morgan's eight organizational metaphors are designed to help us gain a more complete understanding of the ways in which institutions function. The metaphors are also useful in that they provide some important insights into the assumptions held by others concerning organizational behavior and purpose.

We also considered some possible applications of Bolman and Deal's four alternative organizational frames as yet another way to assist proactive supervisors in carrying out their duties. These frames stem from social sciences which have long been studied and used to understand the interrelationships of people and organizations.

Theories of organizational analysis based on *informal* perspectives were also included. First, we reviewed Miles's description of organizational health, which focuses on the relative presence of ten different dimensions such as goal focus, communication adequacy, resource utilization, and so forth. We noted that no school is likely to possess equally high amounts of each of these characteristics. However, an appreciation of the ten dimensions can help the proactive supervisor who seeks to engage in an ongoing diagnosis of the schools and districts with which he or she normally works.

The second construct related to informal organizational behavior is climate as defined by Halpin and Croft, who suggest that schools have identifiable climates analogous to the personalities of individual human beings. These climates, which range from "open" to "closed," are the products of behaviors demonstrated by the teachers and the principal in a school. Again, the value of this perspective is that it offers the supervisor yet another tool in understanding the complex behaviors and relationships that impact on the effectiveness of schools.

All these perspectives, quite different on the surface, have some common aspects. First, all may be used by supervisors to understand succinctly an enormous amount of subtle and complex information about organizational behavior: Formal theory can describe "a lot in a few words." Second, all the models avoid the tendency to provide complete answers. Each attempts to analyze organizations, but none provides recipes for behavior. Finally, none of the models is an absolute unto itself. We present them as but a few examples of frameworks that supervisors might consult as they engage in *proactive* and *analytic*—and therefore *effective*—supervision.

Suggested Activities

1. Make use of the constructs in Hage's theory and prepare a questionnaire to be distributed to the staff of a school to determine their perceptions of the strengths of the various structural variables. Distribute the questionnaire in two or three schools.* Are there differences in terms of structure? What about differences in terms of outcomes?

2. Obtain a copy of the Halpin and Croft OCDQ instrument for measuring school climate, or any other similar scale used to measure this quality in schools. Administer it in two or more schools to see if there are obvious differences.

3. Using either Morgan's organizational metaphors or Bolman and Deal's frames as a guide, interview four or five teachers from your school to see if they reach any consensus regarding the type of organization apparently represented by your school.

---

*With this or any other activity involving research in schools, make sure to obtain permission from the necessary people before beginning and follow all required procedures.

Cases to Consider

Read each case and consider the following:

a. What are the critical issues raised in each case, as they relate to the use of theoretical constructs to analyze organizational structures and processes?

b. How does each case relate to the development of the concept of proactive supervision?

c. In what ways might you suggest a resolution to the issues raised?

Case 5.1:

Opening Things up on Gray Street

One of the things that the general public really seemed to like about Gray Street Middle School was that it never changed much. It wasn't an exciting kind of school, but year in and year out, people knew what was happening at Gray Street, primarily because Dr. Ann Webster, the principal, had been there for so many years. Gray Street was her school, and because Dr. Webster clearly ran the place and did everything, there was little chance that any radical new ideas were likely to get started just because a few teachers wanted to try out a new idea now and then. Indeed, Dr. Webster really controlled the school.

As a result of Dr. Webster's retirement, it was necessary for a new principal to come on board at Gray Street. The superintendent and school board selected Toni Macelli, an experienced middle school principal who had earned an outstanding reputation as a strong instructional leader at Elm Street Middle School in the same district. Toni knew of the reputation for stability at Gray Street, and she truly respected Ann Webster as a good colleague for many years. But Toni wanted to make some changes, a view that was reinforced by the school board during her interviews for the job. She wanted, for example, to encourage her teaching staff to become more involved with running the school and making decisions related to the curriculum, scheduling, and several other issues. After all, the teachers at Elm Street had worked directly with Toni for years, and she believed this to be one of the main reasons why the school was regarded as being quite effective by the superintendent, school board, parents' groups, and even the state department of education. There was even a recent newspaper article which described Elm Street as "one of those rare schools where you felt like you wanted to sign up to be a teacher as soon as you walked in from the street."

As Toni prepared to move across town to Gray Street, she was certain that she wanted to open things up and make some changes. She knew she couldn't come up with a carbon copy of Elm Street, but she knew that Gray Street could no longer be "Ann's school." Her major concern now was related to the strategies that she would use to achieve her goals.

Case 5.2:

Tipping the Balance

The Mill Valley High School had gained a reputation in recent years as one of the most innovative and exciting secondary schools in the country. There were so many visitors coming to the school each year that a policy was adopted to prohibit observers from looking at the school except on Thursdays, a fact that prompted Mill Valley students to refer to that day each week as "Zoo Day."

There were many factors contributing to the innovativeness of Mill Valley. For one thing, it was truly a school where everyone was involved in the decision-making process. Chuck Stowe, the principal, always described himself as the "facilitator of the school" rather than an administrator. That was characteristic of another feature of the school: There appeared to be no differences among the staff in terms of authority. The principal, assistant principals, teachers, classified staff, and instructional aides all referred to themselves as equal members of the Mill Valley Team.

Everything at Mill Valley seemed to be working very well, for the most part. The biggest problem that was developing was the fact that, recently, new homeowners from out-of-state were beginning to complain about some features of the school that did not match the expectations that they brought into the Valley. For example, long-time residents of the community were proud of their school and were content that graduates seemed to be happy and well-adjusted community members when they completed high school. Some went on to college, others to trade schools or the military, and some simply went directly to work in businesses located in Mill Valley. The new residents, however, were expressing grave concerns about the fact that they believed that local high school graduates were not really being prepared for the kinds of post-secondary school experiences desired by their parents. It was less and less acceptable for "some kids" to go on to college. New residents expected most, if not all, to proceed to prestigious colleges and universities.

At a recent parent information night, Chuck Stowe came under considerable fire from many new community members who indicated that they were displeased with the kind of high school program that was being offered. One consistent complaint was that things were simply "too loose." Chuck's first inclination was to let this fire burn out and protect the current practices at the school. But the attack was well organized, and the school board was now directing the superintendent to do something before the disgruntled parents (who tended to be the wealthiest residents of the district) started to hurt other district programs by voting against the annual district budget, school taxes, and other funding proposals. Chuck knew that he would have to act quickly. He now sat in his office thinking about some possible changes. He was also thinking about the consequences that those changes might have at Mill Valley. Would the school continue to have a weekly "Zoo Day," or might the place simply be turned into a zoo?

References

Argyris, Chris (1965). *Integrating the individual and the organization.* New York: Wiley.

Bolman, Lee G., & Deal, Terrence E. (1991). *Reframing organizations: Artistry. choice. and leadership.* San Francisco: Jossey Bass.

Getzels, Jacob W. (1952). A psycho-sociological framework for the study of educational administration. *Harvard Educational Review,* 22:235–246.

Getzels, Jacob W., & Guba, Egon G. (1957). Social behavior and the administrative process. *The School Review,* 65:423–441.

Hage, Gerald (1965). An axiomatic theory of organizations. *Administrative Science Quarterly,* 10(3): 289–320.

Halpin, Andrew W. (1967). *Theory and research in administration.* New York: Macmillan.

Halpin, Andrew W., & Croft, Donald B. (1963). The organizational climate of schools. *Administrator's Notebook,* 11:1–2.

Lipham, James M., & Hoeh, James (1974). *The principalship: Foundations and functions.* New York: Harper and Row.

Miles, Matthew B. (1965). Planned change and organizational health: Figure and ground. *Change processes in the the public schools.* Eugene: University of Oregon, Center for the Advanced Study of Educational Administration.

Morgan, Gareth (1986). *Images of organizations.* Beverly Hills: Sage.

Owens, Robert (1987). *Organizational behavior in education* (3rd ed.). Englewood Cliffs, NJ: Prentice-Hall.

Wynn, Richard, & Guditus, Charles W. (1984). *Team management: Leadership by consensus.* Columbus, OH: Merrill.

Additional Readings

Bolman, Lee G., & Deal, Terrence E. (1993). *The path to school leadership: A portable mentor.* Newbury Park, CA: Corwin Press.

Senge, Peter M. (1990). *The fifth discipline.* New York: Doubleday.

6 Leadership

Many would argue that leadership is synonymous with supervision in school settings. The literature is filled with suggestions, as we shall see in chapter 9, that educational administration represents maintenance of the strategies, whereas supervision involves bringing about organizational change. Unfortunately, the resulting implication is that supervisors are the "good guys" who wear "white hats," while administrators block innovation and creativity and are generally nonprogressive. We do not subscribe to this simplistic notion. Rather, we believe that *effective proactive supervision is compatible with effective administration.* Good supervisors need highly refined administrative skills, and good school administrators must have excellent supervisory abilities. Leadership, however, is a quality that is required of both supervisors and administrators. In fact, leadership is a characteristic increasingly required by all educators—teachers, administrators, and supervisors.

In this chapter, we develop a broad view of leadership by first seeking a definition that applies to a variety of contexts and then reviewing theoretical perspectives from both descriptive and normative perspectives. The chapter concludes with an examination of the concept of instructional leadership.

Alternative Definitions

When we talk about how an organization works, we almost invariably talk about leadership. The presence or absence of this characteristic has a strong and direct impact on the effectiveness of an organization. Nevertheless, organizational analysts struggle to find a basic definition for the concept of leadership. In this section we review several definitions in an attempt to determine some basic features that we need to recognize in analyzing leadership in schools.

Gary Yukl (1985) pulled together a number of different definitions of leadership in his comprehensive review:

- Leadership is "the behavior of an individual when he is directing the activities of a group toward a shared goal" (Hemphill and Coons, 1957, p. 7).
- Leadership is "interpersonal influence, exercised in a situation, and directed, through the communication process, toward the attainment of a specified goal or goals" (Tannenbaum, Weshler, and Massarik, 1961, p. 24).
- Leadership is the "initiation and maintenance of structure in expectation and interaction" (Stogdill, 1974, p. 41).
- Leadership is "an interaction between persons in which one presents information of a sort and in such a manner that the other becomes convinced that his outcomes (benefits/cost ratio) will be improved if he behaves in the manner suggested or desired" (Jacobs, 1970, p. 232).
- Leadership is "a particular type of power relationship characterized by a group member's perceptions that another group member has the right to prescribe behavior patterns for the former regarding his activity as a group member" (Janada, 1960, p. 358).
- Leadership is "an influence process whereby O's actions change P's behavior, and P views the influence attempt as being legitimate and the change as consistent with P's goals" (Kochran, Schmidt, and DeCotiis, 1975, p. 285).
- Leadership is "the influential increment over and above mechanical compliance with the routine directives of the organization" (Katz and Kahn, 1978, p. 528).
- Leadership is "the process of influencing others to achieve mutually agreed upon purposes for the organization" (Patterson, 1993, p. 3).

Although these definitions represent a wide range of ideas about organizational leadership, they display some common themes. First, all suggest that the central feature of leadership is an interpersonal relationship where one individual influences, guides, or controls the behavior of another person. Second, most of the definitions suggest that leader behavior implies some sort of change—that leaders promote movement in the organization or in the behaviors of people in the organization.

James Lipham and James Hoeh (1974) provided yet another definition of leadership that is appealing largely because of its emphasis on the responsibility of a key actor to promote and sustain positive and needed change. For them, leadership is "that behavior of an individual which initiates a new structure in interaction within a social system, it initiates changes in the goals, objectives, configurations, procedures, inputs, processes, and ultimately the outputs of social systems" (p. 196).

Recent research on leadership has emphasized a simple observation: Leaders must have followers. The result of this has been the analysis of a set of behaviors often described in the literature as "followership." We will not dwell on this concept here, but it will be relevant later in this chapter when we talk about the characteristics of effective instructional leaders who empower their followers.

Regardless of the definitions we choose, we must recognize that leadership is a critical issue both in schools and other organizations. Warren Bennis and Burt Nanus (1985), in their study of leadership behavior in many different settings, noted that this issue has particular relevance for at least three reasons:

- Organizations are suffering form a "commitment gap"; people do not believe in what their organizations stand for because leaders have not developed that sense of belief in their followers.

- The level of complexity in modern society is higher than it has ever been before. Predictability and stability are characteristics that are virtually absent from most organizations today.

- Organizational credibility is disappearing. Generally accepted authority figures are being questioned and challenged more often today because so many leaders have disappointed their followers in recent years.

Bennis and Nanus suggest that leadership is no longer a simple academic term to be understood by social scientists but a very real concept that has meaning for everyone. The proactive supervisor has a special interest in learning more about leadership and must develop a genuine and personal definition of this concept.

Descriptive versus Normative Views

There are two fundamentally different ways in which leadership has been analyzed in recent years. The first of these is *descriptive*, where leadership is defined as a particular set of identifiable, observable behaviors, actions, traits, or characteristics. No effort is made to suggest the correct or appropriate ways in which leaders may achieve these features. Descriptive views present "what is," not "what ought to be."

The second way of analyzing leadership is *normative*, where an agenda is provided that is intended to shape future behavior and practice. Normative views suggest "what ought to be," or at least how things are likely to appear, given certain changes taking place in the environment. A normative analysis of leadership behavior might define those activities that should be followed for an individual to appear as a certain type of leader, under certain conditions.

Both descriptive and normative perspectives offer insights into leadership which are helpful to the supervisor. In the context of our discussion about the development of formal theories in chapter 4, however, we note that descriptive theories include only the first two steps in the theory-development cycle (discursive treatment of a topic and simplified listing). Normative theories correspond to the third step in the process, the statement of a juxtaposed taxonomy, because of their emphasis on predictive power. As noted in chapter 4, both description and prediction are necessary if the explanatory values of a theory are to be found.

Before moving into a review of either descriptive or normative theories, let us consider the ways in which leadership has been conceptually developed from an historical frame of reference.

Historical Development of Leadership

The analysis of leadership in organizations has proceeded through at least four major stages: the "great person"; traitist; situational or sociological; and behavioral.

"Great Person" Approach

The "great person" perspective is a psychologically based approach that suggests that leadership is determined primarily by the personality of an individual. If we wish to understand what characteristics comprise leadership, then we should look to how a particular individual, or "great person," demonstrated leadership in the past.

A famous practitioner of this theory of leadership was General George Patton, who often determined how to deal with a problem by reviewing what famous historical characters had done under similar circumstances. An avid student of military history, Patton often charted a path for the American army during World War II based on the strategies of Caesar, Hannibal, or other great military leaders. The "great person" approach to leadership analysis is seen more frequently than we might at first assume. Young children, for instance, have long been advised to read the biographies and autobiographies of famous people in order to learn the ways in which such people lived. If you learn about Thomas Edison, Martin Luther King, Helen Keller, or some other famous "great person," the implication is that you would also grow up to be famous, inventive, brave, or wise.

While this approach to understanding leadership is temptingly simple, it has severe drawbacks that limit its usefulness as a guide to the development of leadership skills. For one thing, we can never find a single "great person" as role model, because the exact circumstances of two lives will never be the same. Reading about the life of Abraham Lincoln does not enable us to follow in his footsteps, because so much of Lincoln's career and behavior was shaped by conditions in early nineteenth century Illinois.

A second limitation to the "great person" view is that the "person" has historically been defined in male terms. The net effect of this sexism has been that women who aspire to leadership roles have been forced, usually in subtle ways, to find male role models; they have been trained to "act like a man." Ultimately this ignores natural differences between ways in which men and women might function most effectively in leadership positions, a major problem identified by Charol Shakeshaft (1987) in her analysis of gender differences in school administration.

Finally, "great person" approaches to leadership limit the creative behavior of present leaders. Instead of asking, "What would Caesar have done under these circumstances?" the modern leader might more profitably explore new ways of facing a problem. By relying exclusively on the past behaviors of others for guidance, people in leadership roles will rarely bring about changes so often needed in dynamic organizations.

Traitist Approaches

The "great person" approach suggests that we study individual leaders; a related view suggests that to understand how leaders behave, we should examine several individuals to determine common characteristics or traits. The student of leadership, for example, might note that leaders of successful corporations are generally tall, attended Ivy League universities, and drive big cars. We might then conclude that a way to the top of a major company would be to enroll at Penn, buy a Cadillac, and, if possible, grow a few inches (or at least buy a pair of elevator shoes!).

Once again, the traitist approach to the study of leadership is appealingly simple and straightforward. It suggests that an educational supervisor who wants to be perceived as an effective leader might constructively spend time finding out which of her or his predecessors were viewed as effective and then identifying and copying traits found in all those individuals. While the realization that "dressing for success" sometimes produces an executive and thus may make trait analyses seem like reasonable strategies, there are some obvious drawbacks.

Traits analyzed in this approach are frequently characteristics over which we have little control. A short follower wishing to acquire leadership characteristics cannot, of course, suddenly become tall. Additionally, there is a danger in generalizing widely from limited examples. The lives of Abraham Lincoln and Lyndon Johnson might reinforce the notion that physical height has a relationship to leadership ability, but how then do we explain the abilities of Napoleon in both the military and political spheres?

Finally, traitist leadership approaches are restrictive. When people focus on specific, similar traits of past leaders, there is a tendency to be unduly biased toward those traits. Perhaps the traits of the leaders even overshadow the other components necessary to run the organization. Thus, traits of new leaders should not necessarily be restricted to the traits of past leaders. Consider the following example: If we were to select school superintendents and principals based on traits common to past holders of these positions, we would limit our search to white, married males who had previously been coaches. The fact that the majority of present school administrators possess these traits is probably testimony to the popularity of the traitist perspective. Popularity, however, is no excuse for the maintenance of a delimiting practice.

Situational Approaches

In sharp contrast to the "great person" and traitist approaches that emphasize physical and psychological characteristics in the study of leadership, the situational or sociological approach maintains that leadership is determined less by the characteristics of individuals than by the requirements of the group or the setting in which the individual works. According to this view, acts of leadership are the direct result of situations that arise in groups or organizations that call for those acts. Thus, an individual's exercise of leadership is brought about by the demands of the group with which that individual must interact. John Hemphill (1949) conducted a comprehensive sociological study of the impact of leaders according to differences of groups. He found such variables as viscidity (the feeling of cohesion in a group), hedonic tone (the degree of satisfaction of group members), size of the group, homogeneity of group members, and intimacy among individuals in the group to correlate significantly with leadership effectiveness. Inevitably, however, researchers realized that if the study of leadership focused purely on such situationally specific issues as how particular groups react to particular individuals, then the study of leadership, per se, would end.

A good deal of situational leadership analysis is found in the actions of the World War I hero, Sergeant Alvin York. York might never have been recognized in history had he remained a poor Tennessee farmer. As a result of the war he enlisted in the army. He then was in the right place at precisely the right time to capture more German prisoners of war than any other soldier. The clear limitation on this theory that situation alone evokes leadership is that it ignores almost completely the individual's characteristics as a leader. Alvin York would not have been a military leader without World War I, but his leadership potential might have been realized in some other field. We have no way of knowing.

Behavioral Approaches

Recent analyses of leadership examine the behavior of the leader and balance elements of both the psychological ("great person" and traitist) and the situational approaches. This perspective, reflected in Lipham and Hoeh's definition cited earlier, recognizes that a leader's behavior is the result of a blend of both personal characteristics and situations in which the leader must act. The basic assumptions of this view are:

- People behave according to different leadership styles. This occurs because people differ in how they perceive a situation, accomplish tasks, interact with others, and make decisions.
- People behave differently depending on contextual circumstances. Consequently, behavior changes.
- There is no single "right way" for people to behave.
- What is comfortable and "right" for one person may feel uncomfortable and "wrong" to another.
- An organization functions best when it capitalizes on the strengths of each individual, encouraging the recognition and celebration of differences.

Additional Issues

No matter what approach we use to analyze leadership, we must also consider certain basic issues including locus, frequency, potency, and scope of leadership. The *locus* of leadership is the social system in which leadership occurs—be it classroom, school, school district, or entire community. The *frequency* of leadership, or how often a leader engages in certain behaviors, is also important. On the one hand, leaders may attempt too many acts of leadership too often without actually implementing or evaluating all of the elements necessary for achieving effective outcomes. On the other hand, some people in leadership positions may rarely engage in any active leadership attempts at all. There is no consensus as to what constitutes the optimal balance between "too frequent" and "not often enough." *Potency* refers to "the extent to which an initiated change by a leader represents significant departure from that which exists, i.e., the magnitude of an initiated change" (Lipham and Hoeh, 1974, p. 186). Finally, *scope* or *range* of leadership is significant. Leadership may be functionally diverse or functionally specific; some leaders have defined and virtually unlimited responsibilities and obligations, whereas for others, the obligations, breadth, and depth of the leadership role are limited and functions circumscribed.

Alternative Descriptive Models

We have selected four alternative leadership perspectives as illustrations of descriptive models. Three are examples of approaches that make use of behavioral terms. They were developed by Andrew Halpin and J. A. Winer, D. J. Bowers and S. E. Seashore, and Robert House. We have also included a popular recent description by Stephen Covey which we believe represents an example of a traitist descriptive approach to leadership.

Halpin and Winer

According to these two researchers, a leader's behavior is composed of two basic dimensions: initiating structure and consideration. These two concepts reflect Getzels's nomothetic and idiographic dimensions (see chapter 5). Halpin (1957) defined them as follows:

Initiating structure. Behavior that delineates the relationship between the leader and members of the work group and endeavors to establish well-defined patterns of organization, channels of communication, and methods of procedure.

Consideration. Behavior that indicates friendship, mutual trust, respect, and warmth in the relationship between the leader and the staff.

Bowers and Seashore

These researchers (1966) suggested that leadership behavior consists of goal emphasis, work facilitation, support, and interaction facilitation. These four dimensions are defined in the following way:

Goal emphasis. Behavior that stimulates enthusiasm for meeting the group's goals or achieving excellent performance.

Work facilitation. Behavior that helps goal attainment by scheduling, planning, and coordinating.

Support. Behavior that enhances someone else's feelings of personal worth and importance.

Interaction facilitation. Behavior that encourages members of the group to develop close, mutually satisfying relationships.

House

House (1973) used three terms derived largely from the work of Halpin and Winer for describing leadership behavior: instrumental, supportive, and participative.

Instrumental leadership. Behavior that delineates the relationship between the leader and members of the work group and attempts clearly to define patterns of the organization without autocratic or punitive control.

Supportive leadership. Behavior that indicates friendship and warmth toward the work group by the leader.

Participative leadership. Behavior that allows subordinates to influence decisions by asking for suggestions and including the subordinates in the decision-making process.

Table 6.1 suggests some obvious similarities among these three theoretical perspectives derived from the behavioral approach to the analysis of leadership. Subtle distinctions can be found in the individual component dimensions suggested in each model, but the overlap is significant.

TABLE 6.1. THREE DESCRIPTIVE THEORIES OF LEADERSHIP SHOWING THE COMPARABILITY OF THEIR COMPONENT DIMENSIONS.

Halpin and Winer	Bowers and Seashore	House
1. Initiating Structure	1. Goal Emphasis	1. Instrumental
2. Consideration	2. Work Facilitation	2. Supportive
	3. Support	3. Participative
	4. Interaction Facilitation	

Covey

There are many authors who are popular and who have attempted to isolate, identify, and describe the qualities demonstrated by effective leaders of organizations. Among these are Peters and Waterman (1982), Bennis and Nanus (1985), and Kouzes and Posner (1987). We believe that each of these perspectives represents a blend of analysis reflecting the traditional traitist view of leadership, although each work is careful to note that leadership behavior must be appreciated in light of a specific contextual reality. As a result, it might be argued that many current descriptions of leadership are also behavioral in nature.

The example of popular leadership analysis that we have selected for a brief review here is the work of Stephen Covey (1991). We believe that his work is founded on many of the same basic assumptions that we have identified as central to proactive supervision. Covey notes eight characteristics of "principle-centered leaders" (pp. 33–38):

1. *They are continually learning.* Principle-centered leaders are constantly educated by their experiences.
2. *They are service-oriented.* Principle-centered leaders view their roles as providing for the needs of followers, as career stops.
3. *They radiate positive energy.* Principle-centered leaders are happy and enthusiastic people.
4. *They believe in other people.* Principle-centered leaders endeavor to find the best in others, not the faults of others.
5. *They lead balanced lives.* Principle-centered leaders are not "married to their work;" they enjoy a full range of social, intellectual, familial, and work-related experiences.
6. *They see life as an adventure.* Principle-centered leaders see things that occur in their lives as challenges, not problems.
7. *They are synergistic.* Principle-centered leaders are able to pull together the vast resources of talent and energy found in people and events that surround them so that they can make organizational life more productive, as the sum of many individual parts.
8. *They exercise for self-renewal.* Principle-centered leaders engage in regular exercise to strengthen themselves physically, mentally, emotionally, and spiritually.

   Each of these theoretical perspectives related to the description of leadership can help us understand some of the basic characteristics of leadership behavior. All are descriptive in nature and as such are somewhat limited because they only present ways of stating what can be observed concerning leadership. Of greater value to the practicing educational supervisor or administrator are normative perspectives of leadership behavior, three of which we consider in the following section.

Alternative Normative Models

The three analyses presented below extend the basic descriptions of leadership attitudes and behavior so that they may be used to predict more or less desirable ways in which people "ought" to behave. These three views are the Leadership Grid of Blake and

Adams McCanse, Reddin's 3-D Theory of Leadership, and the Behavior Matrix developed by the Northwest Regional Laboratory for Educational Development.

Leadership Grid

As is true of most conceptualizations of leadership, the Leadership Grid model of Robert Blake and Anne Adams McCanse (1991) suggests that leadership consists of two attitudinal dimensions: a concern for people, or interpersonal relationships and a concern for tasks, production, or things. This conceptualization of leadership is based on earlier work by Blake and Jane Mouton (1985) who developed the Managerial Grid. Blake and Adams McCanse's Leadership Grid, depicted in Figure 6.1, particularly resembles Halpin and Winer's two-dimensional managerial theory.

The Leadership Grid allows us to analyze leadership attitudes in terms of both concern for people and concern for product, on a continuum of 1 (low) to 9 (high). According to Robert Owens (1987), Blake and Mouton made it clear in their earlier work that 9,9 (high in both areas) is the leadership attitude pattern likely to be most effective in most organizations to achieve the best results:

> "Results" means the effectiveness of the organization in (1) achieving its goals and (2) maintaining a high level of morale. Goal achievement might be measured by such indicators (in schools) as test scores, rate of dropouts, percent of graduates going on to further education, employee-management relations, community support for bond issues, and feedback from employers on the performance of graduates. Morale may be indicated by such things as absenteeism, number of grievances, employee-management relations, and cohesiveness of the group. (Owens, 1987, p. 134)

The Leadership Grid model does not simply provide more terms to describe leadership approaches; rather, its implications about the relative effectiveness of certain behaviors provide useful directions for any individual seeking to perform as an effective educational leader. A Grid rating of 1,1 ("Impoverished Management"), for instance, would hardly be an appropriate pattern approach for a supervisor or administrator called upon to provide direction to a school staff. A 9,9 rating ("Team Management"), on the other hand—where equivalent emphasis is placed both on the needs of teachers, students, and staff and on school outcomes—would be optimal. Variations on this most desirable level are likely, of course; a supervisor who is a proponent of the human relations philosophy

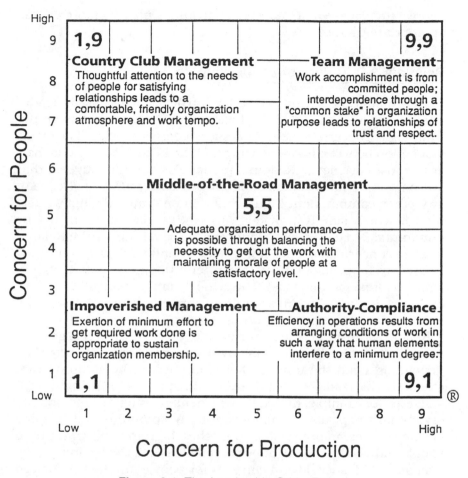

Figure 6.1 The Leadership Grid® Figure

SOURCE: The Leadership Grid® Figure from Leadership Dilemmas—Grid Solutions, by Robert
R. Blake and Anne Adams McCanse (formerly The Managerial Grid Figure by Robert R. Blake
and Jane S. Mouton). Houston: Gulf Publishing Company, p. 29. Copyright © 1991, by Scientific
Methods, Inc. Reproduced by permission of the owners.

would probably come closer to a 1,9 ("Country Club Management")
attitude rating—high concern for people, low concern for
production—while a supervisor who believes in scientific
management might achieve something closer to a 9,1 ("Authority-
Compliance")—low concern for people, high concern for production.

The Leadership Grid is widely used in both public and private
management circles not only as a diagnostic, descriptive device to
help individuals understand their attitudes, but also as a way to

appreciate places where one set of attitudes may be more or less appropriate than others.

Reddin's 3-D Theory of Leadership

The normative 3-D Theory of Leadership developed by W. J. Reddin (1970) goes a step beyond the Leadership Grid, yet builds on the same logic (concern for people versus concern for tasks). The major distinction between Reddin's view and the Leadership Grid is that, at its most basic level, Reddin's model also does not suggest that any one single combination of behaviors is necessarily better than any other combination. Figure 6.2 demonstrates Reddin's basic model, which simply provides descriptive classification in four quadrants: Separated (low in concern for people and task); Related (high in concern for people, low in task orientation); Dedicated (low in concern for people, high in task orientation); Integrated (high in concern for people and task). The critical point to remember is that, at this basic stage, Reddin's quadrants are purely descriptive; none is better or worse than any other.

Reddin's theory becomes normative, however, when it goes on to suggest that the basic four behaviors are more or less appropriate depending upon the unique characteristics of the situation that exists in the leader's organization. As the model in Figure 6.3 suggests, for example, the leader who demonstrates an "integrated" style might appear to be inappropriately compromising in some circumstances; in other situations, the "high in concern for both people and task" style might be perceived as truly "executive." The "separated" leader (low in concern for people and tasks), viewed as disconnected and a "deserter" in some situations, might be an effective and organizationally needed "bureaucrat" in other cases. Sergiovanni and Starratt (1983) summarized the overall value of Reddin's 3-D Theory of Leadership:

> At first glance the theory seems complex and the labels chosen by Reddin confusing and on occasion inappropriate. But the language system is worth deciphering, for the concepts and ideas basic to the theory are powerful and important. A key to this theory is the notion that the *same style* expressed in different situations may be effective or ineffective. (p. 183)

The basic problem with Reddin's theory is that "appropriate" and "inappropriate" situations are not clearly defined. Nevertheless, Reddin's view of effective leadership behavior as a dynamic and situational, rather than static, phenomenon is important.

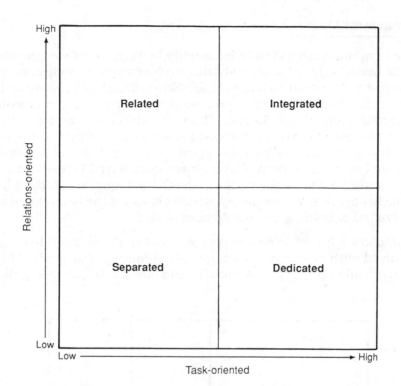

Figure 6.2. Basic model of Reddin's 3-D Theory of Leadership.

When used inappropriately	Basic styles	When used appropriately
Compromiser ⟶	Integrated ⟶	Executive
Deserter ⟶	Separated ⟶	Bureaucrat
Autocrat ⟶	Dedicated ⟶	Benevolent autocrat
Missionary ⟶	Related ⟶	Developer

Figure 6.3. Effective and ineffective expressions of leadership style according to Reddin's 3-D Theory of Leadership.

Behavioral Matrix

The final normative view of leadership behavior that we consider is the Leadership Behavioral Matrix developed by researchers at the Northwest Regional Laboratory for Educational Development in Portland, Oregon, which again suggests that two dimensions comprise leadership behavior. The major difference between this perspective and the ones reviewed earlier in the chapter is that the Northwest Laboratory Matrix suggests that a person is *either* task-oriented or people-oriented and *either* introverted or extroverted in terms of how he or she works with others. Figure 6.4 depicts the basic Leadership Matrix model, which classifies the behavior of an individual according to four distinct styles:

Promoters.   Extroverted and people-oriented, these individuals get involved with others in active, rapidly changing situations. They are typically outgoing and friendly and can get things going, but

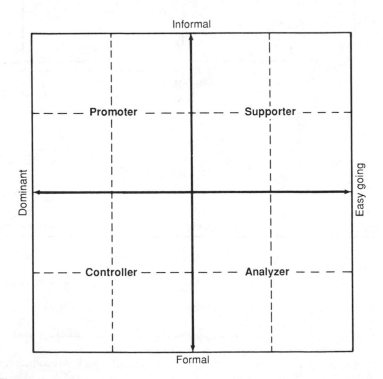

Figure 6.4. Leadership Behavioral Matrix. (Northwest Regional Educational Laboratory. Portland, Oregon. Reprinted by permission of the publisher.)

may settle for less than the best results. Promoters are highly competitive.

Supporters.   Introverted, people-oriented types who value interpersonal relations, these individuals try to minimize conflict and promote the happiness of others.

Analyzers.   They are introverted, task-oriented people who are problem solvers and like to have all the data before making a decision. Thus, some people get frustrated with their slow decision making.

Controllers.   Extroverted and task-oriented, these are individuals who love to run things and have jobs done in their own way. These people will make sure the task is completed on time and to their satisfaction.

The critical observation in this description is that no one leadership style is better than others; there are no "right" or "wrong" styles. Individuals in each of the four quadrants of the Behavioral Matrix have strengths and weaknesses that may be called upon in different situations to create more effective organizational outcomes.

The Leadership Behavioral Matrix is particularly useful in analyzing potential conflicts which are most apt to occur along the diagonals of the quadrants depicted in Figure 6.4. Thus, the most powerful conflicts tend to take place between promoters and analyzers and between controllers and supporters. Consider, for example, the possibility of conflict between a patient, thoughtful analyzer who wants more and more facts before acting, and the more impulsive promoter. Moreover, the action-oriented controller will no doubt have a difficult time dealing with more laid-back supporters. Conflicts are clearly going to take place in schools where all of these various behavioral styles are represented, and they will be increasingly visible and powerful as people become more wedded to the predominant behavioral characteristics of a particular quadrant. More extreme promoters will probably have even more direct problems in dealing with more extreme analyzers.

The Behavioral Matrix, like Blake and Adams McCanse's Leadership Grid and Reddin's 3-D Theory of Leadership, is a behaviorally based, normative model of leadership analysis. All three, properly understood, can provide direction and guidance for effective supervisory leadership practices.

In the next section, we consider ways in which behavioral views of leadership have been applied to school settings by looking at the concept of instructional leadership.

Emerging Leadership Perspectives

In recent years discussions of leadership in the context of educational organizations have built upon the behavioral theories of leadership that we reviewed here. However, these theoretical bases have been directed increasingly toward two specific themes: The supervisor or administrator as an instructional leader (Austin, 1979; Brookover and Lezotte, 1980; Lipham, 1981; Smith and Andrews, 1991) and the supervisor or administrator as moral and ethical leader (Hodgkinson, 1991; Barnett, et al., 1992).

Instructional Leadership

Despite the amount of discussion about, as well as support for, the concept of instructional leadership, little has been done to define the concept operationally. Few studies have been undertaken to determine the specific behaviors of supervisors or administrators who serve as instructional leaders. Early efforts tended to define leadership behavior in very narrow terms. As a result, most early descriptions focused only on the ways in which school principals became directly involved with instructional activities, and the perception grew that only those principals who spent nearly all of their time either teaching classes or observing teachers were legitimately serving as instructional leaders. This view has been more recently rejected for at least two reasons. First, we now recognize that individuals other than principals (e.g., superintendents, supervisors, department chairs, lead teachers, etc.) might engage in instructional leadership behaviors. Second, we have increasingly realized that instructional leadership can take forms that go well beyond direct intervention in classroom activities (Jensen, 1989; Weber, 1989). The definition of instructional leadership suggested by Ching-Jen Liu (1984) is useful in describing this concept. "Instructional leadership consists of direct or indirect behaviors that significantly affect teacher instruction and, as a result, student learning" (p. 33).

Liu divided the tasks of instructional leadership into two categories—direct and indirect. In very broad terms, we might classify *direct leadership activities* as staff development and teacher supervision and evaluation, and *indirect leadership* as instructional facilitation, resource acquisition and building maintenance, and student problem resolution. Examples of specific behaviors related to each of these categories are shown in the following list.

Factor I: *Staff Development*

Work with a committee to plan and implement the staff development program.

Survey staff members to determine topics and activities for a year-long staff development plan.

Provide inservice training for the support staff on how their roles relate to the instructional program.

Factor II: *Resource Acquisition and Building Maintenance*

Acquire adequate resources for teaching.

Allocate resources on the basis of identified needs according to a priority ranking.

Maintain the building in order to provide a pleasant working condition for students and staff.

Factor III: *Instructional Facilitation*

Establish priorities so that, by the amount of time directed to it, instruction is always first.

Work according to the belief that all students can learn and achieve at high levels.

Support teachers who are implementing new ideas.

Factor IV: *Teacher Supervision and Evaluation*

Involve all staff members and people from the community in setting clear goals and objectives for instruction.

Work according to the belief that all teachers can teach and teach well.

Have conferences with individual teachers to review their instructional plans.

Factor V: *Student Problem Resolution*

Assist teachers in dealing with discipline problems.

Enforce school attendance policies to reduce tardiness and absentee rates.

Interact directly with students to discuss their problems about school.

Using these classifications and descriptions of instructional leadership behaviors, Liu studied two groups of high school principals, one "effective" and another "not effective." He found that the effective group engaged in instructional leadership behaviors more often than the other group and that those behaviors reflected both direct and indirect instructional leadership. As a result, we now recognize that the analysis of instructional leadership is considerably more complex than first thought and that supervisors and administrators who strive to exhibit instructional leadership must be prepared to engage in a wide range of activities that support the instructional priorities of the school. We suspect, then, that instructional leadership is as much a product of a personalized instructional philosophy as it is of any particular activities that a person follows.

One of the most comprehensive recent efforts to gain a better understanding of what behaviors comprise instructional leadership was carried out by Jerry Patterson (1993) for the Association for Supervision and Curriculum Development (ASCD), which looked at the work of numerous principals who had been identified as instructional leaders. Five behavioral patterns were identified in those individuals who were viewed as effective leaders.

1. *They provide a sense of vision to their schools.* They demonstrate the ability to articulate what a school is supposed to do, particularly in terms of what it should do to benefit children. Effective instructional leaders leave little doubt that the purpose of the school is to find ways in which children may learn successfully. This vision, or mission, guides all other activities.

2. *They engage in participative management.* They encourage a better organizational climate in the school by allowing teachers and staff to participate meaningfully in real decision making and not merely in an effort to "play at" getting people to be involved when decisions are already made. The staff senses greater ownership in the priorities and programs that are available to help children.

3. *They provide support for instruction.* Instructional leaders are so committed to maintaining quality instruction as their primary organizational focus that when decisions must be made concerning priorities, instruction always comes first. These individuals make it clear to all around them that energy will be expended to assure that resources are available to enable the instructional program of the school to proceed unabated.

4. *Instructional leaders monitor instruction.* They know what is going on in the classrooms of their schools. This monitoring may take several forms from direct, in-class, intensive observation to merely walking around the building and talking with students. The critical issue, regardless of the particular procedures followed, is that instructional leaders are aware of the quality of instruction being carried out in their schools.

5. *They are resourceful.* Instructional leaders rarely allow circumstances in their organizations to get in the way of their vision for quality educational programs. As a result, they tend not to allow the lack of resources, or apparently prohibitive school or district policies, or any other factors from interfering with their goals for their schools.

Instructional leaders carry out these behavior patterns very differently. Thus, people with different personalities, philosophies, values, and attitudes can be equally effective as educational leaders. In addition, entirely different schools can serve as settings for instructional leadership of the type identified through the ASCD work.

Effective school leaders share many behavioral patterns, predictably, with leaders in other organizations. Bennis and Nanus (1985), in a study of a wide variety of effective organizations, discovered five strategies followed by successful leaders:

Strategy I: *Attention through vision.* Leaders create a focus in an organization, or an agenda that demonstrates an unparalleled concern for outcomes, products, and results.

Strategy II: *Meaning through communication.* Effective communication is inseparable from effective leadership.

Strategy III: *Trust through positioning.* Leaders must be trusted in order to be effective; we trust people who are predictable and whose positions are known. Leaders who are trusted make themselves known and make their positions clear.

Strategy IV: *The deployment of self through positive self-regard.* Leaders have positive self-images, self-regard that is not self-centered, and they know their worth. In general, they are confident without being cocky.

Strategy V: *The development of self through the "Wallenda Factor."* Before his death, the famous aerialist Karl Wallenda was said to have become more preoccupied with not falling than with succeeding. Leaders are able consistently to focus their energies on success rather than on simply avoiding failure.

Other researchers have created other lists of successful leadership behaviors parallel to these efforts by Liu, ASCD, and Bennis and Nanus. Such lists typically feature considerable overlap with what we have reviewed here. What is highly significant about all of these efforts is that they represent attempts to move the study of leadership to levels of analysis not found in most past treatments. For educational supervisors, this is good news. It offers the possibility that specific, effective leadership behaviors may now be identified in greater numbers than they were in the past. While such efforts should never be viewed as gospel to be followed for leadership or as panaceas to cure the absence of direction often found in schools, they do provide practitioners with a road map to follow in search for more effective educational programs.

Moral and Ethical Leadership

A new perspective on leadership behavior is appearing in the literature. This view, which we refer to as moral and ethical leadership, appears to have two different ways of looking at the duties of organizational leaders. One characterizes the leader as the model of *moral behavior*—as the person who works to set a proper ethical tone for the organization. The other is related to the leader becoming a servant to meet the diverse needs of those who work in the organization.

With regard to the leader as a moral role model, we find that there is an increasing recognition that, contrary to many conventional images of leadership, it is not sufficient to believe that leaders are simply those who bring about organizational change. Instead, we now find an increased emphasis in the quality and nature of the types of changes that an individual might promote. This view might serve as a response to those who have often claimed that the mere ability of an individual to promote massive societal change (e.g., Hitler or Stalin) made that person a leader. There is now an assumption by many (Sergiovanni, 1990; Hodgkinson, 1991; Barnett, et al., 1992) that a key feature of leadership is that it promotes change toward morally and societally redeeming goals. An understanding of leadership in these terms is highly dependent on the acceptance of a clear vision of the nature of education. Hodgkinson (1991), a proponent of leadership as a moral activity, noted the following:

> Education is not the art of training and subjugating people to serve the profit of others. It is the art of helping people to know themselves, to develop the resources, judgment, and skills of learning and the sense of values needed on facing a future of unpredictable change, to understand the rights and responsi- bilities of adults in a democratic society and to exercise the greatest possible degree of control over their own fate. (p. 16)

Educational leadership, then, is the art of promoting this view of value-based and "value-added" (Sergiovanni, 1990) education.

The second vision of moral and ethical leadership is related to a view which states that the primary goal of the leader is to serve the needs of followers. An example of this perspective is found in the notion of stewardship defined by Block (1993):

> Stewardship is the umbrella idea which promises the means of achieving fundamental change in the way we govern our institutions. Stewardship is to hold something in trust for another. Historically, stewardship was a means to protect a kingdom while those rightfully in charge were away or, more often, to govern for the sake of an underage king. (p. xx)

By separating these two branches of moral and ethical leadership, we do not wish to suggest that value-based leadership is somehow contradictory to stewardship. To the contrary, we find these concepts very compatible. We only wish to indicate that we believe that each of these areas will likely see greater development in the near future, and the proactive supervisor would be well advised to remain aware of this development.

General Comments about Leadership

While we have tried to present an ordered view of the nature of leadership as it has been analyzed in school settings, we have only scratched the surface of a very complex topic. The search for precise understanding of what contributes to effective organizational leadership has been at the center of virtually every analysis of organizations. People always have been and will continue to be fascinated with determining "Who leads?" and "How do they do it?" People will always try to put into some kind of order the notions they have about leadership.

Researchers have only gotten a very brief glimpse into the process of leadership. Many facets of this critical topic have not yet been explored. For example, researchers have tended to look almost exclusively at leadership as demonstrated by those who have formal leadership titles in schools and other organizations. The roles of principals, supervisors, and superintendents have been examined, to the virtual exclusion of the study of others. Anyone who has ever worked in or around schools will recognize that *leadership is not the exclusive property of administrators* (Playko, 1991), and anyone who assumes that it is could be making a terrible error in judgment. A second area where more research is needed is the phenomenon of "followership" and the nature of the dynamic relationships that occur between leaders and others in their organizations. The concept of "transformative leadership" (energy directed toward enabling others to sustain needed change), first described by James McGregor Burns (1978) and expanded into an emphasis on empowerment by Bennis and Nanus (1985) and Block (1989), appears to hold promise for increasing our understanding of how leaders interact with others. Leaders must have followers, and interest must be directed toward that fact.

Finally, a discussion of leadership often includes some views that Bennis and Nanus call the "myths of leadership." We conclude this analysis of leadership by listing these myths and noting why they should not be viewed as limitations.

Myth 1. *Leadership is a rare skill.* In fact, virtually everyone has some leadership potential, and opportunities are great for many people to assume formal and informal leadership roles in a variety of settings.

Myth 2. *Leaders are born, not made.* As we noted when we looked at the "great person" approaches to leadership, the major capacities and competencies of leadership can be learned if there is a basic desire to learn them. Acquiring the knowledge and skills for effective leadership is not easy, but most people have the fundamental capacity to become powerful leaders.

Myth 3. *Leaders are charismatic.* Most leaders are quite human, and they rarely possess any magical talents that are unavailable to the rest of us. In fact, some evidence indicates that what we call charisma is the result of leadership, not the reverse. Good leaders often gain respect and admiration from their followers because of the ways in which they demonstrate leadership qualities.

Myth 4. *Leadership exists at the top of an organization.* As we noted in our review of instructional leadership, successful leaders strive to increase opportunities for staff members to take active roles in schools through conscious efforts at participative management. Leaders are not threatened by allowing others to have some control over the organization.

Myth 5. *The leader controls, directs, prods, and manipulates.* Leadership is not the exercise of absolute power, but rather the empowerment of others to make use of their full potential. As a result, any effort at control for its own sake might not be an activity of leadership at all, but rather an effort to dominate. Ultimately, organizations that are faced with this type of strangling behavior will either cast out the leader or die as organizations.

Summary

In this chapter we reviewed a theory base typically associated with the analysis of educational supervision, that of leadership. Leadership is often referred to as the single most important area to be developed by anyone interested in pursuing a supervisory or administrative role. Supervisors can be neither proactive nor effective without considering some of the basic issues of leadership presented in this chapter.

We looked first at a variety of definitions of leadership found in the literature. We also reviewed the basic differences between descriptive and normative conceptualizations of leadership—a rather subtle shift in recent years from efforts to describe what leadership is to attempts to tell people how to behave as leaders.

In the next section we considered four historical frameworks for the analysis of leadership, including the "great person," traitist, situational, and behavioral approaches. We noted the major limitations for each of the first three approaches and suggested why most current explanations of leadership use the behavioral perspective, which emphasizes the relationships that exist between individual characteristics and the context in which people work.

Next, we considered several descriptive and normative leadership theories. We also reviewed the concepts of instructional leadership and moral and ethical leadership.

The chapter concluded with some general comments and observations on the nature of the complex phenomenon of leadership in schools.

Suggested Activities

1. Interview a group of teachers to determine their perceptions of what leadership should be. Compare the definitions that are presented with the alternative perspectives of leadership discussed in this chapter.
2. Using the list of "leadership myths" that were described by Bennis and Nanus, compose a rating scale that may be used to collect data concerning perceptions of whether people agree or disagree with each of the stated "myths."
3. Talk with people who are not in professional education to determine their perceptions of what "leadership" is. Again,

compare their statements with the "great person," traitist, situational, and behavioral perspectives.

4. Interview at least five practicing school administrators or supervisors to determine their personal definitions of "instructional leadership." How successful do these individuals feel about actually engaging in behaviors that are part of their definitions? What prohibits people from serving as instructional leaders? What contributes to their ability to serve in this capacity?

Cases to Consider

Read each case and consider the following:

a. What are the critical issues raised in each case, as they relate to the use of theoretical perspectives of leadership?

b. How does each case relate to the development of the concept of proactive supervision?

c. In what ways might you suggest a resolution to the issues raised?

Case 6.1:

Who's Running This Place, Anyway?

For many years, the teachers at Jamestown Middle School had earned a reputation as a particularly strong group. They worked together as a unit implementing few changes since the school had opened ten years ago, and they were regarded as extremely competent. On the other hand, they also were viewed as a group of "mavericks" in the school system. Since the school opened, five different principals worked in the school. Many claimed that the cause of this high turnover was the fact that the teachers were so difficult.

The school board and its new superintendent, Dr. Mary Corwin, decided that it was no longer acceptable to have one school where teachers tried to run everything. As a result, when it came time for a new principal to be named for Jamestown, it was decided that someone with a strong will was needed to come "on board" to "straighten out those teachers." As a result, Ernie Carter, a former coach and currently the assistant principal at the high school, was selected as the sixth principal of Jamestown Middle School.

Ernie took charge of his new building in August and immediately went about the task of trying to fulfill his mandate to bring the teachers under control. He scheduled numerous staff meetings for the first two months of the school year. In each of these sessions, he consistently instructed his teachers on procedures and practices that he expected to see implemented. He named a close friend, Dave Spencer, as his assistant principal. Dave was also a former coach who also had a "no nonsense" view of how to lead groups. Dave and Ernie soon became known as an administrative team that knew what it wanted to do. Moreover, the superintendent and board were pleased to note that teachers in the school seemed to be much more controlled than they had ever been in the past. No grievances were being filed, and phone calls of complaints about the new principal were non-existent. This was quite a change from the last few years at Jamestown.

As the year progressed, it was increasingly apparent that things had truly changed at the middle school. A few years ago, it was not uncommon to hear reports of teachers talking directly to the local newspaper about dissatisfaction. Parents often reported that teachers spent conference time lobbying for parental support. All of that now changed with Ernie in charge.

The change in Jamestown Middle School continued into May and June of the school year. However, Dr. Corwin became aware that the results were not necessarily positive. First, she was shocked to find that student scores on the statewide assessment of progress had drastically fallen at Jamestown during the past year. Second, she was now receiving at least three requests for transfers each day from teachers in the school. Even Harry Adams, one of the most respected (and quiet) teachers in the school system for many years had stopped in to share the fact that he was seeking a way to gain an early retirement from teaching this next year.

Case 6.2:

But I Thought They Liked Me!

Bob Cleveland had looked forward to his first principalship for several years. He had completed a masters degree and administrative certification program at the local university three years ago and had taken a position as an assistant principal in one of the district elementary schools as a way to learn even more about the job he eventually wanted to reach. He worked with Ruth Martinez, a principal who had a well-deserved reputation as a very strong leader who really controlled the students and teachers in her school. Bob gained a reputation as a great listener, particularly to those who believed that Ruth had not been sensitive to their needs. Bob considered himself to be a great team player with Ruth; their styles and personalities complemented each other.

This past year, Bob got his wish and became the principal of Big Bend Elementary School, a small but new building. The school's extremely experienced teaching staff moved to Big Bend primarily because it was a beautiful new facility and also because Bob had gained the reputation as a "nice guy" who would not bother teachers, unlike many of the other principals in the district.

As everyone predicted, Bob soon took on his role as principal with many of the same behaviors that he demonstrated as an assistant principal. He rarely confronted teachers. Rather, he took pride in his ability to remain cool under pressure and simply wait for teachers to come to him with their problems. He truly viewed his role as that of a facilitator and supporter of the teachers, and he announced that at all staff meetings at the beginning of the school year.

What Bob did not see at first, however, was that parents were starting to complain to the central office that they were disappointed at what was going on at Big Bend. "You spent all that money on carpeting and equipment at the new school, but we get a bunch of retired teachers to work in it," was one of the more direct comments made to the superintendent after a recent board meeting. Then Bob had a personal revelation that something was seriously wrong when he walked into the teachers' lounge one night after everyone had left and found a reference to "Bob the Wimp" on a cartoon someone had drawn on a piece of scrap paper.

References

Austin, G. R. (1979, October). Exemplary schools and the search for effectiveness. *Educational Leadership*, 35(1): 10–14.

Barnett, Bruce, McQuarrie, Frank O., & Norris, Cynthia J. (Eds.) (1991). *The moral imperatives of leadership: A focus on human decency.* Fairfax, VA: National Policy Board for Educational Administration.

Bennis, Warren, & Nanus, Burt (1985). *Leaders: The strategies for taking charge.* New York: Harper and Row,

Blake, Robert R., & Adams McCanse, Anne (1991). *Leadership dilemmas— Grid solutions.* Houston: Gulf Publishing.

Blake, Robert R., & Mouton, Jane S. (1985). *The managerial grid III.* Houston: Scientific Methods.

Block, Peter (1988). *The empowered manager: Positive political skills at work.* San Francisco: Jossey Bass.

Block, Peter (1993). *Stewardship: Choosing service over self-interest.* San Francisco: Berrett-Koehler Publishers.

Bowers, D. G., & Seashore, S. E. (1966). Predicting organizational effectiveness with a four factor theory of leadership. *Administrative Science Quarterly,* 11(2): 238–263.

Brookover, W. B., & Lezotte, L. (1980). *Changes in school characteristics coincident with changes in student achievement.* East Lansing: Michigan State University, College of Urban Development.

Burns, James MacGregor (1978). *Leadership.* New York: Harper and Row.

Covey, Stephen R. (1991). *Principle-centered leadership.* New York: Simon and Schuster.

Halpin, Andrew W. (1957). A paradigm for research on administrative behavior. In R. F. Campbell & Russell T. Gregg (Eds.), *Administrative behavior in education.* Chicago: University of Chicago, Midwest Administrative Center.

Halpin, Andrew W., & Winer, J. A. (1957). A factorial study of the leader behavior description questionnaire. In R. M. Stogdill & A. E. Coons (Eds.), *Leader behavior: Its description and measurement* (Research Monograph Series No. 88). Columbus: The Ohio State University, Bureau of Business Research.

Hemphill, John K. (1949). *Situational factors in leadership.* Columbus: The Ohio State University Press.

Hemphill, John K., & Coons, A. E. (1957). Development of the leader behavior description questionnaire. In R. M. Stogdill & A. E. Coons (Eds.), *Leader behavior: Its description and measurement.* (Research Monograph Series No. 88). Columbus: The Ohio State University, Bureau of Business Research.

Hodgkinson, Christopher (1991). *Educational leadership: The moral art.* Albany: SUNY Press.

House, Robert J. (1973). A path-goal theory of leader effectiveness. In W. E. Scott, Jr., & L. L. Cummings (Eds.), *Readings in organizational behavior and human performance.* Homewood, IL: Irwin.

Jacobs, T. O. (1970). *Leadership and exchange in formal organizations.* Alexandria, VA: Human Resources Research Corporation.

Janada, K. F. (1960). Toward the explication of the concept of leadership in terms of the concept of power. *Human Relations,* 13:345–363.

Jensen, Mary C. (1989). Leading the instructional staff. In Stuart C. Smith & Philip K. Piele (Eds.), *School leadership: Handbook for excellence.*

144   Theory into Practice

Eugene: ERIC Clearinghouse on Educational Management, University of Oregon.

Katz, D., & Kahn, R. L. (1978). *The social psychology of organizations* (2nd ed.). New York: Wiley.

Kochran, T. A., Schmidt, S. S., & DeCotiis, T. A. (1975). Superior-subordinate relations: Leadership and headship. *Human Relations*, 28:279–294.

Kouzes, J. M., & Posner, B. Z. (1987). *The leadership challenge.* San Francisco: Jossey-Bass.

Lipham, James M., & Hoeh, James A. (1974). *The principalship: Foundations and functions.* New York: Harper and Row.

Lipham, James M. (1981). *Effective principal, effective school.* Reston, VA: National Association of Secondary School Principals.

Liu, Ching-Jen (1984). *An identification of principals' instructional leadership in effective high schools.* Unpublished Ed.D. Dissertation. Cincinnati: University of Cincinnati.

Owens, Robert (1987). *Organizational behavior in education* (3rd ed.). Englewood Cliffs, NJ: Prentice Hall.

Patterson, Jerry L. (1993). *Leadership for tomorrow's schools.* Alexandria, VA: Association for Supervision and Curriculum Development.

Peters, T. J., & Waterman, R. H. (1982). *In search of excellence.* New York: Harper and Row.

Playko, Marsha A. (1991). *The voyage to leadership: Journeys of four teachers.* Unpublished Ph.D. dissertation. Columbus: The Ohio State University.

Reddin, W. J. (1970). *Managerial effectiveness.* New York: McGraw-Hill.

Sergiovanni, Thomas J. (1990). *Value-added leadership.* San Diego: Harcourt Brace Jovanovich.

Sergiovanni, Thomas J., & Starratt, Robert J. (1983). *Supervision: Human perspectives* (3rd ed.). New York: McGraw-Hill.

Shakeshaft, Charol (1987). *Women in educational administration.* Beverly Hills: Sage.

Smith, Wilma F., & Andrews, Richard L. (1989). *Instructional leadership: How principals make a difference.* Alexandria, VA: Association for Supervision and Curriculum Development.

Stogdill, Ralph M. (1974). *Handbook of leadership: A survey of theory and research.* New York: Free Press.

Tannenbaum, R., Weshler, I. R., & Massarik, F. (1961). *Leadership and organizations.* New York: McGraw-Hill.

Weber, James R. (1989). Leading the instructional program. In Stuart C. Smith & Philip K. Piele (Eds.), *School leadership: Handbook for excellence* (2nd ed.). Eugene: ERIC Clearinghouse for Educational Management, University of Oregon.

Yukl, Gary A. (1991). *Leadership in organizations* (2nd ed.). Englewood Cliffs, NJ: Prentice-Hall.

Additional Readings

Bennis, Warren (1990). *Why leaders can't lead*. San Francisco: Jossey Bass.

DePree, Max (1989). *Leadership is an art*. New York: Dell.

Duignan, P. A., & MacPherson, R. J. S. (Eds.) (1992). *Educative leadership: A practical theory for new administrators and managers*. London: The Falmer Press.

Jacobson, Stephen L., & Conway, James A. (Eds.) (1990). *Educational leadership in an age of reform*. White Plains, NY: Longman.

Rost, Joseph C. (1993). *Leadership for the twenty-first century*. Westport, CT: Praeger.

Wheatley, Margaret (1992). *Leadership and the new science: Learning about organizations from an orderly universe*. San Francisco: Berrett-Koehler Publishers.

7 Motivation

Regardless of how individual supervisors look at their work (for example, as "inspectors," or disciples of human relations), and regardless of whether they subscribe to the assumptions and practices of the proactive supervisory process, a key supervisory responsibility is inevitably the fostering of employee motivation. In this chapter we consider a number of alternative theoretical models of motivation. As we have done in earlier chapters, we first provide a definition of motivation and an overview of differing perspectives. The chapter concludes with a discussion of the relationship among the personal philosophy of education developed by an individual to guide professional supervisory behavior, the implementation of proactive supervisory processes, and employee motivation.

Definition of Motivation

Motivation is one of the most important and challenging supervisory responsibilities undertaken in schools or any other organization. Unlike the concepts we explored in earlier chapters, however, motivation can be defined in a relatively simple way. John Lovell and Kimball Wiles (1983) defined motivation as the "level of effort an individual is willing to expend toward the achievement of a certain goal" (p. 50). In attempting to motivate people, we must look for answers to the following three questions, which have been faced by managers, supervisors, and administrators in many different types of organizations throughout history:

- What makes some people work hard, while other people hardly work at all (or at least work as little as possible)?
- How can certain people—educational supervisors, for example— positively influence the performance of the people who work for them?
- Why do some people leave organizations, show up late for work, refuse to be committed, or generally "tune out" of their job responsibilities, while other people tend to get to work early, stay late, and engage in all types of behaviors indicative of a strong commitment to their labor and "go the extra mile?"

Each of these questions is a legitimate aspect of the overall issue of how to increase human motivation. Clearly, there are no "perfect" answers to all, or perhaps even to any of these three questions. There is no way to ensure commitment by all employees all the time. Neither is there a way to guarantee that any single employee will remain highly motivated and committed at all times. The search goes on, however, for the most appropriate motivational techniques. Several theoretical perspectives have been offered to aid in this search. The basic assumptions and features of four of these conceptualizations will be reviewed in the following sections.

Need-Satisfaction Theories of Motivation

Theorists most closely associated with need theories are Abraham Maslow and Frederick Herzberg, each of whom has developed a slightly different scheme for analyzing motivation in organizations.

Maslow's theory of a hierarchy of needs. The basic assumption underlying Maslow's *Motivation and Personality* (1970) are familiar to many. One primary belief is that people are motivated by their individual needs to address certain natural concerns. These concerns, in turn, can be rank-ordered hierarchically in terms of potency.

We need to recognize two important premises in order to understand Maslow's perspective more completely: First, human beings are best defined and understood as "wanting creatures" who are motivated by a consistent desire to satisfy certain needs; second, individuals pursue needs in a linear, sequential progression according to the following levels of intensity and potency.

1. *Safety needs*—the desire to find a safe and secure physical environment
2. *Belongingness needs*—an individual's desire to be accepted by his or her peers
3. *Esteem needs*—the desire to have a positive self-image and to receive recognition from others
4. *Physiological needs*—the most basic human needs such as hunger, thirst, and shelter
5. *Self-actualization needs*—the concern for the development of full individual potential

Figure 7.1 represents the hierarchical relationship of these needs.

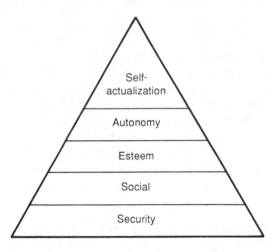

Figure 7.1. Pyramid depicting the hierarchical nature of human needs according to Maslow.

The key concept in Maslow's model is that the needs indicated in the pyramid must be addressed in a hierarchical fashion. Individuals will not be motivated toward a higher level of concern and performance until lower needs are satisfied. If they are not, tension, rather than a positive sense of motivation, is created within individuals. There is little sense in trying to motivate people by focusing on esteem (professional recognition) while they are hungry or apprehensive about being accepted by peers.

Herzberg's need-satisfaction theory of motivation. The research done by psychologist Frederick Herzberg is based largely on the same assumptions about need-satisfaction promoted by

Maslow. In some ways, in fact, Herzberg's (1966) motivation theory represents a natural refinement of Maslow's basic hierarchical framework.

Two major premises or assumptions serve as the basis of Herzberg's theory:

Hygiene factors are those job-related elements that can reduce satisfaction. These factors cannot, in themselves, motivate a worker; they can only prevent dissatisfaction. Hygiene factors are generally defined as those tangible elements such as wages, fringe benefits, and working conditions (see the list below). When an employee's pay is low, for instance, he or she will probably be dissatisfied; raising the pay, however, will not necessarily raise satisfaction (and therefore motivation) proportionately.

Motivators are factors whose presence in a worker's life leads to satisfaction, but whose absence does not necessarily lead to dissatisfaction. Among these are achievement, recognition, responsibility, and advancement.

Hygiene Factors

1. Work environment (organizational climate and physical conditions)
2. Type of supervision
3. Salary and fringe benefits
4. Job security
5. Attitudes and policies of the administration
6. Status

Motivators

1. Achievement
2. Advancement
3. Characteristics of the work itself
4. Growth (personal and professional)
5. Responsibility
6. Recognition

If Herzberg's theory is correct, it implies that such things as salary increases and improvement of fringe benefits must not be ignored, but that these factors alone will not motivate employees to excel in their work.

Three basic criticisms have tended to follow the work of both Maslow and Herzberg and their views of human motivation. First, critics suggest that both Maslow and Herzberg suffer from not providing clear definitions, which in turn hinders the ability to make predictions from their theories. A classic question, asked particularly of Maslow, is, "What is 'self-actualization'?" If we cannot adequately define the term, how can we determine if a person has attained this level? How can we even direct our behavior toward attaining it? It is relatively simple to appreciate the attainment of lower-level goals such as those associated with physiological and safety needs. Higher-order needs such as esteem and self-actualization, on the other hand, are unclearly defined.

Second, the work of both Maslow and Herzberg is criticized as insufficiently dynamic. Inherent in both views is the assumption that individuals wait for needs to arise in their lives before they respond; people do not actively seek ways to increase their effectiveness. These views, then, suggest that needs manipulate people, rather than that people control needs.

Third, critics find in Herzberg's theory no clear-cut distinctions between hygiene factors and motivators. Factors classified as motivators by one organization may be referred to as hygiene factors by another organization, or even by other people who work in the same organization.

Implications of Need Theories for the Supervisor

Educational supervisors can find at least two major values in the concepts defined by need-satisfaction theories. One is the implication that supervisors, administrators, and others engaging in educational leadership should be responsible and held accountable for creating a climate in their schools or districts conducive to the ongoing process of personal growth and self-fulfillment by employees.

A second value is that a supervisor's knowledge of what might satisfy or dissatisfy teachers and other staff members can be an important tool to improve their effectiveness. One major supervisory responsibility is to increase employee motivation; the danger, however, is that the power to motivate might be manipulative. That is, supervisors often have the authority to withhold as well as dispense many of the elements that satisfy staff members' needs.

Equity Theories of Motivation

Equity theories suggest that the most important factor in employee motivation is the extent to which workers perceive a sense of equity in the work environment. If workers believe they are being treated fairly, they will be more satisfied and work harder toward achieving personal and organizational goals.

Implications of Equity Theories
for the Supervisor

If the assumptions on which equity theories are based are correct, then supervisors must determine ways to ensure that their employees believe they are being treated fairly on the job. Employee perceptions of a given situation are important, because "fairness" cannot be entirely based on any objective reality. The supervisor's duty, then, is to make sure people perceive the treatment they are receiving as equitable; to do this requires that the supervisor first determine what people perceive as fair. Equity theories tend to place considerable emphasis on the use of monetary and other tangible rewards, because it is easier to distribute equitable dollars in recognition of valued performance than it is to distribute equitable recognition or esteem. For the supervisor, then, equity theories suggest the need to seek tangible or visible rewards for employees.

One issue that we need to understand in our discussion of equity theories is the difference between "equitable" and "equal." *Equality* implies the need to provide every employee with exactly the same rewards; everyone is treated the same. *Equity* is the concept of finding the fair or right amount of reward for each individual according to need. An equitable workplace is not one in which every employee receives the same treatment, benefits, and rewards. We emphasize this because supervisors frequently attempt to provide equity in the workplace through equal treatment, and this is not what equity theories advocate.

Reinforcement Theories of Motivation

When we talk about motivation through reinforcement, we immediately think of the contributions of B. F. Skinner. Skinner's basic assumptions are quite simple. Reinforcement theory assumes that human behavior can be engineered, shaped, or altered by manipulating the reward structures for various forms of behavior. This manipulation is called *positive reinforcement.*

In this approach, performance standards are first clearly set, and improvement results from the application of frequent positive feedback linked to the attainment of stated performance objectives.

Implications of Reinforcement for the Supervisor

Reinforcement theory probably makes more demands on supervisors than any other popular approach to motivation. The supervisor is largely responsible for manipulating and altering a number of features of the work environment. For example, supervisors must clearly set standards and inform their employees as to which behaviors are desirable in reaching these standards and which are not. The supervisor or administrator who bases practice on reinforcement theories would probably spend a considerable amount of time at the beginning of the school year defining rules and procedures and explaining the consequences of violating those rules. Breaking from policy would bring a swift reprimand, and adherence to policy would be rewarded openly.

In addition, reinforcement theory assumes that performance can be improved by providing continuous feedback to employees concerning the nature and quality of their work with regard to the established goals and standards. In a school setting, then, this suggests that the supervisor would engage in a good deal of monitoring behavior to evaluate teacher performance as a way to start the feedback process. In other words, the supervisor must live by the motto, "When people do good jobs, tell them so."

Reinforcement theories of motivation stand in direct contradiction to equity theories. According to reinforcement theories, supervisors should work to ensure that all employees are not rewarded equally. Instead, they should always be rewarded differently according to their levels of performance. Again, supervisors should be aware of the possibility that their behavior might be overly manipulative or exploitive of teaching staff.

Expectancy Theories of Motivation

According to expectancy theories of motivation, when people value something, they will be motivated to engage in actions based on the strength of that valuing. Porter and Lawler (1965) have been most closely associated with this view of organizational motivation, and they offered the following observations concerning the nature of expectancy theories:

- Behavior is determined by a combination of forces in the individuals and forces in the environment.

- People make decisions about their own behavior in organizations.
- Different people have different needs, desires, and goals.
- People make decisions among alternative plans of behavior based on their own perceptions or expectancies of the degree to which a given behavior is likely to lead to some desired outcome.

Implications of Expectancy

Theories for Supervisors

Because employee behavior ultimately derives from forces in the person and in the environment, a supervisor who subscribes to expectancy theories of motivation must first know the organizational and personal outcomes that each employee tends to value most. The supervisor would therefore need to spend time talking with staff to determine what outcomes have the greatest value. Without such knowledge, the supervisor would be unable to seek a motivational focus. In addition to determining the staff's desired outcomes, the supervisor needs to assess what behaviors and outcomes he or she desires from the staff. To do this the supervisor needs to have a well-articulated personal educational platform to provide guidance and a plan of action.

Expectancy theories of motivation also imply that supervisors must make certain that the goals, behaviors, and outcomes they desire are actually attainable and that the desired outcomes are linked directly to desired levels of performance.

The supervisor adhering to this theoretical framework would need to determine the exact reward structure most likely to ensure that employees will continue to make progress toward the attainment of organizational goals and objectives. The supervisor first needs to analyze the nature of the total work environment to locate any potentially conflicting expectancies. Does one part of the organization value one type of employee behavior while another department suggests rewards for an entirely different behavior? If such conflicts exist, the supervisor might need to make some adjustments to reduce the number of mixed messages being transmitted to the staff.

The supervisor would also need to make certain that, where possible, the changes in organizational outcomes are large enough to motivate and positively change the behavior of employees. Trivial changes and rewards will automatically result in trivial changes in levels of employee performance. This will, in turn, result in trivial outcomes for the organization.

Using expectancy theories for motivating employees also will probably result in some modifications in organizational policies and procedures. For example, pay and reward systems might generally need to be redesigned, with more effort put into rewarding people for organizationally desirable performances. Consequently, extremely precise employee appraisal and evaluation systems would be needed to guide the distribution of employee rewards.

Expectancy theory requires careful reexamination of tasks, jobs, job descriptions, and the roles of employees within the organization. Supervisors must understand the importance of formal and informal employee group structures, because such structures are important determinants of ultimate employee performance.

The final implication for supervisors who buy into the concept of expectancy theory is that they must pay considerable attention to individual employee needs, concerns, and interests. Such sensitivity to individual issues is not found in many organizations, but it needs to be developed and maintained if expectancy theories are to be employed with any consistency.

Individual Professional Philosophy and Approaches to Motivation

In the previous section we reviewed four alternative theories about how people are motivated. Ideally, we could settle on one "best" way to encourage greater commitment to organizational goals and objectives in all structures, but no such satisfyingly simple solution exists. The motivational strategy you select as an educational supervisor will depend largely on your own educational philosophy. In particular, how you view the role of teachers and others who work in schools will determine to a large extent how you try to motivate them. If, for example, you believe that teachers are fundamentally nothing more than employees of the school district and that they need much close direction to control their behavior, then your approach to motivation might well be based on reinforcement theory, which suggests that people can be "conditioned" to operate in a desired manner. If, on the other hand, you view teachers as a highly skilled group of professionals, then you might approach motivation through the needs-satisfaction theory. In particular, Herzberg's views might appeal to you.

Your personal educational platform also comes to play in determining to what extent you support McGregor's Theory X and Theory Y, described in chapter 2. Do you, for example, begin with the assumption that people are basically lazy? If so, your attempts at motivating them would differ significantly from those you would make if you believed that most people really do wish to work hard.

Finally, we point out that no one ever truly motivates another person. There is no causal relationship between your selection of a motivation theory and an outcome of greater staff commitment. Ultimately, whether or not a person works harder rests in that person's own choice. More important, a supervisor's motivational effectiveness depends not on the specific tactic used but on the extent to which the staff believes in the supervisor and on the consistency of the supervisor's performance. In order to achieve the kind of consistency that employees admire, educational supervisors must operate from a foundation of principle and belief about education; again, the development of a personal educational platform is a vital ingredient in effectiveness.

Summary

In this chapter we reviewed a number of theories concerning the motivation of employees in organizations. We noted that motivation is yet another example that reflects how important theory can be in effective supervisory practice, but we also pointed out that motivation is a critically important supervisory responsibility. We stressed that motivation is ultimately the responsibility of those who are to be motivated, but that a knowledge of alternative theoretical perspectives can serve as a critically useful tool for effective supervisors.

We offered four theoretical approaches to motivation in this chapter; the popular *need-satisfaction* theories of Maslow and Herzberg; *equity* theories, which suggest that fairness in the workplace is the most important motivational factor; *reinforcement* theories as developed by B. F. Skinner and others; and *expectancy* theories, which suggest that employees respond favorably to conditions that they value. We concluded with a review of the relationship between motivational strategies and the educational supervisor's individual educational philosophy.

Suggested Activities

1. List the things that someone could do to make you want to work harder than you already do. To what extent are those motivational factors compatible with any of the theories that were reviewed in this chapter? Are you likely to respond to the satisfaction of needs? Describe your sense of fairness and equity? Also, list the things that make you feel unmotivated. Is there a pattern present in the same way as for motivating factors?

2. Interview three or four teachers in a school and determine the same kinds of motivational factors that we reviewed in the exercise above.

3. Watch several television commercials for a number of different products and services. Try to classify the approaches that are used in an effort to motivate you to buy the advertised goods or services.

4. "Motivation" is used very ambiguously in daily discussions. Whenever you hear a reference to this concept, think about whether the person using the term is really referring to the concepts described in this chapter. If the term is being used precisely, classify the strategy for motivation that is being suggested, according to the theoretical models described in this chapter.

5. Observe a teacher's class and keep a record of the motivational strategies that are used with students during a one-hour period.

Cases to Consider

Read each of the following cases and consider the following:

a. What are the critical issues raised in each case, as they relate to the use of theoretical constructs to analyze motivation?

b. How does each case relate to the development of proactive supervision?

c. In what ways might you suggest a resolution to the issues raised?

Case 7.1:

This Will Fix Those Teachers

"It's perfectly absurd to think that every teacher should get paid the same as every other teacher. Some simply deserve more because they work more!" Those were words that were heard during almost every campaign debate and rally in which Hank Gottschalk appeared this past fall. Apparently, his views made a lot of people believe in him, because he won the election. Since taking his seat on the five-member board of education for the Grovedale Schools, Hank has continued with his drive to reward teachers for hard work. After all, he saw such a practice work well in his concrete business for many years. "If you expect more, you pay more."

As the current school year progressed, further discussions took place regarding the possibility of the board implementing a new merit pay system for teachers. Teachers were firmly against the arrangement, and noted that implementing such a system would be inherently unfair. No one could determine precisely the nature of the kinds of things that would distinguish really outstanding teachers from others who simply worked hard at their jobs without necessarily attracting a lot of attention from outside reviewers. The school board, however, with very vocal support from a large percentage of the community, persisted with its vision of more effective ways of "getting better results" from teachers. Paying people for extra effort seemed to make a lot of sense. Test scores had to be maintained or increased, student drop-out rates had to decrease, and in general, schools had to become more effective places. The board felt that the only way to encourage such outcomes would be to reward teachers and other staff members with a pay system that recognized their excellence. After all, they were not going to take anything away from those who were not associated with more effective outcomes—yet.

Case 7.2:

It Worked on the Football Field

Rich Sikorski had enjoyed a great reputation as a very effective high school football coach for six years. As a result, he was not a surprise choice when the school board in Troy Township named him as the new principal of Troy Middle School last year. It was a school with a lot of potential, but also recognized as having a lot of problems. Specifically, the teachers at the school were referred to as "prima donnas" by many who believed that, even with a lot of talent, they did not seem to produce the kind of educational results for which the Troy Township Schools were striving. Instead, the teachers had a reputation for being committed only to their own agenda. They had made life miserable for the past three principals in the school, none of whom lasted more than two years in the position.

When Rich was offered the middle school principalship, he was asked by the superintendent how he planned to work with the teaching staff. "I don't look at this as a problem. Instead, I believe this is a real challenge and an opportunity to accomplish some important things. After all, when I took over the football team up at the high school a few years back, they hadn't won more than two games in a season for ten years. I know how to get the most out of people, and I'm going to put that know-how to work at the middle school."

The first staff meeting saw Rich taking a strong stance with regard to his plans for the next school year. His game plan included the implementing of a wide array of practices that were often associated with effective middle schools, but the Troy teachers had not supported these practices in the past. Multi-age grouping, team teaching, and teacher advisor programs were all going to be part of the new vision of the way things would be at Troy. After all, the school would be recognized "as one of the best middle schools in this state within five years," according to the new principal in his opening day comments to the teachers. The former coach concluded his comments by enthusiastically remarking, "The only way that this dream won't happen is if we all don't get together and work as a team." With that, he walked off the gym stage to the sound of eerie silence. This job might not be as easy as he thought.

References

Herzberg, F. (1966). *Work and the nature of man.* Cleveland: World Publishing.

Lovell, John, & Wiles, Kimball (1983). *Supervision for better schools* (3rd ed.). Englewood Cliffs, NJ: Prentice Hall.

Maslow, A. H. (1970). *Motivation and personality* (2nd ed.). New York: Harper and Row.

Porter, L. W., & Lawler, E. (1966). *Managerial attitudes and performance.* Homewood, IL: Irwin.

Additional Reading

Vroom, V. (1964). *Work and motivation.* London: Wiley.

Part III

The Realities of Supervision
Communication, Change, Power, and Conflict

In Part III, we discuss specific, ongoing concerns of effective proactive supervisors. In contrast with the previous section, emphasis here is on general characteristics of each topic, rather than theoretical aspects.

8 Communication

A discussion of organizational communication directly ties into an analysis of proactive supervision in schools. After all, communication takes place daily on many different levels and within various subsystems. For example, teachers communicate with each other as well as supervisors, students, and parents; administrators share information with community and staff members; there is student to student communication. Examples of the levels and groups participating in the communication process include many different combinations.

Communication clarifies an organization's goals, procedures, and rules for people who are both inside and outside of the organization, bringing to light the unique identity of the organization—what it stands for. Maintaining that identity over time is carried on through ongoing intraorganizational communication patterns. Open channels of communication allow for feedback. Feedback is information which can be used by an organization to alleviate any blurring of its identity or to implement corrective measures. Feedback helps the organization adapt to changing needs.

Basically, communication is the "glue" that holds the organization together. We often hear that a school or other institution has suffered a "breakdown in communication," or that "people aren't communicating with one another." By contrast, when a school is particularly effective, we rarely notice anything related to communication patterns. The need for open and consistent communication in organizations is so great, and we automatically assume that people in effective organizations are communicating. Only when an effective process is disrupted is its importance fully understood.

The practitioner of proactive supervision needs to look constantly at the importance of communication. Supervisors who desire to lead rather than simply react to crises profit greatly from identifying, understanding, and ultimately joining into patterns of communication employed by their school staff. In addition, it is important that supervisors have the ability to comprehend where barriers to effective communication exist and how those barriers might be removed.

Definition of Communication

For our purposes we will define communication simply as the *effort on the part of an individual or group to transmit information to another person or group*. This transmission process, which is often extremely difficult to implement in a satisfying and effective manner with any degree of regularity or clarity, is nonetheless simple to describe and to depict graphically as in Figure 8.1.

Figure 8.1. Illustration of the basic act of communication, or the transmission of a message (M) from a sender (S) to a receiver (R).

As Figure 8.1 indicates, communication involves two major actors, a sender (or speaker) (S), and a receiver (R). The contact between these two ends of the communication process is established by forwarding a message (M) across some recognized channel. As we will see in our subsequent discussion of the types of communication that exist in organizations, our basic diagram can be modified to reflect other communication processes, such as two-way communication. In addition, our description of available modes of communication will reveal a variety of channels available to senders of messages.

Types of Communication

In a review of the characteristics of communication patterns and their implications for school administrators, Russell Spillman (1975) noted that there are essentially three types of communication processes that take place in any organization. The supervisor needs to be aware of the strengths and limitations of each type because all will be required at one point or another in the life of a school. The three types of communication are one-way communication, one-way communication with feedback, and two-way communication.

One-way Communication

Here, the speaker, or communicator, sends a message through some channel or mode directly to a receiver (see Figure 8.2). Although there are likely to be effects from the message, one-way communication strongly implies that the sender is not concerned with the effect and that there is no provision made for the relay of the effect from the receiver back to the speaker.

One-way communication occurs in all organizations from time to time. Someone must occasionally "tell" others some information, regardless of what those others might wish. Nevertheless, there are problems associated with one-way communication, stemming from the quality of the initial transmission of the message at the sender's level. The nature of "what" is to be communicated must be absolutely clear; once the sender transmits the message to the receiver, there is no way to clarify any misconceptions that may occur. One-way communication might be compared to a person firing a rifle shot into the air—not a dangerous practice in itself, but potentially fatal because no one can be absolutely certain where the bullet will eventually land.

Figure 8.2. Representation of the concept of one-way communication. Information proceeds directly from the sender (S) to the receiver (R) and concludes at that point.

Examples of one-way communication are plentiful in schools: Public address announcements, memos in teachers' mailboxes, PTA newsletters, and so on. One-way communication is not "bad" in itself; it is a highly efficient way for schools to share information because it is economical in terms of both time and money spent in preparing the initial message. People in schools often need bits of information presented to them, and one-way communication is highly appropriate in such cases. Problems may arise, however, if there is a virtually total reliance on this limited type of communication. Other methods are needed.

One-way Communication with Feedback

This is one-way communication, but in this process, the receiver transmits a verbal or nonverbal response to the sender, giving the sender the opportunity to modify the message (see Figure 8.3).

Figure 8.3. Diagram showing the concept of one-way communication with feedback. The sender (S) transmits information directly to the receiver (R) and no direct response is expected. However, feedback is provided from the receiver to the sender, although the sender may do nothing with this feedback.

One-way communication with feedback takes place constantly in the classroom. When teachers use formal lecture techniques to instruct students in their classes, there is no dialogue with students. This is essentially one-way communication. However, in most cases, even when students are not deliberately asked to participate, they will exhibit clues suggesting the extent to which they understand the content of the lecture. A puzzled look on some faces will typically nudge the teacher to restate or explain further the phrase just presented. In communication terms, then, the receiver conveys a message—in this case a subtle, nonverbal one—to the sender that, in turn, transforms the nature of the initial message. Good teachers make use of this process constantly.

Utilizing this type of communication to the exclusion of others can, however, have negative consequences. Even if the sender relies on subtle feedback almost exclusively as a way to receive messages from the receiver, the sender is still in control of the act of communication. True learning involves dialogue. On the other hand, as we saw earlier, one-way communication even without feedback is entirely legitimate in some circumstances. If the content and nature of the message being transmitted is such that no adjustment is needed or wanted, feedback is not truly appropriate. We should note, however, that soliciting feedback when you have no intention of modifying the original message is much worse than not providing for feedback in the first place.

Two-way Communication

This type of communication is characterized by the presence of two or more communicators or speakers, each of whom sends messages, and each of whom also receives messages. Diagrammatically, we can see that what takes place in two-way communication is a continuous shifting of the individual's role from sender to receiver to sender, and so forth (see Figure 8.4).

True open dialogue where all parts talk and share ideas with one another is the essence of two-way communication. The most important feature is that, although one party may initiate the communication activity, no one controls the dialogue, and each message is transferred on an equal basis from sender to receiver. True parity is achieved between the senders and the receivers.

Two-way communication occurs in school settings where there is true open dialogue and shared decision making. Team-teaching situations, or administrative councils where all staff members have input into school policies and procedures often exemplify this

Figure 8.4. Diagram of complete two-way communication process. Initial message is transmitted from the sender (S) to the receiver (R). At that point, the receiver becomes a sender (s) and transmits either a new message or a modification of the original message to the initial sender, who now plays the role of receiver (r). The process of communication may end at this point, or it may continue through the same loop again, or with additional senders and receivers added.

process. It may also be seen in individual classrooms where open student-teacher discussion and dialogue take place. Communication processes will break down and be ineffective, however, if two-way communication is "played at" rather than truly enhanced as a valued activity. Token openness—when open, two-way communication is publicly espoused, but one or more parties in the process fail to listen and hear accurately the messages sent by others—probably does considerably more harm than good.

Two-way communication, of course, is not always the best way to achieve a specific goal. When nonnegotiable information must be shared with a school staff (e.g., the district's policy statement regarding students' involvement in field trips), two-way communication is probably not appropriate. The formulation of the policy may indeed have already involved considerable open dialogue. Once formulated, however, that policy needs to be announced in a straightforward manner. The key, we believe, is not using two-way communication in all circumstances but rather knowing how to use this process at the appropriate time to enhance overall organizational communication.

Forms of Communication

Three means or modes of communication are present in most organizations. These may be listed as verbal (or spoken) communication, written communication, and nonverbal communication. All three of the communication approaches reviewed below are found in all organizations, and the effective supervisor cannot hide behind one type to the exclusion of others. Instead, the supervisor must be able to discover the advantages and disadvantages, as well as the likely consequences to the organization, of consciously making use of one means of communication or another.

Verbal Communication

The most prevalent form of intended communication in organizations, verbal communication is used in a deliberate way to send messages between speakers and receivers. This involves certain advantages and disadvantages.

Russell Spillman (1975) noted that verbal communication is spontaneous and reflects the immediate needs of the speaker. We need no advance preparation to articulate an idea verbally, although verbal communication can be planned in advance. One advantage of verbal communication is that a need can be made known "on the spot." In addition, verbal communication takes little or no additional effort by its speakers and receivers, and other than the time that may be expended in the actual process of talking, it uses no greater organizational resources. Verbal communication is momentary. Words shared in haste are, fortunately, so forgotten; permanent scars are less likely when no record exists of what has been communicated.

Obviously, these same advantages can also become disadvantages. For example, the fact that verbal communication leaves no permanent record can be an advantage *unless* what is said is worth remembering. Temporary statements are soon forgotten. Moreover, verbal communication is easily misunderstood by receivers, who might believe they heard one message when something else was actually being said. A final disadvantage is that closure of the verbal communicative act may be difficult, if not impossible, to achieve. There is no exclamation point, question mark, or final period to signal the close of a verbalization.

Written Communication

Written communication is a staple of organizations. In schools, all manners of written notes, forms, and memos are used routinely and extensively.

One of written communication's most powerful advantages is that it provides a permanent record. Minutes of meetings and letters can be filed and referred to at a later date. In addition, written documents serve to accurately preserve information that may be crucial to the operation of the organization. Policies, procedures, and other guidelines that need to be followed to ensure efficient operation are logically kept in a written format so that all members of an organization have a constant reference point to clarify activities. Another advantage is that written methods are a good way to transmit complicated information about hard-to-remember facts or concepts. Imagine providing oral directions for assembling a detailed electronic gadget. Quite a few Christmases would have been ruined if bicycles had not been assembled the night before by parents following *printed* instructions.

A major disadvantage of written communication is its impersonality. Think of a time when a memo was slipped into your mailbox, rather than a message being transmitted through face-to-face confrontation. Written communication can also be relatively slow and expensive to prepare, and the speaker or sender can never be entirely assured that the message has been received, understood, and acted upon. There is no guarantee that a memo will be read.

Nonverbal Communication

Too often we assume that spoken or written words are the only means we have of communicating. These measures are clearly the most widely used in organizations, but increasingly we are realizing the importance of the process of nonverbal communication. Because there are so many nuances associated with nonverbal communication, a more lengthy discussion of this mode is necessary.

Nonverbal communication is the subtle expression of attitudes, emotions, and even the physical state of the sender or speaker (Spillman, 1975) through voluntary and involuntary gestures. A wince, a smile, a glance off into space, or a toe tapping are all examples of powerful, nonverbal signals of what we are feeling or thinking. Nonverbal communication also greatly modifies the words that we utter; it either affirms or denies what is being said. Throughout the history of schooling, for example, students have been masterful in determining if teachers "mean business" by watching *the ways* in which things are said.

It is a major advantage for proactive supervisors to have the ability to sense and analyze nonverbal messages accurately. This means of communication is almost constantly present in all environments, including schools. While nonverbal messages are constantly present, how they are interpreted can be extremely difficult to control. For example, John might interpret Nancy's abrupt exit from a room where they were conversing as an angry reaction to something he said. She, on the other hand, might have realized that she was late for an appointment and rushed out, consumed with the desire to be on time. At that moment, Nancy has no control over the effect her nonverbal message had on John.

Nonverbal messages can and often do contradict what we say in verbal or written form. As a result, receivers tend to use nonverbal cues to judge the accuracy and honesty of verbal statements. If a difference exists between nonverbal and verbal cues, people tend to trust more completely the nonverbal behavior; the old maxim "Actions speak louder than words" is very true.

Nonverbal messages establish the status and honesty of the speaker in the mind of the receiver, who tends to make unconscious decisions about the speaker and his or her intentions. Receivers tend to judge quickly if speakers are egotistical and self-serving or sensitive and caring. Nonverbal messages might disclose hidden agendas that may be held by speakers as well as significant messages about the sender's feelings and attitudes toward the receiver. For instance, a receiver may "hear" that the sender has trust in him or her, but see that the person is actually suspicious or even hostile because the speaker makes no eye contact, drums two or three fingers on the table while talking, and so on.

Potential Barriers to Communication

Proactive supervision involves a constant effort to reduce the potential barriers to effective communication which might be categorized in four groupings: barriers related to the person, barriers based on the role of the speaker, barriers found in the role of the receiver, and barriers caused by situations that inhibit the receiver's accurate reception of the message.

Personal Barriers

The sources of personal barriers, or barriers derived from the speaker, may be classified as *egocentric* limitations, *personality* limitations, or *self-concept* limitations. Egocentric barriers can never be totally overcome. All individuals are somewhat restricted in their ability to communicate absolutely and completely, because each person must judge the world from a unique and highly idiosyncratic perspective. Personality limitations grow out of individual characteristics; some people have difficulty as speakers, for instance, simply because they are timid or shy. Finally, our own self-concepts can serve to prevent us from being completely open, honest, and effective in instigating communication.

Barriers Based on the Role of the Speaker

Roles are normally defined as socially ascribed statuses within the organizational environment. People tend to have preconceived notions about certain *roles*, which are independent from the notions about the *individuals* who are assigned to the roles. The characteristics of the role, whether resented or revered, can become serious barriers to the degree of open communication possible in an organization. The role of the supervisor or administrator is sometimes symbolically more powerful, for example, than the person who fulfills that role might wish it to be. Thus, the designation of someone in a role might very well in itself constitute a barrier to communication. For example, we could point to what happens when a person who has been a teacher for several years is suddenly named to the principalship of the same school. The individual may begin to lose contact with former colleagues simply because he or she is now an administrator.

Receiver Barriers

Sometimes the effectiveness of the communicative act is affected negatively by the receiver, not the speaker. There are a number of ways in which this occurs.

Receivers sometimes simply lack interest in the message being sent; they see no relevance in it. Part of this might derive from the fact that the receiver is not sophisticated enough to appreciate the message or lacks the necessary background or knowledge base to understand it. Also, receivers often have biases that serve to filter out what they really do not want to hear and that, in fact, sometimes prevent the communication process from beginning in the first place. Barriers such as differences in age, sex, social position, or cultural heritage often serve to screen out the real meanings needed for effective communication.

Situational Barriers

Finally, communication may be hindered by specific situational circumstances that screen out a message as it proceeds from speaker to receiver—too much noise, not enough time, additional external distractions, and so forth. Think of the last time you tried to concentrate on a lecture given in a room that was either too hot or too cold, for example. In fact, many people question whether much real communication can take place at all in our modern world because it is so cluttered with what appears to be an overwhelming number of such situational barriers.

Skills to Improve Communication

Regardless of the barriers to carrying out effective communication, people *can* talk to one another. However, understanding and enhancing the communication process is also largely dependent on the development of a set of specific skills employed to increase its accuracy. Richard Gorton (1986) suggested some useful strategies for this important effort:

Paraphrasing.   Restate the main ideas of others to clarify more ideas. ("In other words, what you're saying is . . .")

Perception checking.   Check to see that your perception of what has been said is accurate. ("If I understand what you're saying . . .")

Relating Things to Personal Feelings.   Communication can break down because receivers have a negative reaction to statements; what we say offends, often unintentionally. Confront such negative feelings openly when they occur. ("When you say that, I feel like . . .")

Use Objective Descriptions.   The use of highly subjective terms that imply personal value statements hurts open communication. Use objective terms, when possible, to describe behaviors so that people are less likely to say, "It's not what you're saying that I reject, but rather *how* you're saying it."

Feedback.   Give and accept in return constructive and honest feedback to keep communication channels open between and among all parties.

Summary

A major responsibility of the educational supervisor must be to keep communication going in both the school and the district. We assumed explicitly at the beginning of this chapter that organizations generally will not be effective if people do not know what is going on. Further, the effective leader is committed to open communication. As Warren Bennis and Burt Nanus (1985) noted, leaders communicate at all times, and the more effective the communication, the more effective the leadership.

In this chapter, we began by noting some basic definitions and concepts of the communication act. Next we reviewed types and modes of communication and noted that, depending on circumstances and setting, different modes may be more appropriate than others, even when we generally feel more negative toward some approaches. For example, written memos (one-way communication) might not seem highly desirable, but there are times when this strategy is in fact the most appropriate. The important issue is that a variety of techniques must be used to keep communication channels open.

The chapter concluded with a review of typical barriers to effective communication and skills that the supervisor may develop in an effort to reduce the barriers when they occur.

Suggested Activities

1. Observe the class of a colleague and keep track of how often each of the major types of communication described in this chapter is used. After class, ask the teacher to estimate the percentage of time that she or he spent using both one-way communication and two-way communication, then compare your findings with the teacher's estimate.

2. Carry out the same analysis as above, but follow a practicing school administrator or supervisor for a part of a school day instead of watching a teacher. Again, compare your findings with the administrator's self-perceptions.

3. Conduct a survey to determine why people believe there are barriers to effective communication. Next, question people about the ways in which they believe communication is enhanced. Put together a brief overview of your findings in a way that may be presented to a teaching staff during an inservice day. Make sure that you ask people for some suggestions regarding the possible improvement of communication in your school.

Cases to Consider

Read each case and consider the following:

a. What are the critical issues raised in each case, as they relate to the use of theoretical constructs to analyze organizational communication processes?

b. How does each case relate to the development of proactive supervision?

c. In what ways might you suggest a resolution to the issues raised?

Case 8.1:

Things Have Certainly Changed

Dave Spencer spent twelve years as an elementary school teacher in the Post House Local Schools. He was generally regarded as a very effective teacher, and many administrators in the system had encouraged him to think about a future as a principal. With that support, he enrolled in graduate courses in educational administration at State University. Soon he was certified as an elementary principal. In a short time, he received his first assignment as a building administrator in the Post House Schools.

Dave was extremely happy to receive word that his assignment was to be at Old Hickory School. He had worked there for nine years, so he knew quite a few of the teachers as well as community members. He was aware of a lot of the issues that would face him as a principal. Despite these facts, however, he quickly recognized that he really did not have as good a handle as he believed on how to be an effective leader at Old Hickory.

One of the first things he began to realize was that the teachers, many of whom he had known for several years, looked at him very differently now that he was a principal. As he walked into the teachers' lounge one day, he noticed that all conversations appeared to either cease or at least shift in tone. In the past, he had been the "life of the party" in many lounge conversations. As a teacher, he was always telling jokes, sharing gossip, and serving as the center of attention. As principal, he recognized that his presence had created a chilling effect on the tone of the group. In short, he felt as if the group with whom he used to talk openly was now talking about him.

Case 8.2:

Doesn't Anyone Here Know How to Read?

For several years, the Upper Elroy Schools were known as one of the premier school districts in the state. National test scores, state achievement scores, and large numbers of students receiving scholarships at top-notch universities across the nation were all evidence of a school district with educational programs that were far superior to anything in the area. It was no wonder that the board of education regularly rewarded Dr. Mark Andrews with extensions of his contract as superintendent, along with significant raises in salary.

Dr. Andrews was generally satisfied with his work in Upper Elroy. He enjoyed the community, and he had made many good friends in the business community as a result of his regular participation in Rotary and many other local programs. Last year, he was named one of three "Outstanding Leaders of Upper Elroy." The only thing that he never really understood was the fact that teachers and building administrators often appeared to be quite distant from him. He often visited schools and frequently sent out cards which noted specific accomplishments of different staff members. Further, when he took over the superintendency in the district nine years ago, he immediately instituted a practice of sending out a weekly "Superintendent's Newsletter" where he praised individual accomplishments of teachers and other staff members.

It was truly frustrating for the superintendent to hear, through some feedback that he recently received from one of his assistant superintendents, that he was viewed as quite distant and aloof by the teachers and principals. The thing that was most frustrating for Dr. Andrews was the fact that he truly believed he was communicating with the staff through his newsletter. In fact, he had recently added a special "tear-off" section on the last page so that people could send him notes from time to time. It was, after all, nearly impossible for him to get out to really talk with teachers. Yet, it seemed reasonable to assume that they could read his statements each week.

References

Bennis, Warren, & Nanus, Burt (1985). *Leaders: Strategies for taking charge.* New York: Harper and Row.

Gorton, Richard (1986). *School leadership and administration: Important concepts, case studies, and simulations* (3rd ed.). Dubuque: Brown.

Spillman, Russell (1975, Summer). The nature of communication. *The Administrator*, 5(4): 4–9.

Additional Reading

Katz, Neil H., & Lawyer, John W. (1992). *Communication and conflict resolution skills.* Dubuque: Kendall Hunt Publishing Company.

9 Change Processes

As Lipham (1965) pointed out, the fundamental essence of leadership must be conceived of as the process of bringing about needed change. Implicit within any leadership role, whether director of a private corporation or educational supervisor, is a responsibility to foster the type of change that will stimulate continuous growth and development in an organization. Administration, on the other hand, deals with maintaining the status quo in an organization. This distinction confronts us directly with a perplexing problem that school supervisors must face: Supervisors who wish to be effective must generally engage in administrative duties and behaviors on occasion. As a result, the supervisor who is charged with the responsibility of providing leadership (i.e., organizational change) must also take care to guard the status quo when that is the most appropriate route for a school to follow. Is effective educational supervision an impossibility, then? Or at best a case of trying to walk a narrow line between the competing demands of "changing" and "maintaining?" No change can mean organizational stagnation; change for the sake of change can result in organizational dysfunction. Being effective in this paradox of leadership and administration is like Goldilocks trying to find the perfect bowl of porridge: We need to be careful not to select something either "too hot" or "too cold;" it must be "just right." The supervisor has to know just the right times to push for change, and also when to hold the line.

In this chapter we explore organizational change processes as they relate to the practice of proactive educational supervision. We will review a number of conceptualizations of change that have appeared in the literature and then some of the most consistent barriers to promoting needed organizational change. While change is a necessary condition for the improvement of organizations, it is not an easy condition either to promote or sustain. As a result, this chapter concludes with a consideration of some strategies that may be followed to reduce typical constraints that inhibit needed organizational change.

Alternative Conceptual Models of Change

Douglas Paul (1977) categorized the major descriptions of change in four broad theoretical models: problem solving, social interaction, research-development-diffusion (RD&D), and linkage. In the sections that follow, we look at brief descriptions of the underlying assumptions and most salient characteristics of each of the four principal models of change.

Problem Solving Model

This model suggests that change is a logical effort to provide solutions to problematic states perceived by the organization. The basic view in this model is that, if something is wrong, change must occur. The role of the supervisor is to first determine as much as possible concerning the precise nature of the problems faced by the organization, then suggest modifications in policy and practice that might serve to solve the identified problems.

A rich tradition of support for this conceptualization of change can be found in the work of, among others, Warren Bennis, Kenneth Benne, and Robert Chin (1969), Ronald Lippitt, James Watson, and B. Westley (1958), and Michael Fullan (1973). A major assumption underlying this view of change is that organizational problems, even when complex and threatening, can be identified with sufficient clarity to enable rational solutions to be formulated and applied. This has led to the development of analytical schemes that suggest that organizational dilemmas may be tracked along a predictable continuum, to the extent that the leader can know when to initiate change in the same way that a physician might have a clear idea of when to introduce a new treatment to an ill patient. The Concerns-Based Adoption Model (CBAM) for staff development, devised by Gene Hall and Susan Loucks (1976), is an effective application of this change process. Although we will look at this model in greater depth in chapter 17, we note here that it serves as an excellent example of a practice founded on the problem-solving approach to change. The CBAM suggests that organizations demonstrate clearly identifiable *Levels of Use* of certain activities, and members of organizations experience certain key *Levels of Concern* regarding activities being introduced into their world. Because these two factors are rational, the supervisor (or any other leader) can consciously effect matches between Levels of Use and Levels of Concern, thereby resolving organizational problems and increasing the satisfaction and sense of efficacy felt by the people within the organization.

Gordon Lippitt (1969) identified six basic elements of the problem-solving model of change, including (1) identifying the problem, (2) diagnosing the problem, (3) retrieving related knowledge and discussing its implications for overcoming the problem, (4) forming alternatives to action, (5) testing the feasibility of alternatives, and (6) adopting and implementing the selected alternative. These steps call attention once again to the most obvious characteristic of the model: It makes use of linear and rational thinking as the foundation for change.

Another outcome of the problem-solving perspective is a belief that networking among different organizations is a commendable practice. If we believe that organizational problems are basically rational, then we may assume that many schools, districts, or other organizations face roughly the same problems from time to time. Potentially creative solutions to these recurring problems can come from many systems working together, rather than facing each problem in isolation.

Perhaps the greatest drawback to the problem-solving approach to analyzing organizational change is found in this same absolute faith in the rationality of organizations. The approach firmly suggests that solutions can be identified for all problems and that change can be controlled so as to reduce the negative impact of the problems. The model tends to ignore the fact that solving organizational problems does not always involve selecting the "best" response, but rather involves finding a path that is less imperfect than any others available.

Social Interaction

Change often occurs in organizations solely because people in those organizations talk to other people who convince them to try something a little different. This is the basic assumption found in *social interaction*, a model for change analysis that has its roots in the field of agriculture. Benjamin Ryan and Neal Gross (1943), Everett Rogers (1962), and Everett Rogers and Fred Shoemaker (1971) were among the early proponents of this view, which was first recognized as a process followed by farmers who shared information concerning the development of new hybrid corn seeds. (The process is sometimes called the "agricultural model of change," and change agents are spoken of in the same terms used to describe county extension agents in farming communities.) Douglas Paul (1977) noted three important characteristics of this model, which distinguish it from other conceptualizations of change:

- It strongly emphasizes communication channels and messages to be utilized for diffusing innovations.
- It recognizes interpersonal influence patterns leading to the adoption of innovations as legitimate features of organizational life.
- It focuses on stimuli for adoption of innovative practices that originate outside of the adopting system.

In addition, the social interaction model implies strongly that potential users of an innovation will subject both the innovator and the innovation to a good deal of scrutiny before accepting it, and that this scrutiny will be based to a large extent on the ways in which the potential users of the innovation within the adopting organization "feel" about the possible change.

This explains, at least in part, why the social interaction model is also occasionally referred to as the "organization development" (OD) model of change. This model places a great deal of emphasis not only on the nature of interaction that occurs between the user organization and the external environment that initially introduces the innovation, but perhaps more importantly on the nature of the population within the adopting organization. Richard Schmuck and Matthew Miles (1971), for example, argue in *Organizational Development in Schools* that the user-group population is never a passive body. Instead, innovations are always institutionalized in a school or any other setting because of the workings of the social interaction network within the school. As a result, the supervisor whose notion of change was founded on a belief in social interaction would probably invest considerable time and energy in working with a school staff to increase internal receptivity to desired outcomes.

The application of the social interaction model as a way to stimulate change in an organization normally follows a rather consistent pattern. First, people hear about a new and innovative practice, normally through face-to-face contact with direct users of the innovation or others assumed to have direct information concerning the practice. Next, proponents of the new process engage in a period of attempted persuasion, the goal being to mold the opinion of potential users in a positive and supportive way about the benefits of the new product or practice. Third, potential users make a conscious decision either to use or not to use the suggested innovation. Finally, if the new practice is adopted, efforts are made to determine whether or not the decision was a good one.

A number of theorists in the field of change, including Ronald Havelock (1969) and Milbrey McLaughlin (1976) have raised serious questions regarding the extent to which the social interaction model may be applied realistically to educational settings. The greatest objection is that innovations in schools, unlike new breeds of corn, are generally intangible and therefore difficult to assess and evaluate.

Although this observation may seem to limit the use of the social interaction model as an approach to planned change in schools, the model nevertheless deserves our attention, particularly in its emphasis on personal contact and interpersonal relations. The educational supervisor needs to recognize the power associated with personal relationships formed between people who work within school systems and others outside those systems whose ideas or products may have great value to what goes on in schools. Encouraging others to visit other schools, attending meetings of professional associations, and inviting outside consultants and guests to visit schools serve to increase social interaction between the school and its external environment which, in turn, might provide opportunities for introducing new and effective educational practices from outside. A supervisor mindful of the need to cultivate patterns of positive interaction within the school would probably encourage faculty retreats, staff discussions, schoolwide decision-making processes, and many other approaches to enhancing the quality of interaction inside the school as well.

Research-Development-Diffusion Model

David Clark and Egon Guba (1975) and Ernest House (1974) are most directly associated with what has become known as the research-development-diffusion model (RD&D) of change. The fundamental assumption here is that processes of change based on structured research are begun in order to produce new ideas, practices, or products, which are then disseminated to possible users through a conscientious effort toward diffusion. Ronald Havelock (1973) noted that five basic assumptions underlie the RD&D model of change.

1. Both the development and the application of an innovation are assumed to take place in an orderly sequence that includes research, development, and packaging prior to a mass distribution procedure.

2. The management of this sequence requires extensive planning over a long period of time.

3. A division and coordination of labor are necessary among elements in the RD&D system.

4. A rational consumer is assumed to be one who will adopt an innovation on the basis of a mass dissemination program.

5. High initial development costs are balanced by the long-term benefits that come from an efficient, high-quality innovation that can be used by a mass audience.

In practice, what normally happens is that new users of an innovative practice are assisted by the initial researchers and developers to make certain that the innovation is successfully installed. This approach to understanding change has been particularly influential in national educational policy in recent years. During the mid-1960s the federal government initiated an effort designed to increase the amount of research-validated information available to school practitioners interested in improving practice. One of the tangible results of this initiative was the creation of a network of federally funded research and development centers at major universities across the country, at which faculty served as basic researchers, and another network of regional educational laboratories supported jointly by federal funds and by the sale of contract service to state and local educational agencies. Although subtle differences existed between the centers and laboratories regarding the ways in which they would function and be governed, they both were commissioned to support a strategy for bringing about change in schools that is research-based, rational, and generally in line with the model suggested by Robert Owens (1986), which is shown in Figure 9.1.

The RD&D model of change, not surprisingly, holds a considerable attraction for the academic community, which so often assumes that change without data validated through research in

Figure 9.1. Robert Owens's concept of the Research, Development, Diffusion, and Adoption Model of Change. (Robert G. Owens, *Organizational Behavior in Education*, 3rd Edition, © 1987, p. 211. Reprinted by permission of Prentice-Hall, Inc., Englewood Cliffs, NJ.)

the social sciences is not worth the effort. University faculty tend to place great stock in the linear concepts of research, development, and diffusion because the findings of basic research serve as the starting point for all future progress. Unfortunately, this stance, highly satisfying to many researchers, does not always fit with the reality of school systems, where practitioners need immediate responses to their concerns and have little time for what they see as the time-consuming work of basic research. Proactive supervisors are likely to be caught in some conflict over this issue. On the one hand, they will want to seek validated information to serve as the basis of their work with schools, thus promoting more thoughtful and less crisis-oriented behaviors. On the other hand, crises do arise, and practitioners seek answers even before the last bit of data is collected, the final statistical analysis completed, or the peer-review panel accepts a piece of research for publication.

No matter what its limitations, the RD&D model of change must still be recognized as a potentially powerful conceptualization of how organizations adopt innovative practices. Over time, this model has been modified considerably by proponents like Havelock (1972), who suggested that, in the initiation of organizational change, there should be a rational sequence in the evaluation and application of an innovation; research, development, and packaging of a program change should occur before dissemination of the program change; there should be planning on a massive scale; there should be a rational division of labor and coordination of jobs; and that proponents of the innovation should be willing to accept high initial development costs prior to any dissemination activity.

This brief overview of the research-development-diffusion model of change suggests that there are some clear potential strengths and weaknesses concerning the possible use of this conceptual framework for installing organizational change. We need also to recognize at least one more assumption inherent in the RD&D model, regardless of whether it serves as a plus or a minus: Tremendous emphasis is placed on the adopting organization's ability to implement an innovative practice in line with the stated expectations for "proper" use of a research-based model. As Douglas Paul (1976, p. 27) noted, "the . . . model . . . places responsibility for accurate replication of RD&D products in the user organization." As a result, the supervisor who approaches change from this perspective must be knowledgeable about the research and development carried out to support a particular innovation. In practice, many innovations are not "allowed" to be disseminated to a new setting unless someone from that setting has received substantial training in the proper presentation and use of the innovation.

Linkage Model

Henry Bhola (1965) and Ronald Havelock (1973) are most often associated with the final model of organizational change that we review, namely the linkage model, which is the most recent view of how change may occur in organizations. Linkage borrows some characteristics from each of the other models reviewed, and it assumes that change proceeds through four distinct levels (Lipham & Hoeh, 1974).

1. In a fashion similar to what takes place in the problem-solving model, new knowledge relevant to an identified problem is searched for and retrieved;

2. Educational researchers (as in the RD&D model) carry on the research, development, and diffusion of research findings to a particular school where a problem exists;

3. Attention is focused on the relationship and communication systems among the researcher, practitioner, and consumer, as is true of the social interaction model;

4. The linkage process model is enacted. In this phase, each organizational participant is helped to see what other members of the organization are doing in their respective parts of the process of changing.

It is the fourth step of the model where linkage relationships are formed and supported to serve as a catalyst to innovation being accepted within the user organization. This is also the point in the model that calls for the greatest leadership skill and supervisory involvement. Someone must facilitate the linkage process required for staff within the school, as well as for those who provide information about the innovation from agencies external to the school. The supervisor is a likely candidate for the role of facilitator, or what the literature often describes as a "linker" or "linkage change agent."

The linkage model synthesizes some of the best features of the other three models we reviewed, and as a result, it has considerable value for use by supervisors in school settings. It does have some limitations, however, not the least of which is that it makes tremendous demands on the abilities of individual supervisors who must be directly attuned to the activities taking place in the school in order to determine needs for changes and must also understand the nature of intraorganizational communication that may serve to support desired changes. Supervisors must also be aware of opportunities afforded for change and improvement from agencies in the external environment. Finally, supervisors must possess the communication and interpersonal skills required of anyone who consistently attempts to bridge different groups. In short, the linkage model of organizational change is a powerful one, but it makes heavy and perhaps unrealistic demands on supervisors.

Characteristics of Change

Each model of change reviewed here offers a unique view of how innovation is introduced into a system. There are some common characteristics of organizational change, however, on which all models agree. Gene Hall (1987) suggested the following summary of what is known about the phenomenon of change:

- Change is a process, not an event.
- Change is accomplished by individuals.
- Change is a highly personalized process.
- Change involves developmental growth.
- Change is best understood in operational terms.
- The focus of facilitation should be on individuals, innovation, and the content.

Each of these observations also implies important responsibilities to the supervisor, who must become actively involved in fostering change and not be content merely to sit on the sidelines and wait for things to happen.

Barriers to Organizational Change

One overriding concern about change must be addressed by the proactive supervisor. Because of several possible barriers, change can be difficult to initiate, implement, and maintain in an organization such as a school.

John Lovell and Kimball Wiles (1983) recognized the importance of the educational supervisor's role in stimulating change and identified the following typical barriers to organizational change in schools. For each barrier, we have suggested a way in which this issue is often played out in schools.

1. *Lack of commitment to system goals.* If teachers or other school staff do not either understand or accept the school's goals, they will not endorse a change to ensure that those goals are being met. This often occurs in settings where the administrative team assumes total control over the establishment of

goals. Teachers typically will do little to support an agenda mandated by others, particularly if substantive change is required.

2. *Inadequate feedback.* Teachers frequently lack concrete information and evaluative feedback concerning their performance. We consider this problem in detail in a later chapter, but it has implications for change processes as well. Teachers' feelings of being left to drift lead to tension, anxiety, and the type of low morale that causes people to withdraw into their roles and avoid any risks required for change.

3. *Inadequate knowledge about the conditions of teaching and learning.* Change implies that some ideal way of behaving is fixed in people's minds as a goal. A high percentage of classroom teachers and others in schools, while serving quite successfully, are nevertheless lacking in the kind of knowledge base that would suggest desirable goals for improved performance and change.

4. *Attitudes toward or values about the proposed change.* If people start out with negative views about an innovation, that attitude will be hard to change. When the concept of team teaching was introduced as an innovation to teachers several years ago, it did not take root in many settings because teachers started with negative assumptions even before the practice was formally introduced.

5. *Satisfaction with status quo.* Teachers demonstrate the same reluctance to change their behaviors that others do. The old saying, "If it ain't broke, don't fix it" applies equally to educators who are not always convinced of the need to change the way they have done things in the past. This phenomenon is likely to be strongest in schools where there is a stable and mature teaching staff.

6. *Inadequate skill development.* If people lack the skills needed to carry out a new program, they will resist change. A teacher who has little ability to work with groups of gifted students, for example, will resist being required to do just that as part of a new thinking skills program.

7. *Strong vested interests in the status quo.* People may believe that they will lose something for which they have worked if changes are made in the system around them. Consider, for example, a case where a teacher foresees losing leadership status as the head of a department in a junior high school under

a new organizational pattern for a middle school that proposes to dissolve departments.

8. *Lack of organizational support.* People will resist supporting a change if they believe that the larger system will not reward or endorse the change. Teachers often express resentment toward engaging in practices that they believe the central office will not wholeheartedly endorse.

9. *Closedness rather than openness in the system* Teachers who work in schools in what Andrew Halpin (1967) calls an "open" organizational climate will be more likely to accept change. "Closed" climate schools offer fewer opportunities for social interaction that might, in turn, spark greater interest in and support for change.

10. *Lack of compatibility between the change proposal and other dimensions of the organization.* When a change is introduced to one grade level team of teachers, for example, other teams may be affected by the change. If the reports from the first team are not positive, resistance will follow. On the other hand, when a small group gets "turned on" by an idea, others may follow readily.

11. *Threat to individuals.* The issue here is simple yet powerful: People fear new situations. Even a seemingly minor innovation introduced into school practices represents a new situation, and some resistance can be anticipated.

12. *Inadequate knowledge about restraints and possibilities in a situation.* People sometimes avoid participating in a change process because they assume that some unknown conditions will necessarily prohibit the change from being successfully implemented.

13. *Static organizational role structure.* Organizations do not always enjoy the kind of leadership that supports needed change. The majority of a teaching staff may push for some type of curricular or program change, but the principal may prohibit the change from taking place.

14. *Inadequate expertise for solving problems.* Change often brings with it certain problems related to transition. For the most part, people lack expertise in working with ambiguity and other problems that often accompany organizational change. In schools, teachers are generally well prepared to serve in their assigned instructional roles, but they have had little or no preparation in handling the acceptance of innovation.

15. *Threat to officials in the organization.* The implementation of change in an organization implies significant modifications in existing power structures. Traditional leadership roles and the agendas held by those who inhabit these roles may need complete revision. Such modification, or even the possibility of such change, often carries with it great threats to those who have been "in charge" in the past. This potential "changing of the guard" causes the old guard to dig in its heels and resist. In schools, we often see resistance when principals or other administrators who have held their leadership positions for a long time are suddenly confronted with a change that they believe will erode their control of the schools. Teacher union activities in recent years have caused a considerable amount of negative reaction among some administrators who believed that teachers wanted to change things "too fast and too much." Recent suggestions by educational reformers that the role of the principal as now defined is obsolete are, of course, not winning many administrative supporters.

16. *Inadequate rewards change efforts.* People are often aware of the need for some type of organizational change and have the competence to bring the change about, but they do nothing simply because they decide that the rewards of the change effort will not be sufficient. Teachers might be asked to adopt a new language arts curriculum, for example, but decide that the costs for doing so, in terms of extra meetings, lack of additional pay, and so forth, far outweigh possible rewards.

These identified barriers to organizational change are useful to us in more accurately understanding the nature of organizational behavior. Simply stated, people generally have a tendency to remain constant in their behaviors. Change requires effort; it is easier not to move. Fortunately, people sometimes do engage in innovative practices. To encourage them in that process, proactive supervisors may find recent research on the phases of planned change useful.

Phases of Change

To this point, we have looked at organizational change as if it were a singular event, introduced in sum into the lives of people in an organization. In reality, however, change usually occurs slowly and in clearly defined, deliberate steps. Understanding the nature of these steps may prove helpful to the educational supervisor interested in reducing some of the typical barriers identified above.

Many conceptual frameworks have been developed to analyze the sequential patterns through which change occurs. Everett Rogers (1962) suggests that planned change and innovation efforts proceed through five identifiable and discrete steps: awareness, interest, evaluation, trial, and adoption. Gerald Hage and Michael Aiken (1970) modified this view to suggest that four steps—evaluation, initiation, implementation, and routinization—were in fact present in the introduction of innovation. Gerald Zaltman, Robert Duncan, and Jonny Holbek (1973) proposed two major stages and five substages of change, as the following list shows:

Initiation Stage

Knowledge-awareness substage. Potential adopters of an innovation must be aware that the innovation exists and that there is an opportunity to utilize it in the organization.

Formation of attitudes toward the innovation substage. Organizational members form attitudes toward the innovation. Once the initial search has taken place, the attitudes taken by organizational members are important.

Decision substage. The information concerning the potential innovation is evaluated.

Implementation Stage

Initial implementation substage. The organization makes the first attempt to utilize a particular innovation.

Continued sustained implementation substage. If the implementation has been successful because organizational members understand it and have information about implementation, the innovation will continue to be important.

Table 9.1 compares the stages of change in these three conceptual frameworks. In addition, there has been some effort to examine the links between a given substage and the typical barriers to innovation through each of those substages.

At the "knowledge-awareness" substage, for example, Ronald Havelock (1969) noted not only the strong tendency that organizations show toward trying to maintain stability but also the constant personal threat that change suggests to organization members; people wonder, "What is this going to do to *me*?" Barriers at the "attitude formation" and "decision" substages often stem from organizational tendencies to modify the nature of messages so that the meaning of those messages might be ignored. Because

TABLE 9.1. COMPARISONS OF THE VARIOUS STAGES OF CHANGE AS DEFINED AND CONCEPTUALIZED IN THREE DIFFERENT THEORETICAL MODELS.

Rogers (1962)	Hage and Aiken (1970)	Zaltman, Duncan, and Holbek (1973)
Awareness		I. Initiation Stage
		1. Knowledge-Awareness
	1. Evaluation	2. Formation of attitudes
Interest		toward the innovation
Evaluation		3. Decision
Trial	2. Initiation	II. Implementation Stage
		1. Initial implementation
Adoption	3. Implementation	
	4. Routinization	2. Continued-sustained implementation

they feel unprepared, organizations often do whatever they can to subvert any effort toward change.

When an innovation reaches the "initial implementation" substage, it intersects with organizational disequilibrium at its highest point; members find it hard to know what they have really gotten themselves into. In other words, people at this point may not be absolutely clear as to the precise reasons why they ever began the change process in the first place. Finally, the greatest barrier to change at the "continued-sustained implementation" substage is undoubtedly the fact that people often lose interest quickly in any innovation.

Overcoming the Barriers

Despite the most effective of supervisory efforts, change is difficult to initiate, implement, and maintain in any organization for a multitude of reasons. There are many different barriers to change in general, as well as particular inhibitors that are characteristic of each identifiable stage in the process of adopting innovations. Although it is unlikely that all barriers can be totally overcome, Goodwin Watson (1966, pp. 145–146) identified twelve different ways in which people in leadership roles might be able to minimize the resistance to change found in their organizations.

1. Resistance will be less if administrators and managers [and supervisors] feel that the project is their own—not one devised and operated by outsiders.

2. Resistance will be less if the . . . innovation clearly has whole-hearted support from top officials in the system.

3. Resistance will be less if the [organizational] participants see the change as reducing rather than increasing their present burdens.

4. Resistance will be less if the [innovative] project accords with values already acknowledged by participants.

5. Resistance will be less if the program offers the kind of new experience which interests participants.

6. Resistance will be less if participants feel their autonomy and security are not threatened.

7. Resistance will be less if participants have joined in diagnostic efforts leading them to agree on what the basic problems are and their importance.

8. Resistance will be less if the project is adopted by consensual group decision.

9. Resistance will be reduced if proponents are able to empathize with opponents; to recognize valid objections; and to take steps to relieve unnecessary fears.

10. Resistance will be reduced if it is recognized that innovations are likely to be misunderstood and misinterpreted, and if provision is made for feedback of perceptions of the project and for further clarification of need.

11. Resistance will be reduced if participants experience acceptance, support, trust, and confidence in their relations with one another.

12. Resistance will be reduced if the project is kept open to revision and reconsideration, and if experience indicates that changes will be desirable.

One theme is apparent in all of Watson's recommendations: Overcoming resistance to change requires sensitivity by the supervisor to the personal concerns of people in the organization. In terms of proactive supervision, we cannot overemphasize the importance of knowing not only one's own priorities, values, philosophy, and action plan, but also those of the people who work in the organization. While such an awareness will not conquer all resistance to change, we can assume that the more we know about and are sensitive to the concerns of individuals, the less they will resist change.

Summary

We assume in this chapter that "change for the sake of change" should not be promoted, but that innovation and change are inevitable and necessary for the continuing growth of any organization. Without periodic improvements, organizations will stagnate.

In the first part of this chapter, we reviewed four conceptual models of change: problem-solving, social interaction, research-development-diffusion, and linkage. We suggested that all four models have strengths and weaknesses in terms of their potential to describe ideal strategies for implementing organizational change, but that the linkage model offers particular advantages, because it incorporates elements from each of the other three.

We also examined a number of typical inhibitors to change, including general satisfaction with the status quo and lack of adequate rewards for participating in change. We also suggested that educational supervisors might find particularly helpful the recent efforts to define stages in the change process.

Finally, we concluded by suggesting a number of strategies that might be employed by supervisors who are intent on reducing, if not eliminating, resistance to change efforts in schools.

Suggested Activities

1. Talk with a group of teachers in a school who have experienced some type of change in their school, for example, a new reading curriculum. The actual change itself is not important, but try to ascertain the strategies that were used by supervisors, administrators, other teachers, or whoever was responsible for introducing the innovation to the school. Compare the strategy with the various change processes described in this chapter.

2. Visit three different schools and make an assessment, after interviewing the principal and two or three teachers in each school, as to whether the schools might be classified as belonging to any of the change phases or stages described in

this chapter. Remember that a school does not necessarily have had to go through a very dramatic change recently to qualify as having undergone change.

Cases to Consider

Read each of the cases and consider the following:

a. What are the critical issues raised in each case, as they relate to the analysis of change processes?

b. How does each case relate to the development of proactive supervision?

c. In what ways might you suggest a resolution to the issues raised?

Case 9.1:

I Thought I'd Make the Place Nicer!

Mary Cochran was furious. She had just come back from the faculty room and found the new table cloth she had purchased with her own money folded up and hidden in a drawer in the old cabinet that stood next to the kitchen table where the teachers ate their lunch each day. The nerve of that group of ungrateful . . .

It all started six weeks ago, the day Mary took over Woodson Avenue Elementary School as the new principal. Woodson, a small old building in a blue-collar school district, did not exactly look like the Taj Mahal, but it was a beautiful sight to Mary in her first job as a school administrator. It was a building with a lot of potential for improvement. The walls around the building seemed to be painted a shade of "perpetually institutionally gray and dull," and the bulletin boards seemed not to have been changed for almost a year. Her office looked quite functional, but it really resembled a locker room more than it did the place where she would be spending much of her life. Because she was a "new kid on the block" and, like most new principals, was likely to enjoy a brief honeymoon period with the central office where she could ask for a special favor now and then, she worked hard to get some new painting done in the halls, new coverings for the bulletin board, and even a few new pieces of furniture in her office to brighten things up. As she looked around the building a week before the teachers came back, she began to see a little hope in the old place. She had one last challenge to address, namely improving the appearance of the faculty room.

Mary really wanted to do something extra special for the teachers in her new school. She knew that, as a rookie principal, a lot of her success on the job would be derived from her ability to have a good relationship with teachers. In addition, she had heard that the staff at Woodson was a particularly tough group. They had made it clear to the central office that they were tired of being viewed as a "training ground for new principals." As the smallest building in a district where principals were paid based on building size, Woodson had not had a principal remain for more than three years for quite some time. Mary was determined to win over the teachers by showing that she really did care for them and that, with her as principal, things would be a lot better.

The faculty room was the place where she decided to invest her energy to provide people with a clear indication of where her heart was. The room, which she discovered when she took the job, was a mess. The paint was dull, cracked, and chipped. The windows (one of which was broken) had no drapes or shades. As a result, the old furniture laying around the room was faded. Year-old announcements filled the bulletin board. Perhaps most noticeable, however, was the kitchen table in the middle room. It was covered by an old plastic table cloth which was torn and worn, seemingly ready to disintegrate due to age at any moment. Mary decided that, as a subtle indication of her commitment to her teachers, she would make the improvement of the faculty room her personal project. She didn't have a lot of extra money due to the fact that she had just finished her doctorate at a local university, but she had a lot of energy and will power. She and a friend spent much of an entire weekend painting, scrubbing, and cleaning the faculty room. She convinced her custodian to postpone his other jobs and replace the broken glass in the window which she decorated with an old set of curtains from home. She couldn't afford any new furniture, but she could at least do something about the ugly table cloth so visible in the middle of the room. After everything else in the room was completed, she went to a local store and bought a new covering to place on the kitchen table. To finish the job, she made certain to bring in some fresh flowers from home to place in the middle of the table for the first day, when all the teachers were to report back to work. She believed that the new appearance of the faculty room would be a subtle but important statement to let the faculty know that she would be a different, caring principal who believed that they were important.

The first day with the entire faculty was, of course, a busy day for Mary. It wasn't until Tuesday of the first week, long after the teachers had gone home, that she decided to walk down to admire her work in the staff room one more time. She walked into the room and immediately noticed the table cloth. She hadn't taken time on Sunday evening to throw out the old table cloth. Instead, she had left it folded on a shelf in the little cabinet where teachers often left their lesson books and other paraphernalia while they ate lunch. The old cloth was back on the kitchen table, and her purchase was now on the shelf. She was so mad, she nearly ripped down the drapes. Although she resisted the temptation, she was still angry and hurt.

Case 9.2:

Research Says . . .

Dr. Neil Collins was truly excited about his new job as the director of teaching and curriculum for the Spencer Mountain Schools. As a former teacher and principal in the district, he had always wanted to get into a position in the system where he could really have a direct impact on the instructional practices used in classrooms. He knew last spring that he would be stepping into his new job this summer as the result of the retirement of Rita Goodman, a fine administrator who had been the director for nine years. Rita was a great person and an outstanding manager, but Neil (and many others) believed that she was not particularly creative and sensitive to improvement in the curriculum and teaching practices in the district.

Throughout the last several months, Neil spent as much time as he could reading, viewing videotapes, talking to faculty at the local university, and attending workshops dealing with new instructional techniques. He was going to be ready to serve as a true resource person for the teachers and administrators in the district when he came on board in August. He wanted to know as much as he could, and with as much authority as he could, to answer questions about new practices adopted in the district, such as authentic assessment procedures and outcomes-based education. He read the recent research on both topics so that he could be ready to speak with authority.

It was now early October. Neil sat in his office, thoroughly discouraged. Earlier in the day, he had provided one of his weekly inservice sessions for interested principals and teachers. During that session, he presented some recent data just collected by researchers at Mountain State University to show how the use of portfolios had a relationship to pupil and parent satisfaction in overall school goals. He believed that this was the kind of information that would convince a lot of skeptics that the portfolio preparation and review process would be worth it. After his presentation, however, there was not a single question or comment regarding the research findings. Instead, the principals wanted to know how they were supposed to get more money from the central office to pay for the paper and duplicating costs which would result from compiling portfolios. They also wanted to know if they would be paid for the extra time they would spend on portfolio reviews.

References

Bennis, Warren G., Benne, Kenneth D., & Chin, Robert (1969). *The planning of change* (2nd ed.). New York: Holt, Rinehart, & Winston.

Bhola, H. S. (1965, October). *The configuration theory of innovation diffusion*. Columbus: The Ohio State University, College of Education.

Clark, David L., & Guba, Egon G. (1975, April). The configurational perspective: A new view of educational knowledge production and utilization. *Educational Researcher, 4*(4).

Fullan, Michael (1973). Overview of the innovative process and the user. *Interchange, 3*:1–46.

Hage, Gerald, & Aiken, Michael (1970). *Social change in complex organizations*. New York: Random House.

Hall, Gene, & Loucks, Susan (1976). *A developmental model for determining whether or not the treatment really is implemented*. Austin: Texas Research and Development Center for Teacher for Teacher Education.

Hall, Gene (1987). *Taking charge of change*. Alexandria, VA: Association for Supervision and Curriculum Development.

Halpin, Andrew W. (1967). *Theory and research in administration*. New York: Macmillan.

Havelock, Ronald G. (1969). *Planning for innovation through dissemination and utilization of knowledge*. Ann Arbor, MI: Institute for Social Research, Center for Research on Utilization of Scientific Knowledge.

_____ (1972). *Bibliography on knowledge utilization and dissemination*. Ann Arbor, MI: Institute for Social Research, Center on Research on Utilization of Scientific Knowledge.

Havelock, Ronald G. (1973). *Training for change agents.* Ann Arbor, MI: Institute for Social Research, Center for Research on Utilization of Scientific Knowledge.

House, Ernest, R. (1974). *The politics of educational innovation.* Berkeley: McCutchan.

Lipham, James M. (1965). Leadership and administration. In Daniel Griffiths (Ed.), *Behavioral science and educational administration.* Chicago: National Society for the Study of Education.

Lipham, James M., & Hoeh, James (1974). *The principalship: Foundations and functions.* New York: Harper and Row.

Lippitt, G. (1969). *Organizational renewal.* New York: Appleton-Century-Crofts.

Lippitt, R., Watson, J., & Westley, B. (1958). *The dynamics of planned change.* New York: Harcourt Brace Jovanovich.

Lovell, John T., & Wiles, Kimball (1983). *Supervision for better schools* (5th ed.). Englewood Cliffs, NJ: Prentice Hall.

McLaughlin, Milbrey (1976). Implementation as mutual adaptation: Change in classroom organization. *Teachers College Record,* 77:339–351.

Owens, Robert (1986). *Organizational behavior in education* (3rd ed.). Englewood Cliffs, NJ: Prentice Hall.

Paul, Douglas (1976). Change processes at the elementary, secondary, and postsecondary levels. In J. Culbertson & N. Nash (Eds.), *Linking processes in educational improvement.* Columbus, OH: University Council for Educational Administration.

Rogers, E. M. (1962). *Diffusion of innovations.* New York: The Free Press of Glencoe.

Rogers, E. M., & Shoemaker, F. F. (1971). *Communication of innovations: A cross-cultural approach.* New York: Free Press.

Ryan, B., & Gross, N. (1943). The diffusion of hybrid seed corn in two Iowa communities. *Rural Sociology,* 8:15–24.

Schmuck, Richard A., & Miles, Matthew B. (1971). *Organizational development in schools.* Palo Alto, CA: National Press Books.

Watson, Goodwin (Ed.) (1966). Resistance to change. *Concepts for social change.* Washington, DC: National Training Laboratories.

Zaltman, Gerald, Duncan, Robert, & Holbek, Jonny (1973). *Innovations and organizations.* New York: Wiley-Interscience.

10 Exercising Power and Authority

Although supervisory activities in schools promote needed change, the concepts of power and authority inherent in supervision frequently evoke negative reactions. Classroom teachers intent on exploring alternative career options in the field of education seem particularly concerned about the need for supervisors to exercise power and authority, perhaps because of a long-standing reluctance among educators to think in terms of trying to control others.

In this chapter we explore the concepts of organizational power and authority in more descriptive and, it is hoped, less threatening ways. A formal leadership role, such as that of a school supervisor or administrator, carries with it the responsibility of authority, and that authority brings a degree of power, whether earned or delegated. In short, anyone who finds it unpleasant to think in these terms should probably eschew a career in supervision or administration.

We explore the dual issues of power and authority as well as how the judicious exercise of these by supervisory personnel may bring about more effective organizations. As we have done in previous chapters, we will first consider some definitions of power and authority and then present the characteristics of each concept in greater detail. The chapter concludes with a consideration of some of the immediate, practical applications of these concepts for the individual interested in engaging in more effective and proactive supervisory practices.

Alternative Definitions

"Power" and "authority" are terms that occur often in discussions of organizational leadership, but they are used with a surprising lack of precision. Many people, classroom teachers frequently among them, express distrust of those who appear to possess either characteristic. However, any fundamental understanding of the nature of supervision, whether in schools or other organizations, must include an understanding of power and authority.

In simple terms, Max Weber (1947) defined power as "the probability that one actor within a social relationship will be in a position to carry out his own will despite resistance" (p. 52). *Power*, then, is the fundamental ability of one person to command some degree of compliance on the part of another person. By contrast, *authority* suggests a much less general concept. Clayton Resser (1973) defined authority as "a right granted to a manager to make decisions, within limitations, to assign duties to subordinates, and to require subordinates' conformance to expected behavior" (p. 311). Based on the distinctions suggested in these definitions, we can make some important generalizations about the distinctions between power and authority.

Everyone has power, or at least the *potential* for exercising power. Each of us potentially has the ability to encourage another person to behave in some particular way. Even a person whose role in society seems most unimportant may effect some change in others or in society in general.

When we speak of power we tend to think in terms of its use. We think first of those whose roles automatically provide a potential for influencing others. Everyone has power, but not everyone makes use of it or develops the know-how required to exercise power effectively from a position that does not appear to be strong. This observation is true regardless of the way in which power was acquired in the first place, whether by assuming a position where formal authority is normally delegated or by demonstrating competence in a typically "nonpower" role.

Not everyone, on the other hand, has access to authority, which is a condition possessed by a relatively small percentage of people. According to Herbert Simon (1945), a person with authority has and "uses the formal criterion of the receipt of a command . . . as his basis of choice" (pp. 108–109). Authority is a legitimized statement of one (or more) person's formal designation to control the behaviors in an organization, and it derives from certain societal sources to be reviewed later in this chapter.

The primary distinctions between authority and power are fairly straightforward. *Power* is the *ability* to make others behave in certain ways and is available to most people in society, regardless of whether or not they have formal authority. *Authority* is the *right* to make others behave in certain ways and is not available to everyone but rather is formally conferred on some. Interestingly, however, the fact that people have authority does not necessarily guarantee that they will exercise power.

In the next two sections we consider some specific features of these characteristics of organizational life, beginning with the unique properties of power.

Characteristics of Power

In this section we examine the broader concept of power by looking at its traditional sources. French and Raven (1960) suggested five sources of social power, and we look at how these are related to the role of an educational supervisor.

French and Raven: Sources of Social Power

Reward power is the capacity to provide rewards to others in the organization as a way to influence their behavior. In a school setting, for example, a school board might offer bonus pay to teachers who perform at a level consistent with established district goals. Merit pay proposals are fairly clear examples of attempts to exercise reward power in schools. In the context of our earlier discussion contrasting supervision with administration, we should note that supervisory personnel are traditionally thought to have very limited access to the use of reward power in organizations, whereas administrators generally are thought to control it. This perspective is limiting, however, because the concepts of "rewards" can mean things others than the financial incentives usually controlled by school administrators or boards of education. Supervisors often exercise reward power in more subtle ways, such as assigning some teachers to more attractive communities or distributing newer, more attractive curricular materials. Richard Gorton (1980) identified the following assumptions inherent in the use of reward power:

- The strength of the reward power will increase with the magnitude of the rewards that one person perceives another can obtain for him or her.
- The strength of the reward power will depend on the actual rewards that a person can produce, not on what he or she hopes or would like to produce.
- Unsuccessful attempts to exert reward power will tend to decrease the perceived strengths of that power in the future.

Coercive power is the capacity of one person to provide punishment or negative consequences to another in a deliberate attempt to control the other person's behavior. Again, this form of power is usually associated with administrators, not supervisors. However, supervisory personnel make use of coercive strategies when they do such things as write negative evaluations of teacher performance or reject new curricular programs that may be desired by some teachers. Gorton noted the following assumptions related to the use of coercive power:

- The strength of coercive power will increase with the magnitude of the punishments or costs which the other person perceives that the person exercising power may apply.
- The strength of the coercive power will depend on the *actual* sanctions or punishments that are applied, not only on what one hopes to apply.
- Unsuccessful attempts to exert coercive power will tend to decrease the perceived strength of that power in the future.

Legitimate power is most similar to what shall later be described as formal authority. Control of one person by another is based on the assumption that the person exercising the power has a legitimate right to do so and is supported by a statement of policy, law, or even historical precedent and tradition.

Referent power is the tendency of other individuals to be attracted by and to identify closely with the person who exercises the power. A certain emphasis is therefore placed on the charismatic qualities of the supervisor, administrator, or other person who is making use of the power. Simply stated, this is power derived largely from the extent to which people like or respect the person in charge. Gorton's assumptions related to this source of power include:

- The greater the perceived attractiveness of the person exercising power by another person or group, the more likely that there will be identification with the leader.

- The stronger the identification with the leader by another person, the greater will be the likelihood that referent power can be successfully utilized by the leader.

Finally, *expert power* is the ability to influence others' behavior based on special knowledge. This is the power source most often linked to the supervisor's role. Because supervisors do not enjoy formal authority, the belief is that they must rely on public perceptions of their expertise and competence as a way to influence others. Teachers yield to the power of a supervisor of language arts, for instance, because they believe that the supervisor has special knowledge in the field of language arts. Gorton's assumptions concerning the application of expert power follow:

- The strength of the expert power of a person will vary with the actual knowledge and skill that he or she might possess, along with others' perceptions of his or her expertise.
- The stronger the perception by others that the leader possesses expert power, the higher will be their satisfaction and evaluation of him or her as a leader.

French and Raven's five sources of social power can be understood from both a descriptive and a normative perspective. They provide certain insights into how power may be classified for further analysis, and they can also provide the supervisor with a way of understanding the implications to be derived from reliance on one source or another. Understanding the differences that exist between referent power and reward power, for example, and the likely effect that each is likely to have on people who work in organizations is a powerful guide to behavior. Consider the probable response to a supervisor who works at increasing his or her expert powers by learning more about a particular topic as contrasted with the probable response to a supervisor who tries to "pull rank" by using threats, punishments, or other efforts associated with coercive power strategies.

Compliance Theory

Amitai Etzioni (1961) analyzed power relationships in organizations through the concept of *compliance theory* which suggests that power sources should be matched with organizational types for more efficient use. Etzioni identified three major types of organizations, defined by their fundamental goal as "economic," "order," or "cultural." If the primary goal of an organization is to preserve order (political, moral, financial, or any other type), for example, the most appropriate source of power would be coercive. To understand this, we might look at how police use coercive power (or implied coercive power) in their work, which is primarily directed toward fostering order and control. In the case of schools, people make use of the value of learning and the goal is most often cultural; power might be most often seen as expert power. However, we can see where an assistant principal in charge of student discipline for a high school would make much greater use of coercive power than of any other type, according to Etzioni's theory.

Characteristics of Authority

The legitimized and sanctioned use of power normally referred to as authority may also be understood according to certain characteristics.

Authority Types

The German sociologist Max Weber, whose definition of authority we noted earlier, suggested that there are three major types of authority utilized in different organizations:

1. *Traditional Authority.* Authority derived from tradition. People accept the control of others because it is assumed that those "others" have some sort of traditionally legitimate, absolute right to exercise that authority with no challenge. In school settings, for instance, a parent may tell a child to obey a teacher for the simple reason that the person *is* a teacher, and a teacher always deserves respect. Although this may not hold true in classrooms on a daily basis, many such forms of reliance on traditional authority types may still be seen.

2. *Charismatic Authority.* Authority based on the assumption that the leader has some special gift, or even supernatural powers. Examples of this type of authority are religious leaders and some televangelists who, despite apparent inconsistencies in their personal lives, continue to attract millions of followers and their money because the leaders have successfully established in the minds of their adherents that they possess special gifts from God.

3. *Legal Authority.* Authority derived from laws, policies, or statutes. Military officers have authority because such authority is decreed by regulation. As many enlisted personnel recognize, superior officers may lack identifiable skills or charisma; they are, however, in charge simply because they *are* officers.

Educators can use these descriptions of different types of authority in understanding why we defer to certain individuals. In addition to determining "type" of authority, however, we also need to determine whether it is "formal" or "functional."

Formal versus Functional Authority

Robert Peabody (1962) defined *formal* authority as authority derived from such sources as the organizational hierarchy, laws, a person's position in an organization, or office. *Functional* authority comes from such things as a person's professional expertise and competence, interpersonal skills, and suggestion of great experience in handling a particular situation. The tendency to assume that functional authority is "softer" or "better" is really not warranted. People who exercise authority make use of both approaches. On the other hand, a person may deliberately select one particular strategy in order to effect a desired goal. A school superintendent, for example, who might normally rely on his or her formal authority to bring about changes in the behavior of the teaching staff might choose instead to seek a more indirect way to influence changes in behavior. The superintendent, in other words, might consciously seek to exercise functional rather than—or in addition to—formal authority.

We do not mean to suggest that an effective supervisor should shift between formal and functional authority patterns. Such inconsistency is unwise, if not impossible. Deliberate switches from a formal to a functional approach are often perceived by staff members as manipulative just as the game of "good cop-bad cop" is a staged strategy used to manipulate criminal suspects. Selecting one pattern rather than the other might be impossible for those supervisors who have no, or at best limited, access to formal authority strategies. The critical issue for the practitioner of proactive supervision is always to recognize the strengths and limitations of both formal and functional authority patterns.

Implications for Supervisors

Power and authority are central issues in understanding the field of educational supervision. In chapter 3 we noted the continuing controversy in the study of supervision over whether or not supervisors ever really get anything done. We suggested that the critical concern in assessing a supervisor's potential power rests in our appreciation of how much the supervisor can motivate others to do something.

Supervisors and others involved with supervisory activity can in fact be very effective, and they can be effective without any formal authority. Supervisory effectiveness can rest in functional authority and power. If the supervisor learns to engage primarily in behaviors that influence others, then he or she will bring about change. In school settings, the adoption of techniques designed to have an impact based on expertise, competence, and interpersonal skills will probably result in longer-lasting change on the part of teachers and other staff members who are well educated, sophisticated, and accustomed to performing in settings where they must think for themselves. The supervisor who relies solely on formal authority and "pulls rank" to try to make others perform in a particular way will rarely be effective and, with professional employees, will often actually do more harm than good. Teachers who are "told" what to do will often rebel against what they perceive as an effort to manipulate their behavior.

Proactive supervision assumes that a practitioner will carefully weigh the outcomes that are likely to result from the use of different types of power and authority. Proactive supervision is an effective approach because it leads us toward finding ways of influencing as many people as possible within an organization. Power and authority are central to the questions of motivation or influence, and anyone who is uncomfortable with analyzing these topics in a school setting might well be advised to look at alternative professional roles.

Summary

In this chapter we considered some definitions of two inescapable concerns of supervisory personnel—power and authority. We emphasized the supervisor's need to understand and appreciate the most appropriate and judicious ways to exercise power and authority in school settings.

We reviewed the salient characteristics of power, including the sources of power offered by French and Raven and compliance theory as developed by Etzioni. The section dealing with authority included a brief overview of Weber's definitions of three types of authority—traditional, charismatic, and legal—and a discussion concerning the distinction between formal and functional authority. Finally we noted how the concepts of authority and power are germane to the development of understanding educational supervision, particularly proactive supervision.

Suggested Activities

1. Interview a group of supervisors and a group of administrators and ask them to describe the strategies and techniques that they would follow when trying to encourage teachers to comply with a new school district policy. As each group describes its practices, make an assessment of the types of power (according to French and Raven's conceptualization) that are being used. Are there differences between what the supervisors would do, as contrasted with the administrative group?

2. Talk with four or five teachers and present brief descriptions of the different authority types presented in this chapter. Ask each person to identify situations in which they would expect supervisors or administrators to rely on one or another type of authority.

Cases to Consider

Read each of the cases and consider the following:

a. What are the critical issues raised in the cases, as they relate to the concepts of power and authority in educational supervision?

b. How does each case relate to the development of proactive supervision?

c. In what ways might you suggest a resolution to the issues raised?

Case 10.1:

It Was Supposed to Be Easier

When the superintendent called Malcolm Fredericks and offered him the job as Apple View's new district coordinator of curriculum, it was a happy moment for Malcolm. Although he had been an elementary principal in the system for the past three years, he was not very comfortable in that job. He liked the children in the school and found satisfaction in the work related to curriculum development. However, Malcolm hated the times when he had to act like "the boss" and confront teachers or other staff members. It was really difficult for him to "pull rank" and order others around.

It was because of this overall discomfort with being in the too powerful role of principal that made Malcolm look forward to his new position where he could get involved with improving the district's curriculum and instructional practices. "No more hassles, and no more need to push anyone around," thought the new district administrator.

It was three weeks into the new school year, and Malcolm sat in his office wondering why he still didn't seem to be as happy with his new job as he thought he should be by now. Two weeks ago, at the request of the superintendent, he initiated a districtwide review of the mathematics curriculum. He then received several complaint calls from teachers across the district who stated that they saw no need to "waste a lot of time" going over the math program again. They had been involved with a comprehensive review only five years ago. Yet the school board had made it clear to the superintendent that something had to be done with the math program in the school district. Now, Malcolm was in the "hot seat" and had to push the agenda along.

Malcolm believed that the curriculum review process was warranted, and he really did not object to leading the effort. Still, he was less than happy over the fact that he had to "get tough" with the teachers again.

Case 10.2

That's Another Way to Get It Across

The teachers in Hooten Hollow Middle School had been frustrated over the past few years. They were generally recognized as some of the most competent teachers in the school district, but they had experienced two consecutive principals who rarely sought their opinions. They felt that the past two administrators did not appreciate their hard work and dedication to the job.

Cheryl Gomez was now the next principal at Hooten Hollow. She was walking into the job with her eyes open to the problems with staff morale. She knew that her predecessors, Walter Fitzsimmons and Grace Flores, had experienced a lot of problems, and she had heard stories about how the teachers expressed their frustration with not being involved in decisions. Nevertheless, Hooten Hollow was recognized as one of the highest achieving middle schools in the state, and Cheryl wanted to come on board and do an outstanding job—maintain the school's excellent reputation and make the teachers happy.

It was now the night before Cheryl's first appearance in front of her new staff. She was reviewing several different alternative strategies that she might follow tomorrow when she announced her goals for the next year to her new colleagues. She was not normally a harsh person, but she knew the results that such behavior had brought about in the past. She didn't want to foul up a good thing, but, she wanted to be herself. How could she resolve this dilemma?

References

Etzioni, Amitai (1961). *A comparative analysis of complex organizations*. New York: Free Press.

French, J. R. P., & Raven, B. (1960). The bases of social power. In D. Cartwright & A. Zander (Eds.), *Group dynamics: Research and theory* (2nd ed.). Evanston, IL: Harper and Row.

Gorton, Richard A. (1980). *School administration and supervision: Important issues, concepts, and case studies*. Dubuque: Brown.

Peabody, Robert L. (1962, March). Perceptions of organizational authority: A comparative analysis. *Administrative Science Quarterly*, 6(4).

Resser, Clayton (1973). *Management: Functions and modern concepts.* Chicago: Scott, Foresman.

Simon, Herbert (1945). *Administrative behavior.* New York: Macmillan.

Weber, Max (1947). *The theory of social and economic organization* (Talcott Parsons, Translator). Glencoe, IL: The Free Press.

11 Dealing with Conflict

A great deal of "pop" management literature features self-improvement prescriptions for leaders and would-be leaders to follow, and among the most frequently stated is the notion that effective managers must learn to reduce, or even eliminate, conflict from their personal and professional lives. These books suggest simple steps, similar to time-management techniques, which may be followed to clean up conflict-riddled lives.

We are always amused by these "sure-cures" for managers. It is, simply put, impossible to take on a leadership role in an organization without confronting conflict. In fact, the more successful a manager or supervisor becomes, the more likely it is that she or he will experience more intense, frequent, and visible forms of conflict. Even for those not in formal organizational leadership positions, conflict is an unavoidable fact of life.

Some organizational theorists argue that conflict is not only an *inevitable* feature of organizational life but is also a *desirable* ingredient of functioning organizations. Life without periodic change is stagnant, and the development of conflict is one way to force necessary change. Leaders are legitimately held responsible not for reducing or eliminating organizational conflict, but rather for using it to promote institutional improvement and growth.

The issue that we address in this chapter is not how to avoid conflict, but rather the ways in which a supervisor can minimize the negative consequences of conflict. First we will explore what conflict is, in conceptual terms, and present four different types of conflict. In the second half of the chapter, we focus on a model designed to help us understand how to handle conflict in our lives.

211

What Is Conflict?

Morton Deutsch (1973; cited in Owens, 1987) noted that "a conflict exists whenever incompatible activities occur" (p. 133). For Deutsch, then, conflict is little more than a state of disagreement between two parties. The word can describe a range of phenomena all the way from a simple difference of opinion to war. Kenneth Boulding (1962) suggested that the factor which distinguishes types of conflict is the amount of hostility present in the disagreement. Conflict between two people who want to drive their cars in the same space on an expressway may range in potency from simple annoyance (low hostility) to the violent and destructive behavior seen recently in some cities where drivers have shot at one another (extremely high hostility). We cannot avoid this kind of conflict entirely, unless we decide never to drive. Many of us must drive on freeways in order to get around cities like Chicago, Houston, or Los Angeles. Therefore, we must put ourselves "at risk" to encounter conflict. The key is to remain at the annoyance or low end of the continuum.

Owens (1987) further distinguished among low and high hostility events by noting that the major difference

> . . . lies in the motivation behind them, often not easily discernible. Although considerable (and often vigorous) conflict may erupt over such issues as improving school performance, ways of desegregating a school system, or how to group children for instruction, the parties to the conflict may well be motivated by essentially constructive goals. The key is whether or not the parties involved want to work with the system or are motivated by a wish to destroy it. (p. 246)

If conflict is an inevitable organizational reality, what effects will it have? Obviously there may be good or bad consequences of any institutional characteristic, including conflict. When disagreements (marked by either high or low hostility) occur, two things may happen. The lack of consensus may lead to improvement in the organization, because communication takes place, and compromise or further appreciation of opposite views is achieved. In this case, the consequence of conflict might be described as "good." On the other hand, disagreement may result in polarization of viewpoints, the end of communication, and personal animosity among members in the organization. Here, the results of the conflict are clearly "bad." The responsibility of the leader, particularly a proactive educational leader, is to guide the conflicts that will always be present toward a lower level of hostility and therefore toward a higher probability of serving as positive forces for the organization. To try to avoid or eliminate conflict is, simply put, to avoid a legitimate supervisory responsibility, and the results of such an activity will almost always be negative. For instance, think of the school principal who wants to avoid conflict and therefore simply sits in an office all day with the door closed, shutting out the potential disagreements taking place in the corridors and classrooms. This behavior may be satisfying to the principal, whose blood pressure does not rise in response to the events taking place outside the office, but its consequences to the organization, which consists of both children and teachers, are ultimately negative; opportunities for growth through resolution of conflicts are lost. In short, schools where the principal's door is always closed are rarely exciting schools. We are not suggesting that supervisors should deliberately stir up conflict, but when conflict occurs, no effective leader should run from it.

Sources and Types of Conflict

Proactive supervisors need to understand two additional dimensions of organizational conflict: the sources of conflict and types of conflict most frequently faced by educational supervisors.

Sources of Conflict

Educational supervisors typically face conflict from three sources: within the organization, outside the organization, and within one's self. Robert Owens (1987) defined the sources of conflict in this way:

> Conflict can occur *within* persons or social units; it is *intrapersonal* or *intragroup* (or, of course, *intranational*). Conflict can also be experienced between two or more people or social units: so-called *interpersonal, intergroup,* or *international* conflict. (p. 92)

The only conflict described above that does not appear almost daily in the school leader's life is international, although even in this category there may be situations where conflict is felt by supervisory personnel.

In the context of our overall goal of identifying ways to reduce the negative consequences of conflict, we will explore strategies for the supervisor to follow. Fundamentally, the effective supervisor is one who develops the capacity to remain aware of what is occurring within the organization so that potential conflicts may be identified in advance whenever possible. Developing a *sensitivity* to potential conflicts both inside and outside the organization does not guarantee the prevention of future conflict, but it does ensure that the supervisor will not be surprised (or frustrated) when something happens. There will never be, for example, a school in which every teacher gets along with every other teacher or is totally satisfied with every supervisory or administrative decision. When a leader makes a decision, someone will probably disagree. Poor leadership practice is anticipating neither the likely source nor the potency of the conflict that a decision will engender. Proactive supervisors have a sense of where the "land mines" are located, not in order to defuse them all in advance, but rather to find a path among them which will cause the least damage.

Analyzing conflict that arises from within one's self necessarily grows from an individual's ability to "know thyself." As we indicated in chapter 2, many important values may be defined in the process of developing and reviewing an individual philosophy of education. One of the greatest benefits of such continuous self-assessment is that it can alert us to both our values and likely sources of personal conflict.

Types of Conflict

In the discussion of Getzels's social systems model in chapter 5, we indicated that organizations are best understood as the products of an ongoing and dynamic interactive process involving individual (idiographic) and institutional (nomothctic) dimensions. Getzels defined effectiveness as the extent to which congruence (or lack of disagreement or conflict) was present in the interactions between the component elements of the theoretical model. From this view of effectiveness we can identify four major types of organizational conflict: interrole, intrarefernce group, interreference, and role-personality.

Interrole conflict is the "disagreement between two or more roles simultaneously fulfilled by one person" (Lipham and Hoeh, 1974, p. 133). The supervisor feels the effects of trying to "wear too many hats."

High school subject department chairpersons often suffer from interrole conflict. Some released time from teaching is normally provided for chairpersons to engage in supervisory and administrative duties, but chairpersons are still usually expected to teach classes, advise students, serve on assorted governance and planning committees in the school or district, and, in many cases, do a duty assignment each day, coach a sport, or moderate some student activity. These assignments and expectations are only those encountered during the workday; personal and professional commitments—family, graduate education, community activities, and so forth—add fuel to feelings of conflict and stress. Naturally, the many competing demands cannot always be kept separate from one another. At some point, for example, the department chair may find it impossible to grade student papers before the next class and also fill out a purchase order to get materials requested by department faculty before the deadline imposed by the district business office. These professional pressures are often accompanied by the additional demands of personal activities and responsibilities. The department chairperson may also owe a paper for a university course, have two children who need attention, and be a soloist for the church choir.

Such situations, where people are trying to "juggle several balls at once," are by no means infrequent. Most of us occasionally find that we have more commitments than time, and we sense some degree of interrole conflict. The more competent we are at what we do, the more likely we are to feel this type of pressure; the conflict serves almost as a recognition of ability. Nevertheless, the consequences can be negative. Important jobs are not completed, psychological stress intensifies, and our ability to fulfill our responsibilities is greatly impaired. We can take steps to reduce this type of conflict as well as its negative consequences.

People facing interrole conflict need to take stock of their various competing personal and professional commitments, set priorities, and decide which activities may be removed from their personal agendas. Must we sing in the church choir while taking graduate courses, or can we look forward to solos after completing the degree? Sometimes activities that are important must be dropped, at least temporarily, to provide time for activities of greater personal or professional value.

Another way to reduce interrole conflict is to engage in time management activities. Many schemes exist to help people control their personal uses of time. Larry Hughes (1984) provides a plan that we find particularly useful:

1. *Analyze your job* to clarify precisely what it is you are supposed to do in a particular setting. Formal job descriptions should be

viewed as starting points in determining what is *really* expected in a school or district.

2. *Determine the difference between managing and doing.* Remember that efficiency (doing things well) must be consciously combined with effectiveness (getting the right things done well).

3. *Set personal goals and objectives* and develop strategies for achieving them. Define the goals precisely enough so that they may serve to guide continuing behavior.

4. *Conduct a personal time audit* as a way to see how you have really been using your time.

5. *Avoid interruptions on the job.* Watch out for "drop in visitors" and unwanted telephone calls that divert you from your focus on effective use of available time.

6. *Delegate.* Organize yourself, your subordinates, colleagues, and bosses to accomplish necessary work most effectively.

7. *Plan and conduct effective meetings.* Meetings should serve the needs of the organization and the people who work in it, not be roadblocks to effective use of time. Consider how meetings might be arranged to reduce interrole conflict.

8. *Organize productive committees and task forces.* A primary cause of interrole conflict is that one person tries to do too many things. Increase effectiveness not only by delegating particular responsibilities to others but also by assigning tasks and projects to well-organized committees. Consider how others in the organization might be enlisted to reduce competing demands.

No matter how efficient your use of time management techniques may be, ultimately you can gain control over your commitments and the dysfunction caused by interrole conflict only through reviewing and assessing the personal principles that guide your choices. No one can do everything. At some point you need to decide which involvements are most important, and which ones may be ignored.

Intrareference group conflict is "conflict or disagreement within a reference group in their expectations for the role of the supervisor" (Lipham and Hoeg, 1974, p. 133). The supervisor is "caught in a crossfire." Once again, we might focus on the chairperson of a high school subject department. There may be a dozen or more teachers in the department, some of whom believe that the chair is simply "one of the teachers" who happens to hold a title, and others who may look at the department head as a stock clerk, responsible for doing nothing more than securing materials and equipment for the teachers. Yet another group of teachers may expect direct instructional monitoring from the chair, such as observing teachers in their classrooms. No clear, common vision of the role of the department chair exists, and intrareference group conflict may well be the result.

Interreference group conflict is the "disagreement in two or more (different) reference groups in their expectations" for the role of the supervisor (Lipham and Hoeh, 1974, p. 101). Here, the supervisor is "caught in the middle." A central office supervisor, for example, who visits teachers in schools may be seen by these teachers as a trusted colleague who can help them address their instructional concerns. The same supervisor may be viewed by administrators in the central office as a perfect person to get out into the schools and "get the dirt" on teachers. The supervisor is thus viewed as a potential "snoopervisor" by one group, and a "human relations specialist" by another group. This is a precise example of interreference group conflict.

Conflicts that arise from a supervisor's relationships with groups can be particularly frustrating and damaging to supervisory effectiveness. When groups have differing expectations about how a job will or should be carried out, the conflict is rooted in the perceptions of others; it is beyond the supervisor's immediate control. Nevertheless, some techniques can help reduce the potentially negative consequences of conflicts involving groups.

Many group conflicts can be headed off if jobs are precisely defined before they are begun. What are the formal, stated expectations listed as part of a high school subject department chairperson's position? Is there any suggestion that it is appropriate to be a "gofer?" An instructional leader? Is the job defined so vaguely that such wildly divergent expectations might exist? If so, try to clarify those expectations—and your own—at the outset. For the central office supervisor mentioned above, find out how teachers have traditionally viewed the responsibilities of central office supervisors and ask central office administrators directly about their views concerning proper performance by supervisors.

Group conflict can also be reduced if the individual supervisor has a well-developed concept of what it means to be a supervisor. Again, there is no real substitute for a well-articulated personal philosophy. We can rarely be forced to juggle many competing expectations for a job if we have clearly defined our own role. This personal clarity may have the immediate consequence of angering some people in the organization who do not appreciate the supervisor's self-definition of role. This anger will typically be relatively short-lived, however, and considerably less dysfunctional over time than chronic uncertainty over what is proper behavior in a job.

Role-personality conflict is the "disagreement between the expectations for the role of the . . . [supervisor] and his [or her] personality need-dispositions" (Lipham and Hoeh, 1974, p. 133). Here, recalling the characteristics of Getzels's social systems model is particularly helpful. Figure 11.1 indicates that considerable incongruence can exist between the two elements of role and personality: The job may not fit the person.

Figure 11.1. Illustration of the role-personality conflict shown in the social systems model of Getzels.

Role-personality conflict may be the most frustrating of all, because it suggests that a person has made an error in judgment by selecting the wrong career path. A teacher, for example, decides to leave the classroom for a supervisory or administrative position, based on an assumption of what the role responsibilities of the position will be, only to find out that the assumption was incorrect. We might argue, of course, that the new supervisor can simply return to being a teacher, but going back may be extremely difficult. A teacher who goes into a supervisory position has typically invested a lot of time and money in additional university courses and has moved into a position with greater financial rewards. Turning away from the new status and prestige of a leadership role may be next to impossible—achievable, certainly for some, but hard for most.

Again, there are ways in which the negative impact of this kind of conflict can be reduced. It is most important to pay serious attention to the nature of a position *before* assuming it. We need to question the personal assumptions and review the motivations that underlie a choice of a new job. Are our expectations realistic? Do our assumptions match the actual tasks performed?

Those who are responsible for training people for new roles also have an opportunity—and a responsibility—to acquaint applicants with the realities of their intended positions well in advance of a move. Apprenticeships, training in clinical settings, and numerous other forms of field-based situations help people understand their roles before assuming their new jobs on a full-time basis. Lawyers go through clerkships, and physicians do residencies and clinical internships. In professional education, aspiring teachers must take part in student teaching, and increasingly, future administrators and supervisors engage in internships, planned field experiences, and numerous other activities which allow them to "taste" the new job before coming on board permanently. The primary purpose of these activities is to help people learn how to use certain practical skills that are related to the effective performance of their jobs, but we believe that a second, equally important purpose is fulfilled by a preservice practicum: It allows people to see and try a job in a *low-risk* setting, where no "loss of face" is attached to a decision not to pursue a career, which has been based on actual experience rather than on false expectations. Preservice "tryouts" provide opportunities for people to drop out before experiencing the type of role-personality conflict that damages not only the organization but also the future administrator or supervisor. Those responsible for such programs must emphasize and safeguard their low-risk status, and must condone in nonjudgmental ways the decisions that some participants may make *not* to continue.

Conflict-Handling Styles

We have reviewed techniques for reducing personal conflict and for decreasing potential negative impact on the overall organization. In addition, we would propose that the destructive power of conflict can be reduced by further analysis of the nature of conflict and the ways in which people address conflict situations in their lives.

One of the most frequently employed diagnostic procedures for analyzing organizational conflict is a model that assesses the nature of conflict-handling styles. The model, designed first by Kenneth Thomas (1974), suggests that people react to conflicting settings in one of two basic ways: (1) People deal with conflict assertively, by becoming aggressive about their own needs, rights, and interests; they exercise their own needs above those of others; or (2) people deal with conflict cooperatively, by playing down their own needs and trying to satisfy the concerns of others. Figure 11.2 illustrates how conflicts may be handled along a continuum, from

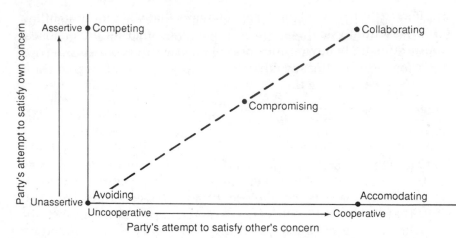

Figure 11.2. Reprinted with permission from NTL Institute, Power and conflict in the student-teacher relationships by D. W. Jamison and K. W. Thomas, p. 326, *Journal of Applied Behavioral Science,* Vol. 10, No. 3, Copyright 1974.

addressing one's own needs to addressing the needs of others.

As the Thomas model suggests, people may engage in behavior of five different types: avoiding, competing, collaborating, accommodating, or compromising. The three points at which there is a balance between equal efforts toward assertiveness and cooperativeness are represented by the points along the doted line in Figure 11.2: avoidance, compromise, and collaboration. Robert Owens (1987) describes these points in the following ways:

Avoidance (low assertiveness and low cooperativeness) suggests withdrawal, peaceful coexistence, and indifference. Avoidance is useful when (a) the latent conflict probably cannot really be resolved ("live with it"), or (b) the issues are not so important to the parties as to require the time and resources to work them out. As Blake and Mouton (1964) pointed out, avoidance can serve as a form of "cease fire." Ultimately, however, this is not a valid way to deal with unresolved conflict; it only serves to suppress conflict momentarily.

Compromise (medium assertiveness and medium cooperativeness) suggests "splitting the difference." Compromise has some elements in common with collaborative problem solving: (a) the parties must be willing to engage in the process; (b) there is some move toward collaboration; and (c) the process is basically conciliatory and not in flagrant conflict with the organization's well-being. Compromising behavior is useful because it does represent an effort to find a set of long-term behaviors that will reduce conflict, but it essentially looks at the parties in conflict as adversaries. Compromising behavior does not move toward resolution; it tries to "keep a lid" on the problem.

Collaboration (high assertiveness and high cooperativeness) suggests that the conflicting parties work together to define their problems and then engage in mutual problem solving. This process requires, first, that parties involved must actively want to use problem-solving techniques and second, that the parties possess (a) the necessary skills for communicating and working in groups, and (b) attitudes that support a climate of openness, trust, and frankness in which to identify and work out problems.

Thomas's model does not provide a prescription to deal with conflict. Indeed, there is no suggestion that one conflict-handling style is necessarily better than others all the time. On the contrary, we believe that the model suggests that a wide range of behaviors may be needed to deal effectively and positively with whatever conflicts arise in the life of the educational supervisor.

Summary

Conflict is a very real—and unavoidable—part of organizational life. We noted that, because conflict is inevitable, supervisors need to know how to *work with* or *reduce* conflict, not how to eliminate it totally from their lives.

We defined conflict as disagreement between two parties. Conflict becomes more intense with the introduction of additional emotional commitment and hostility, so an important supervisory skill is the ability to reduce the *emotional level* in all conflicts. In this chapter we reviewed typical sources and types of conflicts and suggested how each type of conflict might be rendered less harmful. We suggested throughout this discussion that a key element is the supervisor's ability to know his or her personal educational values and philosophy. We concluded with an explanation of Thomas's theoretical model, which was designed to enable us to diagnose the nature of conflict.

Suggested Activities

---

1. Using the list of time-management techniques proposed by Hughes, compile a survey questionnaire and distribute it to a number of administrators in your district. Ask people to check the items that they do exceptionally well and also the items that they do not follow. See if any patterns exist in the responses.

2. Find examples of conflict that are found in the local newspaper over a few days. Classify these conflicts according to the typologies presented in this chapter.

3. Use the concepts found in Thomas's model of conflict-handling styles and ask a group of teachers, supervisors, and administrators to estimate the predominant strategies that they use, according to the model, when faced with conflict in their professional lives. Do the same regarding personal conflicts. Are there differences in how people believe they handle conflict "at work" as contrasted with "at home?"

Cases to Consider

Read each of the cases and consider the following issues:

a. What are the critical issues raised in each case, as they relate to organizational conflict?

b. How does each case relate to the development of proactive supervision?

c. In what ways might you suggest a resolution to the issues raised?

Case 11.1:

How Can I Be Everything?

David Carson was eager to begin his new job as the supervisor of mathematics for the Forest Glen Schools. He had spent nineteen years in the classroom in the district, and as result, he believed he had a handle on what the school system needed to do to bring about needed change in the curriculum. He was looking forward to next Monday when he would walk into the central office and assume his new role.

The only thing that was now bothering David was the feeling he had deep in his mind. He wanted the job as supervisor, but he knew that once he accepted that title, many of his teacher friends would become aloof. He had seen this pattern before: One of the "troops" went into the administration building, but never came back to the rank and file. He was afraid that this new job would make him an outsider forever.

David was also concerned about other aspects of his new job and life. As a classroom teacher, he knew that he would always be home from work at about the same time every day. This was always important because he enjoyed playing with his four daughters, puttering around the house and, in general, being a good family man. His new job would require many evening meetings with curriculum committees, appearances before the school board, and so forth. It also meant that David would have little time to devote to his work at his church on weekends and to his graduate studies at State University. In short, David Carson had achieved a most important milestone in his professional life—prestige and a greatly enhanced salary, but he also started to feel the pressure that would surely accompany his new world. Was it going to be doable? More importantly, would it all be worth the price?

Case 11.2:

But That's Not What Greg Did!

Allison Binder stepped into her new office and was pleased to realize her ambition of several years. She was an elementary school principal. This represented a dream come true for a woman who had spent sixteen years as a classroom teacher and had nearly killed herself by working night and day to complete a graduate degree in educational administration at the local university. She had given up many hours with her three children and husband to finish her graduate studies and complete the requirements for a state administrative certificate. Now she was actually going to be a principal!

She knew that her job at Hawthorne Elementary School would

be challenging. After all, Hawthorne was a relatively poor school in a blue collar district which had clearly seen better days. Fortunately, she was following in the footsteps of a well-respected principal, Greg Spencer, a man who had spent the last five years effecting a strong sense of pride at Hawthorne. Now, being a Hawthorne "Trailblazer" was no longer viewed as being part of a school with no sense of purpose and dignity. Mr. Spencer had made the school orderly; student discipline was the most visible characteristic.

As Allison moved into her office, she noticed that many of Greg's belongings were still there. The bookshelf contained all of his books, for example. Allison noted that every item on the shelf dealt with some aspect of student discipline and behavior management. She was annoyed that in the middle of her office remained two carrels which had been used to provide space for student in-school discipline suspensions. Greg had taken on the job of serving as the primary disciplinarian for the past five years, and so it was not a surprise that part of his work environment contained the carrels. However, Allison needed the space, and besides, she did not want to begin her new life as a person who only worked with "bad boys and girls." The books were sent to Greg at his new school, and the carrels were sent into storage.

The school year started calmly. After all, the kids at Hawthorne were still used to a setting where no nonsense was allowed, and the teachers were happy to start another year. The teachers barely recognized that Greg had left and that they had a new administrator in the building.

The last week of September started to see a few changes. Mrs. Quincy, a fourth grade teacher with more than twenty years of experience in the classroom, suddenly charged into Allison's office to demand that something be done with "that awful Charlie Fenster." Allison quickly determined that Charlie was a boy who had spent a good part of the last two years as a fixture in Greg's office. He was off and running, trying for a third straight year. Mrs. Quincy made it quite clear that the principal was supposed to do something about Charlie—right now. After Allison had listened to Mrs. Quincy, Allison simply looked at her and asked her what she proposed to do with this student in her class. Allison's question was not what Mrs. Quincy expected. As she turned to go back to her class, she looked the novice principal in the eye and said coldly, "Greg would have taken care of this right now. The other teachers will be very disappointed to know that you're not really one of us. Thanks for nothing, Ms. Binder."

References

Blake, Robert, & Mouton, James (1964). *The managerial grid*. Houston: Gulf Publishing.

Boulding, Kenneth (1962). *Conflict and defense: A general theory*. New York: Harper & Row.

Deutsch, Morton (1973). *The resolution of conflict: Constructive and destructive processes*. New Haven, CT: Yale University Press.

Hughes, Larry W. (1984). Organizing and managing time. In James M. Cooper (Ed.), *Developing skills for instructional supervision*. White Plains, NY: Longman.

Jamison, Larry W., & Thomas, Kenneth W. (1974). Power and conflict in the teacher-student relationship. *Journal of Applied Behavioral Science*, 10(3): 326.

Lipham, James M., & Hoeh, James A. (1974). *The principalship: Foundations and functions*. New York: Harper and Row.

Owens, Robert G. (1987). *Organizational behavior in education* (3rd ed.). Englewood Cliffs, NJ: Prentice-Hall.

Additional Readings

Blake, Robert R., Shepard, Herbert A., & Mouton, Jane S. (1964). *Managing intergroup conflict in industry*. Houston: Gulf Publishing.

Likert, Rensis, & Likert, Jane Gibson (1976). *New ways of managing conflict*. New York: McGraw-Hill.

Thomas, John M., & Bennis, Warren G., (1972). *Management of change and conflict*. Baltimore: Penguin Books.

Working with People
Process, Program, and Evaluation

Much of what educational supervisors do involves organizing, motivating, understanding, evaluating, and planning for instruction. All of these processes imply great understanding of the people with whom the supervisor must work. In Part IV we will discuss strategies for working with teachers, staff, and others who are engaged in or around school settings in order to improve the educational climate and, ultimately, to provide a better education for our children.

12 Working with Groups

We often think of the educational supervisor as working almost exclusively with one-to-one contacts. Up to now in this book, we have emphasized the individualistic dimensions of supervision—the personal action plan, leadership, the need to deal with conflict as an ingredient of individual effectiveness. Proactive supervision places great emphasis on the actions of a single person engaged in shaping a more effective organization. We need to remember, however, that a large proportion of the proactive supervisor's professional life is spent working with, for, and through groups. This reality tends to complicate organizational life—after all, it is easier for most people to work on a one-to-one basis—but there is a compelling need to develop insights into the nature of groups, both as components of larger organizations and as organisms unto themselves.

The purpose of this chapter is to explore the nature of groups, which are the building blocks of organizations. We will examine some alternative definitions of groups and then explore group characteristics and some of the ways in which they can be classified, along with some of the roles and responsibilities within them. We will consider characteristics of group effectiveness and conclude with some specific suggestions about how the analysis of groups may apply to the process of proactive supervision.

Definition of a Group

There are many "bunches" of people in society. Not every one of these may accurately be called a group, however. For our purposes, we will define a group quite simply as a *condition wherein two or more people join together in the pursuit of a common, shared purpose*. The definition is similar to a classic view offered by Michael Olmstead and Paul Hare (1978) in their oft-cited work on the nature of small groups. "A group . . . may be defined as a plurality of individuals who are in contact with one another, who take one another into account, and who are aware of some significant commonality" (p. 51).

We suggest the "commonality" that must knowingly be shared by all members of a group is an overriding sense of *purpose*. Further, the more strongly the purpose is established and accepted by all, the stronger a group will be; it is relatively simple to tear apart a group when its members are uncertain why they have been brought together in the first place.

Groups exist throughout schools and school systems, some strong and some weak. Consequently, educational supervisors need to develop a sensitivity to various kinds of groups. Our definition is simple enough and general enough not to exclude groups currently in place. On the other hand, it provides a distinction between what may legitimately be called a "group" and what are simply "bunches of people," or what sociologists commonly refer to as "collectivities." The key difference is the extent to which there is a clearly identified emphasis on a common purpose. Collectivities can become groups; a number of people who happen to be in the same place at the same time may quickly form a shared identity and purpose. Consider the way in which airline passengers who receive repeated notice that their flight will be delayed begin to form a common purpose of complaining to the airline.

By contrast, groups can also become collectivities as once-shared common visions and purposes diminish. This occurs all too frequently in school settings; a faculty that has existed as a strong and cohesive group for a long time eventually loses its identity and sense of purpose, and finally becomes nothing more than a collection of individual teachers "doing their own thing." This might be caused by some event such as a teachers' strike where half of the staff stays in the classrooms while their colleagues (and former group members) walk on the picket line for several days.

Basic Considerations of Groups

Now that we understand what a group is, we need to explore more specifically its typical characteristics. In the following sections, we review some commonly accepted classifications of groups and then look into the special properties of groups and the behavior of people who belong to them.

Classification of Groups

Researchers have tried to develop classifications for groups as a way to understand some of their essential features. One of the most famous of these efforts is the work of Charles H. Cooley (1909), who noted the existence of *primary* and *secondary* groups.

> By primary groups I mean those characterized by intimate face-to-face association and cooperation. They are primary in several senses, but chiefly in that they are fundamental in forming the social structure and ideals of the individual . . . Primary groups are primary in the sense that they give the individual his earliest and completest experience of social unity, and also in the sense that they do not change in the same degree as more elaborate relations, but form a comparatively permanent source out of which the latter are ever springing . . . (p. 212)

Olmstead and Hare (1978) suggest that primary group members tend to have warm, intimate, and personal ties with one another; family, for instance, is a clear and immediate example of a primary group. However, other primary groups are formed in society when individuals are drawn together in highly personalized settings. What does the effective supervisor need to know about primary groups? First, primary groups are never created artificially; the supervisor cannot create a primary group, regardless of whatever sincere desire exists to knit strong bonds among individuals. Second, primary groups are rarely found in school settings, but supervisors still need to understand how primary groups work because when they do exist, they represent powerful forces that supervisors may use in order to channel organizational energy toward the attainment of organizational goals. Some school faculties have worked together for so long and so well that they have truly become a "family unit," in Cooley's terms. Supervisors who are not sensitive to such a group's strength will soon learn how it may subvert or support their agendas.

The secondary group complements the primary group. Olmstead and Hare (1978) noted:

> Relations among (secondary group) members are "cool," impersonal, rational, contractual, and formal. People participate not as whole personalities but only in delimited and special capacities; the group is not an end in itself but a means to other ends. (p. 94)

Most groups are best classified as secondary groups. They gather to achieve some identified objective, and then they dissolve. They are not necessarily unfriendly, but members do not serve together as a matter of personal survival or fulfillment. People drift in and out according to highly personalized agendas. Most school faculties form secondary groups. Cordial and professional relations exist among group members, but the absence or presence of the group has little long-term effect on the satisfaction of the needs of its members. What are the implications for supervisory practice? When working with most school staffs, supervisors need to recognize that, while teachers may show commitment to the goals of the group, they probably have stronger allegiances to other groups outside the school.

Groups may also be classified as *formal* or *informal*. Formal groups tend to be sanctioned by a particular organization to carry out one or more of the functions and responsibilities associated with that organization. In a school setting, examples of such formal groups might be the school board, the district administrative team, the local teachers' association, the PTA, a subject department in a high school, or the National Honor Society chapter. Membership requirements to such groups tend to be firmly established and identified, and it is relatively simple to determine who is and who is not a member. English teachers are not members of the math department; building principals are not members of the school board. In addition, the practices and behaviors of these groups tend to be well defined and openly shared with members. Formal groups, then, display generally clear standards of both membership and behavior.

Informal groups tend to rise out of the immediate needs or interests of individuals. Such groups may or may not have titles. They are fairly constant in their lack of precision concerning membership; people tend to drop in and out of informal groups in somewhat erratic and unpredictable fashion. Finally, informal groups tend to have short lives due to the frequency with which their purposes and memberships fluctuate. Some informal groups do last for several years, but typically "here today, gone tomorrow" is an appropriate description of their fundamental character.

For the researcher, formal groups are easier to identify, name, track, and analyze than are informal groups; as a result, we know a considerable amount about the nature of formal groups but little about the precise nature of informal groups as organizational components. This lack of knowledge could be disastrous for the practitioner of supervision, of course. Imagine a situation where the supervisor assumes that a formal, recognized group (e.g., a subject department in a high school) is the only group with an interest or stake in the subject area it represents. Unhappily, such assumptions are frequently made, rarely correct, and the source of almost inevitable conflict. The effective proactive supervisor is aware of who really has control of and interest in issues, not merely what responsibilities are listed on a formal organizational chart.

W. J. Reddin (1967) attempted to classify groups and suggested that the following eight types might appear at any time in any organization:

1. *Problem-solving group.* All group members demonstrate deep commitment to each other and to finding best solutions for whatever problems they face. This group, generally viewed as the most desirable, is high in both *interaction* effectiveness and *task* effectiveness.

2. *Production group.* This group is focused on accomplishing the task, with little or no emphasis on the needs of group members as people.

3. *Creative group.* The purpose of this group is the development of group members and their ideas. It is generally seen as a direct reverse of the production group, because little emphasis is placed on the completion of identified tasks.

4. *Procedural group.* Group members are more interested in complying with stated guidelines and procedures established for group behavior than in successfully completing a task, promoting individual growth and development, or keeping the group together in a harmonious fashion. Meeting the letter of the law and following regulations are critical goals for the group.

5. *Mixed group.* This group's behavior is typified by compromise and vacillation between hurting the feelings of group members and getting a particular job done. As a consequence, such a group achieves very little in terms of either interaction or task effectiveness.

6. *Fight group.* This group exhibits almost constant conflict, argument, and disagreement, usually based on the personalities and values of individual group members rather than the substantive issues being considered by the group. Virtually nothing of substance is accomplished.

7. *Dependent group.* Similar to the creative group, this group focuses almost exclusively on achieving interaction effectiveness. The critical difference here is that discussion regarding even slightly controversial substantive issues is altogether

avoided. Only issues on which the group is likely to achieve immediate and absolute agreement are ever introduced. This lack of risk taking can quickly lead to group stagnation.

8. *Group in flight*. This group barely qualifies for the title of group in the first place. Members are not committed to any common purposes, and there is a general corresponding avoidance of participation.

We make two observations concerning Reddin's group types. First, despite the images evoked by the descriptions of the eight classifications, we do not mean to suggest that under *all* conditions in *all* organizations one group is necessarily and absolutely "better" than another. The problem-solving group may appear more efficient, and being a member of such a group might seem more appealing than participating in a fight group: But there are times when disagreement might actually be more appropriate.

Second, we note that these descriptions are not absolutes. Any grouping of people, formal or informal, goes through a periodic metamorphosis from one classification to another. For example, a board of education might be characterized as a fight group because its members frequently engage in much conflict and petty bickering. That same group of five or seven people, however, might quickly close ranks and become a productive group or a problem-solving group when forced to deal with a commonly felt challenge. Personal feuds might cease when the district needs to develop a policy concerning AIDS, for instance. By contrast, a subject department might normally appear to be a creative group, devoting most of its attention to providing for the continuing professional development of faculty, but the introduction of certain issues that require absolute adherence to district policy might turn the department into a procedural group. Any group, regardless of its longstanding tradition of behavior, will become an in-flight group if it loses its common purpose and shared vision.

Properties of Groups

Regardless of classification, any group tends over time to take on *characteristics* similar to those of individual human beings. We can talk about "mature" groups, for example, in the same way we discuss mature people. A mature group might be one that has been in existence for a long time, or one that demonstrates particularly well reasoned patterns of behavior, or both. An "immature" group, by contrast, might be a newly formed or particularly unpredictable one. As in the case with a person, of course, a group may become increasingly mature over time.

Groups also possess certain identifiable value orientations, defined as *norms*. In some groups it is acceptable for members to be argumentative; in others, members tend to nod and agree with everyone else. All members of some groups are expected to go to lunch together each day and behave as a unit at all times in public; other groups allow members to act independently and expect them to come together only on rare occasions. At some universities, for example, professors come to the office every day and keep consistent and predictable hours for student contact. In other institutions, the norm calls for faculty to "stay home and write and rarely come into the office at all." A supervisor's ability or inability to identify accurately the existing norms of a particular group may be particularly relevant to successful interaction. If the supervisor assumes that a particular group is loosely knit and that one person speaks for everyone, the implications he or she draws from a conversation with that person may be absolutely false.

Group value patterns may shift rapidly at times, or they may not move for many years. The introduction of new members to a particular group may or may not have an immediate and observable impact on established beliefs and practices. As Dorian Cartwright and Alvin Zander (1960) explained in their classic analysis, *Group Dynamics*, group norms or standards must be understood both by members of the group and also by outsiders (such as educational supervisors) who work with the group for at least three reasons:

1. Norms are consciously utilized by the group to help accomplish its goals;

2. The norms are part of an ongoing self-maintenance process used by groups;

3. Norms help group members develop validity or "reality" for their opinions.

In addition to human characteristics and norms, groups possess a third common property: They always have *leaders*, or at least exhibit the pretense of something termed leadership. Herbert Thelen (1954) considered leadership as the ultimate focusing agent of groups: "Leadership is a set of functions through which the group coordinates the efforts of individuals" (p. 6). The implication is that groups would fail to exist if no evidence of leadership toward goal achievement were present.

Although formal leaders may be designated to serve groups, informal leaders may emerge in these same groups. This phenomenon begs the attention of the practitioner of proactive supervision. Consider, for example, a high school foreign language department with a formally named chair, but one or more teachers who wield such influence over their colleagues' behavior that they also enjoy group leadership status. In fact, these individuals may have considerably more power then does the formal leader. An outsider must then be extremely sensitive to the nuances of leadership—to the fact that the formal leader may not really be in charge, or that multiple sources of leadership may exist in the group. Determining who is really in charge is a critical task in any organization, whether it is a huge city school system or a four-member teaching team in an elementary school. Assuming that the person at the top of an organizational chart is always in fact in charge could be an embarrassing error that makes effective contact and working relations with a group nearly impossible to achieve.

Properties of People in Groups

People in groups tend to play identifiable roles. Kenneth Benne and Paul Sheats (1948) noted three major classifications for group roles:

1. *Group task roles.* Individuals primarily concerned with "getting the job done" usually take on one of the following roles: initiator-contributor—developing and contributing new ideas or in some other way stimulating the group to undertake new directions; information-seeker; information-giver; coordinator; energizer; procedural technician; or recorder.

2. *Group maintenance roles.* People particularly attentive to the business of "keeping the group together" take on the following specific roles: gatekeeper—helping to keep the group "on track" and to move forward toward the achievement of group objectives; or clarifier—helping group members understand what is being said or what is happening in the group.

3. *Individual roles.* People interested almost exclusively in their own self-interests take on these roles, including that of blocker (preventing the group from making progress toward its goals).

People in groups often play different roles in different groups or even shift roles over time in the same group. Most people belong to many different groups in society. Teachers may also be members of church congregations, parent associations, bridge clubs, community councils, and other formal and informal groups, some of which may have been around for years, and others of which have popped up overnight to accomplish a specific task. The same person may serve one group as a compromiser (group maintenance role), trying to help others achieve agreement and harmony, and another as an information-giver (group task role), committed to helping the group become productive. That same person may leave a meeting of either group and move directly to a third setting where he or she is so "tuned out" from the proceedings that personal recognition-seeking (individual role) is the only identifiable activity. We all serve as members of many groups, and we perform different functions at different times. This complex shifting of roles occurs for many reasons, including the extent to which a person feels personal affiliation with other group members, the level of acceptance demonstrated by the group members toward the individual, and external issues such as the amount of time available to participate in group activities.

The fact that people serve different roles in different groups has certain serious implications for the supervisor. A teacher, for example, might be perceived by the supervisor as "out of it" and uninvolved in the larger group of the school faculty, and the supervisor might make assumptions about how that teacher might be treated (or ignored) based on those assumptions. This same teacher might play an entirely different, more positive (and more powerful) role as a member of a curriculum committee, however. A supervisor who is unaware of the frequency with which such shifts occur runs the risk of ignoring a very important contributor to the goals of the organization.

Group Effectiveness

As we have noted throughout this chapter, an important responsibility for the effective supervisor is to analyze the ways in which groups function. Supervisors also play a critical role in assisting existing or newly created groups to find ways to attain their goals.

For Bernard Bass (1960), group effectiveness consists of two characteristics: *interaction* effectiveness and *task* effectiveness. Interaction effectiveness measures the extent to which group activities reduce conflict and enhance harmony within the membership of the group. A group is "good" or effective to the degree that positive, open, and friendly interaction occurs among its members. Task effectiveness measures the extent to which group activities promote, define, clarify, pursue, and accomplish the group's goals. Groups high in task effectiveness focus on "getting the job done," almost at any cost.

The balance between these two dimensions of group effectiveness determines a group's success. A *creative* or even *dependent* group may result from too high emphasis on interaction effectiveness; while these designations are acceptable for brief periods and may even be highly desirable under specific conditions, groups generally cannot exist merely to satisfy members' personal needs for affiliation with others. On the other hand, a group too high in task orientation might be cold and impersonal and ultimately might become an absolute productive or even fight group, with members so caught up in doing a job that they ignore the needs of others. Effective groups balance an appropriate amount of both interaction and task effectiveness.

The relevance of this is important for the practitioner of school supervision. Educational personnel and classroom teachers, in particular, tend to look at the quality of interaction patterns as a primary indicator of the effectiveness of a particular group. If things are going smoothly and no one is angry with anyone else, then the group is likely to be judged "good," and no further effort is made to analyze the group. Whenever complacency sets in, whenever a school staff, task force committee, subject department, or any other group is satisfied with positive interaction as an outcome, the effective supervisor prods the group by demanding to see outcomes and concrete results of the group effort. The operating theme needs to be, "So you like each other, but what have you *done*?"

On the other hand, supervisors must be able and willing to introduce strategies for more positive interactions among group members when the group becomes so blindly focused on accomplishing a given task that all concern for other group members is ignored. The danger in totally ignoring interpersonal needs is that, once a given task is completed, group members will rarely want to work together again toward achieving another goal. Such situations often occur in fields, such as engineering, where a high premium is placed, perhaps stereotypically, on purely technological skills. Engineers may join forces to design a new product and focus so intensely on the project that no one on the team gets to know anyone else. When the job is done, which may take months, the group immediately dissolves, although maintenance of the group might be useful for the organization to deal with future tasks. This phenomenon was witnessed many times in the aerospace industry during the early 1970s, where engineers who had worked side by side to send the first astronauts to the moon found that they knew little about their co-workers when the mission was accomplished. Great isolation and, frequently, personal depression resulted. The educational supervisor facing such a situation must encourage group members to look at each other as people from time to time so that task accomplishment does not block communication.

Applications to Supervision

Supervisors need to understand how groups function, for they will spend a considerable part of their professional lives working with people in this social pattern. Effective supervisors are able to do a number of things regarding groups:

1. *Supervisors know how to "read" groups.* Educational supervisory personnel often work with the teaching staffs of many different schools or even school districts, with frequent shifting from one setting to another and many brief encounters with different groups. The luxury of spending a lot of time getting to know groups is rarely available. Supervisors need to be able to determine quickly whether a group is truly a group or merely a collectivity, who is really in charge, whether a group is too high in either task orientation or interaction orientation, and who is playing what role for what purpose in the group.

2. *Supervisors need to create groups.* Supervisors often need to pull together people to engage in a particular task—an ad hoc committee to review the math curriculum for the district, for example. The first responsibility in creating a group is to establish as firmly as possible the purpose for convening it. If members don't understand the group's purpose from the outset, little further progress will be possible.

3. *Supervisors need to keep groups going.* Once a group has been fashioned from a collectivity, the supervisor needs to keep it going toward its shared purpose. As we noted earlier, groups will periodically shift from problem solving to groups in flight. When this happens, and group members lose their focus on the group's goals, the supervisor must intervene to reestablish the structure and purpose of the group. As a result, knowledge of group process skills and group developmental activities is extremely useful for effective school supervision.

Summary

In this chapter we emphasized the vital need for educational supervisors to understand groups. The reason for this emphasis is that groups are found everywhere in the supervisor's environment—in administrative and teaching teams, subject departments, school boards, parent associations, student councils. Dozens of formal and informal staff groups are constantly forming and reforming. Supervisors must recognize the powerful potential that groups have for contributing to the school environment and the quality of organizational life in schools. Supervisors who do not recognize this potential will rarely be entirely effective.

We began by considering some definitions of groups and settled on one that defines a group as two or more people assembled for a common, shared purpose. We considered some basic features of groups and of the people who form their memberships, and we reviewed the concepts inherent in group effectiveness. Finally, we listed some essential skills needed by any supervisor who wishes to build and maintain groups that will effectively aid in reaching the stated goals and objectives of the school in which the groups operate.

Suggested Activities
---

1. Analyze any group (at a school or in your personal life) of which you are a member to determine if it conforms to the characteristics of groups described throughout this chapter.

2. Interview a practicing supervisor or administrator to determine the numbers and types of groups with which he or she interacts during a typical work week. To what extent are the various types of groups listed by Reddin present in this listing?

Cases to Consider

Read each of the following cases and consider these issues:

a. What are the critical issues raised in each of case, as they relate to the need to understand the nature and behavior of groups?

b. How does each case relate to the development of the concept of proactive supervision?

c. In what ways might you suggest a resolution to the issues raised?

Case 12.1:

That's Not on the Organizational Chart

Nick Kelly was happy about his new job as the supervisor of science in the Marytown Schools. He had been recognized as a very effective high school teacher and science department chair in the neighboring Frankton school district. He was excited about the opportunity to work in the very well respected Marytown school system and about the considerable raise in his salary. In addition, he didn't even have to move. His office in the Marytown central administration building would be closer to his house than Frankton Senior High was.

The first few months on the job were extremely pleasant. Nick's main duty consisted of meeting the building principals, teachers, and department chairs at all the secondary schools in the district. He also found that he enjoyed the lifestyle of the central office. No bells and no set time schedule meant that he could actually control his daily work life. He even had the luxury of making phone calls during the day and going to the restroom whenever he needed!

Nick knew that one of the reasons he was hired was to assist the Marytown Schools in the implementation of a new biology program as part of the high school science curriculum. He recalled that this was a painful process when he was back at Frankton; the new program involved a lot of team teaching, and teachers were not always extremely happy about what that would mean for them. Fortunately, he had heard that the same frustrations were not likely to occur in Marytown. The department chairs at the three high schools had already met with him to assure him that they were highly supportive of the new program and curriculum.

Nick was extremely confident on the morning of the day he was to have an extensive discussion with the teachers in all of the high schools regarding the new biology program. After all, he was "one of them" just a few months ago, and he knew that the department chairs were on his side. He had positive feelings as he stepped into the meeting with the teachers at Marsh High School, but felt a sudden chill in the air shortly after being introduced to the teachers. This was going to be a long meeting, a long day, and a longer year.

Case 12.2:

We're All One Big Happy Famly

"You'll think you've died and gone to heaven. They're really like one big happy family here at Wood Valley Elementary." Those were the words that Emily Schaeffer, the assistant superintendent, shared with Mark Richards, the new principal. Mark was an experienced classroom teacher who was now taking on his first principalship after nearly twenty years in the classroom. He was glad to hear Emily's description, but he was a bit skeptical, based on his experiences of the past.

The year began quietly enough. Despite being the "new kid on the block," Mark did not feel as if the teachers had any resentment toward him. All encounters were cordial. Nevertheless, he didn't feel the kind of enthusiasm and "family atmosphere" described by Emily during the job interview.

Wood Valley was a small school. There were only fifteen full-time teachers, one custodian, a part-time librarian, and a secretary. In one sense, it was a great place to begin a career as a school administrator, but Mark quickly realized that smallness could also be a restriction. Everybody knew everything about everyone else in the school. Every time Mark walked into a teachers' meeting, he felt as if he was intruding on a private set of conversations. He began to understand that each teacher played a certain role, too. Bobbi Wilcox, for example, would always challenge Mark at some point during the meeting. It didn't seem to matter if the issue was a weather report or the new district policy on outcomes-based education; Bobbi would object. And Chuck Starr, a third grade teacher for many years, would always agree with whatever Mark said. Anne Forsyth would say nothing, but her first grade teaching partner, Sylvia Martinez, would always explain what Anne's silence meant on every issue. It was truly an amazing set of behaviors that reminded Mark of the family dinners he had attended after he had moved out of his parents' home when the best part of the meal was not the dessert, but the opportunity to head back to his own place.

References

Bass, Bernard M. (1960). *Leadership, psychology, and organizational behavior*. New York: Harper & Row.

Benne, Kenneth D., & Sheats, Paul (1948, Spring). Functional roles of group members. *Journal of Social Issues*. 4(2): 41–49.

Cartwright, Dorian, & Zander, Alvin (Eds.) (1960). *Group dynamics: Research and theory* (2nd ed.). Evanston, IL: Harper & Row.

Cooley, Charles H. (1909). *Social organization*. New York: Scribner.

Olmstead, Michael S., & Hare, A. Paul (1978). *The small group* (2nd ed.). New York: Random House.

Reddin, W. J. (1967). *Team analysis*. Fredericton, New Brunswick: Managerial Effectiveness.

Thelen, Herbert A. (1954). *Dynamics of groups at work*. Chicago: University of Chicago Press.

13 Teachers and Supervisors

In 1974, Arthur Blumberg published his analysis of the nature of working relationships between teachers and supervisors. The title of his book, *Supervisors and Teachers: A Private Cold War*, is a straightforward description of a truly unfortunate reality in the area of supervisory practice. The relationships that have existed historically between teachers and supervisors in schools have tended to be negative or, at best, typified by uneasy tolerance. There are many probable explanations for this. The earliest historical image of supervision as a form of inspection has provided a powerful continuing image of how supervisors view teachers (i.e., mostly as incompetent and untrustworthy employees). More recently, the lack of friendly relations between supervisors and teachers has been reinforced by collective bargaining agreements outlining clear distinctions between "labor" and "management." General societal factors also play a role. For example, recent financial constraints and enrollment declines in several districts have raised anxieties for many teachers, creating automatic adversarial relationships in many school systems, and demands for greater accountability placed on social institutions including schools have further widened the gulf between teachers and supervisors. However, we must recognize that whatever the unique emphasis on the differences between teachers and formal school leaders is, this emphasis cannot ultimately prevent cooperation. Supervisors must develop strategies that permit teachers, supervisors, administrators, and other school staff members to work together as colleagues. Collaboration is clearly an essential ingredient in proactive supervision.

In this chapter, we look at the world of teachers and teaching to

244

provide you with some insights into the professional life of the people with whom you work. Virtually everyone who serves as a supervisor or school administrator has spent some time as a classroom teacher. Living the life of a teacher, however, does not necessarily provide the kind of understanding required by a *leader*, who must appreciate those subtle features of the world of teaching that will affect the relationships between supervisors and teachers. This chapter does not deal with analyses of the activity of teaching per se; the emphasis here is on who teachers and supervisors *are*, not *what* teachers *do*.

To begin, we review some characteristics of teachers identified by numerous demographic studies and emphasize particularly those factors identified as having attracted people to the field of teaching in the first place. Finally, we examine the professional environment in which teachers work each day and examine strategies that may be employed by supervisors who are interested in finding more effective ways to work with teachers as colleagues. Our goal in each section is to provide insights into the nature of the life of teachers—the people who ultimately "make things happen" for children in schools.

Who Are Teachers?

Researchers have tried to answer this question many times over the years. A classic, frequently cited review of the characteristics of teachers was undertaken by Willard Waller (1932) in *The Sociology of Teaching*. Blanche Geer (1965) and Dan Lortie (1975) carried out similar investigations. These reviews and many others have yielded remarkably similar observations, all of which are relevant for those who invest a large amount of time and energy in working with teachers.

First, research has shown that teachers have often come from humble backgrounds. Historically, teachers have been depicted as representatives of the middle class or even lower middle class, but these designations are generally meaningless in present-day society; what is clear is that the majority of teachers today do not come from wealthy families.

Unsurprisingly, then, a large number of teachers have tradition-ally represented the first generation of college graduates in their families. Some evidence suggests that this is changing, as more people in society are able to pursue university studies. Nevertheless, while physicians and attorneys often come from families with a long tradition of access to higher education, the same cannot generally be said of teachers. Lortie (1975) suggested that controlled access to a college education is an important characteristic of teaching. Socioeconomic constraints typically reduce the range of career choices available to those who eventually become teachers.

> Few occupations are in as good a position [as teaching] to take advantage of socioeconomic constraints which limit access to college education. The system of colleges for teacher training turns out to be more than an institution of socialization—it also recruits. One finds a kind of "entrapment" as such colleges draw in students of limited opportunity whose initial interest in teaching is low. (p. 48)

Lortie's observation suggests not only that teachers often come from families who cannot be selective when it comes to choosing a college, but that this characteristic serves to entice people into teaching in the first place. People from humble family backgrounds who can barely pay for post- secondary education are still able to look at teaching as a realistic professional goal. The extent of the financial outlay required for medical school or law school prevents most people from pursuing those careers. Professional preparation for teachers, however, is widely (and relatively inexpensively) available at public universities; any student can aspire to a teaching career.

Not surprisingly, this observation has come to play in the controversies surrounding recent reports such as that of the Holmes Group (1986), which recommended an increase in status and professionalism for teachers, often including postbaccalaureate education. Critics of such proposals have suggested that efforts to force prospective teachers to undergo significantly greater formal preservice preparation at the university level will automatically close access to teaching to those who are unable to afford such advanced training. An old saying suggests that the only career options available to inner-city residents are those of "preacher, teacher, or social worker." Clearly this situation is changing, but the fact remains that teaching is more easily accessible to more people than most other professional roles.

Research also suggests that teachers select the classroom as a career goal fairly early in their lives. Women tend to identify teaching as a likely career while still in elementary school, and men at least tentatively choose teaching by the time they leave high school. More recent surveys suggest that current teachers made these choices at a slightly later point in their lives, in part, no doubt, because women now have more options available than they once did. Evidence continues to suggest, however, that people who select teaching as a career tend to stay with it, even if that choice is made slightly later in their lives than it once was.

Profiles of the teaching field in the United States, which have been developed by state departments of education and professional organizations substantiate several other enduring characteristics:

1. *Racial characteristics*. Overwhelmingly, teachers in the United States are white, although the 10 percent of teachers who are African Americans come closer to proportionately equalling the nearly 12 percent of the general population that is also African American. Of black teachers, more are female than male. Further, members of nonwhite or nonblack racial groups make up even smaller percentages of the classroom teacher population in this country.

2. *Sex distributions*. Nearly 60 percent of American teachers are female. In addition, there is a historic tendency for the percentage of male teachers to increase at the more advanced levels of schooling (i.e., as one moves from elementary to secondary schools).

3. *Age levels and teaching experience*. Although recent shortages of teachers in some areas of the country and in some subject specializations are beginning to have an impact on the average ages and years of experience of teachers in the United States, those averages continue to rise. In 1911, the average age of teachers was twenty-four, and the typical teacher had five years' experience in the classroom (Rodgers, 1976). Today, the typical teacher is slightly more than thirty-five years old, with approximately eleven years' experience. These figures are higher in larger school systems where there is traditionally less turnover among teachers.

These assorted characteristics provide us with an interesting snapshot of the people who work in America's classrooms. Teachers do not generally come from wealthy backgrounds, and they often work hard to pay for the education that will enable them to reach their goal—a goal that they have typically established early in life. The "typical" teacher is white, female, in her mid-thirties, and usually married. For the most part, teachers come from a relatively homogeneous pool of people; they tend to be more similar to, rather than dissimilar from, one another. Research also suggests that most are politically conservative but are registered Democrats and are regular churchgoing Protestants. Obviously, these "typical" traits go only a short way toward providing valid and usable data to educational leaders; they tend to obscure the huge numbers of teachers who are liberal Republicans (or even unaffiliated anarchists), who are Jewish, Catholic, or atheist, or who are unmarried—in other words, those who deviate from the statistical norm. To some extent, however, such research-based information can inform supervisory "hunches" or guesses about how teachers may react in different situations.

Why Do People Become Teachers?

Once again, we can identify patterns in response to this question, but the differences that exist are as wide-ranging as the number of people who are teaching. Still, supervisors can gather some insights into the nature of teachers from the research available.

An extremely important study of why people become teachers was carried out by Dan Lortie during the 1960s and reported in his work, *Schoolteacher* published in 1975. In this work, five major attractors to teaching were identified:

1. *The interpersonal theme.* Perhaps the response most frequently given by teachers to questions about their selection of teaching as a career is based on their desire for continuing contact with young people. Other professions also enable people to maintain steady interactions with the young, but as Lortie (1975) noted, "Unlike other major middle-class occupations involving children, such as pediatric nursing and some kinds of social work, teaching provides the opportunity to work with children who are neither ill nor especially disadvantaged" (p. 27).

2. *The service theme.* Some people select careers in teaching because they believe that, by devoting their lives to this work, they can fulfill some special mission in society. The aspiring teacher is taking on a responsibility to provide service by engaging in what many societies in the world view as an honored (if not well-compensated) vocation.

3. *The continuation theme.* Some individuals become teachers because they were comfortable as students sheltered in the world of schools. As they grew, they continued to be so attached to life in schools that they could not bear to leave that environment. Lortie summarized this phenomenon by

observing, "Some [teachers] said they 'liked school' and wanted to work in that setting; others mentioned school-linked pursuits and the difficulty of engaging in outside educational institutions" (Lortie, 1975, p. 29). Supervisors should recognize that those who choose to teach because they wish to stay where they are comfortable are unlikely to engage in activities that will change the status quo of schools.

4. *Material benefits.* Surprisingly (especially to many teachers!), Lortie discovered that some people selected teaching for reasons of money, prestige, and employment security. This seems to contradict the general perception that teachers suffer anxiety because they lack these amenities, and this anxiety may be a feature in the attitudes of teachers now in the classroom. We can understand how "material benefits" can motivate some people to become teachers if we recall the reviews of background characteristics which show that teachers traditionally come from relatively modest socio-economic groups and that they are often among the first members of their families to attend college. The opportunity for a steady, relatively secure job that offers a beginning salary near $20,000 for ten months of work might indeed be appealing. For many, an entry-level teaching job may be considerably more lucrative than a job that was held by a parent for many years. In short, entering teachers may sometimes look at their chosen profession not as one that "pays well" but rather as one that "pays better." The more time spent as a teacher, however, the less powerful this motivation becomes; teachers see neighbors and friends who are able to move toward financial rewards at a rate and level far beyond that available to a classroom teacher.

5. *Time compatibility theme.* An old saying suggests that the three best reasons for teaching are "June, July, and August." Lortie and many others have found considerable truth in this notion: People find teaching appealing because it does, when compared to most professions, offer more time for the pursuit of other interests and responsibilities. Although teachers may not always admit it, teaching appeals to many because one can go to work each day before most people get on the freeways, arrive home or go shopping before others, and enjoy protracted vacation periods throughout the year. Teaching has traditionally been recognized as a job that allows women to raise children while working full time: They can put their own

kids on a school bus in the morning, go to work, and return home at about the same time their children do.

Lortie's study of the reasons why people enter teaching remains a milestone for those interested in learning more about the realities of classroom life. Other motivating factors have been identified in other studies. David Armstrong, Kenneth Henson, and Thomas Savage (1981) suggested the following ideas:

1. *Nice working conditions.* Many teachers comment on their favorable impression of both the physical environments in which they work and the kinds of people with whom they work. In addition, teaching is perceived as a job that allows for considerable personal autonomy, which many people find appealing.

2. *Lack of routine.* Teachers who have had to depend on other jobs at other points in their lives, often jobs with great monotony attached, find teaching refreshingly unpredictable. Students are diverse, and as a result, each day in the classroom is to some extent different. In addition, teachers control some of what they do in their classes and can "program in" variety. Finally, the typical school year "life cycle" contains many natural peaks and valleys, sometimes predictable and sometimes not.

3. *Importance of teaching.* As Lortie's "service" theme suggests, some teachers do what they do because they view their work as a way to transmit culture to new generations, provide information to youngsters, serve as positive role models, and achieve scores of other important goals that will ultimately serve as part of the design of a more positive society.

4. *Excitement of learning.* Many teachers were eager learners when they were in school, and they continue to believe in the fundamental value of learning. Many recall their own sense of excitement as they acquired new knowledge, and they assume that, as teachers, they will stimulate the same learning and bring about similar challenges for new generations of students.

What other answers can we provide to the question, "Why do people teach?" In addition to this list of attractors, Lortie also identified certain other factors that tend to direct people toward teaching. He noted, for example, that people become teachers because they have identified with a significant teacher at some point in their schooling, because someone in their family had been a teacher, through "labelling" by significant others, or because aspirations to some other field (e.g., medicine or engineering) have been blocked by socioeconomic or other factors. What is remarkable in most reviews of the reasons people become teachers is the virtual absence of what might be called "negative influences." For example, virtually no teachers suggested that their own early experience with poor teachers had compelled them to try to "do something better" than they had seen in classrooms. This contrasts, incidentally, with the reasons often cited by teachers who move into administration or supervision that they can do better than what they see others do.

What Do Teachers Do?

Teachers instruct students. In addition, they learn how to function in an environment with some very special characteristics— characteristics that need to be appreciated by supervisors who wish to find strategies for enhancing the effectiveness of school staff.

The General Nature of Teaching

Anne Lieberman and Lynne Miller (1984) carried out an extensive analysis of what teachers' lives are like, and they considered the implications of these "social realities" of teaching for supervisors and others who wish to improve the quality of educational practice. Lieberman and Miller noted that to understand teaching we must appreciate the nature of teaching; thus, they identified the following features:

1. *Teaching style is highly personalized.* Because teachers must constantly work with large groups of students (often twenty-five or more at a time) but must do so in as individualized a fashion as possible, teachers often develop highly personalized and idiosyncratic strategies. When teachers settle upon their own ways of dealing with the contradiction between group and individual, they become quite defensive and even militant regarding their strategies. What they do often becomes "the right way" to do things.

2. *Teachers' rewards are derived primarily from students.* Lieberman and Miller (1984) noted that "the greatest satisfaction for a teacher is the feeling of being rewarded by one's students" (p. 2), and these rewards tend to be found in

the affirmation by students that a teacher is doing his or her job properly. Students show support for teachers by participating in class discussions, studying more diligently for exams, or volunteering for special projects. Teachers recognize these behaviors and perceive them as signs that what they are doing is "good." Importantly, teachers usually do not perceive this type of approval as a regular part of their contact with peers, superiors, or other colleagues in their schools.

3. *Teachers are uncertain of the link between their teaching and student learning.* Teaching is much like "shooting an arrow into the air, never knowing where it might fall." Most teachers find continually frustrating their inability to see the ultimate effects of their work. Not knowing "the final product" has for years been one of the most often discussed limitations on teaching as a profession. Teachers never really know whether what they did in the past, or what they are doing now, will serve any truly positive purposes. According to Lieberman and Miller, "A teacher does his or her best, develops curricula, tries new approaches, works with individuals and groups, and yet never knows for sure what are the effects. One hopes the children will get it, but one is never sure. A teacher operates out of a kind of blind faith" (Lieberman and Miller, 1984, p. 3). This characteristic of the workaday life of teachers was also recognized by Joseph McDonald (1992) and Alan Tom (1984) who, in developing the metaphor of "teaching as a moral craft" made the following observation:

> This . . . [relationship of] teacher behavior to student learning . . . is what I call the billiard ball hypothesis. The pool player (teacher) aims the cue ball (his behavior) so that it will strike the target billiard ball (the student) at exactly the right angle to cause the billiard ball to go into a pocket (the achievement of what the student is supposed to learn). (p. 55)

This analogy is flawed only in its failure to recognize the teachers' traditional perception that, just as they strike cue to ball, they are forced to turn their backs to the table and never see if they have met their targets.

4. *The knowledge base of teaching is weak.* Teaching, unlike medicine, law, engineering, and other professions, possesses no unified and highly codified body of knowledge that provides clear direction to those who wish to "cover what is important." Educators agree neither on what should be taught nor on what methods should be used to teach. Is Louis Rubin (1985) correct

in emphasizing the "artistry of teaching?" Are the "scientific" approaches to the analysis of teaching more appropriate? This general lack of consensus concerning the content and techniques of "good" teaching provides a weak knowledge base that in turn impacts negatively on the sense of commitment felt by many classroom teachers. Often, this perception by teachers that they do not have the requisite knowledge needed to have a positive effect on learners must be overturned by a belief in themselves. As McDonald (1992) noted, "Whenever they teach, teachers must to some extent swallow the uncertainty they feel, believe wholeheartedly in their goals and efforts, even though riddled by doubt" (p. 6).

5. *The goals of teaching are vague and often conflicting.* What are teachers "supposed" to do? Disseminate a fixed body of knowledge? Entertain? Babysit? The lack of clarity about a teacher's true role leaves teachers with no true understanding of a single purpose. "When all goals are addressed, no goals are met" (p. 5). Lieberman and Miller noted that, because of this vagueness and corresponding conflict concerning purpose, "individual teachers make their own translations of [educational] policy and this contributes directly to the lack of consensus often found in schools" (pp. 5–6).

6. *Control norms are seen as necessary features of schools.* Educational goals are not always clear, but the end result usually is: Schools are expected to exercise strong control over young people to guarantee that social order is maintained. This educational "fact of life" is demonstrated almost daily in schools where parents, other teachers, supervisors, administrators, and often students hold in high esteem those teachers who "keep the kids in line." By contrast, the inability to "control" students is typically viewed as a serious flaw in a teacher's professional performance, and is in fact often seen as grounds for dismissal.

7. *Professional support is lacking.* Paradoxically, although contact between people (i.e., teacher-to-student, student-to-teacher) is a primary feature of teaching, teachers are remarkably isolated as workers, particularly from colleagues and other adults. This lack of collegiality usually begins with the first classroom assignment, where "rookie" teachers who have just completed student teaching are thrown into the same setting—with the same expectations for professional performance—as considerably more experienced teachers.

Stuart Palonsky left his position as a university professor to spend two years teaching social studies in a suburban high school. In his analysis of that experience, *900 Shows a Year: A Look at Teaching from a Teacher's Side of the Desk* (1986), Palonsky provides a poignant description of the loneliness of teaching:

> Lou was one of the teachers who had retreated from the mainstream of the faculty, and he defined teaching personally and in isolation from other teachers. At one time he had played tennis with Sal, and he considered one of the French teachers to be his friend, but these teachers were now married, and Lou was divorced. He claimed he no longer maintained social relationships with his colleagues, and he rarely went to faculty parties. From our conversations, it did not appear that he liked most of the other teachers, but he enjoyed teaching. (p. 17)

Examples such as this are not unique in the world of schools. It is not uncommon to meet teachers with many years of professional experience who have little contact with colleagues. It is not unusual to hear of cases where no one other than administrators or supervisors have ever seen other teachers teach, and even more remarkable and equally lamentable are cases where teachers have never had the opportunity to ever see another teacher teach.

8. *Teaching is an art.* Lieberman and Miller concluded their analysis by suggesting that the efforts to turn teaching into a precise science are wrong. ". . . in the long haul, more artistry . . . is practical as teachers struggle to adjust and readjust, to make routines, and establish patterns, only to recast what has been done in a new form to meet a new need or a new vision. Teachers are best viewed as craftspeople; the reality of teaching is of a craft learned on the job" (p. 94). Efforts to make teachers conform to behavioral patterns that represent "good teaching" are usually futile because artists struggle to express their uniqueness and resist conformity.

Louis Rubin (1985) provided the following list of features normally associated with "artistic teaching." Artistic teachers:

- Focus on the subtleties of teaching—how to motivate, pace, and control students—which invigorate basic instructional methods and subject matter;

- Improvise tactics for reaching objectives and overcoming difficulties and are creative, inventive, and know how to "go with the flow;"

- Take advantage of unexpected opportunities to clarify ideas and reinforce concepts;
- Make use of their intuition and hunches to guide the modification of routine practices and have a special sense of when to throw away the lesson plan;
- Set high expectations for themselves and their students;
- Find the most efficient and expedient ways of getting things done;
- Are good storytellers and are sensitive enough to know how to use temporary digressions on related topics to enrich lessons, stimulate interest, and increase student involvement;
- Base their control of learning activities on the nature of student behavior;
- Take great pride in what they do and in the achievements of their students;
- Concentrate on a few dominant goals that they believe to be central to their purpose as teachers;
- Respect their own convictions;
- Devote as much time as possible to whatever they enjoy most in teaching.

The "Dailiness" of Teaching

Supervisors and others who wish to understand the teacher's world must appreciate, according to Lieberman and Miller, not only its general nature but also its "dailiness."

Predictability. They note, for example, that the life of a teacher follows certain predictable cycles and rhythms—as anyone who has spent time around schools will agree. Teachers begin each day at the same time, drink coffee at the same time, even go to the bathroom at the same time each day; all of these activities are regulated by the need to provide "coverage" for students. "For the majority of the day, they are bound in space and time. In most instances, teachers need the permission of the principal to leave the building during school hours" (Lieberman and Miller, 1984, p. 5). The predictable rhythms of each school day occur in the context of the larger rhythms of the school year. Every day, the excitement of September slows until the holiday season begins at the end of October and continues through early January. Winter doldrums set in, and days are dull until March or April when spring break occurs. The weeks after that vacation are almost always marked by the increasing fatigue of teachers who are trying to cope with the decreasing interest of students, who are working toward summer vacation. This same cycle is found in virtually every school—public and private, elementary or secondary—across the nation each year, and significant change in its peaks and valleys are highly unlikely.

Interestingly, the observable and predictable nature of the normal teaching day and year contradicts the perception of many entering teachers that the classroom represents a way of life free from routine and predictability. Teacher-student relationships within individual classrooms may indeed be unpredictable, but that spontaneity is not characteristic of the large portion of teachers' lives. Palonsky provides a noteworthy portrait of the "grind" of daily school life:

> For the most part, one day blended with the next, with little to distinguish one from another. I saw the same students at the same time every day. I passed the same teachers and students in the hall at the same place and time every day, said hello to the same people as often as a dozen times a day, but rarely engaged any of them in more substantive conversation. I arrived at school at the same time; I ate lunch at the same time; and I left at the same time every day. (1986, pp. 81–82)

Regulation.   The daily world of teachers is also a highly regulated one. Some of these rules are the official policies and procedures specified by the local board of education. In this sense, teaching differs little from other occupations where employees are told when to start work, how many sick days are available, how to complete certain forms, or what to do in dealing with emergencies or crises.

Other "rules" associated with teaching, as Lieberman and Miller point out, are not formal policies but rather informal norms that serve to govern the behavior of classroom instructors. Two important norms are the expectations that teachers will always be practical and private.

Teachers are expected to be *practical* and to find immediately applicable solutions to whatever problems they encounter in the classroom; perhaps the worst thing that can be said about an educator's ideas are that they are "theoretical." As we noted in chapter 2, most educators have a strong antitheoretical bias, which both results from and reinforces the practicality norms found in schools. Most research on how this norm has developed over time might help us determine if teachers tend to be people who view the world in concrete and nonabstract terms in the first place, or if the nature of teaching forces its practitioners to look for practical solutions rather than theoretical concepts.

Privacy in teaching "means not sharing experiences about teaching, about classes, about students, about perceptions" (Lieberman and Miller, 1984, p. 8). Unfortunately, and contrary to Shirley Heck's and Ray Williams's (1984) description of teachers as colleagues, the norm of collegiality has traditionally been absent from most schools; teachers, of course, lose a great deal by not having the opportunity to share their work with co-workers. The strong pull toward privacy derives at least in part from the fact that unobserved people cannot be judged as incompetent. Do teachers believe that they have had inadequate preservice preparation for their roles and consequently spend a large percentage of their professional lives trying to disguise what they fear are inadequacies in their performance? Or do teachers close their classroom doors to others because they have learned, either through personal experience or via oral tradition, that anyone who sees you teach will inevitably find fault? In short, is retreat to privacy one of the strategies employed as part of Arthur Blumberg's (1974) "cold war"?

Limitation of contact.   Interactions among teachers are typically quite limited. The vast majority of interpersonal contact experienced by classroom teachers is with children, not with co-workers. The average time teachers spend with adults each day is usually less than half an hour. If teachers are asked to indicate the amount of time spent in "meaningful talk" with adults (i.e., not lounge chit-chat concerning yesterday's football game, upcoming television shows, or momentary gossip, for example), the average amount of time is generally reduced. Teachers live in a world surrounded by people, but with little opportunity for discussion with peers. A serious consequence of this lack of contact is that teachers assigned to classes with difficult students live daily lives filled to overflowing with negative human contacts. No wonder that teachers at the end of many school days have trouble being animated in discussions about new approaches to math instruction, team leaning, or performance-based education. As Lieberman and Miller (1984) suggest:

> For most teachers in most schools, teaching is indeed a lonely enterprise. With so many people engaged in so common a mission in so compact a space and time, it is perhaps the greatest irony—and the greatest tragedy of teaching—that so much is carried on in self-imposed and professionally sanctioned isolation. (p. 11)

So What Can Supervisors Do?

Throughout this chapter we have painted a picture of the lives of teachers and the business of teaching which, while fairly accurate, is also quite depressing. We could add other brush strokes to this picture, including the "poor public image and inadequate public appreciation" (Geer, 1965, p. 6) faced by teachers and the general lack of esteem, low pay, and social status afforded them. These latter characteristics clearly have a serious impact on the daily lives of educators, but we do not dwell on them because a supervisor, proactive or otherwise, can do little to modify societal perceptions which have emerged over time. A supervisor alone cannot make the public value teachers and pay them more money. A supervisor can, however, modify some of the daily conditions faced by teachers. Even if changes are not always possible, the supervisor who wants to make a difference will be more effective and more readily accepted by teachers if he or she appreciates the characteristics of teachers' lives.

Daniel Duke's thoughtful analysis, entitled *Teaching: An Imperiled Profession* (1984), found many of the same conditions we discussed above not only to be present but also likely to cause paralysis in both teachers and schools. In Duke's view, the greatest constraints to teacher effectiveness are rooted in *ambiguity* (teachers must cope constantly with the lack of rationality and consensus surrounding goals and purposes) and *insecurity* (teachers face instability in jobs, social status, assignments, and finance). In response to these issues, Duke proposed a reconceptualization of teaching as a profession, guided by the following "What if . . ." considerations:

1. *What if we stopped acting as if there were one best type of teacher and began valuing diversity?* If educators believe firmly that schools must deal with the uniqueness of individual children as learners, why do many of these same educators assume comparability and similarity among all teachers? Particular teachers might best be matched with particular students who possess the same values and perspectives on learning. Policy makers and other educational leaders need to acknowledge the true value of individual differences among teachers. Some supervisors spend as much time learning about the individual qualities of the teachers with whom they work as they do watching those same teachers perform in classrooms

and thus more completely appreciate the differences and richness of their teaching staff.

2. *What if teaching were reconceptualized as a set of complex technical skills, including problem solving, hypothesis testing, decision making, information processing, logical analysis, and resource allocation?* We need to define teaching as an activity that requires as much skill as it does pure emotional commitment to children. The latter is clearly important, but society values skills and knowledge as well as commitment. Some supervisors work with their teaching staffs to design and implement action-research projects that not only increase the knowledge base regarding local school issues but also promote thinking and acting by teachers that go beyond traditional patterns and limitations.

3. *What if teachers would be regarded as discipline-based scholars as well as instructors?* Would not the consequence of this reconceptualization of teaching further enhance the strength and positive image of the profession? As Duke noted, "such action might also help bridge the gulf now separating public school teachers from professors" (Duke, 1984, p. 139). In this way, too, teachers may become more actively involved as researchers in their professional fields.

4. *What if part of a teacher's time was spent teaching adults?* One of the traditional limitations on the teaching profession is that teachers work only with children. Could we not redefine schools as total learning communities, where adults and younger people come together on occasion to partake in mutual learning experiences? Such a setting would be consistent with the desirable behaviors of effective organizations described by Peter Senge in his book, *The Fifth Discipline* (1990). Further, teachers might then be seen not only as true specialists with important bodies of knowledge, but also as possessors of special skills for disseminating that knowledge.

5. *What if students came to school with questions and teachers helped them find answers?* Would not such a turnaround in traditional student-teacher roles decrease the familiar patterns of passive learning now found in most schools? Can teachers be viewed increasingly as facilitators of the learning process for students, rather than providers of all knowledge to students? Such a pattern might be an important step toward the goal of making students control their own learning.

6. *What if teachers at age fifty-five did not have to perform the same functions that teachers perform at twenty-two?* Is it not reasonable to assume that some teachers do some tasks better when they are younger, and others have different insights when they are older? In most schools, a beginning teacher is as likely to be assigned an Algebra I class as a thirty-year veteran. Interchangeability of teaching assignments (and teachers) is a time-honored tradition in schools growing out of the Scientific Management era of the early 1900s, but some creative placement of teachers might benefit the quality of interactions between students and teachers and might also serve to make teachers more satisfied with their professional status. Increasingly, supervisors are aware of the particular needs of adults as learners at different times during their lives and realize that beginning teachers and experienced teachers are not the same.

Duke's suggestions are a good way to begin the process of thinking about ways in which the teaching profession might be changed over time. There are also some very concrete and immediate things that supervisors and administrators may do on a daily basis to enhance the quality of teachers' work life in schools.

First, supervisors and administrators must find ways of restructuring teachers' daily schedules so that more prolonged, if not more frequent, contact is possible among the adults on the school staff. At present, teaching assignments were almost universally constructed in ways that make contact impossible; teachers see colleagues only during the mad dash that usually represents a "daily duty-free lunch period." Prep times, when provided, are rarely arranged so that teams of teachers can get together. In many schools, duty assignments appear more highly valued than opportunities for communication and professional dialogue among peers.

Second, supervisors should examine those factors that attract teachers to the field and use that information in promoting a more effective learning environment. What we are suggesting here is that supervisors can structure some elements of the teacher's world so that the factors that attracted teachers to the field in the first place are more evident. As we noted earlier in this chapter, one of the strongest drawing points to teaching for many people is the opportunity to have contact with students. In reality, however, a teacher's life is often filled with so many administrative responsibilities that the ability to spend much meaningful time with young people is severely constrained. We believe that supervisors who can find ways of cleaning administrative tasks off teachers' desks would go far toward encouraging those teachers to feel much happier about their jobs; the long-term result of this satisfaction would be improved teaching and greater student learning. This same strategy may not work for all teachers, but the same basic premise—that supervisors need to become aware of teachers' real characteristics and concerns—is always an effective way for supervisory and administrative personnel to work with staff.

Finally, supervisors and administrators who are intent upon getting better performance from teachers need to spend time analyzing any conflict with teachers that is linked only to the nature of the roles rather than to the people who fulfill these roles. At many times in the life of an organization, people will not get along, but these times should not be based solely or even largely on job titles. Supervisors and teachers do not have to live in a state of constant war, cold or otherwise.

Summary

In this chapter we reviewed the world of teaching and teachers as it relates to the responsibilities of the proactive supervisor. We began by looking at who teachers are and noting that, for the most part, those of us who have spent time in the classroom are more similar than not, in terms of our socioeconomic backgrounds, value orientations, and stated reasons for having gone into teaching in the first place. Next, we reviewed the general characteristics of the life of a teacher, including isolation from one's colleagues and other adults and the expectation that teachers will enforce certain norms not always supported in their own minds. Finally, we considered some of the ways in which supervisors or administrators can increase their sensitivity toward the realities of teaching in order to enhance the quality of the teaching-learning process in their schools.

Suggested Activities

1. Conduct a series of brief interviews with a group of teachers to determine such information as their backgrounds, reasons for becoming teachers, and reasons for continuing in the

classroom. Compare your findings to those presented in this chapter concerning the characteristics of teachers. What generalizations can you make from the similarities and differences found?

2. Using the features of the lives of teachers described by Lieberman and Miller, construct a survey instrument and ask that a group of teachers in your school or district respond in terms of their agreement or disagreement with the views of the authors. Are teachers, for example, as lonely in their work as suggested?

3. Review the propositions for improvement listed by Daniel Duke with two or three practicing administrators or supervisors to determine if they have any concrete suggestions for ways in which those strategies for improvement might be implemented in their schools or districts.

Cases to Consider

Read each of the following cases and consider these issues:

a. What are the critical issues raised in each case, as they relate to an analysis of teachers and their work environment?

b. How does each group relate to the development of the concept of proactive supervision?

c. In what ways might you suggest a resolution to the issues raised?

Case 13.1:

Why Aren't They Interested?

Jack Charles had just taken the principalship at Halsted Middle School, one of three middle schools in the Georgetown Schools. This was to be his second principalship. He had spent five very successful years as the administrator of the Daley Intermediate School on the other side of Georgetown.

While at Daley, Jack had developed a positive reputation as a very effective manager. He had taken a school with high student absentee rates and teachers with low morale to a point where it was apparent that things had been totally reversed. Jack's former school was now recognized as a model of positive change. When it was clear that Daley was well on its way to success, Jack decided it was time to move on and seek new challenges. Thus, he applied for the opening at Halsted. Because of his previous work at Daley, Jack Charles was an easy choice as the new principal. The school board and superintendent were confident that, if Jack Charles was able to improve a school with the past bad reputation of Daley, he would do an even better job with the highly experienced, child-centered teachers at Halsted.

One of the reasons for such a significant change at Daley, Jack believed, was that he was successful in getting a lot of involvement and participation from the teaching staff, a group described by many to be totally disconnected from their students and the school over the past several years. At Halsted, Jack was looking forward to the immediate implementation of many new instructional practices, such as team teaching and cooperative learning. Although he had heard the stories about how committed the teachers at Halsted were, he felt that a successful change would be possible only if he could get his teachers involved with the new practices that he was promoting. As he planned for the next school year, teacher involvement was the last thing that Jack worried about. He assumed that, while it was critical, it would be simple to achieve. After all, Jack's predecessor had missed a great opportunity for years; he had rarely asked his staff for input on major issues, despite the fact that the teachers were recognized across the district as outstanding educators. Clarence Stevens, the previous Halsted principal, was a nice person who firmly believed that he was most effective in making certain that "teachers teach while administrators administer."

Jack was really excited about how this year would progress. He was now about to lead his first full faculty meeting where the topic would be how to encourage all teachers to become leaders and seize every moment for true empowerment.

As Jack made his plans for sharing his vision with the teachers, he shared his agenda with his assistant principal, Sarah Lowe. She had fifteen years of experience at Halsted, both as an administrator and teacher. "Jack," she said. "I like your idea of promoting greater involvement by teachers, but get ready for a room full of silence when you start talking that way. It just won't work here at Halsted."

Case 13.2

This Isn't What We Do Around Here!

The board of education of the Lake County Schools had no choice. Due to the fact that the voters would not approve a tax bill increase on real estate to finance the construction of new schools along with the tremendous increase in numbers of residents in the county, there would have to be some significant changes in the ways in which schools were operated. The schools were overcrowded, but there was no immediate hope that money would be found to build any new school buildings. The board acted: Next year, the elementary schools of Lake County would be operated on a year-round basis. Students would go to school for nine weeks in a row, take three weeks off, and so on throughout the year. Teachers' schedules would be readjusted so that no one would be working for more than 190 days each year, the same number of days that had been required of teachers in Lake County for many years.

The school board braced for tremendous community anger at the new plan. After all, they had heard that similar year-round school plans around the nation had met with strong resistance by parents who objected to such major changes in their family schedules. Surprisingly, however, Lake County was different. In fact, mail received by the board ran almost three-to-one in favor of the new plan, and even the *Lake County Express* ran a lengthy editorial supporting the board and its new policy, calling it "one of the first examples we've seen in forward thinking, efficient management of public resources around here in many years."

The switch to year-round schools seemed to be a smooth transition. Everything appeared to be ready for implementation for the next school year. No negative comments had been heard from teachers or any other employees in the district, until the meeting that the Lake County Education Association called with the board.

"What are we doing around here with this year-round stuff?" asked Tim Hess the vice president of LCEA. "We are going to have to change everything that we do in our classes. The kids will suffer from the fact that the whole school year will be changed around."

Similar comments were heard from nearly every one of the teachers who presented their views to the board that evening. It was clear that the teachers were not comfortable with this new approach to schooling. For the most part, the arguments made centered around the notion that the children would suffer because they would not be able to adjust to the new schedule.

The board was now faced with the prospect of very unhappy teachers being expected to carry out a very new approach to the school year. They asked Dr. Corwin, the superintendent, to analyze the situation and present a recommendation at the next school board executive session.

References

Armstrong, David G., Henson, Kenneth T., & Savage, Tom V. (1981). *Education: An introduction.* New York: Macmillan.

Blumberg, Arthur (1974). *Supervisors and teachers: A private cold war.* Boston: Allyn and Bacon.

Duke, Daniel L. (1984). *Teaching: An imperiled profession.* Albany: State University of New York Press.

Geer, Blanche (1965). Teaching. In Sils, E. (Ed.), *International encyclopedia of the social sciences.* New York: Free Press.

Heck, Shirley F., & Williams, C. Ray (1984). *The complex roles of the teacher: An ecological perspective.* New York: Teachers College Press.

The Holmes Group (1986). *Tomorrow's teachers: A report of the Holmes Group.* East Lansing, MI: The Holmes Group.

Lieberman, Ann, & Miller, Lynne (1984). *Teachers, their world, and their work: Implications for school improvement.* Alexandria, VA: Association for Supervision and Curriculum Development.

Lortie, Dan C. (1975). *Schoolteacher.* Chicago: University of Chicago Press.

McDonald, Joseph P. (1992). *Teaching: Making sense of an uncertain craft.* New York: Teachers College Press.

Palonsky, Stuart B. (1966). *900 shows a year: A look at teaching from a teacher's side of the desk.* New York: Random House.

Rodgers, Frederick A. (1976). Past and future of teaching: You've come a long way. *Educational Leadership,* 34:97–99.

Rubin, Louis J. (1985). *Artistry in teaching.* New York: Random House.

Senge, Peter (1990). *The fifth discipline.* New York: Doubleday.

Tom, Alan R. (1984). *Teaching as a moral craft.* White Plains, NY: Longman.

Waller, Willard (1932). *The sociology of teaching.* New York: Russell and Russell.

Additional Readings

Ashton-Warner, Sylvia (1963). *Teacher.* New York: Simon and Schuster.

Cherniss, C. (1980). *Professional burnout in human service organizations.* New York: Praeger.

Goodlad, John. (1984). *A place called school*. New York: McGraw-Hill.

Jackson, Philip W. (1968). *Life in classrooms*. New York: Holt, Rinehart, and Winston.

Kidder, Tracy (1989). *Among schoolchildren*. Boston: Houghton Mifflin.

Lieberman, Ann (Ed.) (1990). *Building a professional culture in schools*. New York: Teachers College Press.

Lightfoot, Sarah L. (1983). *The good high school: Portraits of character and culture*. New York: Basic Books.

McPherson, G. (1972). *Small town teacher*. Cambridge: Harvard University Press.

Rosenholtz, Susan J. (1989). *Teachers' workplace: The social organization of schools*. White Plains, NY: Longman.

Sarason, Seymour (1982). *The culture of the school and the problems of change* (2nd ed.). Boston: Allyn and Bacon.

14 Curriculum Development

Throughout the earlier chapters of this book, we described the ways in which supervisory personnel might improve overall organizational performance by becoming involved in many aspects of organizational life. For example, we talked about the need to examine the nature of leadership, motivation, and the structure of organizations. In each case, we have highlighted the fact that, contrary to many traditional images of educational supervision, an effective and proactive supervisor is involved with a wide variety of issues in a school or school district.

In this chapter, we return to a description of supervisory practice in more conventional terms by discussing how educational supervisors might be active in the development and oversight of the school's curriculum. We begin by presenting alternative definitions of the term "curriculum" to guide you in formulating your own definition. We believe that an individual's personal definition of this term will shape his or her involvement with curriculum development and evaluation. Next, we discuss three stages of curriculum development which, when each is properly carried out, will yield effective results. Particular attention will be directed toward the ways in which the proactive supervisor provides leadership and includes everyone who will be involved in the initial planning and implementation stages of the curriculum development. Finally, we talk about some of the key issues and problems associated with the evaluation and assessment of the curriculum after it has been established.

Alternative Definitions of Curriculum

Our purpose is not to engage in lengthy philosophical treatments of the nature of curriculum. We are not, therefore, proposing that the effective educational supervisor possess a strong foundation in alternative curriculum *theories*. Nevertheless, we believe that proactive supervisors or administrators must come to grips with some critical issues which may serve to shape their behavioral patterns as they appropriately assess whether teachers have taught effectively or whether students have learned any worthwhile body of knowledge. Too often, there is an assumption that the curricular role of the educational leader is simply to oversee that what others (i.e., the local school board, the state department of education, etc.) have determined to be the substance of instruction for local districts and schools is, in fact, the curriculum.

For our purposes, we will define "curriculum" in very simple terms: *"what" schools and individual teachers choose to do in their encounters with children.* Although that definition sounds simple enough, it implies an important delimitation on curriculum development. By specifying that curriculum involves a choice by schools and teachers, we have stated that curriculum represents the product of conscious efforts to include information and experiences that should be acquired by learners. Further, we have taken a stance that suggests educational curriculum is somehow bounded by the planned activities provided specifically by "teachers" or "teaching institutions."

By contrast, it would also be possible to take a much more inclusive view of curriculum. For example, curriculum might be viewed as everything that learners acquire, whether through planned or unplanned events. In this view, students learn not only the content of courses in schools and the products of teachers' lesson planning, but from all they experience on a daily basis— their encounters to and from school each day, the content of television programs and newspapers, and interaction with peers. We do not deny that the power of such events and materials are powerful determinants of the total formation of young people. In fact, we doubt seriously that any child is not influenced considerably by after-school television, perhaps more than by what his or her teachers have tried to share for six or seven hours during that same day. We also know that daily home life is a critical influence upon the development of that child; what is absorbed in life's events is a form of curriculum, whether planned or not.

The alternative perspectives of curriculum must be addressed by every individual serving as an educational leader. Each person must make a conscious decision about incorporating appropriate definitions and must determine the purpose of the curriculum, its scope, and perhaps, its ideal sequence. These issues will not be settled here in absolute terms, any more than they have been settled since the publication of Franklin Bobbitt's classic work, *The Curriculum* (1918) or with other works such as John Dewey's *The Sources of a Science of Education* (1929), Henry Harap's *The Technique of Curriculum Making* (1928), and Ralph Tyler's *Basic Principles of Curriculum and Instruction* (1950). We wish only to signal that, before an individual can be expected to become involved with the responsibility of planning, implementing, and evaluating a school's curriculum, he or she must think about what that means in personal terms. If the curriculum is viewed in narrow terms (i.e., incorporating only a few learning orientations), the supervisor or administrator takes on curriculum development duties which might be very narrowly determined. An inclusive perspective of curriculum would call for educational leaders to assume greater responsibility for all the things that students might learn in and away from school by designing the curriculum to incorporate everyday experiences. We take no stance regarding which perspective is correct. We only call this issue to the attention of those who aspire to hold roles of leadership in school settings. It is a critical "plank" in an educational platform.

While our intent is not to provide any single definition of curriculum which would be appropriate for all practitioners, we do believe that a conceptual framework might be helpful as people go about deciding what to teach, to whom, and for what purposes. Elliot Eisner (1985), for example, offers the following five alternative orientations to curriculum:

1. *Development of cognitive processes.* "In this view, the major functions of the school are (1) to help children learn how to learn and (2) to provide them with the opportunities to use and strengthen the variety of intellectual facilities that they possess" (Eisner, 1985, p. 62).

2. *Academic rationalism.* The orientation of the school must be to foster intellectual growth through the rigorous study of challenging issues.

3. *Personal relevance.* The curriculum is a personal quest for individual meaning. The school makes a wide variety of stimuli possible so that learners can select a relevant path.

4. *Social adaptation and social reconstruction.* The content of schooling is derived from an analysis of issues that are to be faced in "real-life" by each learner.

5. *Curriculum as technology.* ". . . conceives of curriculum planning as being essentially a technical undertaking, a question of relating means to ends once the ends have been formulated. The central problem of the technological orientation to curriculum is not to question ends but rather to operationalize them through statements that are references to observable behavior" (Eisner, 1985, p. 79).

William Schubert (1986) offers three differing perspectives on alternative visions of curriculum:

- *Intellectual traditionalist*—subject-oriented, disciplined approaches to what is to be taught, consistent, perhaps with Eisner's first two orientations noted earlier

- *Experientialist*—promotes the learner's constant acquisition of knowledge through a variety of planned and unplanned events and appears most related to Eisner's concept of the curriculum as a form of finding personal relevance

- *Social behaviorist*—holds that it is legitimate to construct patterns of desirable social behavior on the part of learners, consistent with Eisner's social adaptation and reconstruction views

Other perspectives and frameworks are found in abundance in the literature associated with curriculum theory and curriculum development. Perhaps the classic framework which has guided so much thinking in this field over the past half century is the work of Ralph Tyler (1950) who proposed that three data sources must be consulted in making decisions about curriculum development: society, the student, and the nature of the subject matter. Whatever framework might be reviewed, however, we note that the primary work of the educational supervisor or administrator is not to engage in philosophical discussions of what factors should be considered, but how to enact a plan which exposes students in some meaningful way to a body of knowledge that will promote personal growth and development. We leave the determination of which perspectives and orientations to use to each of you as you proceed through the development of your personal platform statement.

Making the Curriculum Happen in Schools

The educational leader must, above all, be a practitioner of curriculum. That is, it is not sufficient for the supervisor or administrator to ponder theoretical perspectives. Once the decision has been made to identify one or another orientation to what should be learned, the real work of putting that "what" into place must be carried out. In this section, we offer a strategy that may be followed by the proactive supervisor as he or she proceeds with the business of moving forward with curriculum development at the local school level. In very simple terms, we divide this process into three phases, namely initial planning, implementation, and evaluation. Our focus here is not on theoretical or philosophical issues but on practical issues that might guide local school leaders in their work.

Initial Planning

To the extent that it may be possible for the educational supervisor or administrator to become involved with the broad, creative process of planning a curriculum (a starting point where ideas are generated, assimilated, and assessed), we suggest that the following steps be consulted:

1. *Scan the nature of the environment for curriculum develop-ment.* Here, the role of the supervisor might be to review the three possible sources of curriculum—the nature of society, the nature of students, and the nature of the subject matter itself—identified by Tyler (1950). It is the role of the educational leader not to change any of these variables, but rather, appreciate the realities found in each one and lead the curriculum in the proper direction. For example, efforts to develop a high-powered college prep curriculum will not likely lead to a high degree of success in communities where the students' and parents' prevailing goals and objectives are not necessarily directed toward the completion of a college or university degree. Devising a curriculum with a strong emphasis on the study of classics, therefore, might be a less-than-productive activity.

   The same concerns might also be voiced with regard to the need for effective supervisors and administrators to take stock of the nature of learners served by their schools or school districts. We are not suggesting that effective curriculum development must be based on simply maintaining the status quo with regard to learning objectives. We are concerned, however, with the temptation to project unrealistic expectations about what students can achieve. The accurate assessment of student abilities should be considered when developing curriculum.

Finally, we recommend that supervisors or administrators examine the nature of the subject matter to be included in the planned curriculum. For example, there are some subjects which need to be learned in a relatively sequenced fashion. Mathematics and foreign languages might be in this category. On the other hand, social studies, for the most part, can be learned in a variety of sequences. We suggest that, during the initial planning of curriculum, the effective supervisor or administrator includes the input of experts from the fields of study that are being reviewed to achieve the maximum benefits from the curriculum.

2. *Develop a strategy to include interested parties.* One of the surest ways to make certain that a curriculum development project will ultimately fail is to avoid including those who might have a stake in the delivery of the curriculum from its initial planning. As a result, effective curriculum leadership necessarily involves making certain that teachers, parents, board members, other citizens, and students themselves be able to voice their opinions regarding the potential value (or lack of value) that might be derived from including certain elements and issues in the established curriculum. Recent cases where local citizens have formed groups to ''bring back the basics'' to schools are often examples of situations where people felt disenfranchised from the planning of curriculum in the past, to the extent that great dissatisfaction was the final result.

3. *Clarify the relationship between learning objectives and the curriculum.* This step has two implications. First, it suggests that there has been a determination of what learning outcomes are to be—for example, teachers might work with parents to identify desired cognitive, affective, or psychomotor outcomes for students at different points in the educational program. On the other hand, learning outcomes can be the result of standards which are identified and mandated by agencies external to the school. Such groups might include the state department of education or even the state legislature. For our purposes here, it makes little difference as to who identifies

what students should learn in school. The simple but critical fact is that, as part of an effective planning process, a conscious decision must be made to find ways of linking those desired outcomes for learners and the way in which the content will be delivered. How does the curriculum match objectives? If, for example, it is decided that an appropriate and important outcome is for learners to demonstrate proficiency in fundamental arithmetic processes, it is likely that corresponding curriculum will include addition, subtraction, multiplication, and division skills.

It is not our purpose here to promote any specific learner outcomes, or even the "best" way to specify those outcomes. For example, we do not wish to take sides in ongoing controversies regarding "outcomes-based education" versus "standards-based education" versus "basic education." Instead, we wish to indicate only that it is absolutely essential to include a clear identification of learning objectives as part of the planning phase for effective curriculum development.

4. *Anticipate political consequences.* Traditionally, educators have insisted that they are somehow involved with a profession that is apolitical. Yet, it is not uncommon to hear teachers lamenting the fact that they could be much more effective if they could only avoid "playing politics." Such a view of the world of schools is unrealistic. In our view, "politics" and political behavior means being able to anticipate and deal with those who may have different opinions or negative feedback and who may apply pressure to achieve *their* goals.

Whether politics *should* be a part of education is not an issue. Politics *is* related to what goes on in schools each day, and those who are involved with curriculum development need to be aware of this fact. If there is an assumption that curriculum can be developed in a type of sterile environment that deals only with higher educational ideals, this assumption will soon lead to frustration and disenchantment. If there is any doubt about this statement, we recommend that one look at virtually any daily newspaper reports of how local community action groups have been successful in intervening in educational reforms because there was a sense that the school had a different agenda than the community.

Proactive leaders may not be able to change the agendas of community interest groups. However, if during the initial planning phase educators are sensitive to the kinds of pressure they are likely to face during the implementation of new educational practices and curricula, they may be able to divert potential criticism and achieve their ultimate goals smoothly and successfully.

Implementation

During this stage, the curriculum is fine-tuned and molded to fit within the specific parameters dictated by the many factors affecting its actual delivery. The steps that need to be followed during this phase of a curriculum process are quite similar to the activities that we suggested as part of initial planning.

1. *Identify relevant parties.* If a new curriculum is to be implemented, either in an individual school or across an entire school district, the first thing that must be done is to identify accurately all those who will likely have a part in or be affected by that implementation process. Who will make use of the new curriculum? In response to this question, it is wise to think more inclusively than exclusively. In other words, changes in the mathematics curriculum of a high school (or for the secondary schools of a district) will not only involve mathematics teachers in the secondary schools, but have a potential impact on the math teachers in the elementary schools of that district. Also, how changes in the curriculum will affect other subject specializations, such as science, must be examined.

   Identifying those who will have a legitimate role in the implementation of any part of a new curriculum is critical and will have an important impact on whether or not implementation efforts are ultimately successful.

2. *Consider resource issues and potential limitations.* The central purpose of the initial planning phase of curriculum development is meant to be very creative and devoid of the type of bounded thinking that takes into account the practical issues of "how much will it cost for our students to learn X?" During the implementation phase, such realistic concerns must be brought back into full view because ignoring the potential costs associated with curricular change (in terms of financial costs as well as human resource expenses) is a certain way of ensuring that change will not occur. Before moving forward with an ambitious agenda related to technology in the curriculum, is it likely that a school system can afford to invest in massive amounts of new computers, video equipment, and so forth? Or, will it be necessary to develop linkages with

agencies outside of the district as a way to provide opportunities for students to have access to the latest technical equipment and expertise needed to develop a new curriculum? Such questions must be addressed as part of the implementation phase.

3. *Identify staff development support that may be needed, and provide it.* The previous step noted that implementation efforts must be guided by a review of resources needed to enhance the likelihood of a new curriculum being adopted. One of the central resources in any school is the staff who will be responsible for carrying out change on a daily basis. Consider, for example, cases where new programs have been initiated in the area of computer technology, perhaps at the insistence of local community groups who fear that their students will fall behind other children if new computer courses are not added to a district's curriculum. The bulk of costs associated with the implementation of these new courses and programs typically involves massive investments in hardware and software, perhaps even capital investments in remodeling large portions of school buildings in order to accommodate additional computers and printers. After such expenses are incurred, little is left in the budget to pay for what may be the single most critical factor associated with effective curriculum adoption, namely the training of teachers and other staff. In short, it makes no sense to invest time and money in new programs if teachers are not prepared to deal with the changes. An effective and ongoing support system and staff development programs must be a major part of any effort to implement new curricular practices in schools.

4. *Maintain effective communications.* We have seen many unfortunate examples of school districts where parents, pupils, staff members, and the community at large are promised that certain outcomes will occur "if only" the district is allowed to engage in one program refinement or another. Often, these promises for improvement are more ambitious than are immediate results. After all, test scores do not leap to appreciably higher levels overnight, and high school drop-out rates are not suddenly eliminated simply because a school system has adopted a new reading program in the elementary schools or has taken steps to implement a new program in computer technology. Thus, if overstated claims are made by district administrators, it is understandable that the public will quickly become disenchanted with educational practices.

While it is certainly not an absolute guarantee to widespread and enduring public support for curricular change, we suggest that a critical part of any program development process is carrying out effective and accurate communication designed to maintain linkages between the schools and the public.

5. *Make certain that accepted practices related to curriculum development are reflected in the implementation plan.* Here we focus on the actual delivery of curriculum, defining what needs to satisfy and the best way to meet those needs. Among the most critical issues that must be incorporated are the following:

   • Traditional curriculum perspectives and foci (e.g., information processing, cognitive development, human development, and constructionism) are addressed.

   • Concepts of curricular scope (How much material should be included, and in what time frame?); sequence (In what order should content be presented?); balance (How much selected subject content should be presented, as compared with other areas?); alignment (How does identified content fit with broader educational goals?); and integration (How does everything fit together?).

   • Matching occurs between curriculum objectives and teaching styles on an ongoing basis.

Evaluation

The final stage in the curriculum development process is to design an evaluation procedure to answer the critical question, "Did what we plan actually work?" Again, a number of important steps are suggested to assist you as you serve as an effective and proactive supervisor.

1. *Return to stated objectives.* The first step in designing an effective assessment or evaluation tool involves a consideration of what the initial goals of the curriculum were to be. It is for this reason that we suggested that during the initial planning phase, the learning objectives and goals to be achieved as a result of changes in the curriculum be stated as clearly as possible. The important question to be answered here is simply, did what we want to happen actually take place? In order to respond, it is essential that "what we wanted to achieve" is fixed in everyone's mind.

2. *Decide the audience for the evaluation.* Will evaluative data regarding a newly implemented curriculum be used to inform teachers and administrators (and other professional staff) who work in the schools on a full-time basis? Or, is the primary audience for the curriculum evaluation to be the school board, a group with an interest in overseeing program efficiency? Perhaps, the real audience for the evaluation will be the general public with an interest in knowing "how the schools are doing" in very general terms.

   Clearly, the audience for the evaluation is a critical issue to be determined by educational leaders. If data is to be made available to professional staff, then it might be assumed that the nature of data can be a bit more technical in nature. School boards, on the other hand, may be filled with very intelligent people, yet they may not be ready to appreciate what is meant by stanines and percentiles on criterion-referenced tests. We have seen too many examples of well-intentioned presentations of curriculum evaluation projects being presented by district officials to bored board members. We advise strongly that thought be put forth regarding the most effective strategy for communicating results with policy makers. Finally, the larger public in the community will likely respond more favorably if they can appreciate how a local district initiative appears to compare with results in other similar districts.

   The critical issue, then, is not changing an evaluation process to get the "right" results, but rather, looking at who will be listening to evaluative data and deciding how to use the data to inform those who will be affected by the outcomes of curricular renewal.

3. *Decide appropriate timelines.* This involves determining what information will be necessary *when.* A common error in many evaluation schemes is to assume that assessment results are needed sooner than when they are actually required. The consequence of such an error may be the collecting and analyzing of data prematurely, a practice which may have serious negative consequences. An example might be a rush to provide data relative to the "success" or "failure" of a new reading program before the next school year so that an adoption decision might be made across all schools in a district. There are numerous unfortunate examples where this type of rush to find the answer has led to school systems making costly errors based on too few cases of new programs being tried for too little time.

4. *Settle on appropriate techniques for obtaining information.*
A common public perception is that all that must be done to
validate a new program is to "try it out" and than "take a look
at test scores to see if the kids have learned any better." While
this approach appears logical, reliance on gains in student
achievement scores is generally an overly simplistic approach
to evaluating new programs, particularly if a new program is
not meant to be directed toward the improvement of student
cognitive achievement alone.

Depending on the nature of the curriculum development
project, a wide array of strategies and techniques may be
selected as part of the evaluation process. Test scores can be
examined, of course, but so can results of locally developed
surveys administered to teachers and others who were involved
with implementing a new curriculum. Parents and students
themselves might also be surveyed to determine their
perceptions regarding new programs and practices. In addition
if long-term data (for example, showing academic trends over
a several-year period) is desired by evaluators of new curricula,
longitudinal evaluations might be developed.

5. *Decide what next steps will be followed after the evaluation.*
The ultimate purpose of an evaluation process is to provide data
to assist people in making further decisions about what was
evaluated. After evaluating any aspect of a planned curriculum,
the issue that needs to be addressed is not simply whether or
not new practices appeared to "work," but what to do as a
consequence of a practice "working" or "not working." For
example, if a new mathematics curriculum is effective in one
school for one year, the decision might be made to implement
the same program districtwide. By contrast, even if a program
does not appear to have achieved its goals and objectives,
evaluative data might prompt decision makers to refine the
new program, or try it as designed but with a different group
of users, or totally reject it for future use.

Summary

In this chapter, we considered some fundamental issues associated
with the analysis of curriculum. Included were some of the
competing philosophical perspectives and definitions which have
tended to surround (and often confine) conversations related to

curriculum for many years. The remainder of the chapter consisted of looking at a number of specific steps that might be followed by educational leaders who would go about the business of planning, implementing, and evaluating programs.

Although the curriculum development process and the role of educational administrators and supervisors are issues which deserve considerably more attention than we are able to give in these few pages, we want to make it clear that certain principles can be consulted on a continuing basis to guide the overall curriculum development process. One of these principles involves making certain that clarity is achieved between purposes and processes. In other words, it is essential that links be established and maintained between the objectives of new programs and the programs themselves. Second, we noted consistently that the development of curricula cannot be done effectively in isolation by professional administrators. We firmly believe that all those who have a stake in a new curriculum for a school or district should be involved in its planning and shaping. Finally, we caution throughout the chapter that decisions made about the adoption of programs, changes in practices, or the rejection of programs cannot be done quickly and without serious thought regarding practical, financial, social, or political consequences. In short, we hold that when appropriate time and effort is spent on curriculum development, the results will be enduring.

Suggested Activities

1. Attend a school board meeting and keep track of the number of decisions that are made concerning the curriculum of the school district. Review minutes and agendas from several recent past meetings of the board and document curricular decisions. Is there any pattern concerning the kinds of issues that are best classified as "curricular" in nature? What percentage of a school board's time is devoted to a review of curriculum?
2. Review any recent adoption of new curricula in a school or district and assess the extent to which the steps discussed in the chapter (initial planning, implementation planning, and evaluating) appeared to have been followed.
3. Interview some teachers and administrators in your school district and ask them to define what they mean by

"curriculum." Do most definitions suggest one or another fundamental philosophy of the inclusiveness of a curriculum. If these various definitions were represented among teachers in a school in which you were a supervisor or administrator, what types of problems might emerge as a result of this diversity of views?

Cases to Consider

Read the two cases and consider the following:

a. What are the critical issues raised in the cases, as they relate to the supervisor or administrator's role in curriculum development?
b. How does each case relate to the development of proactive supervision?
c. In what ways might you suggest a resolution to the issues raised?

Case 14.1:

But the State Requires This Stuff

Amy Hartley was really enthusiastic about her new job as the coordinator for elementary schools in the Porter Grove Schools. She had enjoyed her last ten years as a classroom teacher, but she was ready for a change. Becoming a coordinator would enable her to move out of the classroom into a new leadership role, while at the same time, she could also "keep her hands dirty" with the instructional programs of the district.

Although her new job would include a wide array of assigned activities (including "those duties not specifically identified in the job description, but assigned to her by the Director of Curriculum), she knew that her principal job would be to lead the district in a review of the reading curriculum so that a more effective program could be designed in the future. Amy would be responsible for going out to all of the elementary schools in the district to determine the kinds of changes that teachers wanted to see in the reading curriculum.

She was not quite ready for her first encounter with the teachers in the district. Last Thursday, she met with the staff at Bloomington School. After about twenty minutes, she was truly concerned that she had made a terrible mistake by leaving the classroom for her new role. As soon as she announced to the teachers that she was going to lead a review of the district's reading curriculum, she was met by a series of objections. There was quite a bit of hostility among the teachers, half of whom wanted to know why the district wanted to "disrupt" a very effective program that had worked for years. The other half immediately reminded Amy that there was no sense in trying to change the district curriculum. After all, what was now required of students was consistent with the objectives and material required by "the state curriculum." Why bother trying to change what was already there?

Case 14.2:

I Thought Everybody Bought the Vision

When Jim Snow was recruited to come to the Graystone Local Schools as the new superintendent, the promise was made by the board to support his vision of a more effective instructional program for the children of the district. The way in which Jim wanted to improve education was to initiate a system which focused on students demonstrating the adequacy of learning through the attainment of desired outcomes. In this way, traditional practices of promoting students through the educational program of the system automatically would be a thing of the past. Jim Snow was going to make a difference by instituting a system of outcomes-based education (OBE) in the Graystone Schools. In short, this would improve the quality of education available to students, and it would make Graystone a national model. Some critics immediately noted that Jim Snow would also become considerably more visible as well, and that would enable him to find an even better superintendency in a few years.

The first two years of the new OBE program in Graystone appeared to work pretty well. Teachers modified traditional instructional practices so that greater attention could be placed on individual students and their ability to master learning objectives at their own pace. However, the truth is that many teachers were unhappy with the amount of work they now had to do as students tended to become increasingly "spread out." It was harder to plan and carry out instruction when, at any time, within a group of twenty students there might be ten to fifteen subgroupings of students, each with a different learning objective.

At first, parents also seemed to like Jim's vision of focusing the program on individual student learning rather than traditional lock-step learning. After about two years, however, disenchantment began to appear as many parents were confused about what certain indicators of student progress really meant. Traditional letter grades were no longer being used, and periodic reports sent home contained what many mothers and fathers believed to be very confusing statements regarding how well children had apparently mastered individual learning goals and outcomes. The general view of many was summarized by the statements of one elementary school parent who commented to her principal, "But I really don't know how well my daughter is doing in fourth grade this year if I can't see her progress compared with the rest of her peers."

Outcome-based education in the Graystone Schools was in trouble. In addition to the criticism it had been receiving from parents and from a growing number of teachers, it was now appearing on the agendas of many right-wing conservative groups as an example of how schools were no longer reflecting traditional family values. Even religious fundamentalist groups were pointing to the OBE program as positive proof that public schools were somehow bastions of secularism and immorality.

Jim Snow grew increasingly depressed and now contemplated leaving the superintendency in Graystone. He recently had been contacted about an opening at a nearby educational research center. He truly had a dream and vision concerning how a school district could be restructured—how the curriculum and instructional practices could be made more responsive to the real learning needs of students. Jim had worked so hard to share his vision with the board, administrative team, and teachers. Now, it was all starting to fall apart.

References

Bobbitt, Franklin (1918). *The curriculum*. Boston: Houghton Mifflin.
Dewey, John (1929). *The sources of a science of education*. New York: Horace Liveright.
Eisner, Elliot W. (1985). *The educational imagination* (2nd ed.). New York: Macmillan.

Schubert, William H. (1986). *Curriculum: Perspectives, paradigm, and possibility.* New York: Macmillan.

Tyler, Ralph W. (1950). *Basic principles of curriculum and instruction.* Chicago: University of Chicago Press.

15 Evaluation

Educators often assume that educational supervision is virtually synonymous with evaluation—that supervisors do little more than evaluate teachers and curricular programs, and when we talk about an administrator's supervisory responsibility, we often mean how that administrator goes about evaluating teachers. As we have seen throughout this book, supervision in schools is in fact much more than evaluation. To be sure, a strong relationship exists between supervision and evaluation. Supervisors do have a responsibility to carry out evaluation. In this chapter, however, we will establish a context for the evaluation duties of the proactive educational supervisor. We will see that evaluation is simply one important aspect of the effort to match individual human abilities with organizational goals, objectives, and priorities, and we will try to defuse the notion that educational evaluation automatically and necessarily involves evaluation of the teaching staff for the purpose of making employment decisions.

How does the proactive supervisor carry out evaluation responsibilities? To answer that question, we begin with a brief overview of three different types of evaluation, which we match to common educational foci, or objectives. Then we will look at the most prevalent problems in the area of staff evaluation and conclude with suggestions to supervisors on how to deal with common problems.

Evaluation is simply the process of determining worth—goodness or badness—of something. Blaine Worthen and James Sanders (1987) provided further explanation of the basic concepts of educational evaluation by noting:

... in education, [evaluation] is the formal determination of the quality, effectiveness, or value of a program, product, process, objective, or curriculum. Evaluation uses inquiry and judgment issues, including: (1) determining standards for judging quality and deciding whether those standards should be relative or absolute; (2) collecting relevant information; and (3) applying the standards to determine quality. Evaluation can apply to either current or proposed enterprises. (p. 22)

Evaluation implies the necessary existence and use of a *criterion* or standard to which the "something" being evaluated may be compared to determine *relative worth*. Evaluation thus differs from another term with which it is often confused, namely *assessment*, which describes a process of judging something with or without an external standard or guide. All evaluation, therefore, is a form of assessment, but not all forms of assessment are examples of evaluation. Both organizational evaluation and assessment have basically the same purpose, which is to collect data that people in the organization may use to make decisions. In *educational* evaluation, the purpose is to enable decision makers to determine the value of certain activities and processes used in educating children.

Types of Evaluation

The three basic types of evaluation are diagnostic, formative, and summative.

Diagnostic Evaluation

Diagnostic evaluation is normally used to determine the *beginning* status or condition of something. It is carried out prior to the application of intervention or treatment in order (1) to determine what intervention or treatment may be necessary (as a physician diagnoses an illness to establish needed medical treatment), or (2) to determine the nature of an object or person prior to taking an action that affects the object or person so that after the intervention is completed, its effectiveness can be assessed (as physical scientists note the nature of an environment before they conduct an experiment so they know what effect their experiment has had at its conclusion). Social scientists make use of this same research strategy that, in turn, increases the overall importance of precision in the conduct of diagnostic evaluation.

The educational supervisor frequently uses diagnostic evaluation procedures for both purposes. Supervisors are often called upon to suggest treatments, remedies, or other approaches to "fixing" things that are going wrong in schools. In the same way that a physician uses diagnostic data to determine treatment, then, the supervisor is expected to prescribe solutions on the basis of a diagnosis. Diagnostic evaluation also provides a picture of conditions before anything is done, so the effect of an intervention can be determined. In both cases, care and precision in the diagnosis are vital, or the treatment and/or its results will be in error. A physician must have precise data concerning a patient's weight, heart beat, blood pressure, and so forth before the patient undergoes any medical procedure. Only in this way can the attending physician ascertain if critical aspects of a patient's condition have changed over time. Observed changes provide the diagnostician with a place to look for the cause of the malady.

Similarly, in a school setting, the supervisor can profit considerably from a careful and precise analysis of changes that occur in, for instance, student achievement on some evaluation instrument after a period of instruction. The whole concept of pretest and post-test measurement is based on the logic of using preliminary diagnostic evaluation information as a baseline to examine the net effect of instructional intervention.

Formative Evaluation

Michael Scriven (1967) first distinguished between "formative" and "summative" evaluation, and Worthen and Sanders (1987) noted the importance of keeping these two evaluative forms, which often appear similar in practice, apart.

Worthen and Sanders (1987) point out that "formative evaluation is conducted during the operation of a program to provide program directors evaluative information useful in improving the program" (p. 34). We use formative evaluation to gain intermittent feedback concerning the nature of some activity or practice while it is in progress. Activities can be evaluated many times, and feedback from this kind of evaluation is usually supplied to whoever is in control of the activity being evaluated. Unfortunately, formative evaluation is the least frequently employed of the three forms of evaluation reviewed, and when educational supervisors do employ it, they rarely follow through with appropriate feedback to their teaching staffs. Supervisory and administrative personnel have not traditionally worked with teachers in formative ways.

Formative evaluation implies that the project or activity being reviewed could be improved if properly analyzed and assessed. Business and industry have long used the concept of formative evaluation, particularly in assembly lines. Consider, for example, the supervisor who oversees the production of automobiles. It is this person's responsibility to note minor flaws in the assembly process before the automobile proceeds too far down the line and major revision is necessary, or a flawed total product results. "Mid-course correction" does not always occur on assembly lines, and evaluative feedback is not always acted upon, but the value of periodic formative evaluation is clear. For the most part, this conscious effort to employ continuous evaluation has not been implemented in the field of education.

Educational supervisors would do well to find more opportunities for formative evaluation procedures. Supervisors need to become "sensors," or monitors of work in progress. They also need to develop the skills and strategies necessary to feed information gained in this way back to the teaching staff. In most schools, such practices have not traditionally existed.

Summative Evaluation

"Summative evaluation is conducted at the end of a program to provide potential consumers with judgments about the program's worth or merit" (Worthen & Sanders, 1987, p. 34). Summative evaluation is the process of collecting data in order to make final decisions about the future status of whatever is being evaluated. It is the "last chance," the final point where an ultimate disposition concerning a person or thing is made. Data collected as part of summative evaluation is directed exclusively toward the goal of final judgment.

In both private corporations and public organizations such as school systems, newly hired employees are generally given a standard probationary period during which the new person can decide if the organization is the kind of place in which he or she wants to work, and the organization can look at the performance of the new person and decide if, over time, he or she can "fit in" and be successful in the organization. Some type of formative evaluation is probably carried out from time to time to let the new employee see if his or her work is generally proceeding up to the expectation levels of the company. Finally, at the conclusion of the agreed-upon probation period, the organization takes one last serious look at the employee's work. That summative evaluation is a final, "go-no go" decision point. Virtually every summative evaluation we undergo in our lives represents a major milestone, because of the final nature of the decision that is made.

Summative evaluation differs from diagnostic and formative evaluation precisely in its emphasis on finality. Because it represents an absolute endpoint or a final decision, summative evaluation typically carries with it a sense of anxiety and seriousness, whether or not these feelings are warranted.

Objectives of Evaluation

The four major educational areas most frequently evaluated are students, curricular programs, curricular materials (which are often evaluated with programs), and staff. In this section we will examine each of these objectives and provide examples of each of the evaluation types matched with these objectives.

Student Evaluation

Students are evaluated almost continuously in most schools, and all three processes are employed. *Diagnostic* student evaluation might involve a simple pretest administered by a classroom teacher at the outset of a chapter or unit to determine the level of students' awareness of central concepts to be taught; this pretest might then guide the teacher in selecting appropriate instructional strategies. Special education teachers use multiple techniques to diagnose the nature of individual learning handicaps so that future instruction can be directed more precisely, and standardized achievement test scores serve as a baseline to plan instruction.

Formative student evaluation is an ongoing practice in most schools. Teachers give "pop quizzes" precisely because they want to get some sense of how well students are learning during the course of instruction and also to give students some hints concerning the teacher's expectations for student mastery of course content. Formative evaluation need not necessarily be confined to written tests or other evaluative instruments. Good teachers use formative evaluation techniques constantly; they watch student behavior patterns, and they invite particular students to participate in class discussion to assess their progress. Teachers can then adjust instruction accordingly.

A typical example of *summative* student evaluation is the traditional final exam that concludes a marking period, the results of which are used to make a summary "pass/fail" decision for a student. Similar judgments are made at the end of instructional units in subject areas and at the end of the entire school year, when most schools use comprehensive examinations to evaluate student success across all subjects. Standardized achievement tests are frequently used to make summative judgments about student learning—an undesirable and perhaps invalid form of evaluation, but one we must recognize is widespread in schools.

Curricular Programs and Materials

Schools frequently assess the quality of their overall curriculum as well the materials available to assist students in attaining the stated goals of the curriculum. As we pointed out in chapter 14, committees of teachers and administrators may work together to review the adequacy of the curriculum and the books that fit it. These activities are all basically *diagnostic* in nature.

A school or department might also review a new textbook midway through the year in which it is initially used. The results of that review would be used, not to decide whether to continue using the text, but rather to determine if it could be used more effectively. Do students need supplementary readings? A workbook? Should the speed with which teachers cover the material be varied? This "mid-course" evaluation is *formative.*

At the end of the school year, teachers and administrators who suggested new curricular programs or products earlier in the year might reconvene to decide if their recommendations were effective. *Summative* evaluation would provide data to assist the committee in making its final decisions and recommendations.

Staff Evaluation

Many educators believe that making decisions about staff is the supervisor's sole evaluative responsibility. Staff evaluation is clearly a critical area and one which may cause considerable anxiety for both the supervisor and the people supervised. However, as we have seen in the previous sections of this chapter, it is far from being the only area of evaluative responsibility for supervisors.

The traditional employment interview carried out before an individual is hired by a school district is an example of *diagnostic* evaluation. Other methods frequently used to determine if an individual is suited for a particular job include employment exams to determine basic competency, psychological profiles, or in recent years for teachers in some states, statewide teacher competency tests. Districts also review letters of recommendation submitted on behalf of candidates for staff positions, academic records, and employment files from earlier positions. Most of these forms of diagnostic evaluation provide information for the employing school system about potential staff members before they are hired. In addition, such evaluation also allows the candidate to learn more about a particular school system.

Formative evaluation of staff is one of the most poorly developed features of the entire range of supervisory responsibilities. Periodic evaluation designed to provide teachers and other school staff members with feedback to encourage better performance sounds like a simple thing to do. In practice, however, few schools provide constructive criticism to their staffs in an open, nonthreatening fashion. Several explanations account for this. First, a high percentage of supervisors and administrators are untrained in how to provide feedback to staffs that would encourage "mid-course correction" and improvement. For administrators and supervisors to undertake an "improvement" responsibility is foreign to the traditional image of the supervisor as an authority figure who makes final judgments about job performance. Second, when administrators and supervisors do provide formative assistance, they are generally expected to make final judgments concerning staff competence at the same time. This dual responsibility means that, when supervisors offer feedback, ask teachers to share problems, or urge them to take "creative risks" to improve their performances, supervisors are expected at the same time to be "filing away" information on which to base future decisions on adequacy or inadequacy of performance. It is virtually impossible for the same practitioner of supervision to engage in both formative and summative evaluation responsibilities with equal effectiveness, yet school systems tend to hold supervisors and administrators accountable for making the difficult decisions associated with summative evaluation. Finally, formative evaluation is a time-consuming process that emphasizes interpersonal skills and communication between the supervisor and the persons being supervised. In many cases, supervisors do not have—are not willing to invest—enough time or interpersonal skills to make formative techniques effective. Whatever difficulties formative evaluation may engender for supervisors, it is important and well worth doing frequently and regularly in schools. Various models have been developed to help supervisors increase opportunities for this type of evaluation.

As we noted above, supervisors are often perceived as engaging in *summative* evaluation of teachers and others. Principals, for instance, regularly make class observations for teachers being considered for tenure or a continuing contract. Because tenure decisions are normally made only once in a teacher's professional life, the evaluation process carried out in this case is clearly summative in nature. In reality, it is generally administrators with formal personnel responsibilities who make summative career decisions about members of their staffs. There is no doubt that summative evaluation is important in the traditional job descriptions of supervisors, but it is typically a rarely employed skill for a person classified as a supervisor.

Figure 15.1 suggests the potential relationships between types and objectives in school evaluation.

Figure 15.1 Model depicting three different types of evaluation in relation to three typical objectives of educational evaluation.

Current Problems and Issues in Evaluation

The area of staff evaluation presents some very tangible and special concerns to the practitioner of educational supervision. On the one hand, we generally accept that, to improve practice, we need to determine the worth and effectiveness of that practice. On the other hand, we are all aware of the trauma that frequently surrounds discussions of evaluation. This paradox will probably never be resolved. The supervisor may, however, reduce the negative stigma associated with evaluation of educational personnel by remaining aware of significant current problems in the area, as well as suggested ways of avoiding these problems.

Mixing Purposes

Evaluation effectiveness often suffers because the objectives of evaluation are mixed. This is particularly true of formative and summative staff evaluation. Formative evaluation suggests a climate of openness and trust between supervisor and staff member, to the extent that staff members can admit their deficiencies openly and request feedback that might lead to improved performance. If staff members suspect that information collected as part of the formative evaluation will come back to haunt them during a summative, personnel decision-making part of the evaluation cycle, trust and openness will be either destroyed or damaged to the point where open communication between supervisor and staff member is no longer possible. Consequently, supervisors should strive to separate formative and summative evaluation as completely as possible, even to the extent of involving different people at each stage.

   For staff evaluation to be truly an effective activity, and one that conforms to our idea of proactive supervisory processes, we must first clearly understand what evaluation is supposed to do. Gary Borich (1977) suggested five legitimate functions of evaluation, the first two of which are formative in nature, and the last three summative. According to Borich, evaluation may be used to

1. Guide self-improvement efforts by the teachers;
2. Assist a supervisor in the process of improving someone else's teaching;
3. Advise potential "consumers" of teaching, particularly students;
4. Guide personnel decisions by present or potential employers or superiors;
5. Provide data to external audiences interested in self-effectiveness, accountability considerations, or the success of a particular project.

Lack of Teacher Involvement

Teachers often report that they feel they have not had significant involvement in the development of district staff evaluation programs. This problem is on the wane in many school systems where teachers have become more and more involved with committees and task forces convened to review evaluation practices. The fact is increasingly recognized that, as primary consumers of the evaluation process, teachers have a legitimate stake in the design of procedures.

Lack of Self-Evaluation

Traditionally, little consistent emphasis has been given to the concept of staff self-evaluation. The predominant view suggests that evaluation is "done to" staff by administrators or supervisors. In fact, evaluation conducted by a person regarding his or her own performance is a much more powerful activity than evaluation conducted by an external source. Supervisors designing formal staff evaluation programs need to emphasize self-evaluation as well as the review and evaluation carried out by supervisors and administrators.

Inadequate Evaluation Criteria

Criteria used for staff evaluation often come from the supervisor's personal preferences. Some supervisory personnel, for example, tend to judge the effectiveness of teaching performance according to the extent to which the teacher's activities resemble how the supervisor would have taught the same material. An example of reliance on personal preference criteria, or at least on criteria that are extremely subjective, is illustrated in the teacher evaluation checklist shown in Figure 15.2. Note the number of items that are to be interpreted solely by the supervisor.

  In fact, staff evaluation criteria and instruments should be based primarily on teacher effectiveness research rather than on personal preference. David Berliner and William Tikunoff (1976) proposed the following list of effective teacher behaviors:

1. The teacher reacts constructively (in overt, verbal, or nonverbal ways) to students' feelings and attitudes.
2. The teacher actively listens to what a student is saying, reading, or reciting.

CLASSROOM OBSERVATION

Teacher _____ Subject _____ Date _____

	Always	Frequently	Seldom	Hardly Ever	
					1. Shows specific interests in students as they enter and leave the classroom.
					2. Calls students by name.
					3. Looks at class when in discussion with them.
					4. Makes an effort to involve all students.
					5. Provides a variety of classroom activities and experiences.
					6. Provides a comfortable and attractive environment for the students.
					7. Uses room arrangements appropriate to the teaching-learning techniques employed.
					8. Displays disturbing mannerisms and expressions.
					9. Directions are clear and understandable.
					10. Learning materials are readily available.
					11. Responds appropriately to unplanned occurrences.
					12. Goals for activities are clearly communicated.
					13. Teacher is enthusiastic.
					14. Contacts students individually to observe, answer questions, etc.
					15. Maintains adequate supervision for activities.
					16. Encourages and develops each student's point of view.
					17. Demonstrates interest in activities of students (curricular and co-curricular).
					18. Displays an appropriate sense of humor.
					19. Handles classroom management efficiently.
					20. Maintains order and discipline within the class.

Figure 15.2. Typical example of items utilized in a checklist designed to guide teacher observation and evaluation.

3. The teacher gives a direction or a threat and follows through with it.

4. The teacher seems confident in teaching a given subject and demonstrates a grasp of it.

5. The teacher checks a student's progress regularly and adjusts his or her instruction accordingly.

6. The teacher expresses positive, pleasant, and optimistic attitudes and feelings.

7. The teacher seems to perceive the learning rate of students and adjusts his or her teaching pace accordingly.

8. The teacher encourages students to take responsibility for their own class work.

9. The teacher capitalizes instructionally on expected incidents that might arise during class time.

10. The teacher prepares students for a lesson by reviewing, outlining, explaining objectives, and summarizing.

Research has shown that all of these behaviors have a high relationship with student outcomes, as measured by performance on standardized achievement tests in mathematics and reading. This is certainly not intended as a "perfect" listing of all characteristics shown by effective teachers, but these behaviors may be observed in a more objective fashion than the items presented in the checklist we reviewed earlier in Figure 15.2.

Effective teaching has been conceptualized recently as something other than specific in-class instructional behaviors that produce improved student outcomes on standardized achievement tests. Instead, researchers have emphasized a more subtle, "holistic" pattern. Elliot Eisner (1982) described "artistic supervision" as an approach to evaluation that requires the following:

1. Attention to the muted or expressive character of events, not simply to their incidence or literal meaning

2. High levels of educational connoisseurship; that is, the ability to see what is significant yet subtle

3. Appreciation of the unique contributions the teacher makes to the educational development of the young, as well as those contributions a teacher may have in common with others

4. Attention to the process of classroom life and observation of this process over extended periods of time so that the significance of events can be placed in a temporal context

5. Establishment of rapport between the supervisor and those being supervised so that dialogue and a sense of trust can be established between the two

6. An ability to use language, to exploit its potential so as to make public the expressive character of what has been seen

7. An ability to interpret the meaning of events so that their educational importance may be fully appreciated

8. Recognition of the fact that the individual supervisor with his or her strengths, sensitivities, and experience is the major "instrument" through which the educational situation is perceived

These basic principles of artistic evaluation are further developed by Louis Rubin (1985), who defined a series of behaviors that suggest artistic teaching. In Rubin's view, "artistic teachers" are those who

1. Focus on the subtleties of teaching (i.e., motivation of student, pacing control) which invigorate basic instructional methods and subject matter;

2. Improvise tactics for reaching objectives and overcoming difficulties;

3. Take advantage of opportunities to clarify ideas and reinforce concepts;

4. Make use of intention and hunch in modifying routine practice;

5. Set high expectations for themselves and their students;

6. Find the most efficient and expedient ways of getting things done;

7. Use temporary digressions on related topics to enrich lessons, stimulate interest, and increase pace;

8. Base their control of learning activities on student behavior;

9. Take pride in what they do and in the achievement of their students;

10. Concentrate on a few dominant goals that are central to their purpose;

11. Respect their convictions;

12. Devote as much time as possible to whatever they enjoy most in teaching.

Whatever perspective the supervisor values—artistic or more scientific—the point here is that a consistent, research-based, and objective set of standards should serve as the basis for evaluation of staff.

Evaluation Procedures Not Communicated

In many schools, the purposes, criteria, and processes of staff evaluation are not adequately communicated to staff members. School systems often take great pains to improve the quality of their evaluation procedures. In Colorado, for example, state law requires local school districts to form committees of teachers, administrators, supervisory personnel, and community representatives to design effective evaluation programs for staff. Efforts are made to find objective evaluation criteria that reflect local educational priorities and values. Often, such staff evaluation programs are excellently "packaged." Yet many of these attempts fail, simply because once the new evaluation programs are designed, they are not sufficiently communicated to the entire staff of the district. Districts frequently develop new evaluation procedures one year and then fail to "reeducate" staff about these procedures in following years, assuming that "we all know about those practices around here." Unfortunately, that assumption is often incorrect. Supervisors should ensure that the purposes, criteria, and procedures of any staff evaluation program are clearly communicated periodically to all staff. Such practice increases the likelihood that staff will "buy into" evaluation practices and, more importantly, will raise suggestions for improving the status quo from time to time.

Insufficient Expertise

Staff evaluation procedures often experience difficulties because the administrative or supervisory personnel called upon to implement these procedures lack sufficient technical expertise in the area of evaluation. For years, school administrators were trained to serve as managers of their buildings. As we noted in chapter 6, the expectation that administrators and supervisors will engage in behaviors more reflective of instructional leadership is relatively recent. Thus, few present educational leaders have had extensive training in evaluation practices. Those who do have a background in this area tend to have had specific training primarily in summative staff evaluation procedures. Aspiring administrative and supervisory personnel currently in training must receive additional specialized training and preparation in all types of evaluation and for all objectives. Present administrators and supervisors who feel that they lack sufficient knowledge about how to evaluate or what to evaluate must utilize the expertise of others in evaluating staff. In secondary schools, for instance, a principal with a teaching background in math may need to observe and evaluate a teacher of German. The obvious solution here is to ask help from someone with greater subject area expertise—a department chairperson, subject supervisor, or senior teacher—in providing both criteria for the evaluation and specific feedback regarding mastery of the instructional content.

Due Process Issues

Considerable evidence suggests that, with the advent of negotiated teacher contracts and other more sophisticated efforts to take into account the rights of teachers as employees, the concern that due process is not always observed in staff evaluation has been alleviated. The concern is particularly powerful, predictably, in the area of summative evaluation, from which final decisions concerning employment may result. Effective supervisors ensure that due process is always observed in staff evaluation by following these recommended procedures:

1. Whenever a teacher is evaluated, provide that teacher with a written identification of strengths as well as a diagnosis of weaknesses. In addition, provide specific recommendations for the ways in which weaknesses might be improved.

2. Offer intensive follow-up to the teacher so that he or she can, in fact, implement the specific recommendations provided by the supervisor or administrator. The supervisor or administrator is responsible for documenting this follow-up.

3. If the results of the evaluation and improvement plan still warrant an unfavorable or adverse personnel decision, communicate advance notice of this decision in writing to the staff member. Also provide notice of the staff member's rights to a hearing with the supervisor or administrator responsible for making the adverse recommendation.

4. Specify appeal procedures should the staff member be dissatisfied with the outcome of the hearing.

5. Communicate all these procedures in writing, as well as any additional information unique to the local setting, to all staff members.

In addition to following the specific procedures listed above, adherence to a few general principles will alleviate much of the anxiety supervisors and administrators may feel about this issue of due process and legal responsibilities in general.

1. Evaluation of teaching must be based on a sense of equal respect between supervisor and teacher. (Teachers and other staff members are human beings who possess certain rights. All evaluation procedures must respect the simple human dignity of school staff members.)

2. Evaluation of teaching must be reasonable. (Evaluation procedures must be neither arbitrary nor capricious. Decisions based on information gathered for evaluation must be warranted by that information.)

3. The purpose of evaluation must be clearly identified with educational effectiveness. (Evaluation procedures must promote good education. Evaluation should assure that the aims of the school are being met in an effective manner.)

Inadequate Follow-up

Throughout this discussion we have assumed that the ultimate purpose of any educational evaluation (staff, student, or curricular; diagnostic, formative, or summative) is to enhance the quality of education available to children. To ensure that such enhancement actually occurs, sufficient follow-up about instructional improvement must be provided to teachers, after they have been evaluated by administrators or supervisors. Unfortunately, current evaluation practice is often marked by a decided lack of feedback.

As we will see in chapter 16, the clinical supervision model is designed largely as a formative evaluation technique that stresses direct feedback from supervisors to teachers. Keith Acheson and Meredith Gall (1987) note that effective feedback in postevaluation conferences requires three kinds of activities. The first of these must take place before and during the observation or evaluation session itself; the second and third must take place during the postevaluation conference.

The following activities, according to Acheson and Gall, must occur before and during the evaluation session.

1. In a preevaluation planning conference, the teacher and supervisor must set goals for the year, identify concerns, establish a rationale for working together, consider strategies the teacher has been using and intends to use, and translate abstract concerns into observable behaviors that the supervisor can record.

2. Before the observation session, the teacher and supervisor must identify the nature of the lesson to be observed, make the

objectives explicit, discuss what the teacher will be doing, predict what the students will be doing, consider specific problems or concerns that the teacher anticipates during the lesson, and select appropriate observation techniques and recording systems.

3. During the observational visit, the supervisor must employ one or more devices from a repertoire of data-recording techniques, use appropriate recording devices for the specific situation as related to the goals and concerns, and record data unobtrusively and without disruption of the class.

The above activities are normally included in the first two stages of the clinical supervision model, and they represent what should occur in order for an effective conference to take place.

For Acheson and Gall, the second set of activities that represent part of effective follow-up to evaluation are the following, which form the general, conceptual basis for postevaluation feedback.

1. The supervisor must provide the teacher with feedback using objective observational data.

2. The supervisor must elicit the teacher's opinions, feelings, and inferences about the observational data.

3. The supervisor must encourage the teacher to consider alternative lesson objectives, methods, and reasons.

4. The supervisor must provide the teacher with opportunities for practice and comparison.

Finally, Acheson and Gall suggest five specific activities that should occur at the postobservational conference.

1. The observer displays the data recorded at the observation. This is done without evaluative comments.

2. The teacher analyzes what was happening during the lesson as evidenced by the data. The supervisor simply helps to clarify what behaviors the recorded data represent.

3. The teacher, with the help of the supervisor, interprets the behaviors of the teacher and students as represented by the observational data. At this stage the teacher becomes more evaluative because causes and consequences must be discussed as desirable or undesirable.

4. The teacher, with assistance from the supervisor, decides on alternative approaches for the future in order to attend to the dissatisfaction with the observed teaching or to emphasize those aspects that were satisfying.

5. The supervisor reinforces the teacher's announced intentions for change when the supervisor agrees with them or helps the teacher modify the intentions if there is some disagreement.

We do not suggest that such detail needs to be included in every case of postevaluation follow-up; indeed, effective conferences can consist of an informal chat in the hallway after an observation. There is a critical need, however, for adequate feedback to be made available to staff members as soon as possible after evaluation has been carried out.

We should also mention that, although Acheson and Gall use a clinical model that employs in-class teacher observation as the sole data-gathering technique, observation is certainly not the only way in which evaluative data may be collected. Self-evaluations by teachers (probably the most potent form of evaluation), student evaluations of teaching, and even informal discussions with staff members outside of their normal teaching responsibilities also represent ways in which information can be gathered and structured as part of staff evaluation.

Evaluation of Evaluation

Evaluation programs themselves are rarely evaluated. Procedures are often followed primarily because "we've always done it that way around here," rather than because a solid history of effectiveness argues for the continuation of existing practices.

Richard Kunkel and Susan Tucker (1977) suggested five criteria by which supervisors and administrators might evaluate the quality of their own evaluation activities. We suggest these as an appropriate and natural starting point for the development of a strategy for periodic review of existing evaluation practices:

1. *Holism.* Does the evaluation activity look at the total picture without an undue emphasis on quantification, or on only a few variables?

2. *Helpfulness toward program improvement.* Does the evaluation program promote growth, improvement, increased effectiveness, and other similar types of positive benefits, rather than serving only as a ranking, judging, or criticizing technique?

3. *Acceptance of hard and soft data.* Does the evaluation process emphasize both empirical and intuitive methodologies?

4. *Evaluation vulnerability.* Is the person responsible for conducting the evaluation able to grow as much as the persons being evaluated?

5. *Vision of the future.* Does the evaluation activity have a future orientation, directed toward helping improve things later rather than "fixing" things now?

Regardless of the criteria selected, evaluation practices must be reviewed periodically to determine if they are continuing to serve the same purposes that they were originally designed to serve.

Summary

Evaluation is a critical responsibility for the practitioner of educational supervision. Although evaluation is far from being the only duty for a supervisor, it is clearly one of the most important. Only through effective evaluation can data be obtained to assist the supervisor in making appropriate educational decisions; only through evaluation can the quality of instruction—and of education overall—be improved. Quality education demands continuing efforts at improvement, and improvement often implies changing existing practices. To make correct and effective changes, accurate evaluative information is vitally important.

We began this chapter by defining evaluation as a process for determining the basic worth of something by measuring that "something" against established standards or criteria. We described three types of evaluation: *diagnostic*, which determines the nature of something prior to an intervention; *formative*, which determines how well something is working in progress; and *summative*, which determines whether or not something has ultimately succeeded. All three types or stages are vital activities for improving schools— although, as we noted, too much attention is typically directed toward summative activities and too little toward formative activities.

Primarily, educational evaluation assesses students, curricular programs and materials, and staff. We provided examples in this chapter of evaluative activities directed at each of these three areas. Finally, we concluded with a review of some typical problems associated with evaluation in schools, including confusion over the purpose of evaluation, lack of objective criteria, and lack of strategies to evaluate the evaluation activities themselves.

The most important point made in this chapter is this: We need to work to improve evaluation processes in education because effective educational evaluation will ultimately result in better teachers—and better education—for our children.

Suggested Activities

---

1. Collect descriptions of the teacher-evaluation procedures used in at least four school systems. Analyze these descriptions in terms of the criteria for determining the effectiveness of evaluation practices specified by Kunkel and Tucker.

2. Interview a sample of teachers from your school to determine what they believe are areas that need improvement in staff evaluation practices for your district. Engage in the same activity with a group of principals and other administrators in your school district. Make sure to ask people for suggestions regarding the ways in which improvement may be carried out.

3. Ask a number of administrators to estimate the percentage of their weekly time that is devoted to the different types and objects of evaluation described in this chapter. If they had more time to spend on evaluation, which types would they do more and why?

Cases to Consider

Read each of these cases and consider the following issues:

a. What are the critical issues raised in each case, as they relate to the understanding of evaluation practices of the proactive supervisor?

b. How does each case relate to the development of the concept of proactive supervision?

c. In what ways might you suggest a resolution to the issues raised?

Case 15.1:

It Seems to Work . . . So Far

The administrators in the Buena Vista School District were quite pleased with the work that they had been involved with over the past five years. Under the direction of their superintendent, Dr. Sylvia Moreno, the district had been able to implement what many across the country were now referring to as one of the most extensive programs of outcomes-based education in any public school system. Traditional grading systems and lock-step promotion of children from one grade to the next, regardless of whether any true learning had occurred, were gone. This was truly a remarkable accomplishment in a school system where there had always been a history of ultra-conservative practice. Dr. Moreno had come to the district with a vision, and that vision included OBE.

Little by little, however, rumblings were being heard in the community. Letters to the editor of the local newspaper began to question the wisdom of discarding all the time-honored traditions of the past. "How will we know if our kids have really learned anything now that grades are gone?" "This outcomes-based stuff is for the birds. What outcomes are being taught?" "What was so wrong with the way we learned in the past?" "Why are schools out there teaching these values as outcomes? Where are the basics?" These are only a few of the many different questions that were being asked in the district by a wider and wider segment of the community.

Criticisms of the outcomes-based education program in Buena Vista were now being given greater credibility by the school board, particularly since the district was facing a critical bond election for capital improvements in only six weeks. Dr. Moreno, therefore, was not surprised to be summoned to a special executive session of the board. During that meeting, she was asked to explain how important the OBE program was, in her professional judgment.

"The OBE effort here in Buena Vista is central to a long-term vision of more effective schooling. We cannot turn around now, just because some in the community don't like what we're doing," she said. "We are now a national model."

Tom Gresham, the board president, responded to Dr. Moreno by stating, "Sylvia, we are not using this as a referendum on your performance as the superintendent. All we are asking now is the same question that a lot of voters are also asking. Do you have any evidence to show that this innovation has made any real difference in what's going on in our schools? I'm assuming that you have some data, so please be prepared to make a public presentation within the next month. I'm sure that we'll all be relieved when you can start to answer some of the objections in a more objective fashion."

Sylvia Moreno walked out of the board meeting knowing that she had a lot of work to do in the next few days.

Case 15.2:

Can You Really Do the Job?

Carl Franklin had spent his first three years as a school administrator in Crawford township, a blue-collar community. While he enjoyed his experience, he was getting increasingly tired with the daily two hours of time wasted driving between his home in the suburbs of Clarksville and Crawford. He had taken the job three years ago because it was the only principalship available in a community where he would be able to maintain residence in the Clarksville area. This was important because he wanted to realize his ambition of a principalship, but he could not relocate because of his wife's job.

Carl had been keeping his eyes open for an administrative position in a community closer to Clarksville for the past three years. Finally, he saw an opening in the very prestigious Wellington Estates school district. It was a principalship of a medium-sized elementary school, with a considerable increase in pay. Even more important, Carl would be working a little closer to home. He had begun to feel like a stranger in his own home in recent months. The Wellington job would mean an end to being so far from home, better money, and more time with his wife.

Not surprisingly, Carl was called in for an interview, a clear indication that he was one of the finalists for the Wellington job. He was extremely confident that he was exactly the person who would be a great choice for the district. The only thing that really bothered Carl after the first round of interviews were the kinds of questions that he seemed to be getting from the administrators on the interview committee.

Specifically, Carl was asked about his "philosophy of supervision." While he spent a considerable amount of time responding to that question by talking about the kinds of things that he had done at Crawford with the teachers, he didn't seem to be answering the questions in the ways that people wanted. Carl talked about teacher empowerment, staff development, observing classes, inservice sessions, and so forth, but the interviewers kept returning to questions about "supervision experience." In every instance, the main concern seemed to be whether or not Carl was the kind of principal who could really get rid of some bad teachers.

Although he wanted to work in Clarksville, Carl was more than a bit uneasy as he drove back to his house following the interviews. He was afraid he would have to tell his wife that he would be driving a lot again next year.

References

Acheson, Keith A., & Gall, Meredith D. (1987). *Techniques in the clinical supervision of teachers* (2nd ed.). White Plains, NY: Longman.

Berliner, David, & Tikunoff, William (1976). The California beginning teacher evaluation study: Overview of the ethnographic study. *Journal of Teacher Education, 27.*

Borich, Gary D. (1977). *The appraisal of teaching: Concepts and process.* Reading, MA: Addison-Wesley.

Eisner, Elliot (1982). An artistic approach to supervision. In Thomas J. Sergiovanni (Ed.), *Supervision of teaching.* (1982 Yearbook of the Association for Supervision and Curriculum Development). Alexandria, VA: The Association.

Kunkel, Richard C., & Tucker, Susan (1977). A perception-based model of program evaluation: A values-oriented theory. Paper presented at the Annual Meeting of the American Educational Research Association, New York.

Rubin, Louis J. (1985). *Artistry in teaching.* New York: Random House.

Scriven, Michael (1967). The methodology of evaluation. In Robert E. Stake (Ed.), *Curriculum evaluation.* American Educational Research Association Monograph Series on Evaluation. Chicago: Rand McNally.

Worthen, Blaine R., & Sanders, James R. (1987). *Educational evaluation: Alternative approaches and practical guidelines.* White Plains, NY: Longman.

Additional Reading

Tracy, Saundra J., & MacNaughton, Robert (1993). *Assisting and assessing educational personnel: The impact of clinical supervision.* Needham Heights, MA: Allyn and Bacon.

Part V

Models for Supervision
Now and the Future

In Part V we review *clinical supervision*, a supervisory model that many see as a cure-all for the ills of educational supervision, as well as other emerging models in the field. Finally, we will review the important issue of staff development and inservice training and look quickly at future trends and issues.

16 Clinical Supervision

As we noted in the previous chapter, educators have rarely had a strong record in formative evaluative practices. Well-developed strategies guide diagnostic and summative staff evaluation, but strategies for formative evaluation are less clear. Even though researchers generally recognize that intervention to improve any activity is most effective if undertaken while that activity is in progress, formative evaluation of staff has not been given high priority in most school systems. This situation has begun to change during the last twenty years, and one reason is the general acceptance of the supervisory model we discuss in this chapter.

Underlying Assumptions of Clinical Supervision

Many educators endorse clinical supervision as a perfect approach to the supervision of teachers. In Ohio and Colorado, for example, the most recent standards for the certification of educational supervisors and administrators require candidates seeking administrative or supervisory licenses to receive special, intensive training in the use of the clinical supervision model. We do not agree that clinical supervision will cure all of our current ills, but we do think that it offers some very useful strategies for the improvement of supervisory practice. Throughout this chapter we will suggest that clinical supervision must be understood in an appropriate context, and that context is defined largely by the assumptions and historical background upon which this model is based.

Clinical supervision is typically presented as the brainchild of Robert Goldhammer, Morris Cogan, and Robert Anderson, who worked together at Harvard University during the late 1950s and early 1960s. They were responsible for the development of curriculum and instructional practices for Harvard's experimental Master of Arts in Teaching (M.A.T.) Program, normally referred to as the Harvard-Newton Summer School Project (Cogan, 1961). Cogan, Goldhammer, and Anderson were charged specifically with the development of a practicum that would be a part of this new program. We need to point out that the Harvard-Newton Program was never designed for all teachers; it was a highly selective project intended to refine the teaching skills of some of the best teachers in the country. From its inception, the Harvard effort was directed toward the *enhancement of excellence*, never at "fixing" mediocre or poor teachers, and the practicum was an important way in which excellent, experienced teachers could become even better.

Cogan, Goldhammer, and Anderson were faced with a critical dilemma. How could they design a field-based learning program that was not established, like traditional student-teaching arrangements, to provide basic hands-on learning in real, live classrooms? The participating teachers were master teachers in their own districts, and were often called upon to work with weaker colleagues. How could anyone hope to provide feedback to people of this quality who were returning to student teaching?

The answer to this was what Cogan, Goldhammer, and Anderson—later joined by Robert Krajewski—called "clinical supervision." Cogan (1973) defined their model as supervision "focused upon the improvement of the teacher's classroom instruction. The principal data of clinical supervision includes records of classroom events: what the teacher and students do in the classroom during the teaching-learning process" (p. 9). The notion of "clinical" as opposed to "general" supervision was selected to suggest an emphasis on supervision related specifically to classroom observation, analysis of events taking place within the classroom, and the in-class behavior of teachers and students. The primary goal of this model was to provide an opportunity for teachers to gain feedback that would allow them to improve already good teaching skills. Noreen Garman (1982) notes, "In the clinical approach to supervision, the supervisor provides the practitioner with a service that is concerned with the quality of his or her practice" (p. 35).

Weller (1977) identified the following elements of clinical supervision:

1. To improve instruction, teachers must learn specific intellectual and behavioral skills.

2. The supervisor should take responsibility for helping teachers to develop
   a. skills for analyzing the instructional process based on systematic data;
   b. skills for experimentation, adaptation, and modification of the curriculum;
   c. a broader repertoire of teaching skills and techniques.

3. The supervisor should emphasize what and how teachers teach, to improve instruction not to change the teacher's personality.

4. Planning and analysis must center on making and testing instructional hypotheses based on observational evidence.

5. Conferences should deal with a few instructional issues that are important, relevant to the teacher, and amenable to change.

6. The feedback conference should concentrate on constructive analysis and the reinforcement of successful patterns rather than on the condemnation of unsuccessful patterns.

7. Feedback must be based on observational evidence, not on unsubstantiated value judgments.

8. The cycle of planning, observation, and analysis should be continuous and cumulative.

9. Supervision is a dynamic process of give-and-take in which supervisors and teachers are colleagues in search of mutual educational understanding.

10. The supervisory process is centered primarily on the analysis of instruction.

11. The individual teacher has both the freedom and the responsibility to initiate issues, analyze and improve his or her own teaching, and develop a personal teaching style.

12. Supervision can be perceived, analyzed, and improved in much the same manner as teaching can.

13. The supervisor has both the freedom and the responsibility to analyze and evaluate his or her own supervision in a manner similar to a teacher's analysis and evaluation of his or her instruction.

Acheson and Gall (1987) noted five major goals implied by the clinical supervision model. Clinical supervision is designed to:

1. Provide teachers with objective feedback on the current state of their instruction;
2. Diagnose and solve instructional problems;
3. Help teachers develop skill in using instructional strategies;
4. Evaluate teachers for promotion, tenure, and other decisions;
5. Help teachers develop a positive attitude about continuous professional development.

All of these assumptions and goals accurately reflect the nature of supervisory practice that follows the clinical model. In addition, we want to point out two other considerations. First, clinical supervision is not for everyone; it is designed to support and provide feedback to experienced, reflective, and generally very good classroom teachers. Second, clinical supervision presumes that teachers should direct the supervisory process precisely because, as users, they are experienced and effective. This teacher-controlled model should not be used to judge teaching quality, but rather as a resource for good teachers to refine their instructional techniques. Effective supervisors should be capable of making these practices available to teachers any time the teachers request them.

Clinical supervision is best viewed as a collegial practice, not as something that a superordinate (an administrator or supervisor, for example) does to a teacher, but as a peer-to-peer activity. Thus, some practitioners suggest that the clinical supervision model is best used between teachers, and that supervisors or administrators have no real ongoing role in it.

We do not mean to reduce the potential value of this model. Rather, we wish to emphasize that the best use of clinical supervision must be based on its documented strengths, and not on assumptions that have in fact never been present. The clinical model, for instance, cannot be used effectively with a first-year teacher, and we doubt that true clinical supervision is an appropriate way to provide feedback to a teacher judged as incompetent. Because of these limitations, we must approach with considerable caution those wholesale suggestions that clinical supervision should automatically be used with all teachers in all schools under all circumstances.

Developing an Appropriate Climate

Before we can legitimately consider the structure of the clinical supervision model, we need to define those conditions that must exist to make use of that model effective. Just as clinical supervision is not appropriate for every teacher, it is also not appropriate for every school setting. Under certain conditions, clinical supervision may cause more harm than good.

Clinical supervision is collaborative, collegial, and teacher-centered. As a result, clinical supervision can only be effectively used if supervisors or administrators truly trust the teachers in the school, to the extent that they are willing to allow those teachers to define and control the analysis of their own instructional behavior. Moreover, teachers must feel comfortable enough in the school environment to "act naturally." Improvement can only take place among those who are willing to admit to their own imperfection.

If no climate of trust exists, then any clinical practices employed in supervision will be without substance. John Lovell and Kimball Wiles (1983) noted the importance of this condition in discussing potential pitfalls of clinical supervision:

> Sometimes supervisors are not willing to take the time, or do not have the ability, to establish a basis of mutual trust. Such a condition is essential. However, there is also a need for mutual respect for professional competence. Without these two conditions, it is impossible to have effective clinical supervision. (p. 182)

Many supervisory schemes make use of the structural steps of clinical supervision. Without the proper climate, however, true clinical supervision simply is not taking place. As Lovell and Wiles (1983) observed:

> Some organizations like the "sound" and the "glamour" of clinical supervision but do not have the conviction and/or ability to provide the human and material resources. To implement clinical supervision, it is essential that supervisors and teachers have *time* to participate in various kinds of activities on a continuing basis. Time is needed for pre-observation conferences, observations and analysis of teaching, and post-observation feedback and corrective procedures. Clinical supervision requires in-depth thinking and working together over an extended period of time. If it is going to work, the organization must provide the necessary personnel, arrangements, rewards, equipment, leadership, and support. (p. 211)

Stages of the Clinical Supervision Model

Cogan's (1973) initial design of a clinical supervision model included eight steps.

1. Establishing the teacher-supervisor relationship
2. Planning with the teacher
3. Planning the strategy of observation
4. Observing instruction
5. Analyzing the teaching-learning process
6. Planning the strategy of the conference
7. The conference
8. Renewed planning

Robert Mosher and David Purpel (1972) reduced these eight steps to three stages or process activities:

1. Planning
2. Observing
3. Evaluating or analyzing

Acheson and Gall (1987) also simplified the clinical supervision model by suggesting only three stages:

1. Planning conference
2. Classroom observation
3. Feedback conference

Peter Oliva (1993) summarized these competing descriptions of the component elements of clinical supervision by suggesting that, regardless of the particular approach, all possess certain essential ingredients: (1) contact or communication with the teacher prior to an observation; (2) classroom observation; and (3) follow-up of the observation.

Practitioners will no doubt continue to disagree over the "official" number of steps in the clinical supervision model. For our purposes, we find useful the five-stage description first presented by Goldhammer (1969), and maintained in the more recent work of Goldhammer, Anderson, and Krajewski (1993):

1. Preobservation conference
2. Observation
3. Analysis and strategy

4. Supervision conference
5. Postconference analysis

Preobservation Conference

The first stage allows participants to form a mental framework in anticipation of the observation of teaching that is to follow. This stage has the following specific purposes:

1. Communication can be opened (or reopened) between supervisor and teacher. Goldhammer suggested that "it can be useful for [the] teacher and [the] supervisor to talk together . . . to renew their habits of communication, their familiarity with one another's intellectual style and expressive rhythms . . ." (Goldhammer, 1969, p. 57).

2. Supervisor and teacher may become familiar with each other's goals and intentions, as well as reasons, premises, doubts, motives, and ultimate expectations, and interpersonal communications may become more fluent.

3. Teacher and supervisor can rehearse what will take place during the actual episode of classroom observation.

4. Last-minute revisions of the teacher's goals, objectives, and lesson plan may be carried out.

5. The nature of specific practices to be followed in the observation can be determined and a "contract" regarding the ground rules (i.e., how long the supervisor will observe, at what time during the school day, when the supervisor will enter the classroom, and so forth) made between the teacher and supervisor.

In short, this first stage is when teacher and supervisor plan the clinical supervision cycle. It is here that the teacher articulates (often in a vague and ill defined way) his or her reasons for requesting someone to observe a class. During this step, supervisors should avoid any tendency to make demands and place restrictions on teachers in anticipation of the observation. Instead, the supervisor primarily listens to the teacher specify what is wanted. If this is not well-defined, the supervisor helps the teacher articulate concerns more completely. The following outline, developed by Goldhammer, Anderson, and Krajewski (1993, pp. 86–87). offers a sample agenda for a well-designed pre-observation conference.

1. Establish a "contract" or "agreement" between the supervisor and the teacher to be observed, including

    a. Objectives of the lesson

    b. Relationship of the lesson objectives to the overall learning program being implemented

    c. Activities to be observed

    d. Possible changing of activity format, delivery system, and other elements based on interactive agreement between supervisor and teacher

    e. Specific description of items or problems on which the teacher desires feedback

    f. Assessment procedures of activities and problems

2. Establish the mechanics or ground rules of the observation, including

    a. Time of the observation

    b. Length of the observation

    c. Place of the observation

3. Establish specific plans for carrying out the observation

    a. Where shall the supervisor sit?

    b. Should the supervisor talk to students about the lesson? If so, when? Before or after the lesson?

    c. Will the supervisor look for a specific action?

    d. Should the supervisor interact with students?

    e. Will any special materials or preparations be necessary?

    f. How shall the supervisor leave the observation?

Observation

This step, so simple to describe (the supervisor observes the teacher) may be the most difficult and complicated for the supervisor actually to carry out. Observation is difficult and complicated because it requires the supervisor to make use of many different skills, which we can cluster into two basic categories: determining *what* to observe and determining *how* to observe.

    Deciding what to observe should be guided by the discussion between the supervisor and teacher at the preobservation conference. As Oliva (1993) notes:

> If we follow through with the cycle of clinical supervision the teacher and supervisor in the preobservation conference have decided on the specific behaviors of teacher and students which the supervisor will observe. The supervisor concentrates on the presence or absence of the specific behaviors. (p. 502)

This is, at least in theory, the proper focus for classroom observation—but only if what the teacher indicated in advance is in fact an accurate description of the major issues that exist in the classroom. If the teacher suggested, for example, that his or her major problem is knowing whether or not she is using sufficiently demanding questions to elicit high-level thinking skills from students, and if the observer finds that this indeed is the major classroom issue, then the observation can be nondirective. If, however, the observer finds many other classroom problems that need to be addressed, then the observer needs to make an immediate decision: Will he or she observe the teacher's stated problem, or will he or she note instead the true problems that the observer perceives in the classroom?

The issue of how to observe also deserves attention. The best intentions of supervisors will be pointless if their efforts at observation are not guided by the overriding realization that data must be gathered in an efficient and objective fashion. The ultimate goal of data gathering is to obtain information to share with the teacher after the observation has concluded, so that the teacher can analyze his or her own activities in the classroom. One recent development of interest to us in refining classroom observation techniques is the research focus on analyzing classroom activities. Researchers with no particular interest in supervision (or for that matter in any processes that have the goal of modifying teaching behavior) have nonetheless developed instruments that enable supervisors to engage in more sophisticated in-class observations. Acheson and Gall (1987) reviewed many of these techniques and suggested their potential application for clinical supervision.

1. *Selective verbatim.* The supervisor makes a written record of exactly what is said, in a verbatim transcript. Not all verbal events are recorded; the supervisor and teacher, as part of their preobservation conference, have decided what kinds of verbal events ought to be written down in a "selective" fashion. For example, if a teacher believes that he or she is not asking sufficiently difficult questions to challenge the very bright students in a class, the supervisor may spend the entire observation doing nothing but transcribing the questions used by the teacher. This transcription can take place while the class is in progress, or from a review of a taped recording of a class.

2. *Observational records based on seating charts.* The supervisor documents the behaviors of students as they interact with a teacher during a class session. A considerable amount of complex behavior and interaction can be described

pictorially. An application of this approach might be in a case where, during a preobservation conference, a teacher expresses concern about the fact that some students are more involved in class discussions than others. Using a seating chart observation form, the observer may document graphically that the teacher is in fact interacting more frequently with a handful of students, suggesting that some students are not receiving much attention. This may serve as an explanation for why some students are not as involved as others.

3. *Wide-lens techniques.* The observer makes brief notes of events in the classroom that answer, in a very broad fashion, the question, "What happened?" Wide-lens notes are also called *anecdotal records.* The observer makes no effort to record precise events, but rather writes down overall impressions and big events. This technique might be particularly appropriate when the teacher does not have a precisely defined concern or problem related to teaching. Often a teacher will simply recognize that "something just isn't going well in my class." The wide-lens technique might then be employed by a supervisor who wishes to collect data that reflect broad impressions of what is going on in the classroom. These broad impressions might then serve to assist the teacher in more precisely describing his or her concerns.

4. *Checklists and timeline coding.* The supervisor observes and collects data about the teaching behavior being observed and categorizes these activities according to predefined classifications. A famous example of this procedure in supervisory observation is the Flanders Interaction Analysis scale (Flanders, 1970), which suggests that teaching behavior may be understood in terms of the extent to which classroom activities fit into three broad categories—Teacher Talk, Student Talk, and Silence. Each of these categories is further divided in the illustration of the Flanders Interaction Analysis Categories (FIAC) instrument in Table 16.1.

Another checklist used to guide classroom observation is the timeline coding technique developed over the past twenty-five years, principally as part of research designed to study teaching strategies. Here, the observer notes certain predetermined behaviors of either teacher or students at particular times during a class. These techniques, once again, can provide data to teachers who are unable to articulate precisely what they feel should be observed in their classes. These widely validated instruments can

Table 16.1 FLANDERS INTERACTION ANALYSIS CATEGORIES.

Teacher Talk	**Response**	1. *Accepts feeling.* Accepts and clarifies an attitude or the feeling tone of a student in a nonthreatening manner. Feelings may be positive or negative. Predicting and recalling feelings are included. 2. *Praises or encourages.* Praises or encourages students; says "um hum" or "go on"; makes jokes that release tension, but not at the expense of a student. 3. *Accepts or uses ideas of students.* Acknowledges student talk. Clarifies, builds on, or asks questions based on student ideas.
		4. *Asks questions.* Asks questions about content or procedure, based on teacher ideas, with the intent that a student will answer.
	Initiation	5. *Lectures.* Offers facts or opinions about content or procedures: expresses his own ideas, gives *his own* explanation, or cites an authority other than a student. 6. *Gives directions.* Gives directions, commands, or orders with which a student is expected to comply. 7. *Criticizes student or justifies authority.* Makes statements intended to change student behavior from nonacceptable to acceptable patterns; arbitrarily corrects student answers; bawls someone out. Or states why the teacher is doing what he is doing; uses extreme self-reference.
Student Talk	**Response**	8. *Student talk—response.* Student talk in response to a teacher contact that structures or limits the situation. Freedom to express own ideas is limited.
	Initiation	9. *Student talk—initiation.* Student initiates or expresses his own ideas, either spontaneously or in response to the teacher's solicitation. Freedom to develop opinions and a line of thought; going beyond existing structure.
Silence		10. *Silence or confusion.* Pauses, short periods of silence, and periods of confusion in which communication cannot be understood by the observer.

SOURCE: *Based on Flanders, Ned A. (1970). Analyzing teaching behavior, as printed in Keith A. Acheson & Meredith Damien Gall (1987). Techniques in the clinical supervision of teachers, 2nd edition. White Plains, NY: Longman.*

guide supervisors in their observations and provide specific feedback within accepted classifications.

As we have attempted to indicate here, a wide variety of techniques may be used to direct the observation stage of clinical supervision. The effective supervisor should be aware of many approaches in order to choose one that fits the concerns of the teacher. What we see from time to time is, unfortunately, the reverse. In many settings, supervisors learn about one technique such as verbatim scripting or the Flanders Interaction Analysis Scale and become wedded to that approach. Techniques have clear strengths, but these strengths quickly disappear when a supervisor insists on using a single approach to guide every observation process, rather than allowing the teacher's instructional concerns to dictate the tool for observation.

Despite the limitations inherent in this stage, observation is absolutely critical for many reasons. As Goldhammer noted when he first described the purpose and rationale for observing teaching in classes:

> In the most general sense, observation should create opportunities for supervisors to help teachers to test reality, the reality of their own perceptions and judgments about their teaching. I have argued that supervision should result in heightened autonomy for teacher and, particularly, in strengthened capacities for independent, objective, self-analysis, and that supervision which increases teacher's dependency upon supervisor to know whether his teaching is good or bad, that is, supervision in which supervisor's unexamined value judgments predominate, is bad supervision. But the supervisor's perceptions and evaluations, rather than counting for nothing, represent a potentially excellent source of data from which consensual validation can be obtained; given his own perceptions of what has taken place. Teacher can test "reality" by ascertaining whether supervisor's observations (and later his value judgments) tend to confirm or to oppose his own. (Goldhammer, 1969, p. 61)

This description of the potential value of observation suggests another issue: Is clinical supervision in fact primarily an activity of staff *development* rather than staff *evaluation*? One theme that permeates existing explanations of the model is that teachers may use clinical supervision to assume increasing control over their own professional development. Recent years have witnessed the creation of numerous programs across the nation which have built upon teachers' wishes to engage in positive collegial relationships on the job. These schemes have made use of the structure and assumptions of the classical clinical supervision model.

Analysis and Strategy

In the third stage of the clinical supervision model, supervisor and teacher independently reflect on the nature of what has just transpired and assess the extent to which the observation was related to the goals and objectives developed during preobservation. Goldhammer's initial description of this stage noted that there are two general purposes to be addressed. The first, *analysis*, involves making sense out of the observational data. In the second, *strategy*, supervisor and teacher plan the agenda of the conference that will follow: "that is, what issues to treat, which data to cite, what goals to aim for, how to begin, where to end, and who should do what" (Goldhammer, 1969, p. 63).

Supervision Conference

As soon as possible after the actual observation, supervisor and teacher meet for a follow-up conference primarily designed to permit the two actors in the clinical model to "de-brief" about what has taken place to that point: Were the goals and concerns of the teacher identified during the preobservation conference accurate? What was seen during the observation? What do we now know as a result of the observation?

Lovell and Wiles (1983, p. 179) identified the following specific goals of the supervision conference:

1. Anticipated teacher and student behavior and actual teacher and student behavior are compared.
2. Discrepancies are identified between anticipated teacher and student behavior and actual teacher and student behavior.
3. Decisions are made about what should be done about discrepancies and congruencies between anticipated and actual behavior.
4. Comparisons are made between projected use of subject content, materials equipment, physical space, and social environment with their actual use, with emphasis on the identification of congruencies and discrepancies, and plans for their future use.
5. Comparisons are made regarding desired learning outcomes with actual learning outcomes within the context of other appropriate factors in the situation, as described by observation.

Goldhammer, Anderson, and Krajewski (1993) acknowledge that, in addition to providing feedback to the teacher and a basis for the improvement of future teaching, the conference can meet at least five additional goals.

1. Teachers can be provided with adult rewards and satisfactions. A supervisor may say to a teacher, in essence, "You are worth my time, and I value you as a colleague sufficiently that I am glad to work with you." As we noted in chapter 13, teachers rarely receive this kind of signal from others with whom they work.

2. Issues in teaching may be defined more precisely. The supervisor can affirm that what the teacher sensed as a problem is indeed something that needs attention.

3. If appropriate, the supervisor can offer to intervene directly with the teacher to provide didactic assistance and guidance. Depending on a number of circumstances (particularly the level of trust between the supervisor and the teacher), the supervisor may usefully suggest specific changes to be made by the teacher.

4. The teacher may be trained in techniques for self-supervision. The clinical supervision model is, ultimately, to be replaced by the ability of the individual teacher to "do without" the supervisor. Good teachers, of course, will always value feedback from colleagues, but an effective clinical supervisor aims at making teachers increasingly responsible for their own improvement. The postobservation conference can be used to increase capability in this area.

5. Teachers can be provided with additional incentives for increasing future levels of professional self-analysis.

Postconference Analysis

Four basic objectives may be achieved in this fifth and final stage, which is structurally part of the supervision conference. First, teacher and supervisor reconstruct the salient features of the conference so that they understand what took place and determine what agreements were made. Second, the participants assess the supervision conference to decide whether or to what extent the objectives of the observation were attained, and to what extent the conference was of value to the teacher. Third, supervisor and teacher consider whether or not the entire process of clinical supervision has had any value to the overall professional development of the teacher. Finally, teacher and supervisor assess the quality of the supervisor's skill in carrying out each of the stages in the model. In short, this final stage in the clinical supervision model allows teacher and supervisor to relax, reflect, and consider the strengths and weaknesses of the process in which they have just been involved. Was it worth all the effort? Did it have any payoff? Should it be done again in the future? In what ways might the process be changed? These questions and others might be considered by teachers and supervisors during the postobservation analysis phase.

These five stages of clinical supervision are not absolute requirements. As we noted earlier, different theorists have included more or fewer steps, but virtually all these descriptions can be logically structured into three stages: preobservation conferencing; observation; and postobservation conferencing. Adherence to every step in a model is not a critical issue; in fact, the specific steps are much less important than the precondition described earlier, namely the establishment of a climate of mutual trust and open communication.

Conversely, then, we can point out that merely employing the five stages (or eight, or three, or whatever particular description is selected) does not produce clinical supervision. Many evaluative programs require supervisors or administrators to hold conferences before observing staff, and also to conduct de-briefing conferences after the observation has taken place. Unless this sequence occurs in a setting where the *basic assumptions* of clinical supervision are observed (i.e., that it is a formative activity, teacher directed, and carried out in an environment where collegial trust is present), the model has not been implemented.

Limits of Clinical Supervision

As we noted in the opening of this chapter, the process of clinical supervision holds considerable promise as a technique for stimulating teachers to take more control of their own development and, as a result, improve the quality of their teaching behavior. However, clinical supervision is not a panacea to be applied to all teachers in all circumstances. We have already noted why some teachers might not be appropriate participants in the clinical model. Other basic limitations of the model also exist.

Ben Harris (1976) presented a precise review of the limitations inherent in the clinical supervision mode. He suggested restrictions in three broad categories: the settings in which the model is deployed; the personal abilities of those involved with the model; and the strategies that need to be followed to make clinical supervision work.

Limitations in Settings

The day-to-day realities of life in schools make clinical supervision exceedingly difficult. As should be evident by now, the model requires considerable time to implement—from two to five hours to carry out in its entirety. If that amount of time is multiplied by the number of times any given teacher might wish to be clinically supervised (remember that the true model is "on demand"), little would go on in a school other than teacher conferencing and observations. This problem can be substantially reduced in situations where the role of the supervisor is broadly enough defined to include the possibility of teachers observing other teachers in peer programs. Some educators suggest that, most supervisory and administrative time in schools should be devoted to precisely the activities of the clinical model. Nevertheless, the fact is that time is limited in schools, and this restricts the unbridled use of clinical supervision.

Harris (1976) also suggest that, because of the press toward conformity felt by teachers at most schools, the highly individualistic nature of clinical supervision makes the model appealing to many who feel it sets them aside as "special" from their peers. From their initial preservice programs, teachers are trained to do what everyone else on the faculty does. Clinical supervision threatens to violate this norm by asking that teachers think of their own needs differently from those of their co-workers.

Personal Limitations

Not every teacher is motivated enough to make the intense time and energy commitment required of clinical supervision. Teachers can be quite talented, experienced, and generally fit the profile of those who may profit from the model, but they simply may not wish to go through all the bother.

Other teachers may simply not be, as Harris (1976) points out, "intelligent, creative, imaginative, open [or] uninhibited" (p. 87) enough to engage in the model. These teachers are not capable, for example, of reflecting on their teaching to the point of sophisticated analysis.

Personal limitations can also restrict the supervisor. Some supervisors are not sufficiently creative or reflective to use the clinical process. Also, the model implies a strong ability to be nondirective in encounters between supervisors and teachers; the fact is that many in supervisory positions have neither the patience nor the inclination to allow teachers to direct the supervisory process.

Strategic Limitations

The fundamental assumption of clinical supervision is that the quality of education in a school can be improved through intervention into the behaviors of teachers in classrooms. The model ignores the fact that other factors contribute to the quality of life in schools. More than observation and analysis of in-class phenomena must be taken into account in the strategies employed to supervise teachers.

Lovell and Wiles (1983, pp. 181–182) described other "pitfalls" inherent in the ways in which the clinical supervision model is carried out in many schools:

1. Some organizations have yielded to the temptation to use "clinical supervision" as a system for evaluating teachers for personnel decisions. Such a decision precludes the use of privileged information, can be threatening and can limit willingness to share problems and concerns, can put teachers in a role of dependency and inferiority, and can limit the hoped-for outcome of teachers becoming better functioning and self-improving professionals.

2. Sometimes clinical supervision is delivered in a rigorous and inflexible series of steps, which may not take into consideration the needs and concerns of a teacher, or his or her readiness to participate in things like observation and analysis of his or her teaching, feedback, and corrective procedures. This practice could be a "turnoff" for some teachers and downright "shattering" for others. Supervisors need to be sensitive to the individual differences among teachers.

3. Sometimes supervisors think that the way they observe a situation is the way it is. It is impossible ever to see things as they are. We can only see them the way we think they are. Thus, it is necessary for supervisors to share their observations with teachers and get teacher feedback, with the hope of reshaping data toward agreement. The teaching situation is too complex and filled with stimuli to see everything. We need to remember that observational data are rough and incomplete at best, and we need to keep working to improve it.

4. The possibility of tenseness and fear are present when teachers are getting feedback about their behavior. Supervisors must

take appropriate steps to ease these situations by stressing the positive aspects of a teacher's performance before making any statement that could be perceived by the instructor to be negative feedback.

Summary

Clinical supervision is a powerful way to provide formative evaluative feedback to classroom teachers. In this chapter we reviewed assumptions of this model in the context of its original design and noted that, from the first, clinical supervision was not a practice intended for all teachers. A struggling first-year teacher who finds it nearly impossible to specify clearly what things are going well in the classroom let alone what things are problematic is hardly capable of engaging in clinical supervision. Only teachers able to articulate fairly specific concerns about their own instructional behavior can constructively enjoy the process of self-directed analysis. We also noted that clinical supervision's use in a school is always contingent upon the extent to which a climate of openness and trust exists in that school between supervisors and teachers. The model may be used only when teachers and supervisors share a fundamental respect for each other.

The chapter also described the stages normally included in clinical supervision and accepted Goldhammer's five stages as appropriate for our review. They are preobservation conference, observation, analysis and strategy, supervision conference, and postconference analysis. Finally, we considered some ways in which the effective application of clinical supervision is limited by ongoing conditions in schools.

Suggested Activities

1. Interview a group of practicing school principals to determine the extent to which they are familiar with the concepts and practices of clinical supervision in this chapter. Are they using the model in their schools? Why or why not, and to what extent?

2. Role-play a preobservation conference with a teacher and practice strategies for asking the teacher to articulate as clearly as possible the things that you might observe in his or her class.

3. Observe a teacher's class, using at least two different techniques described in this chapter.

Cases to Consider

Read each of the following cases and consider these issues:

a. What are the critical issues related to each case, as they relate to the understanding of clinical supervision as a tool for the proactive supervisor?

b. How does each case relate to the development of the concept of proactive supervision?

c. In what ways might you suggest a resolution to the issues raised?

Case 16.1:

The New Evaluation System in Greenville City

The Greenville City Schools board of education was clear in its expectations: Poor teachers would no longer be welcome. In order to make good on this promise, the board directed Stu Callahn, the superintendent, to come up with a teacher evaluation system that could be used in the schools. At the same time, however, they didn't want any trouble with the teachers' association. As a result, Stu would have to come up with a program that would be strong enough to rid the system of poor performers without ruffling any feathers. He directed Mary Carson, his assistant superintendent, to begin the process of initiating a new, more effective teacher evaluation program.

Mary was an excellent manager of details related to the operation of the district. However, she had little knowledge related to alternative approaches to teacher evaluation programs. The challenge that Stu had directed to her was not going to be an easy one to meet. Her only background in teacher evaluation was through her work as a principal, but she honestly could not say that she was an expert. She also learned a bit about effective teacher supervision and evaluation by reading a few articles now and then.

As Mary got ready for her new assignment, she noticed that the state administrators' association was sponsoring a weekend seminar on clinical supervision. When she read the description of the session, she noted that this technique was supported by the state teachers' association as well as the administrator group. Considering that Stu had made it clear that the new evaluation system would have to be sensitive to teachers, Mary thought that the clinical supervision model would have a lot to offer the district as a way to find a new, fool-proof teacher evaluation system that would make teachers happy. She happily sent in her registration fee for the weekend seminar. Soon she would convene a committee of teachers, administrators, and other staff members to begin the work of establishing the kind of system envisioned by the school board. However, Mary knew that if she could learn enough through the training seminar, she could easily direct the committee to adopt the principles of clinical supervision.

Case 16.2:

Visiting Mr. Greeley's Class

Sara Gallagher, the principal of South Central High School, had always been impressed with clinical supervision as an effective approach to teacher evaluation. She was impressed that this was a most effective way to provide teachers with the kind of formative feedback that would help them increase their effectiveness in the classroom. She also subscribed to the notion that clinical supervision must be a process controlled by teachers. It is a non-directive approach, so she always promoted the idea that she was a resource to teachers who were best prepared to identify their concerns.

Harry Greeley was new to the math department at South Central. Sara was really looking forward to observing his class for the first time. She did not know much about his past work at other high schools in the district. He was a last minute hire in the summer. Ordinarily, Sara spent a lot of time looking over the past teaching records of any instructors brought into her school. However, because of the need to locate a new math teacher just before the school year started, she had not looked too deeply at Harry's file. Besides, he was the only certified math teacher seeking a transfer within the district, and the district policy made it clear that a principal could not refuse such a request for transfer unless there was clear evidence of past unsuccessful performance. Harry's personnel folder carried no such warning.

Now, Sara was about to see her new math teacher in his class. Her preobservation conference had gone extremely well with Mr.

Greeley. He was articulate about the kinds of things he wanted Sara to observe. He indicated that he was concerned about the ways he was involving students in his class presentations. He was concerned that his examples were not clear enough for some of the less able students. After all, most of Harry's previous experience had been with more advanced math classes than the ones assigned to him at South Central.

Sara was prepared to go into Mr. Greeley's class to observe and record the illustrative examples used by the teacher so that Harry could assess the quality of his work during the postobservation conference. However, what she saw in the class was considerably different from what she expected to see. It was many years since Sara had taken a math class, and she did not consider herself an expert in algebra or geometry. However, what she saw in Mr. Greeley's class shocked her. For one thing, Mr. Greeley was clearly disorganized. He had no clear lesson plan in mind. Moreover, his explanations of math were wrong. He made mistake after mistake in explaining some of the principles of geometry that were covered in this class session. And students knew it. They continually interrupted him with comments about discrepancies between "what it says in the book" and what Mr. Greeley was saying.

Sara had quite a headache as she sat in her office waiting for her postobservation conference with Harry Greeley. This was going to test her belief in clinical supervision!

References

Acheson, Keith A., & Gall, Meredith D. (1987). *Techniques in the clinical supervision of teachers* (2nd ed.). White Plains, NY: Longman.

Cogan, Morris (1961). Supervision at the Harvard-Newton Summer School. Unpublished mimeographed paper, Harvard Graduate School of Education.

Cogan, Morris (1973). *Clinical supervision.* Boston: Houghton Mifflin.

Flanders, Ned A. (1970). *Analyzing teaching behavior.* Reading, MA: Addison-Wesley.

Garman, Noreen B. (1982). The clinical approach to teaching. In Thomas J. Sergiovanni (Ed.). *Supervision of teaching.* (1982 Yearbook of the Association for Supervision and Curriculum Development). Alexandria, VA: The Association.

Goldhammer, Robert (1969). *Clinical supervision.* New York: Holt, Rinehart, and Winston.

Goldhammer, Robert, Anderson, Robert H., & Krajewski, Robert J. (1993).

Clinical supervision: Special methods for the supervision of teachers (3rd ed.). San Diego: Harcourt, Brace, and Jovanovich.

Harris, Ben M. (1976). Limits and supplements to formal clinical supervision. *Journal of Research and Development in Education.* 9(2): 85–89.

Lovell, John T., & Wiles, Kimball. (1983). *Supervision for better schools* (5th ed.). Englewood Cliffs, NJ: Prentice Hall.

Mosher, Robert L., & Purpel, David E. (1972). *Supervision: The reluctant profession.* Boston: Houghton Mifflin.

Oliva, Peter F. (1993). *Supervision for today's schools* (3rd ed.). White Plains, NY: Longman.

Weller, Richard. (Ed.) (1977). *Humanistic education: Visions and realities.* Berkeley: McCutchan.

Additional Readings

Bellon, Jerry J., Eaker, Robert E., Huffman, James O., & Jones, Richard V. (1978). *Classroom supervision and instructional improvement: A synergistic process.* Dubuque: Brown.

Clinical supervision. (Theme Issue). (1977, Fall). *Contemporary Education.* 49.

Clinical supervision. (Theme Issue). (1976). *Journal of Research and Development in Education.* 9(4).

Cooper, James M. (Ed.) (1984). *Developing skills for instructional supervision.* White Plains, NY: Longman.

Sullivan, Cheryl Granade (1981). *Clinical supervision: A state of the art review.* Arlington, VA: Association for Supervision and Curriculum Development.

Tracy, Saundra J., & MacNaughton, Robert (1993). *Assisting and assessing educational personnel: The fact of clinical supervision.* Needham Heights, MA: Allyn and Bacon.

17 Emerging Models of Supervision

An important consequence of recent reports and discussions about the importance of instructional leadership in schools has been an increasing focus on educational supervision. One by-product of this focus has been the development of some exciting new conceptualizations of supervisory practice.

In this chapter we review two emerging conceptual models of supervision: Carl Glickman's view of developmental supervision and Allan Glatthorn's description of differential patterns of supervision.

Developmental Supervision

The basic assumption in the developmental supervision model initially proposed by Carl Glickman in 1981 is simple: Teachers are adults, and the supervision of adults must acknowledge the nature of their ongoing developmental process. This model suggests that any educational supervisor must recognize the individual differences among clients of supervisory behavior—in other words, teachers—in schools. This relatively simple notion is nevertheless powerful, and Glickman's contribution has been significant because his is that rare formal system designed to take into account *human development* and *individual differences*.

The core of developmental supervision is that two basic factors have an impact on whether supervisors provide more or less effective treatment: the supervisor's basic beliefs about supervisory practice and the teacher's characteristics.

Supervisory Beliefs

The first factor that influences supervision consists of those basic beliefs that any given supervisor holds when working with teachers. Ten different behaviors are indicative of these beliefs, which in turn suggest three basic orientations toward supervision: *nondirective, collaborative*, and *directive*.

Nondirective

1. *Listening.* The supervisor says nothing when working with a teacher but might give slight nonverbal cues such as a nod of the head to indicate that the teacher should continue to speak without interruption.
2. *Clarifying.* The supervisor asks questions but only to the extent that these will draw the teacher into giving information that provides fuller understanding of his or her problems.
3. *Encouraging.* The supervisor encourages the teacher to talk about those factors that may be a part of the problem.
4. *Presenting.* The supervisor offers a limited number of personal perceptions and thoughts about the difficulties that are expressed by the teacher.

Collaborative

5. *Problem Solving.* The supervisor initiates discussions with the teacher by using statements that are aimed at exploring possible solutions to the teacher's problems.
6. *Negotiating.* The supervisor attempts quickly to get to the matter at hand by prodding the teacher to resolve his or her problem immediately.
7. *Demonstrating.* The supervisor physically shows a teacher how to act in similar circumstances, thus eliminating the teaching problem.

Directive

9. *Directing.* The supervisor details simply and exactly what the teacher must do in order to address a problem and improve performance.

9. *Standardizing.* The supervisor explains to the teacher what must be done in order to comply with the behaviors of all others in the school.

10. *Reinforcing.* The supervisor specifically delineates the conditions and consequences for the teacher's improvement.

The relationship between specific supervisory behaviors and general orientations to supervision is shown in Figure 17.1. Note how behaviors signify a gradual shift of control over the supervisory encounter from the teacher to the supervisor. Those practicing supervision generally have a preferred approach to supervisory behavior, which is in line with some specific point on the continuum. Glickman refers to this as the *predominant supervisory belief.*

In order to understand the developmental supervision model more thoroughly, we need to look more closely at the three major orientations to supervision. These three orientations—directive, collaborative, and nondirective—have great impact on the ways in which an individual interacts with the teachers in a school.

Directive supervision.   In this orientation, the supervisor tends to exercise great control in the relationship with the teacher. This does not necessarily mean that the supervisor acts in an authoritarian or arbitrary fashion, but rather suggests that the supervisor sets very precise standards for teachers and then openly explains his or her expectations that those standards will be met. As Glickman (1981, p. 21) noted, "The approach presumes that the supervisor knows more about the context of teaching and learning than the teacher does. Therefore, the supervisor's decisions are more effective than if the teacher is left to his or he own devices."

Collaborative supervision.   This approach suggests that either teacher or supervisor may appropriately take the initiative to require a meeting to discuss concerns. The critical issue is not who requests a supervisory contact, but that the product of the supervisor-teacher meeting is an actively negotiated plan of action. If negotiation between the two parties is not possible, then some third party must be invited to work with the teacher and supervisor to mediate any major difference.

Nondirective supervision.   The nondirective orientation is based on the primary assumption that teachers are capable of initiating their own improvement activities by analyzing their own instruction. The supervisor acts as a facilitator helping teachers

	1	2	3	4	5 Problem solving	6	7	8	9	10	
s	Listening	Clarifying	Encouraging	Presenting		Negotiating	Demonstrating	Directing	Standardizing	Reinforcing	t
T											S

Orientation to
supervision: **NONDIRECTIVE** **COLLABORATIVE** **DIRECTIVE**

KEY:
T = Maximum teacher responsibility   t = Minimum teacher responsibility
S = Maximum supervisor responsibility   s = Minimum supervisor responsibility

Figure 17.1 The Supervisory Behavior Continuum in the Developmental Supervision Model. (From *Developmental supervision: Alternative practices for helping teachers improve instruction*, p. 10, by Carl Glickman. Alexandria, VA: Association for Supervision and Curriculum Development. Copyright 1981 by ASCD. Reprinted by permission.)

control their own improvement. As Glickman (1981, p. 35) notes, "a nondirective orientation ultimately assumes that the teacher makes the wisest and most responsible decisions for his or her own behavior; thus the final determination is still left with the teacher." We believe that the true clinical supervisory model (discussed in chapter 16) with its emphasis on teacher control of the supervisory process fits well with the inherent assumptions of nondirective supervision.

Teacher Characteristics

In addition to supervisory beliefs, a second important factor needs to be recognized in the analysis of supervisory practices, the characteristics of teachers—clients of the supervisory relationship. Glickman's model suggests that the characteristics of teachers are best understood as the product of two features: level of commitment and level of abstraction.

Level of commitment.   Based on research by Gould (1972), Loevinger (1976), and Levinson (1978), and observations by others such as Sheehy (1976), Fuller (1969), and Hall and Loucks (1978), we can identify a number of fairly specific stages through which teachers progress during their professional lives. Glickman has built his developmental supervision model upon these recognized stages of teacher development and has indicated that identifiable characteristics parallel the increasing intensity of individual commitment to a teaching career. "Low commitment" is demonstrated by such things as little concern for other teachers, little time or energy expended toward the job, and great emphasis directed toward simply keeping one's job. These low-commitment characteristics interestingly parallel lower-level needs on Maslow's hierarchy (see chapter 7). At the other end of the continuum, those teachers "high" in professional commitment display high degrees of concerns for students and other teachers in the school, interest and willingness to spend more time and energy on job-related activities, and a primary concern with being able to do more for others.

Level of abstraction.   A continuum also defines the range of teachers' abstract thinking ability, which Glickman (1981, p. 35) defines as "levels of cognitive development, where abstract/symbolic thinking predominates (as a way) to function with greater flexibility in the classroom."

Teachers described as "low" in level of abstraction are easily confused by the professional problems they face, tend not to know what choices can be made to solve problems, need specific direction from others, and often have one or two habitual responses to problems, regardless of the complexity of issues involved. Teachers with a "moderate" level of abstract thinking ability are better at defining the problem at hand, can think of two or more possible responses to a professional problem, but have trouble developing a comprehensive plan for dealing with complex and multifaceted problems. These teachers can usually define a problem in their own terms and then develop a limited range of potential solutions. Finally, teachers with "high" levels of abstract thinking ability can look at a problem from many different perspectives; they can, for example, see things from the perspectives of other teachers, of students, and of parents. As a result, they are able to generate many alternatives and viable solutions to complex problems, to choose a plan of action, and to think through each step in that plan.

The continuums of abstraction and commitment combine to form four typical teacher profiles that generally describe the staff of virtually any school:

Teacher Dropouts. Low in both level of commitment and level of abstract thinking ability

Unfocused Workers. High commitment, but low abstract thinking skills

Analytical Observers. High thinking skills but low level of commitment.

Professionals. High in both level of commitment and abstract thinking skills.

Figure 17.2 demonstrates the relationships between teacher characteristics and supervisory orientations.

The developmental supervision model has great potential to help proactive supervisors do their job better and be more sensitive to the needs of the teachers in the school. At various points throughout this book we have suggested that certain conditions are likely to have an impact on how we engage in supervisory responsibilities. Your personal philosophy and platform, for example, considerably influence how you approach supervision (for example, as "snoopervision" or perhaps from a human relations perspective). We have also suggested that organizational and environmental features have an impact on our choice of a supervisory orientation. Practitioners in business-oriented communities with business-

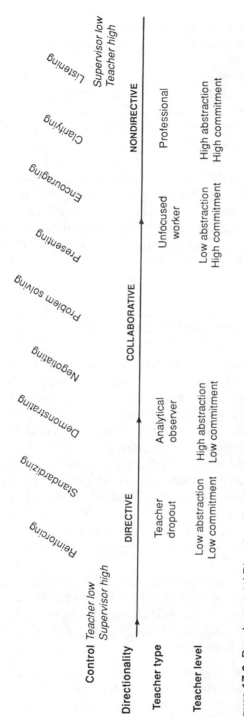

Figure 17.2 Developmental Directionality of the Supervisory Behavior Continuum. (From *Developmental supervision: Alternative practices for helping teachers improve instruction*, p. 49, by Carl Glickman. Association for Supervision and Curriculum Development. Copyright 1981 by ASCD. Reprinted by permission.)

oriented school board members may be tugged toward those practices that are consistent with the beliefs and assumptions of scientific management.

We have also suggested that some supervisory practices and models, such as clinical supervision, are appropriate only in fairly limited circumstances. The value of Glickman's model is that it suggests that the best and most appropriate supervisory strategies ace those that recognize not everyone should receive the same treatment under all circumstances. Developmental supervision is not an easy model to follow at all times, but, perhaps because of that, it is a good one. It stresses the need to develop sensitivity to the backgrounds, abilities, needs, and characteristics of a heterogeneous teaching staff which possesses many special skills and talents and, when properly analyzed, will provide excellent learning opportunities for children.

Differentiated Supervision

Allan Glatthorn (1984) developed an approach to appropriate supervisory strategies which was widely distributed by the Association for Supervision and Curriculum Development in a monograph entitled *Differentiated Supervision*. As was true of Glickman's work, the basic premise in differentiated supervision is quite simple: Different circumstances require different approaches. Research conducted by a number of workers, including Lovell and Phelps (1976), Young and Heichberger (1975), Cawelti and Reavis (1980), and Ritz and Cashell (1980), has made it abundantly clear that teachers have traditionally viewed supervisory activities in schools as rigid and inflexible. Options are needed that will address a variety of needs, interests, skills, and backgrounds.

In response to these assumptions, Glatthorn proposes four types of supervisory practice for schools: clinical supervision, cooperative professional development, self-directed development, and administrative monitoring. Glatthorn (1984, pp. 4–5) defines these approaches in the following ways

> *Clinical supervision* is an intensive process designed to improve instruction by conferring with a teacher on lesson planning, observing the lesson, analyzing the observational data, and giving the teacher feedback about the observation.

Cooperative professional development is a collegial process in which a small group of teachers agree to work together for their own professional growth.

Self-directed development enables the individual teacher to work independently on professional growth concerns.

Administrative monitoring, as the term implies, is a process by which an administrator monitors the work of the staff, making brief and unannounced visits simply to ensure that staff are carrying out assignments and responsibilities in a professional manner.

Certain situations arise in which each of these four models might effectively be used.

Clinical Supervision

Although we described clinical supervision in detail in chapter 16, we include it again here because Glatthorn suggests it as one of his alternative models. Many understand clinical supervision as a practice narrowly defined by Cogan or Goldhammer and requiring absolute adherence. Glatthorn, however, suggests that the structure of the clinical model is compatible with a number of other recently developed supervisory models including scientific supervision, accountable supervision, and artistic supervision.

Scientific supervision is typified most directly by the views of Madeline Hunter (Russell & Hunter, 1980), who has suggested that the activity of teaching might best be assessed according to the extent to which a classroom teacher engages in each of nine specific activities:

1. *Diagnosis.* Identifying a general objective and assessing pupils' present attainment in relation to it

2. *Specific Objectives.* On the basis of the diagnosis, selecting a specific objective for the daily lesson

3. *Anticipatory Set.* Focusing attention, reviewing previous learning, and developing readiness for what is to come

4. *Perceived Purpose.* Clarifying the objective for the pupils, explaining its importance, and relating it to previous learning

5. *Learning Opportunities.* Choosing learning opportunities that will help learners achieve objectives

6. *Modeling.* Providing both a verbal and a visual example of what is to be learned

7. *Check for Understanding.* Assessing the extent to which pupils are achieving objectives

8. *Guided Practice.* Guiding pupils' practice of learning and checking to see that they can perform successfully

9. *Independent Practice.* Giving pupils the opportunity to practice the new skill on their own

This "scientific" approach to the supervisory evaluation of teaching has achieved considerable popularity in recent years, in large part, because it appeals to our sense that there must be "right ways" to do certain things. It is reassuring to think that teaching can be assessed according to certain tenets that have been shown "by research" to be true. Hunter's views have also engendered criticism, however, from researchers who suggest that teaching involves many activities performed well beyond the boundaries of observable teacher-student interactions in a classroom setting (Fenstermacher, 1978; Peterson, 1979). Robert Calfee (1981, p. 53) provided the following criticism of the "narrowness" of the Hunter model:

> The investigations (from which the direct instruction model derives) have tended to be empirical, behavioral, correlational, and prescriptive: the typical study lacks theoretical foundation, focuses on action more than thought, entails interventions that are poorly controlled, yet proposes eventualities in advance to the teacher on how to conduct classroom instruction.

Accountable supervision emphasizes a supervisory focus not on the teacher's behavior as much as on the apparent student outcomes derived from the instructional activity. John D. McNeil (1971) indicated that an accountable approach would involve the following steps:

1. The supervisor helps the teacher determine what learning objectives will be emphasized during a given lesson.

2. The teacher and supervisor agree on how student learning will be assessed.

3. The supervisor visits the teacher's classroom for the primary purpose of observing and determining whether or not the pupils have achieved the intended objectives.

4. The overall assessment of the teacher's activity is made almost exclusively in light of whether or not students achieved stated objectives, not on whether or not there was any "goodness" or "badness" in the instruction itself.

Those who disapprove of this perspective suggest, once again, that it is a highly narrow view of what should take place in the teacher-student interaction. The notion that measurable student outcomes can serve as the criterion for whether or not a teacher is doing a good job is the basis of considerable criticism. Despite these objections, however, others suggest that the emphasis on the accountable approach is squarely where it should be, on the "bottom line." If students are not learning, then there must be something wrong with teaching.

Artistic supervision, the third perspective that Glatthorn suggests, is compatible with clinical supervision. Artistic supervision was developed by Elliot Eisner (1982), who defined it this way:

> [Artistic supervision] is an approach to supervision that relies on sensitivity, perceptivity, and knowledge of the supervisor as a way of appreciating the significant subtleties occurring in the classroom, and that exploits the expressive, poetic, and often metaphorical potential of language to convey to teachers or to others whose decisions affect what goes on in schools, what has been observed. (p. 59)

The fundamental value of the artistic approach to supervision is that it defines teaching much more holistically than other models do: Teaching is an art that changes according to a variety of conditions which do not always fit in to preconceived, lock-step models of how teachers must teach. Critics of Eisner's perspective point to its almost total emphasis on subjective assessment and ask, predictably, "If the model does not say what is *right*, what can be *wrong*?" Glatthorn (1984) and Sergiovanni (1982) both recognize limitations in the artistic view and suggest that, at best, it can function as a supplement to the scientific and accountable approaches, providing a kind of balance to be narrow foci implied in other views.

The basic assumptions of scientific, accountable, and artistic supervision are all compatible with the overall assumptions and structure of the clinical supervision process. The questions that Glatthorn then asks are: Who should receive clinical supervision: Who should provide clinical supervision? Glatthorn (1984, pp. 35–36) believes those who should receive clinical supervision include the following:

- Experienced teachers who have just begun to teach at a particular school. They are unknown quantities—and should at least begin with clinical supervision until the supervisor is assured of their basic competence.

- Experienced teachers who are encountering serious problems of teaching and learning. They need the intensive help that clinical supervision can provide.
- Competent, experienced teachers who believe they can profit from intensive supervision. Even these teachers can learn from effective supervision—but, for them, clinical supervision should be an option that they choose.

In answer to the second question, who should provide clinical supervision, Glatthorn suggests the following:

- Ideally, a trained supervisor, not an administrator, should provide clinical supervision. Clinical supervision is an improvement model, not a form of evaluation, and administrators are typically charged with the duty of evaluating, so their involvement with this model is not advisable.
- Experienced classroom teachers may be trained in the clinical model, and may be asked to provide this service to their colleagues. This solution is particularly useful in school systems that are too small to employ regular full-time supervisory personnel in addition to administrators.
- If the school is large enough, one administrator may be assigned the single responsibility of providing clinical supervision to teachers and be relieved of any teacher evaluation duties. This solution, however, ignores much recent research on instructional leadership, which suggests that such leadership will never be a forceful reality in schools if it is delegated to only one member of an administrative team (Liu & Daresh, 1985).
- Following the recommendations of Sturges (1978), a specialized role of "consultative supervisor" might be created to designate one staff member who is always "on call" to provide clinical supervision.
- Principals may "swap schools" and go to different buildings in the same district to provide clinical supervision, thus avoiding the assumed conflict between the clinical model and the administrative duty of evaluating staff.
- Principals and other administrators might develop skills to do both jobs—clinically supervise and evaluate teachers—provided that they are able to avoid mixing these two very different practices.

All of these suggestions have apparent merit, but the realities of most present school systems, in our opinion, dictate that the currently typical solution, where principals do two jobs, will continue to prevail.

Cooperative Professional Development

Glatthorn defines cooperative professional development as "a moderately formalized process by which two or more teachers agree to work together for their own professional growth, usually by observing each other's classes, giving each other feedback about the observation, and discussing shared professional concerns. Often in the literature it is referred to as *peer supervision* or *collegial supervision*" (Glatthorn, 1984, p. 39). Four essential characteristics serve as the basis for a supervisory program of cooperative professional development:

- The relationship that is developed between or among cooperating teachers is moderately formalized and institutionalized. It is not simply an informal exchange of occasional visits by a few teachers who are close associates.
- At a minimum, the teachers agree to observe each other's classes at least twice and to hold conferences after the visits.
- The supervisory relationship is among peers. Although an administrator or supervisor may be involved in organizing and occasionally monitoring the program, the observations, conferences, and follow-up discussions involve only teachers.
- The relationship is purely nonjudgmental and nonevaluative. It is intended to complement, not take the place of, traditional evaluation systems. None of the observation or conference data are shared with administrators or made part of the evaluation process.

The approach to supervision inherent in this cooperative development model speaks to a very serious problem found in most schools. At a number of points in this text, we have commented on the unfortunate isolation of teachers from their colleagues in most schools. Cooperative professional development offers several ways for teachers to work together to improve their performance, thus considerably reducing this kind of professional separation.

In this model, for example, teachers—professional peers—can serve as informal observers and consultants to their colleagues. Teachers may also serve as true clinical supervisors of their colleagues, an approach that has become increasingly popular as evidenced by recent peer supervision programs in many communities. Peer clinical supervision has become a highly formalized program, negotiated between district administrators and local teachers' associations, with the particular purpose of helping new teachers or teachers experiencing difficulty on the job.

Yet another strategy for implementing cooperative professional development is the use of teachers as focused observers of classroom instruction. Perhaps the best example of this is the widely disseminated Teacher Expectations and Student Achievement (TESA) model designed by Sam Kerman (1979), in an effort to formalize the exchange of observation data among teachers who interact frequently in coaching arrangements. An even more formal and institutionalized arrangement to encourage cooperative professional development can be found in what Lawrence and Branch (1978) describe as "peer panels," in which teachers guide the inservice and developmental activities for their colleagues in a school or district. The final strategy to encourage teachers to interact with each other is one that has existed in many schools for a long time, the result not of any intended plan for peer supervision, but rather of normal organizational patterns. Here, teachers who work together in instructional teams also observe each other as peers, plan together, and make suggestions for improvement.

Like most other models, the cooperative professional development approach to supervision has considerable potential value, but not necessarily for all teachers in all schools. It provides another option for some situations in some settings, most notably in those schools where a demonstrated climate of openness and trust already exists among the teachers.

Self-Directed Development

Glatthorn (1984, pp. 49–50) defines self-directed development as a process for professional growth characterized by the following four basic features:

1. *The individual teacher works independently on a program of professional growth.* Although a member of a leadership team acts as a resource for the teacher, the teacher is not supervised by others, in the conventional sense of the term, and the teacher does not work cooperatively with other members of a team.

2. *The individual develops and follows a goal-oriented program of professional involvement.* The goals of this program stem

from the teacher's own assessment of professional need; there is no need for the teacher's goals to be derived from organizational goals. It is assumed that any professional growth will contribute at least indirectly to the school's goals.

3. *The individual has access to a variety of resources in working toward those goals.* Based on the nature of the goals set, the leader and the teacher may decide that one or more of the following resources and experiences might be appropriate: videotapes of the teacher's teaching; feedback from students; professional books and computerized information services; graduate courses and intensive workshops; support from school and district supervisors and administrators; intraschool visitations.

4. *The results of the self-directed program are not used in evaluating teacher performance.* The program is entirely divorced from evaluation; it is assumed that the teacher will be evaluated by whatever district program is in place.

A number of ways exist in which the basic concept of self-directed development may be effectuated. The most familiar approach is probably formal or self-appraisal systems such as management-by-objective programs (MBO) or the Redfern (1980) evaluation plan. The following appear to be common steps followed in most similar programs in use in school districts around the nation:

1. District goals are established for the following school year. (For example, a district's goal for the next year might be to increase student reading comprehension scores on standardized achievement tests.)

2. Individual staff members review the district goals and formulate individual performance targets and objectives that are in harmony with the district's priorities. (An individual teacher examines his or her instructional goals and priorities for the year and decides how the increase in reading scores might be supported.)

3. Individual members develop performance (or appraisal) contracts that specify how the individual job targets will be achieved and how they will be evaluated. (If, for example, a teacher suggests that he or she will spend fifteen minutes more per day on activities related to the improvement of reading comprehension, the teacher's appraisal will be based on the extent to which this target is met.)

4. Staff members review their performance contracts with their organizational superiors. (In a nonjudgmental and nonthreatening fashion, teachers hold individual conferences with supervisors or administrators to see how well they followed their job targets.)

5. Progress toward the attainment of the stated goals is periodically reviewed.

6. The individual staff member meets with a superior at the conclusion of the cycle to evaluate, in a summative fashion, the extent to which the overall and specific goals were achieved. A new goal-setting cycle may then begin. (The ultimate question to be asked in this context is not whether the teacher was "good" or "bad," but rather whether or not the targets were appropriate and, if they were not achieved, what prevented their attainment.)

Teachers can also analyze their performances on the basis of videotape recordings. Once pupils (and teachers) lose their overawareness of the presence of cameras in classrooms, this technique is a powerful way for individual teachers to assess their performance under nonthreatening circumstances.

As with Glatthorn's other supervisory approaches, self-directed development has both strengths and weaknesses. For example, critics cite research suggesting that teachers have not traditionally been very skillful in appraising their own teaching (Carroll, 1981). On the other hand, supporters stress the value in recognizing teachers as adult learners and of putting them in charge of their own learning and development. Further, teachers are individuals with distinct needs, and self-directed development allows for the highly individualized aspects of teacher development (Bents & Howcy, 1981).

We would not suggest that self-directed improvement would serve as a replacement for all other forms of supervision. We concur, however, that this strategy represents yet another potentially powerful way to foster improvement in schools.

Administrative Monitoring

Glatthorn recognizes that some situations call for a more directive approach to supervision by school administrators. He refers to this as administrative monitoring, or "drop-in supervision," the brief and informal observations of teachers made by principals or assistant principals. Glatthorn (1984, pp. 63–65) has identified four major characteristics as part of this supervisory approach:

1. *Administrative monitoring must be open.* This is not an activity based on the "supervision as inspection" assumptions defined in chapter 1. The purpose here is to see teachers at work under normal conditions, not to catch them doing something incompetent. A basic assumption of administrative monitoring is that, from the outset, the principal and the teacher will speak openly about issues such as:

   • Who will do the monitoring?

   • What kind of behavior can the teacher typically expect from the administrator who will drop in for visits?

   • What kind of feedback may the teacher expect after a drop-in visit?

   • What records will be kept of the monitoring?

   • Will data from monitoring sessions be made part of the formal teacher-evaluation process?

2. *Administrative monitoring should be planned and scheduled, not done randomly and unsystematically.* Certain times during the school week might be established as those when the principal and assistant principals will generally be "out and about" in the school building, and teachers who are to receive administrative monitoring will be visited during those times.

3. *Administrative monitoring should be learning-centered.* If the "drop-in" is not based on the review of learning activities, the visit will not have much purpose. In fact, a principal (or anyone else) who, without any clear purpose, visits a classroom will end up being a dysfunctional intrusion to the teacher's work rather than a help. The following questions may serve to guide an unstructured drop-in visit:

   • What is the teacher's purpose? To what extent is it definite? Attainable?

   • How suitable for achieving these purposes is the plan of instruction that the teacher has prepared?

   • To what extent do the proposed learning experiences promise to help realize the desired purposes?

   • To what extent have students been psychologically prepared, by assignment and otherwise, to participate in this learning experience?

   • What is the atmosphere of the classroom and what is the morale of the students as evidenced by their attitudes toward each other, toward the teacher, and toward the work they are doing?

- Are abundant and rich materials prepared by the teacher or by the pupils in advance?
- Are the pupils gaining adequate guidance by the teacher in directing their own learning? Does each pupil know what to do?
- To what extent is the presentation of new material adequate and clarified by explanation, by obvious order, by illustrations, by relation to the pupils' past experiences, and by application to pupils' needs, immediate or recognized as probable in the future?
- How ready does the teacher appear to be to modify the instructional plan so as to seize the opportunity as it appears for student learning?

4. *Administrative monitoring is likely to be most effective when it is interactive across two dimensions: The administrator gives feedback to the teacher and uses the observational data as part of an ongoing assessment of the instructional program and the school climate.* The teacher involved should receive both negative and positive feedback as a result of the administrator's visit. Some questions that may serve as the basis for this interaction between teacher and administrator are the following:

- Are there certain times during the day when pupils seem inattentive and are disruptive in class?
- Are there certain places in the building where pupils seem easily distracted?
- How much direct instruction goes on across grades, ability levels, and subjects?
- Is monitoring used excessively, insufficiently, or inappropriately?
- To what extent are teachers giving attention to critical thinking and the higher thought processes?
- How much do teachers vary content and method from group to group?

Administrative monitoring is an essential activity in all schools, but not for *all* teachers under *all* circumstances. It may sound like a rather harsh concept—administrators wandering around in teachers' classrooms without any real warning. At the same time, considerable evidence suggests that, when supervisors and administrators know what is going on in an organization, everyone benefits.

Summary

In this chapter we examined the basic assumptions and practices associated with two recent conceptualizations of educational supervision: Carl Glickman's developmental supervision and Allan Glatthorn's differentiated supervision. Both of these perspectives represent emerging views of the ways in which supervisors can work with teachers to achieve the goals of schools.

We selected two models because, in our judgment, they represent coherent *approaches* to supervision and not merely "packaged" models. The recent call for new supervisory and instructional leadership has produced a predictable bombardment of educators with all types of quick-fix schemes to improve supervisory practices—videotape programs, books, and offers for workshops. These cure-alls flood the mailboxes of administrative and supervisory personnel with the promise of immediate improvement in teacher supervision. The fact is, however, that effective supervision is the product not of a weekend seminar but of hard work and serious thought. That is the message of the approaches we have reviewed in this chapter, and it is also the message that we have tried to share throughout this entire book.

Suggested Activities

1. Review Glickman's Supervisory Behavior Continuum presented in Figure 17.1. Ask several teachers to indicate the behavior that they prefer to receive from supervisory personnel (i.e., "listening," "encouraging," etc.) and also the behaviors they believe they actually witness in supervisory relationships. Do the same with two or three supervisors by asking them to indicate the ways in which they believe they interact with teachers, and also the ways in which they wish they *could* interact. What are the differences and similarities among these various perceptions?

2. With the permission of a classroom teacher, observe a class and try to answer the questions listed under "administrative monitoring should be learning-centered" on p. 347. Use the responses to these questions to focus a feedback session with the teacher after the class has concluded.

3. Using the various alternative approaches to supervision provided by Glatthorn, conduct a survey of practices used in your district to determine the percentage of time individual schools spend in using each of the models reviewed.

Cases to Consider

Read each case and consider the following:

a. What are the critical issues raised in each case, as they relate to some of the emerging models of supervision reviewed in this chapter?
b. How does each case relate to the development of proactive supervision?
c. In what ways might you suggest a resolution to the issues raised?

Case 17.1:

Everyone's Different

Dr. Don Westphal has enjoyed an outstanding reputation as one of the most effective principals in the school district for several years, particularly in the area of teacher evaluation. As a consequence, it was not surprising to hear that he had recently been named as the new principal of Luther Hawkins High School, perhaps the most run-down school in the entire system. Although it was an old building in need of repair work, it also was known as a good school because of an outstanding staff dedicated to helping the students in the surrounding inner-city neighborhood learn. In short, Hawkins was a dump, but it was a school where people cared.

Dr. Westphal was looking forward to his new assignment. He had heard so many stories about the quality of the teaching staff at Hawkins, and he believed that this would be a great place for him to achieve many goals that he had never achieved earlier in his career. As he looked over the roster of nearly one hundred faculty members, he saw three individuals with backgrounds and descriptions that seemed to call out for special attention as soon as the year started. All three were experienced teachers who were due for periodic evaluation by the principal, and Don knew that each case would call for a different evaluation strategy.

Lucy Erlich was a science teacher with about five years experience in the classroom. She had several years of experience as a nurse before going into teaching after she lost her husband, a bright young physician, about eight years ago. Lucy was highly regarded as a teacher with considerable expertise in life sciences, but she had an equally strong reputation as a somewhat abrasive person who was often short-tempered and sarcastic with her co-workers.

Craig Mark was also due for intensive evaluation. Craig was clearly one of the brightest classroom teachers that Don Westphal had ever encountered. His work in the American history classroom was superb, and he had received many awards over the years pointing to his excellence as a great instructor. He was also known as one of the great egos in the school district. Other members of the history department respected Craig because of his work in the classroom and his intelligence, but he intimidated his colleagues to the point that he was often isolated from the majority of teachers in the school.

Finally, Don was also due to evaluate Morris Jackson, the youngest of the three teachers on his list. Morris was a young man who seemed to lack any self-confidence. He was bright, cared about his students, and demonstrated considerable skill in the classroom each day. However, he simply did not appear to believe in himself.

What would Dr. Westphal do with this trio?

Case 17.2:

That's Not My Problem

"So what am I? A social worker? I teach and teach well!" With that pronouncement, Amos Carlisle pounded the desk of the principal, Helen Rosenberg, and stormed out of the office. What began as a routine preobservation conference between a teacher and the principal quickly became a loud and unpleasant discussion. Helen sat quietly for nearly five minutes, trying to recall everything that was said which may have led to the blow-up by one of her fifth grade teachers. Perhaps the most frustrating aspect of the situation was that Amos was known as one of the better elementary school teachers in the entire school district, at least with regard to his performance in the classroom.

Helen had called Amos in to her office for two reasons. First, it was time for the two to get together for a prescribed conference prior to one of the two observations which were required for Mr. Carlisle this year. The master contract for the district specified that each tenured teacher would be observed in his or her classroom twice a year, every other year; each observation had to be preceded by a minimum of twenty minutes of conference time between the teacher and the principal.

The second objective that Helen had wanted to attain through this meeting was considerably less formal. For the past three years, she had watched Amos become increasingly separated and aloof from the school in many different ways. At one time, Mr. Carlisle was a teacher who got to work before almost everyone else and left the building long after most other teachers had gone home. He always seemed to be working—putting up new exhibits for class, talking with pupils, visiting with other teachers, or correcting student assignments. All of that seemed to change over the past three years. Now, Amos appeared to be less inclined to do much other than the minimal amount of work outside of what he did simply to get ready for his classes. His work with students didn't seem to be suffering; he was still getting a lot of positive comments from the pupils and their parents, but he was losing ground with his colleagues. Helen was truly concerned as she saw a great talent beginning to fade. That's when she decided to call for this conference and try to find out what was bothering Mr. Carlisle.

The session began peacefully, with Helen following the normal pattern of asking Amos about his instructional goals, anticipated teaching strategies, and so forth. After about ten minutes, however, she interjected her observation about how Amos did not seem to be working with the other fifth grade teachers in the same ways he did in the past. That's when the explosion occurred. Now Helen tried to determine what she should do next. Amos Carlisle was still doing a great job in the classroom with his fifth graders, but now something else had to be done.

References

Bents, R. H., & Howey, Kenneth R. (1981). Staff development: Change in the individual. In Betty Dillon-Peterson (Ed.), *Staff development/ organization development*. Alexandria, VA: Association for Supervision and Curriculum Development.

Calfee, R. (1981). Cognitive psychology and educational practice. In David C. Berliner (Ed.), *Review of research in education, 9*. Washington, DC: American Educational Research Association.

Carroll, J. G. (1981). Faculty self-evaluation. In Jason Millman (Ed.), *Handbook of teacher evaluation.* Beverly Hills: Sage.

Cawelti, Gordon, & Reavis, Charles (1980, December). How well are we providing instructional improvement services? *Educational Leadership,* 38:236–240.

Cogan, Morris (1973). *Clinical supervision.* Boston: Houghton Mifflin.

Eisner, Elliot (1982). An artistic approach to supervision. In Thomas Sergiovanni (Ed.), *Supervision of teaching.* Alexandria, VA: Association for Supervision and Curriculum Development.

Fenstermacher, Gary D. (1978). A philosophical consideration of recent research in teacher effectiveness. In David C. Berliner (Ed.), *Review of research in education, 6.* Washington, DC: American Educational Research Association.

Fuller, Frances (1969). Concerns of teachers: A developmental conceptualization. *American Educational Research Journal,* 6:207–226.

Glatthorn, Allan (1984). *Differential supervision.* Alexandria, VA: Association for Supervision and Curriculum Development.

Glickman, Carl (1981). *Developmental supervision: Alternative practices for helping teachers improve instruction.* Alexandria, VA: Association for Supervision and Curriculum Development.

Goldhammer, Robert (1969). *Clinical supervision: Special methods for the supervision of teachers.* New York: Holt, Rinehart, and Winston.

Gould, R. (1972). The phases of adult life: A study in developmental psychology. *The American Journal of Psychiatry,* 129:521–531.

Hall, Gene E., & Loucks, Susan (1978, September). Teacher concerns as a basis for facilitating and personalizing staff development. *Teachers College Record,* 80:36–53.

Kerman, Sam (1979, June). Teacher expectations and student achievement. *Phi Delta Kappan.* 6:716–718.

Lawrence, Gordon, & Branch, J. (1978, June). Peer support as the heart of inservice education. *Theory Into Practice,* 17:245–247.

Levinson, Daniel (1978). *The seasons of a man's life.* New York: Knopf.

Liu, Ching-Jen, & Daresh, John C. (1985). *Instructional leadership behavior of high school principals.* Paper presented at the Annual Meeting of the American Educational Research Association, Chicago.

Loevinger, J. (1976). *Ego development.* San Francisco: Jossey Bass.

Lovell, John T., & Phelps, M. S. (1976). *Supervision in Tennessee: A study of perceptions of teachers, principals, and supervisors.* Murfreesboro: Tennessee Association for Supervision and Curriculum Development.

Maslow, Abraham (1960). *Motivation and personality.* New York: McGraw Hill.

McNeil, J. D. (1971). *Toward accountable teaching.* New York: Holt, Rinehart, and Winston.

Peterson, Penelope P. (1979). Direct instruction reconsidered. In Herbert J. Walberg (Ed.), *Research on teaching.* Berkeley: McCutchan.

Redfern, George B. (1980). *Evaluating teachers and administrators: A performance objectives model.* Boulder, CO: Westview.

Ritz, W. C., & Cashell, J. G. (1980, October). 'Cold War' between supervisors and teachers? *Educational Leadership*, 38:77–78.

Russell, D., & Hunter, Madeline (1980). *Planning for effective instruction*. Los Angeles: University Elementary School.

Sergiovanni, Thomas J. (1982). Toward a theory of supervisory practice: Integrating scientific, clinical, and artistic views. In Thomas J. Sergiovanni (Ed.), *Supervision of teaching*. Alexandria, VA: Association for Supervision and Curriculum Development.

Sheehy, Gail T. (1976). *Passages: Predictable crises in adult life*. New York: Dutton.

Sturges, A. W. (1978). *The roles and responsibilities of instructional supervisors*. Alexandria, VA: Association for Supervision and Curriculum Development.

Young, J. M., & Heichberger, R. L. (1975, Fall). Teacher perceptions of an effective school supervision and evaluation program. *Education*, 96:10–19.

Additional Readings

Eisner, Elliot (1979). The educational imagination. New York: Macmillan.

Glickman, Carl D. (1991). Supervision of instruction: A developmental approach (2nd ed.). Boston: Allyn and Bacon.

Rubin, Louis J. (1985). Artistry in teaching. New York: Random House.

18

Supervision as Effective Staff Development and Inservice Education

Educational reform requires that we pay more attention to discovering how classroom teachers increase the effectiveness of the learning process for children. For the past few years the relationship of specific practices and behaviors of teachers to student achievement, particularly in the basic skills areas of reading, language arts, and mathematics, have been the focus of considerable research. We are learning more about how teachers organize their classrooms, interact with students, and deliver instruction to elicit positive results. Still, many teachers are not aware of practices that may have the greatest potential for improving their schools. Staff development and inservice education—the traditional systems that support professional development of teachers and other educators—are typically viewed as relatively ineffective. The perception of ineffectiveness hinders our judgment about an activity which can be a potentially valuable contribution to school improvement. As we have stressed throughout this text, the effective practitioner of proactive supervision always focuses on one ultimate goal: the enhancement of school effectiveness for the improvement of student learning.

One of the proactive supervisor's most important ongoing responsibilities is to improve the continuous professional growth and development of all those who are working toward achieving the goals and objectives of the school. In short, supervisors need to be aware of effective practices associated with staff development and inservice teacher education. We generally accept the notion that inservice education and staff development must be improved if schools are to improve. We also believe that, in many ways, the responsibilities of supervisors include staff development, but efforts to make staff development and inservice education more effective tend to be sporadic. Often, little attention is paid to the relationship between professional development for teachers and the improvement of instruction for students. As we noted in chapter 6, research on school effectiveness has shown that the ability of school supervisors and administrators to provide instructional leadership in their schools and districts is an important factor in the improvement of instruction. Yet few educators seem to recognize that positive change occurs when school leaders accept the responsibility of working with their staffs to plan, carry out, and ultimately evaluate inservice and staff development activities.

In this chapter, we consider a number of issues related to the supervisor's ability to provide more effective professional development. We begin by defining educational staff development and examining some of the more positive trends in the design of more effective staff development and inservice education programs. We pay particular attention to recent research findings that focus on the determination of desirable content and delivery in development programs. Finally, we examine two issues associated with more effective staff development and inservice programs: adult learning theories and individual differences among learners. In this regard, we also examine the concept of mentoring as a form of professional development that addresses these two issues.

Finding a Definition

Staff development and inservice education have become hot topics of discussion for educators. Increased attention to an important topic is generally a good thing, but the downside of this phenomenon is that many people talk without always knowing what they are talking about. All sorts of schemes have appeared on the market promising to increase the effectiveness of staff development overnight. We cannot rid the field of professional education of all those profitable quick-fix packages for staff development and inservice education, but we do suggest that educators can take a big step toward improving the quality of staff development and training by more clearly defining just what staff development is.

The distinction between staff development and inservice education is normally based on whether an activity has been designed primarily to address a perceived deficit in professional knowledge or performance or to stimulate long-term improvement and on-the-job growth. The accepted view is that *inservice education* covers those activities directed toward remediating a perceived lack of skill or understanding; *staff development* refers to an ongoing process that promotes professional growth rather than remediation.

This distinction makes inservice education sound somehow "bad," and staff development "good." The fact is, in certain situations each activity may be effective and enhance the quality of education. Inservice education, generally perceived as something done "to" people to "fix them," is in fact necessary and appropriate in some settings and is an entirely positive process. There are times when people need special training to correct deficits in their skills. Consider, for example, the number of very good teachers who have recently taken part in inservice education programs designed to provide skills in the use of microcomputers. Most teachers who graduated from college before the mid-1980s had little or no training in computer technology; as a result, they were "deficient" in a very important area. Inservice education corrected that deficiency positively and appropriately. By contrast, developmental activities, designed to engage teachers in process experiences to provide personal and professional insights, are sometimes totally inappropriate. For example, engaging a beginning teacher who has few classroom survival skills in a developmentally focused, consciousness-raising staff development exercise is both pointless and potentially harmful. The young teacher may indeed grow, but at the cost of not acquiring some basic mechanical skills absolutely vital to teaching.

We want to minimize the artificial distinctions that have been drawn between inservice education and staff development. Suggestions that one activity is better than the other, as we have seen, are false. In the real world of schools, in any case, little difference is made in the use of the two terms. Practitioners face daily problems in implementing more effective inservice and staff development; they are far more concerned with the quality of implementation than with subtle conceptual differences. If we must differentiate between inservice and staff development, we suggest that staff development, or the currently popular "professional development," is a broader term that includes inservice education as a subset. Whatever term we select, we are talking about a learning process designed to assist the professional staff of a school or district in carrying out their duties more effectively so that children are better able to learn.

Research Related to Inservice and Staff Development

The complexities of current educational activities require teachers and other staff members to receive additional opportunities for learning. Simply stated, effective inservice and staff development are needed for effective schools; they may no longer be viewed as "extras" that are made available only if school systems have a few additional dollars to spend. Despite the critical need for effective approaches to staff development and inservice education, however, these activities remain part of a field with few theoretical or conceptual roots (McLaughlin & Berman, 1977; Henderson, 1979), little respect from practitioners (Brimm & Tollett, 1975), and a generally meager research base (Swenson, 1981). Theorists suggest that both staff development and inservice education lack sufficient intellectual rigor, whereas practitioners often complain that what has been written has little practical value for addressing problems faced in the "here and now."

A recent review of research on staff development and inservice education (Daresh, 1987) found that from the many studies that have been conducted, two observations could be made. First, the research techniques used to study staff development and inservice education have been seriously limited. Most work used survey questionnaires exclusively, for example. Second, and more relevant to our concerns in this text, most research has centered on only three targets: (1) the evaluation of specific inservice or staff development models, (2) the content of inservice and staff development activities, and (3) the delivery systems typically used.

Research on specific programs has consisted primarily of individual researchers studying the effectiveness of workshops, seminars, or other forms of inservice education that the researcher designed. Not surprisingly, a large number of these studies indicated that such efforts at providing inservice education were quite effective, but the studies added little to our goal of learning more about improving inservice education and staff development because of the difficulty of generalizing from a single setting to a larger sample. Studies that are focused on content and delivery aspects of staff development and inservice education are of greater interest because their conclusions are more clearly applicable in helping supervisory personnel determine how they might make these activities more positive.

Content of Staff Development and Inservice Education

A review of recent studies on the nature of inservice education and staff development content leaves us with four major observations:

1. Staff development and inservice education are perceived as more effective when content is based on the self-reported needs of participants.

2. Desired staff development and inservice education content reflects topics of immediate concern to practitioners. Great interest was expressed in how to implement externally mandated programs—for example, competency-based instructional programs; less interest was expressed in programs or activities designed to deal with less concrete, more conceptual topics, such as building a more supportive organizational climate for student learning. At a mid-range of interest were topics concerning human relations skills development, such as how to enhance communication skills in the classroom.

3. Few strong relationships appeared to exist between teachers' demographic background characteristics and staff development and inservice education interests. In fact, the only characteristic repeatedly linked to desired content was length of service, or experience, as an educator. Beginning teachers (usually defined as those with one to three years' experience) sought activities that helped them deal with feelings of insecurity, frequent uncertainty, and limited knowledge concerning their immediate teaching environment and the larger field of professional education. Experienced teachers (more than ten years in the classroom), who were generally less favorable toward staff development and inservice education, did express interest in topics that focused on student instructional needs. In other words, the length of teacher experience was an important and accurate predictor of staff development and inservice education interests. Teachers' interests shifted gradually through their careers from teacher-centeredness to greater child-centeredness.

4. Teachers and other educators wanted to be involved in planning their own staff development and inservice education programs and activities.

Delivery of Staff Development and Inservice Education

Most of the recent studies addressed methods for planning and carrying out staff development and inservice education activities. Many of these studies were designed to examine the issue of content as well. Our review of these studies produced the following four generalizations:

1. There is a great dissatisfaction with, or at least lack of interest in, existing procedures associated with most staff development and inservice education programs and activities. Studies did not always pinpoint the exact nature of the procedures causing the dissatisfaction; instead, such evaluations concerned the general ways in which staff development and inservice education are "usually" provided.

2. Staff development and inservice education participants want to be involved with planning, implementing, and evaluating their learning experiences. The general finding expressed in many studies was that participants do not wish to have someone "do" staff development "to" them. As we shall see later in this chapter, this attitude correlates with research findings which conclude that adults want to play a primal role as the source of their own learning.

3. Staff development and inservice education participants prefer learning activities and programs that make them engage in a process. They do not wish to be mere passive observers of presentations by others. In addition, demonstrations were more highly valued than lecture presentations.

4. Both staff development and inservice education are viewed as more effective when they are part of training that continues over an extended period of time. Short-term, one-shot sessions were viewed negatively.

Supervisors need to recognize some general issues raised by recent research on staff development and inservice education. We might conclude, for example, that the skills most frequently sought by professional educators, as determined through the research, are knowledge-level skills. More often than not, those knowledge-level skills are related to issues of immediate interest and concern to practitioners. Thus, for a few years, staff development programs and related research were directed almost exclusively to the "hot topic" of mainstreaming students with physical, mental, or emotional disabilities. Now, the emphasis seems to be microcomputers in the classroom. We can only guess at what will be included in the next wave of perceived need and interest for inservice education in schools.

Current research on staff development and inservice education seems focused on collecting information of apparently limited benefit to the improvement of school practices, the ability of educators to be more successful in their roles, or the condition of staff development and inservice education. Despite these limitations, supervisory personnel may cull some important insights concerning the characteristics of effective staff development from the existing research. A number of researchers (Lawrence, 1974; Nicholson, Joyce, Parker, & Waterman, 1976; Paul, 1977; Mclaughlin & Marsh, 1978; Hutson, 1981) have offered useful guidelines:

- Effective inservice and staff development programs are directed toward local school needs.
- Inservice and staff development participants are actively involved in effective programs.
- Effective programs are based on participant needs.
- Effective local school inservice and staff development programs are supported by a commitment of resources from the central office.
- Effective programs provide evidence of quality control and are delivered by competent presenters.
- Programs that enable participants to share ideas and provide assistance to one another are viewed as successful.
- Rewards and incentives, both intrinsic and extrinsic, are evident to participants in programs that are viewed as successful.
- Inservice and staff development activities are viewed more positively when provided during school time.
- Effective inservice education and staff development activities are accompanied by ongoing evaluation.

The above guidelines are general, but they should prove useful to supervisors and others charged with designing, developing, and implementing an effective inservice or staff development program. Other useful research includes that of Sprinthall and Thies-Sprinthall (1983) who also described effective practice for continuing professional development programs to improve educational practice:

Collaboration between participants and programs sponsors.
Building or districtwide professional development councils can

foster collaboration and cooperation in planning effective inservice programs.

Learning needs identified by participants. Professional development programs responsive to the needs of participants will maximize the probability of success. A comprehensive assessment of needs should be undertaken before planning specific programs.

Programs offered at convenient locations. Sites are easily accessible.

Intrinsic and extrinsic rewards provided. Intrinsic rewards are derived by gaining competence (self-esteem) or success (self-actualization). Extrinsic rewards could include certificates, enhanced promotional opportunities, or increments in pay.

Modeling by experts of skills and concepts. Demonstrations by skillful practitioners should be an integral part of professional development programs.

Utilization of participants' talents and abilities. Independent study, role-play exercises, or presentations by participants can be used to draw upon participants' talents and abilities.

Synthesis of content and adaptation to diverse situations. Case analyses, site visits, or guided group discussions may be employed to achieve synthesis of content and to explore its adaptation to diverse situations.

Individualized learning activities. Small group discussions, private counseling, or case studies written and analyzed by participants may be useful.

Significant and challenging role-playing experiences. Role-play can be an integral part of many professional development programs, particularly those dealing with interpersonal relationships or instructional procedures.

Opportunities for reflection. Time for reading and reflection is essential; programming must provide time for this to occur.

Continuity and logical sequencing of activities. All presentations and activities should be carefully planned and coordinated to build on previous learning.

Both personal support and personal challenge. Participants grow through confrontation with challenges; they must have freedom to try, to fail, and to try again without fail.

Assessment of results. The program should be evaluated in terms of its objectives, which might be cognitive, affective, or psychomotor development, or combinations thereof.

Information about useful and effective practices regarding inservice education and staff development is clearly available. However, school districts and other agencies engaged in these activities too often tend to be unresponsive to the practices and guidelines we have noted here. Consequently, professional development efforts are not as effective as they might be. Attitudes are frequently quite negative, Those negative perceptions result in part from lack of attention to two important features of staff development that have traditionally been ignored by school personnel, as we shall see in the next section.

Important Missing Ingredients

After listening to many teachers voice their frustrations about the quality of staff development activities, we have identified two basic ingredients of "good" programs:

- Recognize that adults have specialized learning needs
- Reflect an understanding of the individual differences among learners

Characteristics of Adult Learning

Intuition has long suggested that adults have different learning needs or characteristics from those of children. Malcolm Knowles (1970), a major contributor to the field of adult education, is generally credited with coining the word *andragogy* (the art and science of teaching adults) as distinct from *pedagogy* (the art and science of teaching children). More important, Knowles identified four critical characteristics of adults and their patterns of learning:

1. As a person matures, his or her self-concept moves from one of dependency to one of self-direction.
2. The mature person tends to accumulate a growing reservoir of experience that provides a resource for learning.
3. The adult's readiness to learn becomes increasingly oriented toward the developmental tasks of his or her assigned social roles.
4. The adult's time perspective changes from postponed application of knowledge to immediate application, and accordingly his or her orientation toward learning shifts from subject-centeredness to problem-centeredness.

Predictably, Knowles's work encouraged others to research and write in the field of adult education, and some researchers' work is useful for us in seeking to improve staff development in schools. Fred Wood and Stephen Thompson (1980), for example, reviewed some salient aspects of adult learning:

- Adults will learn when the goals and objectives of a learning activity are considered *by the learner* to be realistic, related, and important to a specific issue at hand.
- Adults will learn, retain, and use what they perceive as relevant to their immediate personal and professional needs.
- Adults need to see the results of their efforts and have frequent and accurate feedback about progress that is being made toward their goals.
- Adult learning is highly ego-involved. When a person is unsuccessful at a given learning task, it is likely that he or she will take it as an indication of personal incompetence and failure.
- Adults always come to any learning task with a wide range of previous experiences, knowledge, skills, and competencies.
- Adults want to be the origins of their own learning, and they wish to be directly involved in the selection of learning objectives, content, activities, and so forth.
- Adults will tend to resist any learning experience that they believe is either an open or implied attack on their personal or professional competence.
- Adults reject prescriptions by others for their own learning.
- Adult motivation comes from the learner and not from any external source. While this may be generally true of motivation of all individuals, it is true that, as a person matures, efforts to motivate from outside the individual will decrease in probable effectiveness.

Taken together, these characteristics of adult learning should provide practitioners of supervision who design and lead staff development experiences with some important insights into how such experiences should be planned and carried out. First, the fact that adults want (and learn best from) experiences that address immediate problems suggests that supervisors should direct activities toward answering the perennial question, "What should I do on Monday morning?" Presentations of the latest research on teacher behavior and school effectiveness, no matter how carefully prepared, will be exercises in futility unless staff members clearly understand how the research relates to their school's immediate needs. However, it can be dangerous to focus too directly on issues of immediate importance to a school or district if the offered solutions are merely prescriptions—quick fixes—to complex problems. As we saw above, adults tend to reject prescriptions. Those planning staff development should understand what the real problems are in a school or district, avoid "band-aid" responses, and be careful not to ignore other serious issues.

The study of adult learning or andragogy also provides some important clues about adult self-concept needs. Teachers frequently complain that staff development and inservice education seem threatening—that participants often feel incompetent. The implication here is that as people become more mature and fixed in their ways, they become increasingly self-conscious in situations where they believe they might experience failure (and perhaps ridicule) in front of others. Staff development and inservice education activities must therefore be planned so that teachers and other staff will not be put in situations where their performance might be compared publicly with that of their co-workers. Thus, we might question the wisdom of using activities, such as role playing, which require people to "perform" in front of others to demonstrate particular techniques, especially when people have not clearly volunteered to do so.

Finally, the literature on adult learning clearly shows that as people mature, they tend to accumulate additional learning experiences. Supervisory personnel involved with a staff which has a variety of adult learning experiences should recognize the potential and varied richness of this previous learning. Nothing is more frustrating to teachers than being asked to participate in activities designed to send everyone "back to square one." Practices that do this not only ignore an important resource for teaching adults but also violate a basic rule of effective staff development, namely that individual differences among learners must be taken into account.

Individual Learning Differences

Although educators frequently affirm the belief that every learner is different, they seem to forget this principle when they plan staff development activities. A recurring message from critics of "bad" staff development is that teachers do not like to be treated as if they were a herd of sheep—a sort of amorphic blob known collectively as "the staff." Supervisors and others who plan development activities often seem to overlook the fact that, with the staff, many different needs, interests, learning styles, and abilities exist. Time and again, teachers report that staff development and inservice sessions are a waste of time because no effort was made to match learning activities with learning needs.

Fortunately, a considerable amount of information is now coming from the research community concerning differences among teachers. This information has much to offer supervisors and other planners of staff development and inservice education. Unruh and Turner (1970) defined four stages of professional growth reflected within most school staffs. These categories should be useful to the supervisor in determining broad groupings of teachers who might be interested in different staff development activities and learning opportunities:

1. *The preservice period.* Within the school, this period is represented by student teachers and interns. Although this is not a period with great immediate implications for staff development, general interest is usually high because much of what happens in education is actually a supplement to what took place (or should have taken place) as part of college training.

2. *The initial training period.* Teachers in this period, who generally have from one to five years' experience, often have "beginner" problems such as discipline, routine organizational and administrative chores, and general class planning and curriculum development. The supervisor aware of the unique concerns of staff in this period might design activities to' address these problems.

3. *The security-building period.* Teachers with five to fifteen years' service might be most interested in increasing their personal knowledge and skills. The supervisor needs to make certain that inservice and staff development experiences are appropriately designed to promote individual growth for teachers in this category.

4. *The maturing period.* "Master teachers" have an undefined number of years of experience but a clear depth of professional expertise. The supervisor would do well to tap into the knowledge and skills possessed by these teachers as additional resources in promoting professional growth.

Although these stages of professional growth suggest differentiated patterns for staff development and inservice education, their usefulness is somewhat limited by the fact that right now the vast majority of teachers in most schools belong to the "security-building" period. We need finer definitions of individual or staff needs to assist in devising more effective strategies.

Promising work in this area has been done by Gene Hall and his associates at the University of Texas Research and Development Center for Teacher Education (Hall & Loucks, 1978). Building on earlier work by Frances Fuller (1969), Hall and his colleagues suggest that an important way to differentiate needs of staff members is according to their levels of concern about a particular educational practice. Hall indicates that teachers might be classified according to the following descending order of "Levels of Concern":

6. *Refocusing.* The teacher believes he or she has some ideas about making good practices even better.

5. *Collaboration.* The teacher is interested in combining his or her good ideas with the ideas of co-workers.

4. *Consequence.* The teacher is concerned with the extent to which there will be a positive impact on student learning.

3. *Management.* The teacher is concerned with getting materials ready for instruction.

2. *Personal.* The teacher is most interested in what personal effect a school practice will have on him or her.

1. *Informational.* The teacher is most concerned with finding out basic information about a practice.

0. *Awareness.* The teacher is not interested in a particular issue or practice.

This classification system is in no sense evaluative. In other words, we should assume that, at any given time, a school's staff will be distributed across all seven levels of concern, *depending on the issue at hand.* Teachers are not automatically better than their co-workers simply because they are at the "refocusing" level; conversely, virtually all teachers may be legitimately classified at the "awareness" level from time to time. In fact, shifting from one level to another depending on the issue may indicate a healthy professional environment, where staff members feel free to act in an honest and open fashion.

The implications of this work for staff development and inservice education should be fairly obvious. It makes it clear that not every staff member will be interested in every topic, and that a particular lack of interest does not constitute a negative evaluation of the school's total staff development plan. A second implication is that the design of any staff development or inservice education activity must be flexible enough so that staff members can approach an issue according to their own levels of concern, without feeling anxious or threatened if they are not interested in a particular issue at a particular time.

Gene Hall and Susan Loucks (1978) summarized the most crucial lessons to be learned in the area of staff development according to the "Levels of Concern" categories:

- The staff development leader must attend to the teachers' concerns as well as to the content to be covered.
- It is all right to have personal feelings.
- Change cannot be accomplished overnight.
- Teachers' concerns might not be the same as those of the staff developer.
- Within any group, there is a variety of concerns.

Finally, Gordon Lawrence (1982) has suggested the analysis of psychological types as a fruitful path for supervisors and other planners of inservice and staff development to explore. Lawrence's work is based on the original premise of the Swiss psychologist, C. G. Jung (1923), who suggested that people's behavior could best be explained through the extent to which they followed certain patterns, or "psychological types." Jung based these types on how people prefer to make and perceive judgments. Lawrence (1982) noted that in Jungian psychology, "all conscious mental activity can be classified into four mental processes—two perception processes (sensing and intuition) and two judgment processes (thinking and feeling). What comes into consciousness, moment by moment, comes either through the sense or through intuition. To remain in consciousness, perceptions must be used. They are used—sorted, weighed, analyzed, evaluated—by the judgment processes, thinking and feeling" (p. 6).

Sixteen different psychological types have been identified, and measures such as the Myers-Briggs Type Indicator (MBTI), designed by Isabel Briggs Myers and Katherine Briggs (1962), help us determine the extent to which individuals fall into one another of the different types by looking at relative strengths in four areas: extroversion (E) versus introversion (I); gathering information through sensing (S) versus intuition (N); making judgments as a product primarily of thinking (T) versus feeling (F); and a desire to live in a world defined mostly through judgment (J) versus perception (P). The possible combinations of these different descriptors, along with typical behaviors associated with each of the sixteen possible types, are shown in Figure 18.1.

ENTJ

Intuitive, innovative ORGANIZER; aggressive, analytic, systematic, more tuned to new ideas and possibilities than to people's feelings.

ESTJ

Fact-minded, practical ORGANIZER; aggressive, analytic, systematic, more interested in getting the job done than in people's feelings.

INTP

Inquisitive ANALYZER; reflective, independent, curious, more interested in organizing ideas than situations or people.

ISTP

Practical ANALYZER; values exactness, more interested in organizing data than situations or people, reflective, a cool and curious observer of life.

ESTP

REALISTIC ADAPTER in the world of material things; good natured, tolerant, easy going, oriented to practical, first-hand experience, highly observant of details of things.

ESFP

REALISTIC ADAPTER in human relationships; friendly and easy with people, highly observant of their feelings and needs, oriented to practical, first-hand experience.

ISTJ

Analytical MANAGER OF FACTS AND DETAILS; dependable, decisive, painstaking and systematic, concerned with systems and organization, stable and conservative.

ISFJ

Sympathetic MANAGER OF FACTS AND DETAILS; concerned with people's welfare, dependable, painstaking and systematic, stable and conservative.

ISFP

Observant, loyal HELPER; reflective, realistic, empathic, patient with details, gentle and retiring, shuns disagreements, enjoys the moment.

INFP

Imaginative, independent HELPER; reflective, inquisitive, empathic, loyal to ideals, more interested in possibilities than practicalities.

ESFJ

Practical HARMONIZER and worker-with-people, sociable, orderly, opinioned, conscientious, realistic and well tuned to the here and now.

ENFJ

Imaginative HARMONIZER and worker-with-people; sociable, expressive, orderly, opinioned, conscientious, curious about new ideas and possibilities.

INFJ

People-oriented INNOVATOR of ideas; serious, quietly forceful and persevering, concerned with the common good, with helping others develop.

INTJ

Logical, critical, decisive INNOVATOR of ideas; serious, intent, highly independent, concerned with organization, determined and often stubborn.

ENFP

Warmly enthusiastic PLANNER OF CHANGE; imaginative, individualistic, pursues inspiration with impulsive energy, seeks to understand and inspire others.

ENTP

Inventive, analytical PLANNER OF CHANGE; enthusiastic and independent, pursues inspiration with impulsive energy, seeks to understand and inspire others.

Figure 18.1. Brief descriptions of the 16 possible psychological types derived from the Myers-Briggs Personality Type Indicator.

For our purposes, the value of the psychological types as noted by Lawrence is that they provide important clues about the individualized concerns of teachers and enable us, once again, to avoid the trap of assuming that all teachers have the same needs and interests. "Staff" development, then, becomes increasingly involved with defining and meeting individual developmental needs and concerns of members of the staff.

In this section, we presented two concepts—adult learning characteristics and differentiation of individual needs—that are often ignored in current staff development programs. It is tempting to suggest that adding these two ingredients will improve all that ails staff development and inservice education in schools, but to do so would be to suggest a quick-fix solution to a complex problem. The comments of many teachers today reflect other and deeper concerns. However, designing staff development that recognizes both adult needs and differences among staff members will certainly address two major clusters of individual complaints.

Promising Practices

Defining Goals

One promising development is not truly a new practice per se but is, nevertheless, an important improvement in the areas of inservice education and staff development—that is, the way in which this topic is defined. We do appear to be coming closer to developing a clear conceptualization of what both inservice and staff development are supposed to be and do—a goal that we noted as critical earlier in this chapter. Kenneth Howey (1985) suggested, for example, the following six critical functions to be served:

1. *Continuing pedagogical development.* Learning about more effective instructional techniques in the classroom, such as classroom management skills and teacher presentation skills;

2. *Continuing understanding and discovery of self.* Learning more about developmental needs; for example, in interpersonal skills;

3. *Continuing cognitive development.* Determining the level of cognitive ability and development of teachers so that future staff development and inservice schemes might be able to address potential differences more completely;

4. *Continuing theoretical development.* Contributing to the attainment of goals set forth in a selected educational theory;

5. *Continuing professional development.* Increasing the competence levels of teachers in a way that would enable these individuals to contribute to a knowledge base which would, in turn, also contribute to the development of teaching as a profession;

6. *Continuing career development.* Creating greater leadership skills and other competencies that might lead teachers eventually to greater career development opportunities.

Other valid assessments of the purposes for staff development and inservice education are no doubt possible; we offer Howey's primarily to indicate that this field has become increasingly sophisticated in recent years. We no longer view staff development as a "chore" that must be done periodically in schools or as a "frill" to be carried out only in wealthy districts. A look at the multiple purposes for staff development and inservice education suggests how critical a responsibility it is for those who provide leadership in schools. The effective practitioner of proactive supervision must not only be well versed in the techniques for implementing staff development but must also settle upon a clear understanding of its purpose.

Program Evaluation

A second promising development in inservice education has appeared in an area often overlooked throughout most of professional education: program evaluation. Bruce Joyce and Beverly Showers (1988, p. 118) suggest a useful conceptual framework for the evaluation of staff development, derived from a review of responses to questions in three categories:

- Questions related to the human resource development system as such. (The purpose of these questions is to determine generally how a system is doing. Is it in good health? Does it succeed in its purpose? How well does it provide for individuals, schools, and district initiatives?)

- Questions related to the major dimensions of the system and the health of those dimensions. (How well are individuals, schools, and system initiatives being served? What can be done to improve each identified dimension within a system?)

- Questions related to the study of specific programs and events within each dimension of a system. (A number of specific questions can be asked here, but only a few may be addressed in a formal evaluation system: Are programs that give teachers the opportunity to study teaching skills and strategies succeeding? Are school improvement programs being implemented and affecting the lives of students in a positive way? Are school district initiatives being implemented, and are they improving the performance of students?)

Once again, we do not suggest that this analytic framework must be followed, but we offer the work of Joyce and Showers as one example of what is being done in one critical area. Staff development and inservice education programs must be evaluated intensively to determine if they are truly worth the effort of maintaining them. Past staff development programs have too often been attempts to provide simple answers to complex organizational problems, and they have not been adequately evaluated according to schemes such as the one presented here. This lack of evaluation contributes greatly to the perception of many teachers that programs are ineffective or at least that they are "snake oil remedies" that promise more than they deliver. Supervisory personnel need to direct their attention to ongoing evaluation if they truly want their efforts to be successful.

Mentoring

We conclude this chapter by noting that there are some very promising practices associated with implementing more effective ongoing professional development opportunities for school personnel. One that we believe is particularly noteworthy is mentoring. We define this practice as the *forming of mutually supportive and learning relationships between two individuals who work together in the same or similar organization*. Others have also called this type of relationship either *peer coaching* or simply *coaching*. Proactive supervisors have an important part to play in designing and promoting mentoring in their school districts or within individual schools.

Many current mentoring programs have been established primarily to provide support to beginning school teachers or, in a few cases, school administrators. In these instances, mentoring has been seen as a way to initiate newcomers to schools by pairing them with more experienced colleagues who can assist others in learning some "tricks of the trade" that are needed for survival and success in a new role.

We agree with the value of mentoring for new teachers and administrators. However, we have also found in our work (Daresh & Playko, 1993) that mentoring relationships can serve as strategies to promote ongoing dialogue and collaboration between educators at all levels of their professional careers. Thus, teachers (or administrators) with several years of professional experience can learn from colleagues who might be willing to serve as "sounding boards" for their co-workers. As we saw in chapter 13, the paradox of education is often that, in spite of a world ostensibly filled with continuing needs for interpersonal contact, schools are indeed typically quite lonely places where teachers and others so often work in complete isolation from other adults. Mentoring programs may reduce this type of problem.

Summary

Effective staff development and inservice education programs are critically important to the development of good schools. As a result, the planning, the implementation, and the eventual evaluation of formal professional development programs are particularly important responsibilities for the practitioner of proactive supervision, whose ultimate goal is always to make schools more effective.

In this chapter we considered the distinction—conceptual as well as practical—that theorists often draw between staff development and inservice education. We pointed out that, although the differences between the two can be both subtle and real, practicing educators rarely make such fine distinctions. We reviewed recent research, defined the characteristics typical of development programs that are considered effective, and noted that recent studies have primarily focused on the content and delivery of effective programs.

We explored the two areas where staff development programs experience their greatest problems: the extent to which adult learning and development principles are ignored and the lack of attention to individual learner differences. We then suggested some useful studies that supervisors might consult to remedy these persistent problems. Finally, we presented some promising recent developments in the areas of definition, evaluation, and mentoring that may lead to eventual refinement and improvement of staff development and inservice education.

Suggested Activities

---

1. Interview a group of teachers to determine their perceptions of the strengths and weaknesses of inservice and staff development programs in which they have recently participated. Compare your findings with the issues related to individual differences and adult learning that we reviewed in this chapter.
2. Using the Levels of Concern description presented here, review how a group of five or more teachers react to the implementation of some new practice in their school. Chart the number of people found at each level as you carry out your interviews.

Cases to Consider

Read each of the cases and consider the following:

a. What are the critical issues related to each case, as they relate to the design of effective staff development and inservice education as a responsibility of the proactive supervisor?
b. How does each case relate to the development of the concept of proactive supervision?
c. In what ways might you suggest a resolution to the issues raised?

Case 18.1:

But This Expert Was Highly Recommended

Kathy Kleinschmidt sat in her office staring out the window. The inservice session she sponsored yesterday for the teachers of Big Salmon High School was the biggest disaster she had seen in her five years as the staff development director for the Big Buckle School District.

Last year, when Kathy attended a national conference on community involvement in local schools, she heard nothing but praise about Dr. Kyle Alexander, a former school superintendent now running his own consulting agency in the west. Staff development directors whom Kathy had known for several years told her what a great job Dr. Alexander was reported to have done in school districts around the country. He was gaining a formidable reputation as a person who could motivate even the most resistant school staffs to get interested in site-based management and community involvement. He sounded like the kind of speaker who was needed at Big Buckle. Kathy made initial contact with Dr. Alexander while at the conference and tentatively invited him to be the keynote speaker for the high school inservice day in the fall.

In the next few weeks, Kathy called the consultant to review the topics that should be addressed in his session. Dr. Alexander agreed to the plans and even sent the Big Buckle Schools a copy of his latest book, *Kyle Alexander's Ten Steps to Community Involvement* at no charge, along with a preview edition of his latest videotape. This was going to be a great inservice session—Big Buckle was finally going to play in the "big leagues" and get a big-time speaker for a change. This would not be the typical day-long session where the teachers simply got together to work in teams to plan their strategies to deal with district goals.

When the day of the inservice session arrived, the high school auditorium was filled with teachers, central office staff, a few board members, several professors from the local university, county office representatives, and some guests from other school systems. Dr. Alexander took the stage and began his session by sharing several brief jokes about his past experiences as a superintendent, as a teacher, as a parent, as a Rotary Club member, as a consultant, as a former high school student . . . The list of stories, many of which convulsed the crowd with laughter, never seemed to end. Between each story, Dr. Alexander introduced one his "Ten Steps" that appeared in his book. In fact, Kathy began to recognize whole sections of the book being presented almost verbatim to the crowd. Not once did Dr. Alexander make reference to any of the local concerns that Kathy shared with him before he arrived. For the first hour and a half, the crowd was attentive to the speaker. After the morning break, it was apparent that something was wrong. The laughter was not quite as loud, and people started to slip away for "urgent phone calls" or other matters outside the auditorium. It was clear that most people were not returning.

Luncheon was served in the cafeteria, and Kathy saw that teachers were speaking to each other in small groups around the room. As she circulated among the tables, she knew that the main topic of conversation was the morning session. At one o'clock, the group reconvened in the auditorium to watch two of Dr. Alexander's tapes. The speaker seemed totally oblivious to the fact that, as he launched into yet another recollection of how his ten steps worked well in another community, the audience was less than half the size it had been at the opening session that morning. By three o'clock, when the audience was invited to question the speaker, the first ten rows of seats were barely full.

Kathy dreaded the thought of reading the evaluations for the day. She received a message to see the superintendent and knew it was not going to be a pleasant meeting.

Case 18.2:

How Much Do You Charge to Talk?

It was mid-October and Dr. Bob Kramer was sitting at his desk in the College of Education at State University. He knew that before the day ended, he would have a chance to make a few extra dollars by being a guest speaker at one of the school districts in the area. After all, it was only a week before the annual regional teachers' inservice day.

Several years ago, the school districts in the central part of the state decided that each year, toward the end of October, they would hold one day in common for teacher inservice in all districts. The idea was that strength could be derived if many small school systems pooled their limited inservice funds to sponsor meaningful learning activities for staffs.

The main problem seemed to be that there was never much coordination of the concept once it became implemented. What started as a good idea was now an annual ritual where students were released from all schools in the area one Friday each fall. In many districts, teachers (and administrators) looked at the day as a holiday; some even quipped that this annual inservice day was the best day of business at shopping malls around this part of the state. It allowed many teachers to get an early start on Christmas shopping.

In a few districts, however, there was still some effort to use the October Friday as a day for teacher inservice. It was these school systems that would call Dr. Kramer and many of his colleagues a week or two before the inservice day and offer an honorarium to talk about an educational issue of possible interest to the staff. This year, the Southeastern Schools needed someone to talk about conflict management. After Dr. Kramer received the call he was waiting for, he noted the time and place in his calendar, and headed to the library to find some appropriate material to guide him in preparing a few overheads.

References

Brimm, J. R., & Tollett, D. J. (1975). How do teachers feel about inservice education? *Educational Leadership.* 30(7): 60–62.

Daresh, John C. (1987). Research trends in staff development and inservice education. *Journal of Education for Teaching.* 13(1): 3–11.

Daresh, John C., & Playko, Marsha A. (1993). *Leaders helping leaders: A practical guide to administrative mentoring.* New York: Scholastic, Inc.

Fuller, Frances F. (1969). Concerns of teachers: A developmental conceptualization. *American Educational Research Journal.* 6:207–226.

Hall, Gene E., & Loucks, Susan (1978, September). Teacher concerns as a basis for facilitating and personalizing staff development. *Teachers College Record,* 36–53.

Henderson, E. S. (1979). The concept of school-focused inservice education and training. *British Journal of Teacher Education,* 5(1): 17–25.

Howey, Kenneth (1985). Six major functions of staff development: An expanded imperative. *Journal of Teacher Education,* 58–64.

Hutson, Harry M. (1981). Inservice best practices: The learnings of general education. *Journal of Research and Development in Education,* 14(2).

Joyce, Bruce, & Showers, Beverly (1988). *Student achievement through staff development.* White Plains, NY: Longman.

Jung, Carl G. (1923). Psychological types. In Jolande Jacob (Ed.) (1970). *Psychological reflections: A new anthology of the writings of C. J. Jung.* Princeton: Princeton University Press.

Knowles, Malcolm S. (1970). *The modern practice of adult education.* New York: Association Press.

Lawrence, Gordon (1974). *Patterns of effective inservice.* Tallahassee: Florida Department of Education.

———. (1982). *People types and tiger stripes: A practical guide to learning styles.* Gainesville, FL: Center for Applications of Psychological Types.

McLaughlin, Milbrey, & Berman, Paul (1977). Retooling staff development in an era of decline. *Educational Leadership,* 34:21–28.

McLaughlin, Milbrey W., & Marsh, David D. (1978). Staff development and school change. *Teachers College Record.* 80(1): 69–94.

Myers, Isabel Briggs, & Briggs, Katherine (1962). *The Myers-Briggs Type Indicator.* Princeton, NJ: Educational Testing Service.

Nicholson, A. M., Joyce, Bruce R., Parker, D. W., & Waterman, F. T. (1976). *The literature of inservice education: An analytic review.* Palo Alto, CA: Stanford Center for Research and Development in Teaching.

Paul, Douglas (1977). Change processes at the elementary, secondary, and post-secondary levels. In Jack Culbertson & Nicholas Nash (Eds.), *Linking processes in educational improvement.* Columbus, OH: University Council for Educational Administration.

Sprinthall, N. A., & Thies-Sprinthall, L. (1983). The need for a theoretical framework in educating teachers: A cognitive development perspective. In Kenneth R. Howey & W. E. Gardner (Eds.), *The education of teachers: A look ahead.* White Plains, NY: Longman.

Swenson, Thomas I. (1981). The state of the art in inservice education and staff development. *Journal of Research and Development in Education,* 15(1): 2–7.

Unruh, A., & Turner, H. E. (1970). *Supervision for one and innovation.* Boston: Houghton-Mifflin.

Wood, Fred, & Thompson, Steven R. (1980). Guidelines for better staff development. *Educational Leadership,* 37:374–378.

19 Future Trends and Issues in Supervision

In this final chapter, we want to explore briefly some of the issues that serve as a basis for analyzing the field of educational supervision and that we believe will impact the direction of future analysis.

Movement toward Reactive Practice

In these days when the headlines of newspapers and the evening television news seem to be filled with story after story of violence in schools, dysfunctional families, and children with all manners of social problems never encountered before, it is no wonder that there is a drift toward schools becoming focused almost exclusively on how to deal with problems other than those we have discussed in this book. When a principal is faced with nightly drive-by shootings in the community surrounding his or her school, it is not surprising that there is not necessarily a strong interest in and commitment to the improvement of the psychosocial climate inside a school by focusing on the constructs of Matthew Miles's view of organizational health.

We understand the nature of these real-life concerns. Nevertheless, if educational leaders adopt a stance wherein they view their roles solely in terms of how to deal with crises which face schools at present, we can only wonder what the nature of educational programs will look like. On the one hand, we are sympathetic to situations where educational leaders have real concerns about the health and safety of the children in their schools because of the threat of gangs, local drug dealers, and so forth. But we now see an increasing number of schools that look like armed camps, complete with metal detectors, police officers in uniform, and attack dogs. Unfortunately, we cannot deny the fact that, in some cases across the United States, such precautions are not only understandable, but essential so that schools may open each day. Although we have not yet reached a point where all schools—or even a large number of schools—must devote their energy to simply keeping the doors open and the students and teachers alive, there is a great deal of talk from both lay citizens and professional educators alike which seems to indicate that an increasing number of schools are only a moment away from such terrible violence, leaving no alternative but armament. In such a scenario, no further concerns about educational programming and the subtleties of effective teaching and staff development will be needed.

Clearly, our concern here is that a proper balance remains between keeping schools as safe and orderly environments and effecting the most sound instruction and learning possible. We believe that it is imperative that educational administrators and supervisors guard their roles as proactive leaders and not fall into the trap of simply worrying about the next headline, police report, or community crisis. We see many cases of school leaders keeping their perspective and avoiding the temptation to deal only with immediate issues. This ability to keep an eye on the truly important aspects of education for children is indeed an example of proactive supervision.

Battles over Standards and Outcomes

One critical issue that has persisted in virtually all discussions about effective educational practice has involved a consideration of what should be the desired outcomes of schooling. For years, there have been many who supported the notion that schools were to be places where students were prepared for particular vocational roles, while others have focused on the role of schools as agencies designed to teach learners about fundamental processes, often referred to as "the basics" (reading, writing, and arithmetic). Still others have identified schools as places where moral and ethical (and religious?) values should be developed within children.

The modern educational supervisor will continue to face this same sort of debate as he or she works with diverse community groups and expectations. Increasingly, discussions may center around the desirability of promoting educational practice directed toward attainment of sound, basic education ("the basics"), religious principles (return prayer and God to classrooms), and broadly defined outcomes which supposedly represent a synthesis of content.

It is not our goal at this point to define the correct outcomes or standards which should serve as the appropriate goals defended by any educational leader. Rather, we simply point to the fact that this type of conversation will continue well into the future. Supervisors and administrators need to be clear about their own personal platforms which guide their work in schools. They may lose some battles with those who hold opposing viewpoints, but at least they will be able to maintain personal integrity in this critical area.

Increased Expectations for Social Roles of Schools

In addition to the constant search for the "ideal" purpose of schooling, as noted above, there are also greater expectations being placed on schools as agencies for the delivery of a wide array of social services in society. Decreased sources of financial support coupled with increased demands that schools serve as stabilizing bodies which deal with numerous problems faced by children mean that the role of the educational administrator or supervisor will increase in complexity. No longer will it be possible for the school leader to pretend as if his or her job consists of duties solely within the walls of the school.

The implication of this observation for proactive supervisory practice is clear. Individual administrators and supervisors must begin to look at the bigger picture of how they approach their important responsibilities. Effective school leaders of the future will need to define their roles not simply as leaders of schools, but rather, as leaders of people; the most important group of people will continue to be the children who attend our schools. Some need education as defined and limited largely by the traditional boundaries of the school day and the established curriculum. On the other hand, more and more children will need opportunities to grow and develop which will come from sources beyond the classroom. The effective educational leader of the future must become aware of this fact and promote a broader vision of education.

Summary

In the first edition of this book, we noted three issues that we believed would serve as important areas to be addressed by proactive supervisors. These included continued calls for educational reform, increased professionalism of supervisors, and more opportunities for professional development of educators. We continue to believe that these are important issues. However, as we noted in this concluding chapter, we are convinced that additional issues and challenges will face those who will provide effective school leadership in the foreseeable future.

We do not wish to infer here that the only problems that will face educators are the ones listed in this chapter. Clearly, other challenges await leaders of schools. Many of these are not yet even imagined by most. However, our goal here has been to identify a few of the issues that are likely to have a significant impact on the ways in which supervisors and administrators will be able to do their jobs. It is through this type of analysis that we believe it may be possible to identify ways in which proactive supervisory practices will continue to flourish in the next several years.

Index